# Soar with Haskell

The ultimate beginners' guide to mastering functional
programming from the ground up

**Tom Schrijvers**

BIRMINGHAM—MUMBAI

# Soar with Haskell

**Group Product Manager**: Kunal Sawant

**Publishing Product Manager**: Teny Thomas

**Book Project Manager**: Manisha Singh

**Senior Editor**: Nisha Cleetus

**Technical Editor**: Jubit Pincy

**Copy Editor**: Safis Editing

**Proofreader**: Safis Editing

**Indexer**: Hemanigini Bari

**Production Designer**: Shankar Kalbhor

**Business Development Executive**: Kriti Sharma

**Developer Relations Marketing Executive**: Shrinidhi Manoharan

First published: December 2023

Production reference: 2240625

Published by
Packt Publishing Ltd.
Grosvenor House
11 St Paul's Square
Birmingham
B3 1RB, UK

ISBN 978-1-80512-845-8

www.packtpub.com

*To my wife, Annemie, for her enduring support.*

*– Tom Schrijvers*

# Contributors

## About the author

**Tom Schrijvers** has been a professor of computer science at KU Leuven in Belgium since 2014, and previously from 2011 until 2014 at Ghent University in Belgium. He has over 20 years of research experience in programming languages and has co-authored more than 100 scientific papers. Much of his research focuses on functional programming and the Haskell programming language in particular; he has made many contributions to the language, its ecosystem, and applications, and chaired academic events such as the Haskell Symposium. At the same time, he has more than a decade of teaching experience (including functional programming with Haskell) and received several teaching awards.

*I would like to thank the Haskell community who have created and fostered this amazing language. They have been a major inspiration. Of course, I am grateful to the Packt team who have followed the development of this book every step of the way. Many thanks also to Alexander Granin for his uplifting technical feedback. Finally, I am indebted to my employer, KU Leuven, who granted me a six-month sabbatical leave. That gave me the opportunity to write the first 10 chapters in the welcoming environment of Kellogg College in Oxford.*

# About the reviewer

**Alexander Granin**, a functional programming expert, is renowned for his fundamental books *Functional Design and Architecture* and *Pragmatic Type-Level Design*. With over 15 years of experience spanning C++, Haskell, C#, and Python, he's evolved from developer to software architect. As an accomplished international speaker, he delivered many talks on software design and functional programming. Alexander's methodology, functional declarative design, provides a pragmatic knowledge of design patterns, principles, and best practices, useful for building applications with functional languages. His mission is to empower developers with practical insights and build a comprehensive software engineering discipline for Function Point (FP).

# Table of Contents

# 3

# Recursion 49

# 4

# Higher-Order Functions 79

# Part 2: Haskell-Specific Features

5

## First-Class Functions                                                                101

6

## Type Classes                                                                          119

# 7

# Lazy Evaluation 153

# 8

# Input/Output 175

# Part 3: Functional Design Patterns

## 9

## Monoids and Foldables                                          199

## 10

## Functors, Applicative Functors, and Traversables          227

# 11

# Monads                                                          257

# 12

# Monad Transformers                                              277

# Part 4: Practical Programming

## 13

## Domain-Specific Languages — 301

## 14

## Parser Combinators — 319

## 15

## Lenses — 337

# 16

# Property-Based Testing                                      355

# Preface

*This book provides an introduction to functional programming in Haskell:*

- **Functional Programming** (**FP**) is one of the main programming paradigms, along with imperative programming and object-oriented programming. It uses functions as its core concept of computation – turning input into output in a predictable and context-independent way. While many non-FP languages also offer functions in some form, in FP, language functions truly have first-class status. They are not only computation but also data, which can be ferried around by other (higher-order) functions, dynamically assembled out of simpler functions, stored in data structures, or data containers themselves.

- Haskell stands out among FP languages in that it unequivocally embraces the FP paradigm. Because it does not make any compromises for imperative programming, Haskell had to come up with entirely new solutions to tackle common programming problems that also turned out to be successful in solving next-level problems. This way, it has become an inspiration for the designers of other programming languages (both FP and non-FP) and libraries in those languages.

Besides being true to the principles of FP, Haskell is also renowned for its sophisticated static type system. This means that Haskell programs are automatically checked for particular kinds of mistakes (known as type errors) before they are run. Moreover, thanks to Haskell's powerful type inference mechanism, programmers have to write little to no type annotations themselves. Taking all the preceding aspects of FP in Haskell into consideration, the common theme of this book is abstraction. It provides many mechanisms for abstraction and powerful examples of abstractions that allow us to converse and reason about common programming patterns, becoming more effective programmers when we (re)use them.

## Who this book is for

This book is for all those who already have some programming experience and want to learn FP in Haskell:

- If you are familiar with imperative or object-oriented programming, this book introduces you to the wonderful world of FP.

- If you are already familiar with other FP languages, you will discover the unique Haskell language features, ideas, and programming style.

- If you have outgrown your current programming language, are ready for a new challenge, or want to fall in love with programming all over again, your journey starts here.

# What this book covers

*Chapter 1, Functions*, explains the core concept of FP – functions. It introduces function definitions and shows how functions are called. This includes an explanation of all the syntactic elements (types, type signature, function body, etc) and their role. Along the way, it also introduces a number of built-in types and functions.

*Chapter 2, Algebraic Datatypes*, introduces Haskell's mechanism for user-defined types – **Algebraic Datatypes (ADTs)**. We build up from simple forms of ADTs such as enumerations and records to their full generality, and we learn the different elements of ADT definitions – the type name, the data constructors, and their fields. We see how ADT values are created and how they are taken apart by pattern matching. Finally, we see how ADTs can be parameterized over other types.

*Chapter 3, Recursion*, presents the functional programming alternative to loops. Recursive datatypes are a natural mechanism to express data structures of arbitrary size, and recursive functions are the way to process these functions. We will focus in particular on structural recursion as a principled use of recursion but also cover alternative recursion patterns.

*Chapter 4, Higher-Order Functions*, explains how repeated patterns in function definitions can be abstracted over, notably by abstracting over higher-order parameters. Special attention goes to commonly used higher-order library functions such as `map`, `filter`, `foldr`, and `foldl`.

*Chapter 5, First-Class Functions*, covers a range of language features and mechanisms that facilitate function-oriented programming, where we program at the level of functions rather than plain values.

*Chapter 6, Type Classes*, presents Haskell's unique mechanism for supporting ad-hoc overloading– type classes. It explains what ad-hoc overloading is and how functions give rise to polymorphic type signatures with type class constraints. Then, we will see how predefined type classes can be instantiated for user-defined types and how new user-defined type classes can be created. Finally, we cover several user-defined type classes and their use in standard libraries.

*Chapter 7, Lazy Evaluation*, reveals Haskell's unique evaluation mechanism – lazy evaluation. It shows how lazy evaluation works and improves upon both call-by-value and call-by-name. Then, it shows how to use the strategy to your advantage by using lists as iterators that supply their elements on demand. Finally, the chapter also points out a pitfall of the mechanism – the build-up of thunks.

*Chapter 8, Input/Output*, explains Haskell's unique way of interfacing with the outside world – its I/O mechanism. First, the chapter explains why the existing approach of other languages is problematic due to the lazy evaluation strategy and the language's purity principle. Then, it presents the Haskell solution using the I/O type and `>>=`/`return` operators. Then, it introduces the `do` notation as a more user-friendly notation for I/O steps. Finally, it covers common I/O operations.

*Chapter 9, Monoids and Foldables*, introduces the notion of foldables. These are collections that support a similar range of frequently used operations. Along the way, we learn that Haskell has a mechanism to abstract over parts of types, called type constructors, and uses algebraic concepts such as semigroups and monoids to design highly general algorithms.

*Chapter 10, Functors, Applicative Functors, and Traversables*, leads us further into the hierarchy of type classes for type constructors. We will first consider functors – data structures that can be mapped over. Then, we will move on to applicative functors, which can merge multiple data structures, and finally, we will see traversables as data structures that can be mapped over with side effects.

*Chapter 11, Monads*, introduces the king of the type constructor hierarchy – monads. We will first cover two well-known examples of monads – the `Maybe` monad for failure and the state monad for state passing. Then, we will generalize from these examples and present the Monad type class. Finally, we will present a number of additional examples of monads.

*Chapter 12, Monad Transformers*, shows how the functionality of different monads can be combined into a single monad. The chapter covers the monad transformer mechanism and gives a range of commonly used instances. Then, it shows how applications can abstract over the implementation details of monads and monad transformers, with monad subclasses. Finally, we will see how the same monad transformers can be combined in different ways to achieve different behavior.

*Chapter 13, Domain-Specific Languages*, documents a powerful problem-solving technique that is appropriate when a range of problems have to be solved within the same problem area – **domain-specific languages (DSLs)** embedded in Haskell. First, we will see several examples of DSLs that are tailored to different problem areas. Then, we will focus on implementation techniques for DSLs. The most general and flexible approach is deep embedding. It contrasts with shallow embedding, which is a more lightweight and efficient technique.

*Chapter 14, Parser Combinators*, introduces parser combinators, a lightweight and convenient DSL in Haskell for parsing. It covers what parsing is and where it is used. Then, we will see a basic definition of parser combinators to get a good idea of how they work. From there, we will move on to the industrial-strength Parsec library. Finally, we see how to tackle common parsing problems with parser combinators.

*Chapter 15, Lenses*, presents an exciting approach to the mundane activity of data access in nested datatypes. First, it demonstrates the basic approach for records that is built into Haskell and identifies its disadvantages. Then, it presents the concept of lenses as a much more convenient alternative for both reading and updating fields. We will show that lenses not only compose trivially to reach deep into data structures but also can be used to seamlessly define virtual fields. Finally, we cover the main lens combinators provided by the well-known `lens` library.

*Chapter 16, Property-Based Testing*, covers property-based testing, the powerful testing technique pioneered by Haskell's QuickCheck library. It explains the advantages of property-based testing over unit testing. Then, it shows how to write properties and examine test outcomes. Then, it shows you how to test your own ADTs by writing generators for them. Finally, shrinking is used to drill counterexamples down to their essence.

# To get the most out of this book

Refer to the Haskell website – in particular, the page at `https://www.haskell.org/get-started/` – for directions on how to set up your Haskell environment. The main installer for GHC can be found at `https://www.haskell.org/ghcup/`.

| Software/hardware covered in the book | Operating system requirements |
| --- | --- |
| Glasgow Haskell Compiler (GHC) | Windows, macOS, or Linux |

**If you are using the digital version of this book, we advise you to type the code yourself or access the code from the book's GitHub repository (a link is available in the next section). Doing so will help you avoid any potential errors related to the copying and pasting of code.**

# Download the example code files

You can download the example code files for this book from `https://github.com/PacktPublishing/Soar-with-Haskell`. If there's an update to the code, it will be updated in the GitHub repository.

We also have other code bundles from our rich catalog of books and videos available at `https://github.com/PacktPublishing/`. Check them out!

# Conventions used

There are a number of text conventions used throughout this book.

`Code in text`: Indicates code words in text, database table names, folder names, filenames, file extensions, pathnames, dummy URLs, user input, and Twitter handles. Here is an example: "The type signature states that the function has the name increment and, given a value of the Int type as input, produces a result of the Int type."

A block of code is set as follows:

```
redSuits :: [Suit]
redSuits = Hearts : Diamonds : []
```

When we wish to draw your attention to a particular part of a code block, the relevant lines or items are set in bold:

```
data Expr = Lit Int | Add Expr Expr
```

Any function call is written as follows:

```
*Main> renderExpr (Add (Lit 2) (Lit 5))
"2+5"
```

**Bold**: Indicates a new term, an important word, or words that you see on screen. For instance, words in menus or dialog boxes appear in **bold**. Here is an example: "What sets FP apart from the other two is that it is a member of the **declarative programming** family."

## Get in touch

Feedback from our readers is always welcome.

**General feedback**: If you have questions about any aspect of this book, email us at customercare@packtpub.com and mention the book title in the subject of your message.

**Errata**: Although we have taken every care to ensure the accuracy of our content, mistakes do happen. If you have found a mistake in this book, we would be grateful if you would report this to us. Please visit www.packtpub.com/support/errata and fill in the form.

**Piracy**: If you come across any illegal copies of our works in any form on the internet, we would be grateful if you would provide us with the location address or website name. Please contact us at copyright@packt.com with a link to the material.

**If you are interested in becoming an author**: If there is a topic that you have expertise in and you are interested in either writing or contributing to a book, please visit authors.packtpub.com

## Share Your Thoughts

Once you've read *Soar with Haskell*, we'd love to hear your thoughts! Scan the QR code below to go straight to the Amazon review page for this book and share your feedback.

https://packt.link/r/1805128450

Your review is important to us and the tech community and will help us make sure we're delivering excellent quality content.

# Download a free PDF copy of this book

Thanks for purchasing this book!

Do you like to read on the go but are unable to carry your print books everywhere? Is your eBook purchase not compatible with the device of your choice?

Don't worry, now with every Packt book you get a DRM-free PDF version of that book at no cost.

Read anywhere, any place, on any device. Search, copy, and paste code from your favorite technical books directly into your application.

The perks don't stop there, you can get exclusive access to discounts, newsletters, and great free content in your inbox daily

Follow these simple steps to get the benefits:

1.  Scan the QR code or visit the link below

https://packt.link/free-ebook/9781805128458

2.  Submit your proof of purchase
3.  That's it! We'll send your free PDF and other benefits to your email directly

# Part 1:
# Basic Functional Programming

This part introduces you to the Haskell programming language. You will get an overview of the basic functional programming language features. In particular, you will start with the key concepts and functions, expanding into the data processed by functions (algebraic datatypes), the way to write loops with functions (recursion), and functions taking other functions as input (higher-order functions).

This part has the following chapters:

- *Chapter 1, Functions*
- *Chapter 2, Algebraic Datatypes*
- *Chapter 3, Recursion*
- *Chapter 4, Higher-Order Functions*

# 1

# Functions

While FP has been around for many decades, its following has only been growing rapidly in recent years. More programmers are picking up functional programming languages or are programming in a functional style in non-functional languages than ever before. At the same time, existing non-functional programming languages are adopting a growing number of FP features and libraries.

In these ongoing developments, Haskell stands out as a reference for all. As a purely FP language, it embodies the ideal of FP. As a trailblazer for new (functional) programming language developments, it sets the bar for other languages to follow in its tracks.

Before diving into practical FP, this chapter gives a brief overview of what FP is and how Haskell fits in. Then, we start with our first Haskell functions. We learn how to define and call functions. This includes an explanation of all the syntactic elements (types, type signature, function body, and so on) and their role. Along the way, we are also introduced to a number of built-in types and functions, and we discover what the type checker does for us when we write programs. Finally, we put together several functions into a larger program.

By the end of this chapter, you will have a basic understanding of what FP is about. You will also be able to write small Haskell programs that consist of one or a few simple functions that act on primitive datatypes such as integers and Booleans.

In this chapter, we are going to cover the following main topics:

- What is FP and how does Haskell fit in?
- What does a minimal Haskell program, a single function, look like?
- What are Haskell's primitive datatypes and what can we do with them?
- What does Haskell's type checker do for us?
- How do we write larger Haskell programs out of individual functions?

# Technical requirements

From the *Writing basic functions* section onward, you will need a working Haskell environment: the **Glasgow Haskell Compiler** (**GHC**) and a code editor (e.g., Visual Studio Code). We refer to the Haskell website (in particular, the page at `https://www.haskell.org/get-started/`) for directions on how to set up this environment. The main installer for GHC can be found at `https://www.haskell.org/ghcup/`.

The code shown in this book can be downloaded from its GitHub repository: `https://github.com/PacktPublishing/Soar-with-Haskell`.

# What is FP?

Before diving into practical Haskell programming, we give a brief overview of FP, its history, and its applications. If you are eager to get your hands dirty, you may want to forge ahead to the next section, then return here at a later occasion when you are ready to put Haskell into context.

## Programming with functions

**Functional programming** (**FP**) is one of the main programming paradigms next to imperative programming and object-oriented programming.

### Declarative programming

What sets FP apart from the other two is that it is a member of the **declarative programming** family. Sometimes, the principle of declarative programming is summarized by saying that declarative programs state *what should happen, not how it should happen*. This means that its programs do not explicitly determine the order in which computation steps are executed; it is up to the language implementation. Haskell particularly stands out among other FP languages because it embraces the declarative programming principle with its lazy evaluation semantics, which *Chapter 7, Lazy Evaluation*, explains in detail.

### Function-based programming

Most members of the declarative programming family use mathematical logic as their basis; programming in the language closely corresponds to writing statements and/or theories in a particular logical framework. FP distinguishes itself from other declarative paradigms in that it uses mathematical functions as its core concept. Functions are a good formalism for expressing computation as a unit of data processing that turns inputs into outputs. Also, as the concept of functions is widely taught in schools, FP can be more approachable for those without a prior programming background than other programming paradigms. This is one of the reasons it is often taught as the first programming language in academic computer science curricula.

FP aims to replicate the mathematical concept of functions. Yet, there are practical reasons why this is not possible in general. Hence, it is important to be aware of the differences between mathematical functions and functions in FP languages. In mathematics, we can define a function without saying how it can be computed; it may even be impossible to compute certain mathematical functions because they rely on unknowable information such as what will happen in the future. This generality is, of course, not useful as the basis of a programming language. Hence, functional programs restrict themselves to functions that are given in a form that makes it clear how they should be computed.

## Referential transparency

One of the key properties of mathematical functions that Haskell has adopted (but that many other FP languages violate) is **referential transparency**. The concept of referential transparency means that if an f(x) function call yields the result y, then it does not matter whether we write f(x) or y anywhere in our program. The two should be indistinguishable and not affect the outcome of the program.

Referential transparency is a valuable property as it guarantees that functions are in some sense easy to reason about. Indeed, it implies that no matter how often the function is called and in what context, if it is given the same input, it will produce the same output. Hence, we do not have to take into account any prior history or any aspects of the calling context. In contrast, functions or procedures in imperative and object-oriented languages can have implicit side channels or side effects. For example, they can access and modify global variables that are not explicitly passed in as parameters. As a consequence, repeated calls with the same parameters can have different results, and these functions are much harder to disentangle from their context.

Referential transparency also allows the compiler to carry out much more aggressive optimizations. Here are just a few possibilities:

- When the compiler sees a repeated function call, it is allowed to replace the second call with the result of the first. This is known as common subexpression elimination.

- When the result of a function call is not used, the compiler can drop the call entirely.

- When there are two independent function calls, the compiler can choose the order in which to execute them. In fact, the calls can even be executed in parallel without causing any interference.

Referential transparency also poses a challenge for programming as many common programming tasks involve side effects. Think of interacting with a user, another process, the filesystem, the operating system, a remote server, and so on. None of these are naturally modeled by means of referentially transparent functions. Nevertheless, Haskell has managed to come up with an unusual but elegant approach to reconciling side effects with referential transparency. *Chapter 8, Input/Output*, will cover this approach in detail.

### First-class functions

While many languages of other paradigms also offer functions in some form, they typically do not embrace them to the same extent as functional languages. Indeed, FP languages give functions a first-class status; they have the same *rights* as other datatypes in the language.

This means that functions blur the line between computation and data; they are both. They not only process data but can also be treated as data constructed during program execution. Indeed, functions can be ferried around by other functions. Such functions, which take other functions as input or produce functions as output, are known as **higher-order functions** (see *Chapter 4, Higher-Order Functions*).

Just like programs dynamically assemble complex data structures, they can also assemble complex functions out of simpler functions by gluing them together in various ways. Finally, functions can also be stored as elements in data structures (e.g., in a list of functions), or themselves be viewed as containers of data. *Chapter 5, First-Class Functions*, explains all these use cases.

### Static typing

The origins of FP in mathematical logic have set the paradigm on the path for developing powerful static type systems. A static type system means that the programs are checked for particular kinds of mistakes (known as type errors) before they are run. This is an effective way of quickly reducing the number of bugs in programs before they are in use.

While not all functional languages have gone down this path, Haskell and many other influential languages have spearheaded the development of such type systems. They have explored various aspects:

- How a process known as type inference can unburden programmers from supplying excessive amounts of type information to make type checking work

- How to reuse code that does not just work with one type of input but that can uniformly work on different types

- How to capture all kinds of relevant properties and program invariants in the type system in order for violations to be caught during type checking

- How to automatically generate boilerplate code based on the structure of types

This means that, often, the focus in Haskell programs is more on the types than on the actual code.

### Abstraction

Taking all the previously mentioned aspects of FP together, there is a common theme: abstraction. Abstraction is an important tool in computer science. It compels us to extract the common patterns and focus on the high-level behavior while putting aside differences and irrelevant details. It gives names to these patterns so that we can replace lengthy descriptions with a single word that can be easily reused and does not inadvertently introduce variations in meaning. We reason about or develop intuition for an abstraction, and reuse that for the many instances of that abstraction. Hence, abstraction will be a common theme in this book.

While abstraction has many good properties, it can also be quite challenging. Indeed, when learning a new abstraction, there may not be an immediate foothold to grasp what the abstraction is about. It may seem pointless or inscrutable at first. This problem is one of the main challenges for newcomers to functional programmers, especially if they do not follow a carefully laid out didactic approach and are overwhelmed by many commonly used abstractions. To overcome this hurdle of unfamiliar abstractions, we should seek out specific instances of a new abstraction that are meaningful to us in their own right. By comparing such different examples, a common pattern may merge, namely the abstraction we are trying to grasp. Only at that point may we start to develop appreciation and intuition for the abstraction itself, and even discover new instances of the abstraction on our own. Then, with experience and practice, it will become easier to pick up new abstractions.

Now that we have a general idea of the key ingredients of FP, let us briefly consider where FP comes from and how it has led up to Haskell.

## Brief history of FP

We will give a brief overview of the three key evolutionary steps that preceded the creation of Haskell and have been highly influential for FP in general. Along with name-dropping several key language features that we will learn about in this book, this brief history conveys two other important distinguishing aspects of FP. Firstly, as one of the oldest programming paradigms, FP pioneered and adopted language features many decades before they became mainstream. Secondly, it is steeped in a long tradition of scientific research that has poured more mathematical rigor and scientific scrutiny into the paradigm than in any other. In short, even though FP may be new to you and most mainstream programmers, it is not new. On the contrary, its maturity and solidity are two of its underappreciated selling points.

### The lambda calculus

The history of FP started in the 1930s when mathematician Alonzo Church developed the lambda calculus to study the foundations of mathematics. This lambda calculus was, in a way, the first FP language, and sits at the core of all functional (and even many non-functional) programming languages today; *Chapter 5, First-Class Functions*, will show this for Haskell. Mind, we do need to be somewhat forgiving to see lambda calculus as a programming language. There was no computer to execute it on, nor was that its intended purpose. It only existed as a concept to reason about and to write about on paper. Moreover, it would not have been convenient to program with, as the lambda calculus is a highly primitive, stripped-down version of a programming language. It would take a lot of effort to use it to write what we consider today simple programs. Nevertheless, in 1937, Alan Turing showed that lambda calculus is as expressive as any other possible programming formalism. Indeed, there is nothing we can compute with any contemporary programming language that we cannot also compute with lambda calculus (provided we have enough patience to encode it and wait for the result). While the initial version of lambda calculus did not feature any types, Church came up with this notion in the 1940s.

### Lisp

Lisp was the first practical FP language, developed by John McCarthy in the 1950s. Lisp was inspired by the lambda calculus and pioneered many practical programming language features that are taken for granted today, including recursion, conditional expressions, and automated garbage collection. The name Lisp itself is a contraction of the words *LISt Processing*, as lists were a prominent data structure of the language; as *Chapter 3, Recursion*, and *Chapter 7, Lazy Evaluation*, show, lists are still quite important in Haskell. Notably missing from Lisp is a static type system. Due to its high level of abstraction, Lisp became popular among artificial intelligence researchers. Lisp has had many descendants (including Scheme, Racket, and Clojure) and is still used today in various flavors.

### ML

After Lisp, many other smaller, experimental, and less long-lived functional languages were developed. Another major milestone, the ML language, was developed by Robin Milner in the 1970s. It consolidated many earlier good ideas for FP language design, notably algebraic datatypes and pattern matching. These made **ML** (short for **Meta Language**) suitable for processing other formal languages (e.g., for compilers that process programming languages or for automated theorem provers that process logical formulas). A key contribution of ML is the work on a static type system that features parametric polymorphism, the Hindley-(Damas)-Milner type system, and a powerful type inference algorithm to go along with it. Haskell has inherited this type system, which we will use throughout this book, as well as algebraic datatypes and pattern matching, which are covered in *Chapter 2, Algebraic Datatypes*.

Now that we know of these key moments in the history of FP, let us move on to the next big evolutionary step: Haskell.

## Haskell

Let us briefly consider the history of Haskell itself and identify the three main characteristics of the language that set it apart from other FP languages.

### Abridged history

The Haskell language was created by a committee of researchers. Following the earlier popularity of the lazy FP language Miranda, which was proprietary, the committee wanted to pool their resources in defining an open standard.

Haskell 1.0 came out in 1990 and subsequently went through several further versions before reaching a stable milestone in 1997 with what is called Haskell 98, and was later published in the Haskell 98 Language Report. During this phase, many different implementations of Haskell were developed to carry out various experiments in language design. Yet, after Haskell 98, most of these projects gradually ended and one main implementation emerged, the GHC.

While minor changes have been made to the official Haskell standard since 1998, GHC has effectively taken over the de facto role of defining the language. Today, it provides more than 100 language extensions on top of Haskell 98.

Apart from laziness as the main rallying point of Haskell, we will next discuss the three main characteristics of the language.

## Main characteristics

GHC's lead developer, Simon Peyton Jones, characterizes Haskell as *pure, principled, and nimble*:

- **Pure**: Haskell is one of the few purely FP languages. Most other functional languages are, in fact, hybrids that also incorporate imperative elements, and sometimes object-oriented ones. The idea is that the advantages of FP only come fully into their own when the language goes all in on the functional paradigm and enforces its core tenets. A consequence of this strict adherence to purity certainly poses challenges to the designers and users of Haskell. Because they could not rely on established approaches from imperative languages to deal with a range of common programming situations, they had to come up with original purely functional approaches.

- **Principled**: As pure FP has a notion of function that is quite close to that of mathematics, many design aspects of Haskell and its libraries can be (and have been) founded on mathematical principles. Indeed, notably, the subareas of abstract algebra and category theory have turned out to offer useful abstract patterns that apply equally to mathematics and programming. As a consequence, Haskell programmers do not use the typical design pattern terminology that is common among many programming languages. Instead, they refer to abstract mathematical concepts such as monoids, functors, and monads. While these mathematically inspired concepts are more and more being picked up by other programming communities, it has for a long time branded Haskell as a language for theoretically-minded programmers.

- **Nimble**: The nimbleness refers to the relatively fast pace at which new language features are explored and adopted in Haskell, sometimes turning back on its steps to replace a suboptimal solution with a better one. This has cast Haskell in somewhat of a pioneering role, trailblazing the path for other programming languages that adopt its novel features after they have proven their worth. In this way, Haskell has become quite well-known among programming language designers and has influenced the design of many other languages.

Now that we have an idea of Haskell's characteristics, let us compare it to other contemporary FP languages.

## Other contemporary FP languages

There are several other prominent FP languages available today. What they have in common is that, unlike Haskell, they all make compromises with respect to purity. They allow destructive updates and other side effects (such as printing) anywhere in the program. Many also incorporate object-oriented features. We briefly mention a few.

### F#

F# is Microsoft's FP language for the .NET platform. It is a member of the ML family of languages with call-by-value semantics and strong static typing that was also partly influenced by Haskell. Because F# supports imperative and object-oriented programming, it is particularly convenient to interface F# with existing C# code and libraries.

### OCaml

OCaml (**Objective Caml**) is another scion of the ML family that is particularly renowned for its emphasis on performance. As the name suggests, OCaml supports object-oriented programming, although this is perhaps not as commonly used as in the case of F#. One of the main contemporary users and backers (besides academic researchers) of OCaml is the trading firm Jane Street.

### Scala

**Scala** is a hybrid functional/object-oriented language for the **Java Virtual Machine** (**JVM**) with static typing. Its design was heavily influenced by Haskell and contains many original ideas for reconciling the two paradigms, such as case classes as an object-oriented presentation of algebraic data types. While among the top five most popular JVM languages in industry, Scala is also increasingly being used in programming education as one of the first programming languages taught.

### Others

There are many other contemporary programming languages that are either seen as functional (Clojure, Racket, Erlang, etc.) or that have been influenced to a greater or lesser extent by FP languages (Swift, Kotlin, Rust, and so on). Moreover, many languages contain libraries whose design has been heavily influenced by similar FP libraries, such as reactive programming libraries, parser combinators, and property-based testing frameworks.

Now that we know the common characteristics of a range of FP languages, let us see what they are good for.

## Prominent application areas

While FP languages such as Haskell are fit for any purpose and have applications in many areas, there are a few that stand out in particular.

Perhaps the most well-developed application area of FP is that of implementing language processors such as compilers and interpreters. This is partly explained by the fact that for a long time, the main users of FP were the language developers themselves. Their main applications were the implementations of the languages they were developing. It is thus not surprising that functional languages and their libraries have been honed for this task. At the same time, many of the common FP language features are a perfect match for language processing. Language processors typically represent programs with tree-shaped data structures called abstract syntax trees. Such abstract syntax trees are easily represented with algebraic data types, taken apart with pattern matching, and processed recursively.

Moreover, the initial conversion of the program text to an abstract syntax tree proceeds via a parser. In the context of Haskell, in the 1990s, a novel approach called **parser combinators** was developed for defining such parsers in a compositional and library-based manner. This approach has now become immensely popular and has been ported far outside FP languages.

By lowering the threshold and cost for implementing new languages, FP has enabled a new problem-solving strategy: **domain-specific languages** (**DSLs**). DSLs are niche languages created to target a specific problem domain and solve problems more efficiently, ergonomically, or in a more accessible way than with general-purpose languages. Functional DSLs are particularly successful in the financial sector where they are used to model both financial and, in combination with blockchain technology, general-purpose contracts.

Now that we have put FP and Haskell in context, let us finally dive into writing our first code.

# Writing basic functions

In this section, we write our first Haskell functions to get acquainted with Haskell's syntax and basic elements.

## Our first function

Let us start with a simple function for incrementing an integer:

```
increment :: Int -> Int
increment x = x + 1
```

This function definition consists of two lines. The first line is the *type signature* and the second line defines the behavior of the function. The type signature states that the function has the name increment and, given a value of the Int type as input, produces a result of the Int type. Here, Int is of course the type of integers such as -1, 0, and 42.

The second line is an *equation* that says that increment x (where x is any possible input) is equal to x + 1. We can read such an equation also operationally: given any x input, the increment function returns the result x + 1. Here, x is called a *variable*; it acts as a placeholder for an actual input to the function. The result x + 1 is called the *body* of the function.

To invoke the function, we put it in the Functions.hs file where the .hs extension indicates it is a Haskell source file. Next, we fire up GHCi, the interactive environment of the GHC Haskell compiler. It provides a so-called repl, a **read-eval-print loop**, that allows us to try out our code:

```
$ ghci
GHCi, version 8.10.2: https://www.haskell.org/ghc/   :? for help
Loaded GHCi configuration from /Users/toms/.ghci
Prelude>
```

After starting up, GHCi prompts us for a command. First, we want to load our source file:

```
Prelude> :load Functions
[1 of 1] Compiling Main                 ( Functions.hs, interpreted )
Ok, one module loaded.
*Main>
```

Now that the source file is loaded, we can use the increment function it defines:

```
*Main> increment 5
6
```

Here, we have called increment on 5 and GHCi tells us the result is 6. Note that the notation for function calls does not involve any parentheses like in so many other programming languages. The function name and the parameter are only separated by a space—the fancy name for this notation is **juxtaposition**. Two or more spaces would also be fine, but a single space is the conventional style.

While parentheses are not part of the syntax for functional calls, they are only used for the purpose of disambiguating the precedence of different operations. For instance, we can call the increment function on the result of 2 * 3:

```
*Main> increment (2 * 3)
7
```

The parentheses here indicate that * has precedence over increment. That is to say, first, 2 * 3 is evaluated to 6 and then the increment of 6 is computed. In contrast, we can change the precedence by changing the parentheses:

```
*Main> (increment 2) * 3
9
```

Now, 2 is incremented to 3 first, and then 3 `*` 3 yields 9. In fact, this is the default precedence and does not require parentheses:

```
*Main> increment 2 * 3
9
```

Indeed, in Haskell, named functions such as `increment` have precedence over infix operators such as + and *.

We have just written a function that takes a single parameter, but of course, we can add more.

## A two-parameter function

Let us write another function, now with two parameters:

```
average :: Float -> Float -> Float
average a b = (a + b) / 2
```

The average function takes two floating point numbers (of the `Float` type) and returns their average. Observe that juxtaposition is used again, putting the function name and its two parameters, a and b, side by side. The same juxtaposition is used when calling the function:

```
*Main> average 2 3
2.5
```

As before, parentheses only come into play to change the precedence:

```
*Main> average (5 - 3) (1.5 * 2)
2.5
```

This first evaluates 5 `-` 3 to 2 and 1.5 `*` 2 to 3 before computing the average of 2 and 3.

Haskell provides special syntax that allows us to treat a two-parameter function as if it were an operator and write it *between* its two parameters rather than *before*:

```
*Main> 2 `average` 3
2.5
```

This notation requires putting the function name (`average`) between backticks.

My recommendation is to make use of this possibility sparingly and only in cases where the function implements a mathematical operator that is usually written with an operator symbol such as a set union.

We have so far mainly focused on functions with ordinary alphabetical names such as `increment` and `average`, but operators are functions too.

## Custom operators

While Haskell comes with a number of predefined operators such as + and *, programmers can also define their own custom operators. For example, we can write the `average` function as an operator:

```
(><) :: Float -> Float -> Float
a >< b = (a + b) / 2
```

We combine the greater-than and less-than symbols into a bowtie-like operator that has no prior meaning in Haskell. Note that in the type signature, we need to surround this operator with parentheses, while we write it between its a and b parameters in the equation. This same infix notation is used when calling the operator:

```
*Main> 2 >< 3
2.5
```

Any sequence of symbols can be used, except for digits, letters, and the following special characters:

```
( ) | , ; [ ] ` { } _ " '
```

Moreover, a colon ( : ) should not be the first symbol in an operator.

While operators are customarily written between their two parameters, Haskell provides a notation that allows writing them before:

```
*Main> (><) 2 3
2.5
```

Indeed, when put between parentheses, the bowtie operator is written before its two parameters, just like the `average` function.

Again the advice is to make sparing use of custom operators. Overuse of custom operators makes your code hard to read for others. Similarly, writing operators before their parameters can be hard to read. Consider, for instance, this alternative definition of `average`:

```
average :: Float -> Float -> Float
average a b = (/) ((+) a b) 2
```

It takes more time to figure out what the body of this function does.

So far, we have worked only with the Int and Float types. Let's investigate a few more handy types that Haskell has to offer.

# Programming with primitive types

Haskell comes with several built-in primitive types that are used in most programs.

# Int and Integer

We have already used the `Int` type of integers in several examples. It supports four common arithmetic infix operators:

- `(+)` – addition

- `(-)` – subtraction

- `(*)` – multiplication

- `(^)` – exponentiation

The `(-)` operator can also be used as a prefix operator to negate a number. Besides these operators, two useful arithmetic functions are as follows:

1. `div` – integer division
2. `mod` – modulo

A common beginner mistake is to use the `(/)` operator for `Int`, but it is only defined for floating-point types such as `Float` and `Double`.

The `Int` type only covers a finite range of integers. The Haskell language specification guarantees that this covers at least the integers in the range from $-2^{29}$ to $(2^{29}-1)$, but the actual range can be implementation dependent. For example, in GHC 8.10.2, the `Int` type covers the integers from $-2^{63}$ to $(2^{63}-1)$. As in most languages, underflow or overflow can yield unexpected results:

```
*Main> 9223372036854775807 + 1 :: Int
-9223372036854775808
```

Here, `:: Int` is a type annotation. It tells Haskell that the expression should have the `Int` type. The reason we have to use it here is that Haskell defaults to the `Integer` type for integer arithmetic.

This `Integer` type covers the infinite range of integers. It is only bounded by the available memory resources:

```
*Main> 9223372036854775807 + 1
9223372036854775808
```

As we can see, no overflow happens for `Integer`. That is why Haskell uses it as the default type for integers when no type information is given; it is simply less error-prone.

These integral types cover whole numbers. In addition, Haskell, of course, also features support for fractional numbers.

## Float and Double

With the `Float` and `Double` types, Haskell provides both single and double-precision floating-point numbers:

```
Prelude> 1 / 3 :: Float
0.33333334
Prelude> 1 / 3 :: Double
0.3333333333333333
```

The default choice for Haskell is `Double`. Hence the preceding type annotation is redundant.

These two floating-point types have the `(+)`, `(-)`, and `(*)` operators in common with `Int` and `Integer`. As already announced, they also support division with `(/)`. A further difference is that the exponentiation operator is `(**)` rather than `(^)`:

```
Prelude> 2 ** 0.5
1.4142135623730951
```

In addition, there is a range of transcendental functions available. Common functions are as follows:

- `pi    :: Float`              – the `pi` constant
- `exp   :: Float -> Float`     – the e constant raised to the given power
- `log   :: Float -> Float`     – the natural logarithm
- `sqrt  :: Float -> Float`     – the square root
- `sin   :: Float -> Float`     – the sine of the given angle in radians
- `cos   :: Float -> Float`     – the cosine
- `tan   :: Float -> Float`     – the tangent

In addition, there are hyperbolic versions of `sin`, `cos`, and `tan`, as well as inverses of both sets: `sinh`, `cosh`, `tanh`, `asin`, `acos`, `atan`, `asinh`, `acosh`, and `atanh`. All these functions are also available for the `Double` type.

While numeric types are instrumental for practical programming, the next primitive type for Boolean logic is perhaps even more widely used.

## Booleans

The Haskell `Bool` type of Booleans has two values: `True` and `False`.

## Comparisons

They are often obtained by all manner of comparison operators – for example, on numeric values. For example, the `passing` function checks whether the given grade is a passing grade:

```
passing :: Float -> Bool
passing grade = grade >= 5.0
```

A grade below 5.0 is a failing grade, and above it is passing:

```
*Main> passing 4.5
False
*Main> passing 9.0
True
```

The available comparison operators are as follows:

- `(==)` – Equal
- `(/=)` – Not equal
- `(>)` – Greater than
- `(>=)` – Greater than or equal
- `(<)` – Less than
- `(<=)` – Less than or equal

## Boolean combinators

Comparisons and other Booleans can be combined into more complex conditions with the following three logical operators:

- `(&&)` `:: Bool -> Bool -> Bool` – Logical and
- `(||)` `:: Bool -> Bool -> Bool` – Logical or
- `not` `:: Bool -> Bool` – Logical negation

The `workingAge` function contains an example of a composite comparison:

```
workingAge :: Int -> Bool
workingAge age = 15 <= age && age <= 64
```

This function implements the definition of working age according to the Organization of Economic Co-operation and Development (OECD), which is between 15 and 64 years old. Observe that the `(&&)` operator has lower precedence than the comparison operators.

## *If-then-else*

Boolean conditions are often used to select between different alternatives. Haskell supports this with `if-then-else` expressions (also called conditional expressions), as shown in the following `discount` function:

```
discount :: Int -> Float
discount qty = if qty >= 10 then 0.10 else 0
```

This function computes the discount percentage based on the quantity purchased. The `if-then-else` expression is used to distinguish between two cases. If the quantity is greater than or equal to 10, then the discount is 10%. Otherwise, there is no discount (0%). These `if-then-else` expressions can be nested to distinguish more cases. Suppose we get a 15% discount when purchasing a quantity of 50 or more items. That is reflected in the following function:

```
discount2 :: Int -> Float
discount2 qty = if qty >= 50 then 0.15
                    else if qty >= 10 then 0.10 else 0
```

## *Guards*

Such nested conditionals quickly become unwieldy. Haskell's guard notation avoids this clutter:

```
discount2' :: Int -> Float
discount2' qty
    | qty >= 50  = 0.15
    | qty >= 10  = 0.10
    | otherwise  = 0
```

In this notation, we get one equation per case (15%, 10%, or 0% discount). Each case is guarded by a condition; the `otherwise` condition of the last case is just a different name for `True`. Haskell picks the first case whose condition succeeds:

```
*Main> discount2' 51
0.15
*Main> discount2' 49
0.1
*Main> discount2' 9
0.0
```

## *Exhaustive cases*

It is essential that you cover all cases when using `if-then-else` or guards. It would not be meaningful for a function not to return a result in some cases; the whole point and the only point of a Haskell function is to return a result for its input. For this reason, Haskell does not allow the omission of the `else` case of `if-then-else`; this is considered a syntax error that is detected by the compiler.

However, the Haskell compiler is, in general, unable to work out whether the guards you have written exhaustively cover all cases. You have to verify this yourself. If you have forgotten a case, this will result in a runtime exception. Suppose we forget the last case of discount2':

```
missingCase :: Int -> Float
missingCase qty
   | qty >= 50  = 0.15
   | qty >= 10  = 0.10
```

Then, we get an error at runtime for quantities below 10:

```
*Main> missingCase 9
*** Exception: Functions.hs:(11,1)-(13,21): Non-exhaustive
       patterns in function missingCase
```

The exception message points to the lines in the file where the missingCase function is defined and states that the given cases are non-exhaustive (i.e., there is a missing case).

Overall, the choice between guards and if-then-else is a matter of taste, with guards perhaps preferred more often than if-then-else, even when there are only two cases.

### Indentation-sensitive syntax

The guarded function definition with two or more cases naturally spreads out over multiple lines. It is worth pointing out that this syntax is indentation-sensitive: the | symbol, which precedes a guard, may not appear at the start of a line but must be indented by at least one space. The following code violates this rule:

```
discount2' :: Int -> Float
discount2' qty
| qty >= 50  = 0.15
| qty >= 10  = 0.10
| otherwise  = 0
```

Loading this code gives rise to a syntax error:

```
Prelude> :load Functions
[1 of 1] Compiling Main                ( Functions.hs, interpreted )

Functions.hs:13:1: error: parse error on input '|'
   |
13 | | qty >= 50  = 0.15
   | ^
Failed, no modules loaded.
```

Unfortunately, the error message is vague about the problem. It only states that the | symbol is not expected at that position, and gives no indication that adding a space fixes the issue. The solution is, of course, to indent the guard by adding one or several spaces.

Now that we have covered numeric and Boolean types, there is only one more class of primitive types we need to cover, for representing text.

## Char and String

The last two primitive types we cover are `Char` and `String`, respectively for single characters and for whole strings of characters. For now, we keep things brief, but we will return to these more extensively in a later chapter.

Values of the `Char` type are single characters written between single quotes:

```
capitalA :: Char
capitalA = 'A'
```

Values of the `String` type consist of zero or more characters between double quotes:

```
emptyString :: String
emptyString = ""

hello :: String
hello = "Hello, World!"
```

Both types use conventional character escape sequences that start with a backslash to denote non-printing characters such as a tab (`'\t'`) or a newline (`'\n'`). The escape sequence is also used to write the single quote character (`'\''`), a string containing a double quote (`"He said: \"Hello\"."`), or either a character or string containing a literal backslash (e.g., `"The backslash is written thus: \\."`).

GHCi just displays a character or string back to us the same way we have written it, including the quotes and escape sequences:

```
*Main> "Speak friend\nand enter"
"Speak friend\nand enter"
```

In *Chapter 8, Input/Output*, we will see how to make GHCi display these without quotes and with the escape sequences interpreted appropriately.

Basic operators supported on characters and strings are equality and non-equality, as well as the comparison operators:

```
*Main> 'a' == 'b'
False
```

```
*Main> "apple" < "banana"
True
```

*Chapter 3, Recursion*, will reveal that the `String` type has more structure than we are showing here. It will exploit this structure to unlock a host of additional `String` functions.

With all the primitive types we have covered, a remaining important question is how to convert from one to another.

## Converting between primitive types

Often, we want to combine data of different primitive types. For example, we want to multiply an `Int` quantity with a `Float` price:

```
*Main> (3 :: Int) * (2.10 :: Float)

<interactive>:22:15: error:
    • Couldn't match expected type 'Int' with actual type 'Float'
    • In the second argument of '(*)', namely '(2.10 :: Float)'
      In the expression: (3 :: Int) * (2.10 :: Float)
      In an equation for 'it': it = (3 :: Int) * (2.10 :: Float)
```

As we can see, this multiplication gives rise to a type error. The problem is that `(*)` is not defined for multiplying an `Int` type with `Float`. If we convert `Int` to a `Float` type, we can, however, use the available multiplication of two `Float` types that yields a `Float` type. Haskell will not implicitly do this conversion for us; we must indicate it explicitly by invoking a conversion function:

```
*Main> fromIntegral (3 :: Int) * (2.10 :: Float)
6.2999997
```

The matrix in *Table 1.1* shows a number of available conversion functions between the primitive types:

| ->      | Int                             | Integer                     | Float           | Double          | Bool | Char | String |
|---------|---------------------------------|-----------------------------|-----------------|-----------------|------|------|--------|
| Int     |                                 | from Integral               | from Integral   | from Integral   |      |      | show   |
| Integer | from Integral                   |                             | from Integral   | from Integral   |      |      | show   |
| Float   | floor, ceiling round, truncate  | floor, ceiling round, truncate |              | realTo Frac     |      |      | show   |

| -> | Int | Integer | Float | Double | Bool | Char | String |
|---|---|---|---|---|---|---|---|
| Double | floor, ceiling round, truncate | floor, ceiling round, truncate | realTo Frac | | | | show |
| Bool | | | | | | | show |
| Char | | | | | | | show |
| String | read | read | read | read | read | read | |

Table 1.1 – Conversion functions between primitive types

The entries in the matrix provide standard conversion functions between different primitive types. Rows correspond to types to convert from and columns correspond to types to convert to. If an entry is empty, there is no standard conversion function available.

The floor and ceiling functions respectively round a floating-point number down or up to an integer. In contrast, round picks the nearest of the two and prefers the even integer in the case of a tie. Finally, truncate rounds to the integer nearest to zero.

With all the types we have covered, we should discuss what Haskell does with type information.

## Putting the type checker to work

Types are very important in Haskell. It is, after all, a statically typed language. This means that programs are (type-)checked before they are run, by a process called the **type checker**. If the type checker finds that the program violates the typing discipline imposed by the language, then it raises a (type) error and the program will not be executed.

The type checker helps in several ways during the programming process.

### Checking function calls

Firstly, when calling a function, it checks that we pass parameters of the appropriate type to that function. For instance, recall that discount has the Int -> Float type:

```
*Main> discount True

<interactive>:44:10: error:
    • Couldn't match expected type 'Int' with actual type 'Bool'
    • In the first argument of 'discount', namely 'True'
      In the expression: discount True
      In an equation for 'it': it = discount True
```

The type checker tells us here that for the first argument passed to the `discount` function, namely the `True` value, it expects a value of the `Int` type while `True` is actually of the `Bool` type. The reason it expects a value of `Int` is that that's what the type signature of `discount` demands.

Observe that the last line of the error is particular to GHCi, which implicitly assigns the entered `discount True` expression to the `it` variable.

## Checking function definitions

The second way in which the type checker helps is when writing a new function definition. Start by writing the type signature of the function. This captures part of your intent for the function in a form that the type checker can compare to the implementation you supply subsequently. If the type checker finds a discrepancy, this either signals a mistake in the implementation or a mistake in the formulated intent. Either way, you will want to make adjustments, either to the implementation or to the type signature, until they are consistent.

## Disambiguating overloaded functions

We have already encountered several overloaded operators (such as `(+)`), overloaded functions (such as `fromIntegral`), and overloaded literals (such as `1`) that work at different types. It is the type checker's job to figure out at which type they are used.

Recall the definition of our first function, `increment`:

```
increment :: Int -> Int
increment x = x + 1
```

This definition features both the overloaded `(+)` operator and the overloaded literal, `1`. The former has types as follows:

```
Int      -> Int     -> Int
Integer -> Integer -> Integer
Float    -> Float   -> Float
Double  -> Double  -> Double
```

Similarly, `1` can be of the `Int`, `Integer`, `Double` type, and so on. Which type has been used here?

The type checker uses information from the context of the use to work this out. Specifically, the function signature says that the input and result of the function are both of the `Int` type. Hence, as `x` is the name given to the input, it is of the `Int` type. Also, as the result of the function is produced by `(+)`, the operator must be used at the `Int -> ? -> Int` type The only available signature for `(+)` that matches this pattern is `Int -> Int -> Int`. From that, it follows that the second argument of `(+)`, which is `1`, also has type `Int`.

## Inferring types

If we have forgotten the type of a function, we can simply ask GHCi with the :t command:

```
*Main> :t discount
discount :: Int -> Float
```

Haskell's type checker is powerful enough to automatically infer the type signature for a function definition in case none is given. However, it is in general not a good idea to omit writing type signatures. After all, you lose the ability of the type checker to find mistakes by comparing the given signature to the given implementation. Also, when the type signature is not present, it takes more effort for us humans to figure out what the implementation does; we are lacking a vital piece of documentation that we have to reconstruct ourselves. Finally, at this early stage in the book, we may not actually be able to understand the inferred type signature. There are, after all, still many features of Haskell's type system waiting for us to discover in the coming chapters. To give a taste of that, suppose we omit the type signature from the definition of discount, then this is what we get from the type checker:

```
*Main> :t discount
discount :: (Ord a, Fractional p, Num a) => a -> p
```

*Chapter 6, Type Classes*, will explain how to read such a type signature.

In summary, a function's type forms a minimal contract that stipulates how a function should be called and what it delivers in return. It is the type checker's job to enforce this contract. This becomes important when we write larger programs by combining several functions that call each other.

# Combining functions

You can write larger Haskell programs by composing simple functions into more complex ones.

## Calling functions from within functions

Functions are composed simply by defining a more complex function in terms of simpler functions. This means that the definition of the complex function calls other functions.

For example, let us write a function to compute the price of a purchase given the price of the purchased item and the quantity at which it is purchased:

```
price :: Float -> Int -> Float
price ip qty = ip * fromIntegral qty
```

This is already an example of the principle that a more complex function, price, calls simpler functions. In this case, the simpler functions are two predefined functions: the (*) operator and the fromIntegral function. Recall that the fromIntegral conversion is needed to convert the Int quantity to a Float type before it can be multiplied by the item price.

When our business logic evolves, we can introduce a discounted price that adjusts the item price. The `discount` function we wrote earlier determines, based on the purchase quantity, by what percentage to discount the price.

Let us write a complementary function that reduces a price by a given percentage:

```
reducePercentage :: Float -> Float -> Float
reducePercentage pct p = (1 - pct) * p
```

Now, we can assemble the three functions into a new one that computes the discounted purchase price:

```
discountedPrice :: Float -> Int -> Float
discountedPrice ip qty =
  reducePercentage (discount qty) (price ip qty)
```

This function computes both the discount percentage and the price before discount and then reduces the latter by the former percentage:

```
*Main> price 1.20 15
18.0
*Main> discountedPrice 1.20 15
16.2
```

While the `discountedPrice` function could have been written entirely from scratch, it becomes more readable if we define it in terms of the three simpler functions. Moreover, if the simple functions are sufficiently general, such as `reducePercentage`, they can be easily reused in other contexts.

## Naming intermediate results

The definition of `discountedPrice` is quite concise because it immediately passes the results of the `discount` and `price` functions to `reducePercentage`. Some programmers may prefer a slightly more verbose version that names the intermediate results. Haskell provides two different syntactic ways of achieving that. The first is with `let-in` expressions:

```
discountedPrice :: Float -> Int -> Float
discountedPrice ip qty =
  let p   = price ip qty
      pct = discount qty
  in reducePercentage pct p
```

Here, the `let` part defines any number of variables. These variables can be used elsewhere in the `let` part and in the `in` part.

The second approach is a `where` clause:

```
discountedPrice :: Float -> Int -> Float
discountedPrice ip qty =
```

```
reducePercentage pct p
  where p   = price ip qty
        pct = discount qty
```

Now, the `where` clause defines the variables. Unlike a `let-in` expression, which can appear anywhere an expression is valid, the `where` clause is always written at the level of an equation. Both notations are indentation sensitive: the local equations must all start in the same column.

Whether or not to name intermediate results is a matter of taste. Generally, experienced Haskell programmers would not do so in cases like this where the functions involved are all relatively simple.

## Local function definitions

Both `let-in` expressions and `where` clauses can be used to define functions that are for local use only. For example, we could make `reducePercentage` local to `discountedPrice`:

```
discountedPrice :: Float -> Int -> Float
discountedPrice ip qty =
  reducePercentage (discount qty) (price ip qty)
    where
      reducePercentage :: Float -> Float -> Float
      reducePercentage pct p = (1 - pct) * p
```

A consequence of this is that `reducePercentage` can only be used within the definition of `discountedPrice`; outside of that definition, it is not defined. Notably, we cannot try it out in GHCi:

```
*Main> reducePercentage 0.10 5.5

<interactive>:54:1: error:
    Variable not in scope: reducePercentage :: t0 -> t1 -> t
```

A local function definition is useful when the function is too specific to be reused and/or can only be understood in the context of the function for which it is defined.

## Summary

This chapter has given us a brief introduction to FP and Haskell. We have written our first Haskell functions, used Haskell's primitive types, and combined individual functions into larger programs. We have also learned about type checking and how it helps us.

In *Chapter 2, Algebraic Datatypes*, we will learn how to define our own custom datatypes, how to create values of these types with constructors, and how to take those values apart with pattern matching. We will also familiarize ourselves with a powerful abstraction mechanism for types that is used ubiquitously in Haskell: parametric polymorphism.

# Questions

1. What are the key characteristics of the Haskell language?
2. What is the purpose of parentheses in Haskell?
3. What is the difference between the `Int` and `Integer` types?
4. How does the type checker help in the programming process?
5. What are the different ways in which we can define local functions?

# Further reading

- Haskell 98 Language and Libraries: The Revised Report. Simon Peyton Jones et al. December 2002. `https://www.haskell.org/onlinereport/`

- A history of Haskell: being lazy with class. Paul Hudak, John Hughes, Simon L. Peyton Jones, Philip Wadler. HOPL 2007: 1-55.

# Answers

1. Haskell is a lazy, purely FP language that is both principled and nimble.
2. Parentheses are used for overriding or disambiguating the precedence of function and operator applications.
3. Because the `Int` type uses a fixed-size representation, it has a bounded range and wraps around when going beyond that range. In contrast, because the size of an `Integer` value is not fixed, it can be arbitrarily large.
4. The type checker makes sure that function definitions conform to their type signature and that function calls likewise respect that type signature. It also disambiguates overloaded functions and operators, and can automatically infer type signatures when none are given.
5. Haskell provides two different syntaxes for this. With `let... in...`, we can define a local function anywhere in an expression. In contrast, a `where` clause can define a function local to an equation.

# 2

# Algebraic Datatypes

While functions are, of course, central in functional programming, they have to have values to process. Haskell classifies values by means of types and provides a number of built-in types such as Integer and Bool. Yet, these built-in types are rather limited and rather generic. For this reason, Haskell provides a facility for defining user-defined datatypes, called **algebraic datatypes**.

This chapter explains how algebraic datatypes work. We first study two simple forms of algebraic datatypes (enumerations and records) that have well-known counterparts in other programming languages. Then, we merge the two features into the full-blown form of algebraic datatypes. We learn about the different elements of an algebraic datatype definition: the type name, the data constructors, and their fields. We see how algebraic datatype values are created and how they are taken apart by pattern matching. Finally, we see how both functions and algebraic datatypes can be parameterized over other types.

The term *algebraic datatype* is often abbreviated to **ADT**. It is not to be confused with the term *abstract datatype* (which is also abbreviated to ADT). The latter is not a Haskell-specific term, but a more theoretical computer science term that is not tied specifically to the features of any programming language.

The adjective *algebraic* in "algebraic datatype" refers to the fact that a new ADT can conceptually be thought of as being a composition of existing types by means of algebraic operations. **Enumeration types** can be thought of as "sums" of their alternatives, and **record types** can be thought of as the "products" of their fields. Hence, algebraic datatypes are sometimes also called **sum-of-product types**, in reference to these two operations. We will not further explore these algebraic operations on types in this book.

In this chapter, we are going to cover the following main topics:

- How do we define and use enumeration types?

- How do we define and use record types?

- How do we combine the features of enumeration types and record types into the general form of algebraic datatypes?

- How can we reuse functions that act uniformly on values of different types?

- How can we define and use datatypes that are parametric in the types of their fields?

# Enumerations

We start with one of the simplest use cases of ADTs, which are often called **enumerations**, or **enums** for short. An enumeration type is a type with a finite number of distinct values. Many programming languages provide specific support for enums, but in Haskell, they are just a special case of ADTs and not especially distinguished from other ADTs.

## A game of rock-paper-scissors

We illustrate the use of enumeration types with the well-known game of rock-paper-scissors.

Rock-paper-scissors is a two-player game. There are three possible outcomes for the first player (and likewise for the second player) – lose, draw, or win:

```
data Outcome = Lose | Draw | Win
```

The `data` keyword signals that this is the definition of a new datatype. Next comes the name of the new datatype, `Outcome`. Finally, the possible values are enumerated: `Lose`, `Draw`, and `Win`. These values are called **data constructors**, **value constructors**, or **constructors** for short. Observe that both the names of the type and of the data constructors must start with a capital letter.

A new datatype such as `Outcome` comes with only minimal functionality. The first is to create a value, which is what a constructor does. For example, writing `Win` creates a winning outcome. The second is to inspect by what constructor a value was created, which is done by means of pattern matching. For example, suppose we want to render outcome as a string:

```
render :: Outcome -> String
render Lose = "lose"
render Draw = "draw"
render Win  = "win"
```

This `render` function is defined in terms of three cases, one for each constructor. Where previously we would have written an equation of the form `render g = ...`, we now write the name of a constructor instead of a variable such as g. The more general term used in Haskell is a **pattern**. When the `render` function is applied to an input, it checks which pattern the input matches to decide what equation to use:

```
*Main> render Draw
"draw"
```

In the preceding call, the `Draw` value does not match the `Lose` pattern in the first equation. Hence, that equation is skipped. The `Draw` value does match the `Draw` pattern in the second equation. As a result, that equation is used and the result `"draw"` is returned.

The outcome of a game is determined by the two players simultaneously making a hand gesture. They can choose between three options: rock, paper, or scissors. We can model these options with another enumeration datatype:

```
data Gesture = Rock | Paper | Scissors
```

The Gesture type's structure is similar to that of the Outcome type. It too has three constructors: Rock, Paper, and Scissors. Despite the similarities, Haskell considers the types to be distinct and does not allow for them or their constructors to be interchanged.

The rules of the game stipulate that rock beats scissors, paper beats rock, and scissors beats paper. We can capture this in a two-parameter function that takes the gestures of the two players and determines the outcome for the first player:

```
play :: Gesture -> Gesture -> Outcome
play Rock     Rock     = Draw
play Rock     Paper    = Lose
play Rock     Scissors = Win
play Paper    Rock     = Win
play Paper    Paper    = Draw
play Paper    Scissors = Lose
play Scissors Rock     = Lose
play Scissors Paper    = Win
play Scissors Scissors = Draw
```

This function has 9 cases, one for each of the 3 × 3 combinations. When calling the play function, it selects the equation that matches the input:

```
*Main> render (play Paper Scissors)
"lose"
```

Just like in the case of guards, we have to make sure that every possible combination of patterns is covered by the equations. Suppose that we had forgotten the Paper-Scissors combination, then we'd get a runtime error:

```
*Main> render (play Paper Scissors)
"*** Exception: ADTs.hs:(11,1)-(19,29): Non-exhaustive patterns in
function play
```

If we launch GHCi with the -W option, it will check the source files we load for several problems, including missing cases, and issue a warning:

```
$ ghci -W
GHCi, version 8.10.2: https://www.haskell.org/ghc/  :? for help
Loaded GHCi configuration from /Users/toms/.ghci
Prelude> :l ADTs.hs
```

```
[1 of 1] Compiling Main                 ( ADTs.hs, interpreted )

ADTs.hs:11:1: warning: [-Wincomplete-patterns]
    Pattern match(es) are non-exhaustive
    In an equation for 'play': Patterns not matched: Paper Scissors
    |
11 | play Rock      Rock      = Draw
    | ^^^^^^^^^^^^^^^^^^^^^^^^^^^^^^^^ ...
Ok, one module loaded.
```

Instead of passing the -W flag to GHCi, we can also include an OPTIONS_GHC pragma at the beginning of our source file, ADTs.hs in this case (a pragma is an instruction for the compiler that is placed in the source code):

```
{-# OPTIONS_GHC -W #-}
```

A good thing about the -W flag is that it also warns us about missing cases when we extend a datatype. Suppose we extend our game from rock-paper-scissors to rock-paper-scissors-lizard-Spock:

```
data Gesture = Rock | Paper | Scissors | Lizard | Spock
```

Then, -W would tell us that the play function needs to be extended with 16 more cases.

## Don't-care patterns

With nine cases, the play function is rather lengthy. We can shorten it somewhat with the help of **don't-care patterns**:

```
play :: Gesture -> Gesture -> Outcome
play Rock      Rock      = Draw
play Rock      Scissors = Win
play Paper     Rock      = Win
play Paper     Paper     = Draw
play Scissors  Paper     = Win
play Scissors  Scissors  = Draw
play _         _         = Lose
```

This definition has only seven cases but it collates all the losing cases into the last equation. This last equation makes use of two don't-care patterns, both written as an underscore. A don't-care pattern matches any possible input. In fact, it behaves essentially like a variable pattern:

```
play x y = Lose
```

The difference is that, with the underscores, the inputs are not given names and thus cannot be mentioned in the body.

When using a don't-care pattern, it is important to be aware that pattern matching proceeds from top to bottom. The first equation that matches the input is used. Hence, if we'd put the don't-care case first, it would intercept all inputs and all other equations would be unreachable. For that reason, don't-care cases usually appear at the end.

A downside of the don't-care patterns is that they silently absorb extensions, such as adding lizard and Spock to the game, without issuing a warning. Either player using one of the two new gestures would always result in the first player losing the game. Hence, you should either avoid using these don't-care patterns with datatypes that are likely to be extended later or, when extending a datatype, carefully check whether any function definitions with don't-care patterns need to be updated.

## Booleans revisited

The `Bool` type we encountered in the previous chapter is a predefined example of an enumeration. Although the type is built into the language, it is conceptually defined as an ADT:

```
Prelude
data Bool = False | True
```

Hence, `False` and `True` are the data constructors of `Bool`, and we can define functions by pattern matching on them. For instance, we can write a function that converts a `Bool` type to an `Int` type, as follows:

```
boolToInt :: Bool -> Int
boolToInt False = 0
boolToInt True  = 1
```

Contrast this with the same function defined with the help of `if-then-else`:

```
boolToInt :: Bool -> Int
boolToInt b = if b then 1 else 0
```

Both functions behave in the same way; the difference is only one of style. Usually, `if-then-else` and guards are preferred, especially when the Boolean expresses a condition. However, sometimes pattern matching is the preferred way, for instance, when writing a Boolean operator as a truth table:

```
xor :: Bool -> Bool -> Bool
xor False False = False
xor False True  = True
xor True  False = True
xor True  True  = False
```

Whenever we need a two-value enumeration type, we can just use `Bool`. However, it is good practice (and relatively easy) to create a new ADT for each purpose. For example, to model the state of a light, we could use `Bool`, and to toggle the light, we could use the predefined `not` function. Yet, it is a good idea to define a custom datatype and function for this purpose:

```
data Light = Off | On

toggle :: Light -> Light
toggle Off = On
toggle On  = Off
```

The name of the new ADT better documents its purpose, and the names of the constructors better convey their meaning than `True` and `False`.

We now know how to define a datatype with a number of different values. Next, we will see how to define a datatype whose values are composite: they contain or group several other values.

# Records

A second use case of ADTs is often called **record** or **struct types**. The purpose of records is to group or structure several related pieces of data.

## People

We create the `Person` ADT as a first simple example of a record datatype:

```
data Person = MkPerson String Int
```

Just like in the previous section, a new ADT is announced by the `data` keyword, followed by the name of the new type, which is `Person` in this case. Whereas the enumeration examples were defined in terms of a number of alternatives separated by | characters, a record type has only one alternative. This alternative is the `MkPerson` data constructor. What's new is that this constructor takes two parameters, also called **fields**, of the `String` and `Int` types, respectively.

We create a new `Person` by calling the constructor on values of the appropriate type:

```
tom :: Person
tom = MkPerson "Tom" 45
```

In fact, the constructor behaves essentially like a function:

```
*Main> :t MkPerson
MkPerson :: String -> Int -> Person
```

The two differences are that the name of a constructor always starts with a capital letter and that a constructor does not perform any computation—it just creates a value.

We can extract the fields out of a record by means of pattern matching, as in the age function here:

```
age :: Person -> Int
age (MkPerson n a) = a
```

The typical pattern to match against a record type consists of the name of the constructor followed by a variable for each of the fields. The body can then refer to these fields by those variable names. The whole pattern is written in parentheses to indicate that it forms a single function parameter rather than multiple ones.

As we are not using the name field of the function, we can use a don't-care pattern for it instead of a variable pattern:

```
age :: Person -> Int
age (MkPerson _ a) = a
```

Finally, observe that the data constructor name of a record type can be freely chosen. We can even use the same name for the type and for the data constructor (e.g., Person) in both cases:

```
data Person = Person String Int
```

Yet, it is a common idiom to use as the data constructor name, the type name prefixed with Mk (short for "make"), as we have done here with MkPerson.

## Named fields

Haskell supports naming the fields of a record with its so-called **record syntax**. For example, suppose we have a datatype of points in a two-dimensional space. We could write in the same way as previously:

```
data Point = MkPoint Double Double
```

Yet, with two fields of the Double type, it may not be obvious which of the two is the x coordinate and which is the y coordinate. Using record syntax, we can name the two fields to document their role more explicitly:

```
data Point = MkPoint { xcoord :: Double, ycoord :: Double }
```

We can still use the datatype as if it did not have named fields. The project function illustrates this:

```
project :: Point -> Point
project (MkPoint x y) = MkPoint x 0
```

This function projects a point on the x axis, by pattern matching on a point and creating a new point with the same x coordinate and a zero y coordinate. The record syntax gives us several alternatives, both for pattern matching and for creating a new record.

Let us investigate a few alternatives:

```
project2 :: Point -> Point
project2 (MkPoint {xcoord=x}) = MkPoint {ycoord = 0, xcoord = x}
```

This second version of `project` uses the named field syntax in the pattern match and in the creation of the point. It shows that in the pattern match, we only have to list the fields we are interested in; in this case, `xcoord` is mentioned but `ycoord` is omitted. Moreover, the creation of the object shows that we can list the named fields in any order we like.

Here is another variant:

```
project3 :: Point -> Point
project3 p = MkPoint {ycoord = 0, xcoord = xcoord p}
```

The third version of `project` does not extract the x coordinate of its input via pattern matching against the `MkPoint` constructor. It just uses a variable pattern, p. To access p's x coordinate in the body, it uses the field name as a function, `xcoord :: Point -> Double`, which extracts the coordinate. Every field name gives rise to such a function.

From GHC 9.2.0 onward, fields can also be extracted with the dot notation, which is a common notation in other programming languages for accessing record fields:

```
project4 :: Point -> Point
project4 p = MkPoint {ycoord = 0, xcoord = p.xcoord}
```

Here, the record value, p, is followed by a dot and the name of the field. This notation is not available by default. It is provided as a language extension that must be explicitly enabled. This can be achieved by adding the following line at the top of the source file that uses the feature:

```
{-# LANGUAGE OverloadedRecordDot #-}
```

It can also be enabled when starting up GHCi by passing the `-XOverloadedRecordDot` flag to the executable:

```
$ ghci -XOverloadedRecordDot
```

We have one final version in store:

```
project5 :: Point -> Point
project5 p = p {ycoord = 0}
```

This is my preferred version. It expresses the intent of `project` most succinctly through the **record update syntax**. The body returns an update of p in which the y coordinate has been set to 0. The x coordinate, which is not mentioned, simply takes its original value. Mind that Haskell does not modify any values in place. Hence, p {ycoord = 0} does not actually modify p. It simply returns a new point with the same field values as p, except for the y coordinate, which is set to 0. We often refer to such a non-modifying update as a **functional update**.

## Nested records

The fields of record types can be record types themselves; we speak of **nested** records. For example, a company can have a name, a manager, and a location:

```
data Company = MkCompany { name     :: String
                         , manager  :: Person
                         , location :: Point
                         }
```

To reach deep inside such a structure, we can use nested patterns. For example, suppose we want to extract the age of the manager:

```
managerAge :: Company -> Int
managerAge (MkCompany _ (MkPerson _ a) _) = a
```

The outer layer of the (MkCompany _ m _) pattern matches against the company, with only the manager of interest, and don't-care patterns for the other two fields. However, instead of a variable pattern, m, for the manager, a (MkPerson _ a) constructor pattern is used to expose the age field of the manager.

While the preceding code is valid, it quickly becomes hard to read. Usually, it is preferable to write code in a more compositional style, with one function per layer of the nesting:

```
managerAge :: Company -> Int
managerAge c = age (manager c)
```

Here, managerAge is defined in terms of the existing functions for extracting the company's manager and for extracting a person's age.

Now that we have studied sum and record types, we are ready to move on to the general case of algebraic datatypes, which are hybrid forms of both.

# Full-blown algebraic datatypes

Full-blown algebraic datatypes combine the capabilities of both enumeration types and record types. Indeed, an ADT can have one or more data constructors, and each data constructor can have zero or more fields.

## Shapes

The following `Shape` datatype features two constructors with a number of fields:

```
data Shape = Circle Double
           | Rectangle Double Double
```

A shape can be either a circle with a given radius or a rectangle with a given width and height. The next function computes the area of such a shape:

```
area :: Shape -> Double
area (Circle r)      = pi * r**2
area (Rectangle w h) = w * h
```

This function has two equations, one with a pattern for each of the two `Shape` constructors. This case analysis is a common template for writing functions over an ADT. The general shape of such a function for `Shape` is as follows:

```
f :: Shape -> …
f (Circle r)      = …
f (Rectangle w h) = …
```

A second instance of this function is the function that computes the circumference of a shape:

```
circumference :: Shape -> Double
circumference (Circle r)      = 2 * pi * r
circumference (Rectangle w h) = 2 * (w + h)
```

A third instance generates a character pictogram of the shape:

```
pictogram :: Shape -> Char
pictogram (Circle r)      = '◯'
pictogram (Rectangle w h) = '□'
```

Mind that we can use the record syntax with all ADTs:

```
data Shape = Circle { radius :: Double }
           | Rectangle { width :: Double, height :: Double }
```

This better documents which of the two fields of the `Rectangle` constructor is the width and which is the height.

## Cards

As an example of nested ADTs, we now model the cards in a standard deck of playing cards.

Cards are classified into four different suits: clubs, spades, diamonds, and hearts:

```
data Suit = Clubs | Spades | Diamonds | Hearts
```

Each card also has a rank:

```
data Rank = Numeral Int | Face Court
```

The rank is either a numeral or a face. The numeral is an integer in the range 1-10, which we model with the Int type. A face is one of three possible court members:

```
data Court = Jack | Queen | King
```

Finally, either a card combines the previous elements or it is a joker:

```
data Card = MkCard Suit Rank | Joker
```

For example, we can create the ace of spades as follows:

```
aceOfSpades :: Card
aceOfSpades = MkCard Spades (Numeral 1)
```

## Showing cards

When creating a new datatype, it is tempting to try it out in GHCi. Yet, this may quickly lead to disappointment:

```
*Main> aceOfSpades

<interactive>:2:1: error:
    • No instance for (Show Card) arising from a use of 'print'
    • In a stmt of an interactive GHCi command: print it
```

The problem is that, off the bat, GHCi does not know how to display the values of a new ADT (here, Card, Suit, Rank, or Court values).

*Chapter 6*, *Type Classes*, will introduce the general mechanism for explaining GHCi how to display new datatypes. For now, we will restrict ourselves to adding the "magical incantation" deriving Show to each datatype declaration that we want GHCi to be able to display:

```
data Suit = Clubs | Spades | Diamonds | Hearts
  deriving Show
data Rank = Numeral Int | Face Court
  deriving Show
data Court = Jack | Queen | King
  deriving Show
data Card = MkCard Suit Rank | Joker
  deriving Show
```

Notice that we must add `deriving Show` not just to `Card` but also to all the types it depends on.

Now, GHCi can show us the card:

```
*Main> aceOfSpades
MkCard Spades (Numeral 1)
```

Now that we have covered algebraic datatypes, we move on to a different type system feature of Haskell: parametric polymorphism. The next section first introduces it in the context of functions, but the one after that integrates polymorphism in algebraic datatypes.

# Parametric polymorphism

While we have so far been focusing on custom ADTs and functions that process them, there are actually other functions that do not care about the type of values they are processing. Such functions are **(parametrically) polymorphic**.

## The identity function

One of the most trivial functions is the identity function, which just returns its input. What should be the type of this function? It works on any possible type of input. Thus we could create many copies of this function, one for each type we want to use it with:

```
idInt :: Int -> Int
idInt x = x


idBool :: Bool -> Bool
idBool x = x


idChar :: Char -> Char
idChar x = x
```

However, this leads to an unfortunate duplication of essentially the same logic. Moreover, our job is never done, as we would have to write another copy whenever we create a new ADT. Hence, instead, Haskell allows us to write a single generic definition that simultaneously works at all types:

```
Prelude
id :: a -> a
id x = x
```

The definition of this `id` function is the same as that of the preceding three specific cases. What is different is the type signature, which does not mention a concrete type of input (or output) such as `Int` or `Bool`. Instead, it uses a type variable, a. A **type variable** is written in lowercase, is usually just a single letter, and is a placeholder for any type.

The type variable is implicitly instantiated when calling the function:

```
*Main> id True
True
```

The preceding call applies `id` to `True`. As `True` is of the `Bool` type, Haskell's type checker works out that the a type variable of `id` is instantiated to `Bool`. In short, `id` is used at the `Bool -> Bool` type.

In a different call, the type variable can be instantiated to any other type:

```
*Main> id 'A'
'A'
```

In this second call, `id` is used at the `Char -> Char` type. While the types are implicit, we can add an explicit type annotation to document our intention and have it verified by the type checker:

```
*Main> (id :: Char -> Char) 'A'
'A'
```

This is useful for Haskell novices, but it is not common practice among experienced programmers.

The advantage of the type variable approach is that we only have to write a single function definition and that it works at all types, even types we have not defined yet. Taking many types is what the term *polymorphism* refers to. This particular flavor of polymorphism is known as *parametric* polymorphism because it works in the same way (uniformly) across all types.

The `id` function is one of Haskell's predefined functions. It may seem useless now, but it will turn out to be a handy building block in *Chapter 4, Higher-Order Functions*, and *Chapter 5, First-Class Functions*.

## The constant function

Another predefined polymorphic function is the constant function:

```
Prelude
const :: a -> b -> a
const x y = x
```

It is called the constant function because it returns the same result (its first input) no matter what the second input is.

The type signature of this function features two different type variables, a and b. The fact that they are different implies that they can be instantiated independently. Hence, the two inputs may be of different types:

```
*Main> const True 'A'
True
```

In the preceding call, the type variable of `a` is instantiated to `Bool`, and the type variable of `b` to `Char`. Following the type signature, the result is then of the `Bool` type as well.

Not only function signatures can feature type parameters but also ADT definitions can. In fact, often polymorphic functions act on such parametric ADTs.

# Parametric ADTs

In this section, we integrate parametric polymorphism in algebraic datatypes.

## Tuples

Haskell already has several parametric datatypes built in. A common family of these are generic record types, where the types of the fields are parameters, known as tuples.

If we were to define such tuple types ourselves as ADTs, we would probably write something like this:

```
data Tuple2 a b     = MkTuple2 a b
data Tuple3 a b c   = MkTuple3 a b c
data Tuple4 a b c d = MkTuple4 a b c d
...
```

However, the actual built-in tuple types come with a special syntax, following the mathematical notation for tuples. The type names are written as a pair of parentheses with a comma-separated list of type parameters between them:

```
(a,b)
(a,b,c)
(a,b,c,d)
...
```

Tuple values are written with essentially the same syntax:

```
*Main> :t ('a',True)
('a',True) :: (Char,Bool)
```

The `('a',True)` tuple value has the `(Char,Bool)` tuple type.

An example of a predefined function that uses tuples is the `divMod` function:

```
*Main> divMod 7 3
(2,1)
```

This function returns both the result of integer division and the modulo. In other words, the result is the same as `(div 7 3, mod 7 3)`, but computing the two results together is more efficient than doing so separately.

There are only two predefined functions for extracting the values out of tuples, and they are only for two tuples:

```
Prelude
fst :: (a,b) -> a
fst (x,y) = x


Prelude
snd :: (a,b) -> b
snd (x,y) = y
```

Here is an example:

```
*Main> snd (divMod 7 3)
1
```

The Haskell 98 Report stipulates that tuples should be supported at least up to size 15, and GHC takes it much further than that. However, it is generally a bad idea to use tuples very much and especially at larger sizes. Instead, it is a good idea to define more application-specific ADTs with meaningful names, and, in the case of many fields, to possibly use nested ADTs that group the data in smaller units. Nevertheless, tuples can be handy when quickly writing some prototype code or when returning multiple results from a function.

## Type synonyms

Functions over parametric datatypes need not necessarily be polymorphic with respect to the type parameters. For example, instead of using a new datatype for points as in the *Named fields* section of this chapter, we could use the representation (Double, Double). Then, the projection function would be written as follows:

```
project :: (Double,Double) -> (Double,Double)
project (x,_) = (x,0)
```

This function only works on tuples of Double values and is clearly not polymorphic.

Of course, it is better practice to create a separate datatype of points for this purpose. The type checker sees to it that such a new datatype cannot be confused with other tuples of Double. Yet, when quickly prototyping new code, the use of tuples can be convenient, especially as the fst and snd functions can be readily used.

In such cases, Haskell provides a middle ground, which allows documenting the purpose of the (Double, Double) type – a type synonym:

```
type PointSyn = (Double,Double)
```

The `type` keyword indicates that this is the declaration of a type synonym. The new synonym's name is `PointSyn`. It is a synonym for the `(Double,Double)` type. All a type synonym does is provide an additional name, an alias if you will, for an existing type. As far as the type checker is concerned, the type synonym and the type it is aliasing are indistinguishable. Hence, with the synonym in place, we can give `project` an alternative type signature without changing its equation:

```
project :: PointSyn -> PointSyn
project (x,_) = (x,0)
```

Whether we give this signature or the previous one has no impact on the program. Its only purpose is to document the intent of the function.

## Maybe

The `Maybe` datatype is often used where `null` is used in other programming languages, to indicate the absence of a value:

```
Prelude
data Maybe a = Nothing | Just a
```

The `Nothing` constructor signals the absence of a value, while `Just` carries a value in its field.

The `Maybe` type can be used to turn functions that would otherwise be partial (i.e., that would raise an error on some inputs) into total functions that always return a result. A good example is integer division, which raises an error when the divisor is 0 as the result is not defined:

```
Prelude> div 4 0
*** Exception: divide by zero
```

With `Maybe`, we can make a safe version of `div` that always returns a result:

```
safeDiv :: Integer -> Integer -> Maybe Integer
safeDiv x y
   | y == 0      = Nothing
   | otherwise = Just (div x y)
```

This function does not generate a runtime error:

```
*Main> safeDiv 4 0
Nothing
*Main> safeDiv 4 2
Just 2
```

While most languages do not use different types to distinguish the possibility and impossibility of getting `null`, in Haskell, the `Integer` and `Maybe Integer` types are different.

A consequence, which may seem a downside but is actually the point of using Maybe, is that we cannot use Maybe Integer where Integer is expected. For instance, we can't just apply + 1 to it. Instead, we have to inspect the Maybe Integer value. If it is Nothing, we need to treat it appropriately. Otherwise, we can extract the Integer value and process it further:

```
incrementMaybe :: Maybe Integer -> Maybe Integer
incrementMaybe Nothing = Nothing
incrementMaybe (Just x) = Just (x + 1)
```

Often, the Nothing case, and thus the Maybe type, is propagated during further processing. *Chapter 11, Monads*, will present useful infrastructure to enable this.

## Either

Our last example of a predefined parametric ADT is Either:

```
data Either a b = Left a | Right b
```

This type has two type parameters, a and b, and two corresponding constructors, Left and Right. A value of the Either a b type is either a value of the a type wrapped up in a Left constructor, or a value of the b type wrapped up in a Right constructor.

The Either a b type can be used to combine any two types into a single type. While this potentially has many applications, it is often more sensible to define a custom ADT specialized to a specific application. Thus, just like tuples, the use of Either is a *bad code smell* that is suggestive of quick and dirty code.

One prominent use case of Either e a is to distinguish an ordinary result of the a type from an explanation of the e type why no result is available. Compare this to Maybe a, where Nothing denotes the absence of a value but does not explain why. We can, for example, define a custom datatype to signify different errors related to a bank transfer:

```
data TransferError = NonPositiveAmount | InsufficientFunds
```

These can be used by a function that performs the transfer:

```
data Account = MkAccount { owner :: String, amount :: Double }

transfer :: Account -> Account -> Double
  -> Either TransferError (Account,Account)
transfer from to amt
  | amt <= 0
  = Left NonPositiveAmount
  | amount from < amt
  = Left InsufficientFunds
```

```
  | otherwise
  = Right (from { amount = amount from - amt }
          ,to   { amount = amount to   + amt }
          )
```

Thanks to the use of `TransferError`, we get an explanation for why a transfer fails and can take remedial action accordingly.

## The unit type

Lastly, we present another predefined type. This type is the simplest imaginable: it has only one value. Hence, it is also called the **unit** type. Haskell provides a special syntax for it: both the name of the type and the one value are written `()`. You can also view this as a nullary tuple.

On its own, this type is not very useful. After all, since it only has one value, we don't need to inspect the value to know what it is. In other words, the values of this type carry no information. Nevertheless, it is sometimes used to instantiate the type parameters of parametric types to obtain degenerate cases. For example, `Either () a` carries essentially the same information as `Maybe a`. Hence, it is a degenerate case of `Either` where we do not exploit the ability to distinguish between different error cases.

We can witness the equivalence (also called **isomorphism**, a mathematical term) with two functions that convert between the two types:

```
eitherToMaybe :: Either () a -> Maybe a
eitherToMaybe (Left ()) = Nothing
eitherToMaybe (Right x) = Just x

maybeToEither :: Maybe a -> Either () a
maybeToEither Nothing = Left ()
maybeToEither (Just x) = Right x
```

This is just a small example of why it is useful to have a trivial type available as a building block. *Chapter 11, Monads*, will have more compelling applications.

## Summary

This chapter has explained to us how to define and use algebraic datatypes, with pattern matching as a notable concept for taking values apart. First, we have seen the restricted forms of enumeration types and record types. Next, we have seen how these can be in their more general form by combining features of the two. We have also introduced parametric polymorphism, a powerful mechanism for abstracting over types, that can be used in function signatures and in the definition of algebraic datatypes.

In *Chapter 3*, *Recursion*, we will learn about recursive definitions, which can be used for both functions and datatypes. Recursive function definitions are the counterpart of imperative loops and enable (both bounded and unbounded) repetition of computation. Recursive datatype definitions enable data structures of arbitrary size and are typically processed by recursive functions.

## Questions

1.  How can you define and use enumeration types?

2.  How does the record syntax work?

3.  What do algebraic datatype definitions look like and how do you use them?

4.  How can the same function definition be reused for different types of input?

5.  How can the same datatype definition be reused for different types of fields?

## Answers

1.  Enumeration types are defined with the syntax `data ET = K1 | ... | Kn`, where `ET` is the name of the type and `K1...Kn` are the names of the data constructors. Each of the constructors is a value of the enumeration type. Values can be distinguished by means of pattern matching, writing one equation of a function per constructor:

    ```
    f K1 = ..

    ...
    f Kn = ...
    ```

2.  Record types are defined with the syntax `data RT = RK {f1 :: T1, ..., fn :: Tn}`, where `RT` is the name of the record type and `RK` is its constructor. The fields are named `f1...fn` and have the `T1...Tn` types, respectively. A value of `RT` is created with the syntax `RT { f1 = e1, ..., fn=en}`, where `e1...en` are expressions of the `T1...Tn` types that yield the values for the fields. Given a value of the record type, a field can be extracted by using the field name as a function, `fi :: RT -> Ti`.

3.  An algebraic datatype is defined with the syntax `data AT = K1 T11... | ... | Kn Tn1 ...`, where `AT` is the name of the algebraic datatype and its constructors are `K1...Kn`. Each `Ki` constructor has zero or more fields of the `Ti1` type, and so on. A value is created by applying a constructor to expressions of the constructor's field types. Constructors can be distinguished and fields extracted by means of pattern matching.

4.  By using type variables, a function's type signature can abstract over types and allow the function to be called at any choice of type for those type variables. This is called parametric polymorphism.

5.  Just like a function signature, a datatype can use type variables in its field types. The datatype is then parameterized in those type variables.

# 3
# Recursion

The functions and datatypes we have written so far are limited in power:

- We lack a mechanism to repeat a number of computation steps. If we want some computation to be repeated five times, we explicitly have to write five function calls. If we want six instead, we have to modify the program and add a sixth call.

- Similarly, we lack a mechanism to arbitrarily extend the size of a data structure. If we want a data structure that holds five values, we have to write an **algebraic datatype (ADT)** definition with a constructor that has five fields. If five is not enough, and we want six instead, we need to modify existing definitions.

These extensions of existing definitions quickly become unwieldy for larger sizes, and we cannot dynamically determine the number at runtime (at least not beyond the cases we have explicitly foreseen while writing the program).

Imperative programs solve this problem in two different ways for repeated computations and data structure sizes. For repeated computations, they provide loops (notably, `for` and `while` loops), while for data structures of arbitrary size, they typically work with a pointer mechanism to create a web of interconnected values.

In functional programming, we have a single unified approach to both problems that is based on a mathematical concept – **recursive definitions**. Recursion is a powerful mechanism whereby an entity, either a function or a datatype, is defined in terms of itself. The fact that the same concept is used for both functions and datatypes means that, when processing recursive datatypes with recursive functions, their structures naturally align. This leads to highly succinct and elegant definitions.

We will first focus on the built-in datatype of lists, which is probably the most ubiquitous recursive datatype in Haskell. We explain how to work with lists using predefined library functions, the succinct list comprehension mechanism, and our own recursive functions. Next, we will move on to writing our own recursive algebraic datatypes and corresponding recursive functions. We will highlight structural recursion, which is a way of defining recursive functions that align with the recursive structure of the datatypes they process, and explore several variations. Finally, we will touch upon freer forms of recursion.

In this chapter, we will answer the following questions:

- How do you work with lists and list comprehensions?
- How do you write recursive functions to process lists?
- How do you define your own recursive algebraic datatypes?
- What is structural recursion?
- What are common variations on structural recursion?
- What recursion patterns are not structural?

## Standard libraries

From this chapter onward, we will more actively see and use code from the Haskell standard libraries. This serves two purposes. Firstly, functions in the standard libraries often serve as good examples of particular programming patterns. Secondly, knowing these library functions (alongside the language features and programming patterns) makes us more fluent programmers.

Haskell comes with a rich set of standard libraries. The most prominent library is called the Prelude. It comes with some of the most heavily used functionality and does not need to be explicitly imported; it is imported by default. Another library that we will use frequently is Data.List, which contains functions related to lists. This library has to be imported explicitly by putting the following declaration at the top of the source file:

```
import Data.List
```

This imports all the functionality provided by the library. If only a small subset of that functionality should be imported, it can be enumerated as follows:

```
import Data.List (nub, tails)
```

Now, we only import the nub and tails functions from `Data.List`.

When showing definitions of library functions, we will annotate them with the name of the library that provides them. For example, here, we indicate that sum is provided by the `Prelude`:

```
Prelude
sum :: [Integer] -> Integer
sum []     = 0
sum (x:xs) = x + sum xs
```

The implementation we give may deviate from the one actually used in the library. This is because we typically want to illustrate a particular programming pattern and do so in its purest form, while the implementation in the library is often somewhat more involved because of performance concerns.

# Lists

As a first example of recursion, we will study Haskell's built-in datatype for lists.

## List syntax

A list is a sequence of an arbitrary number of elements of some type. For instance, `seasons` is a list of strings:

```
seasons :: [String]
seasons = ["spring","summer","fall","winter"]
```

The signature shows that the list type is written as two square brackets, [ and ], with the type of elements between them. In the case of seasons, the element type is `String`. The equation of seasons shows that a list value is written as a comma-separated list of elements between square brackets.

As the notation suggests, the list type is parametric in its element type. For example, `redSuits` is a list of `Suit`s:

```
redSuits :: [Suit]
redSuits = [Hearts,Diamonds]
```

This uses the `Suit` datatype from the previous chapter.

A special case of a list is an empty list – for example, of `Bool` elements:

```
noBools :: [Bool]
noBools = []
```

Another special case is the singleton (i.e., one-element) list – in this case, of `Int` elements:

```
anInt :: [Int]
anInt = [7]
```

## List syntax desugared

The comma-separated list syntax is *syntactic sugar*. That means it is a sugarcoating of more primitive notation, which doesn't look as nice. The primitive syntax for Haskell consists of two data constructors:

```
[]  :: [a]
(:) :: a -> [a] -> [a]
```

The first constructor is that for the empty list, which is written as [], as we already saw. The second constructor is in fact an operator, the colon. It takes an element and a list, and creates a new list. In the new list, the given element is the first element or *head*. The remainder of the new list is formed by the given list or *tail*. Hence, we can think of (:) as adding an element in front of an existing list.

We can write `redSuits` in terms of the primitive notation, as follows:

```
redSuits :: [Suit]
redSuits = Hearts : (Diamonds : [])
```

Reading from right to left, this starts from the empty list, adds `Diamonds` in front, and `Hearts` in front of that. Because the `(:)` operator associates to the right, we can, in fact, omit the parentheses:

```
redSuits :: [Suit]
redSuits = Hearts : Diamonds : []
```

One will rarely encounter a full list written in this primitive notation; the syntactic sugar is much preferred. Yet, the `(:)` operator comes in handy when extending an unknown list. For example, the following `addOne` function adds `1` to the front of a list:

```
addOne :: [Int] -> [Int]
addOne list = 1 : list
```

This extends any given list of `Int` elements:

```
*Main> addOne [2,3]
[1,2,3]
*Main> addOne []
[1]
```

Observe that GHCi also prefers the syntactic sugar when showing us list results. Nevertheless, the primitive syntax has the merit of revealing the recursive nature of lists. The base case is the empty list, `[]`, which exists on its own. However, non-empty lists, created with the `(:)` operator, require an already existing list to create a new one. Hence, lists are compositional in nature, where ever-larger lists can be created by adding more elements to the front. In short, it is the recursive nature that enables lists of arbitrary size.

## Predefined list functions

Haskell comes with a range of predefined functions on lists. We will review a handful of the most important ones here.

Firstly, `null :: [a] -> Bool` tests whether a given list is empty:

```
*Main> null []
True
*Main> null [1,2]
False
```

Next, `head :: [a] -> a` and `tail :: [a] -> [a]` return respectively the first element and the remainder of a non-empty list:

```
*Main> head [1,2,3]
1
*Main> tail [1,2,3]
[2,3]
```

These functions should not be used on empty lists though:

```
*Main> head []
*** Exception: Prelude.head: empty list
*Main> tail []
*** Exception: Prelude.tail: empty list
```

Together, these three functions can be used to process lists:

```
Prelude
sum :: [Integer] -> Integer
sum l
    | null l      = 0
    | otherwise   = head l + sum (tail l)
```

If the input list is empty, the function returns 0. Otherwise, it adds the head of the list to the sum of its tail. While this definition works, it is not the preferred way of writing the function. In the *Custom list processing* section, we will see the more conventional Haskell style.

A further useful function is `length :: [a] -> Int`, which returns the number of elements in a list:

```
*Main> length []
0
*Main> length [True,False,False]
3
```

The `(!!) :: [a] -> Int -> a` operator selects the element at the given position (the *index*) in the list:

```
*Main> [1,2,3,4] !! 0
1
*Main> [1,2,3,4] !! 2
3
```

As the example shows, the first element has index 0, the second element has index 1, and so on. Using an index that is out of range leads to a runtime error:

```
*Main> [1,2,3,4] !! 4
*** Exception: Prelude.!!: index too large
```

While indexing into an array is a common operation in imperative languages, it is not very popular in Haskell, as getting the index right can be rather error-prone. We will see plenty of examples of list manipulation in this book, but hardly any indexing.

While the `(:)` constructor builds up a list one element at a time, it is much more convenient to append two smaller lists to obtain a larger list. This is accomplished with the `(++)  ::  [a]  -> [a]  -> [a]` operator:

```
*Main> [1,2] ++ [3,4]
[1,2,3,4]
*Main> [] ++ [True]
[True]
```

Finally, a range of integers can be obtained using the following special range syntax:

```
*Main> [1..10]
[1,2,3,4,5,6,7,8,9,10]
*Main> [5..7]
[5,6,7]
*Main> [10..1]
[]
```

This yields a list with the consecutive integers in the given range. If the lower bound of the range is larger than the upper bound, the resulting list is empty.

A variation on this notation enables a step size different than 1:

```
*Main> [10,9..1]
[10,9,8,7,6,5,4,3,2,1]
*Main> [1,3..10]
[1,3,5,7,9]
```

The step size is determined by the first two given elements.

## List comprehensions

List comprehensions are a powerful mechanism to define new lists in terms of existing lists, adapted from a similar mathematical notation for sets.

### Generators

Here is the first example:

```
*Main> [ 2*x | x <- [1,2,3]]
[2,4,6]
```

A list comprehension can be recognized by the [ ... | ... ] syntax. The x <- [1,2,3] part is called a *generator*. It draws x from the [1,2,3] list. Hence, x successively takes the values 1, 2, and 3. The list comprehension produces a new list whose elements are of the form 2*x. Given the values that x takes, the resulting list is [2*1,2*2,2*3], or [2,4,6] when fully evaluated.

A list comprehension can contain multiple generators:

```
*Main> [ (x,y) | x <- [1,2,3], y <- [4,5]]
[(1,4),(1,5),(2,4),(2,5),(3,4),(3,5)]
```

This draws x from the [1,2,3] list and, for each value of x, considers all the ways to draw y from the [4,5] list. The example simply returns all combinations as tuples, (x,y). We can, of course, combine x and y any way we like – for example, by adding them:

```
*Main> [ x+y | x <- [1,2,3], y <- [4,5]]
[5,6,6,7,7,8]
```

## Guards

Not all values produced by the generators have to be used in the resulting list. With the help of a guard, we can select those we want and discard the others:

```
*Main> [ 2*x | x <- [1,2,3], odd x]
[2,6]
```

Here, the predefined odd :: Integer -> Bool function checks whether a given number is odd. The odd x Boolean expression is a guard. The guard discards all the numbers that are not odd – that is, the value 2. Hence, the resulting list is [2*1,2*3].

Guards can combine the variables of different generators:

```
*Main> [ (x,y) | x <- [1,2,3], y <- [4,5], odd (x + y)]
[(1,4),(2,5),(3,4)]
```

A more sophisticated example generates all so-called Pythagorean triples in the range of 1–100:

```
triples :: [(Int,Int,Int)]
triples = [ (a,b,c) | a <- [1..100]
                    , b <- [1..100]
                    , c <- [1..100]
                    , a^2 + b^2 == c^2
                    ]
```

While this definition does the job, it is not particularly efficient.

## Symmetry breaking and guard scheduling

The first inefficiency is that it computes every triple essentially twice. For example, both (3,4,5) and (4,3,5) occur in the result. Generally, when (a,b,c) is a solution, so is (b,a,c). We can avoid this by adding an additional guard that only keeps one of the two symmetric results:

```
triples :: [(Int,Int,Int)]
triples = [ (a,b,c) | a <- [1..100]
                    , b <- [1..100]
                    , c <- [1..100]
                    , a^2 + b^2 == c^2
                    , a < b
                    ]
```

With the additional guard, a < b, only (3,4,5) is produced and not (4,3,5); this is known as *symmetry breaking*.

Putting the new guard at the end of the list comprehension is actually not the best idea. We are better off *scheduling* it as early as possible, as soon as both a and b have been generated:

```
triples :: [(Int,Int,Int)]
triples = [ (a,b,c) | a <- [1..100]
                    , b <- [1..100]
                    , a < b
                    , c <- [1..100]
                    , a^2 + b^2 == c^2
                    ]
```

This tests a < b once for every possible combination of a and b, instead of 100 times (once for every possible value of c).

## Interdependent generators

We can take the a < b guard into account even earlier by incorporating it into the generator. Indeed, we can restrict ourselves to generating only values for b that are larger than a:

```
triples :: [(Int,Int,Int)]
triples = [ (a,b,c) | a <- [1..100]
                    , b <- [(a+1)..100]
                    , c <- [1..100]
                    , a^2 + b^2 == c^2
                    ]
```

Observe that the generator for b depends on a. The same idea can be applied to the generator for c, which is bound to be larger than b:

```
triples :: [(Int,Int,Int)]
triples = [ (a,b,c) | a <- [1..100]
                    , b <- [(a+1)..100]
                    , c <- [(b+1)..100]
                    , a^2 + b^2 == c^2
                    ]
```

Together, these optimizations reduce the original search space from 1,000,000 combinations to 161,700, which is a reduction of almost 84%. Perhaps you can think of further ways to reduce this number.

## Strings revisited

Haskell's predefined String type is not actually a primitive type. Strings are just lists of characters, and the String type is defined as a type synonym accordingly:

```
type String = [Char]
```

The only thing that is special about strings, as opposed to other lists, is how we write them and how GHCi renders them. In fact, we can write strings with the square bracket notation just like other lists:

```
*Main> ['H','e','l','l','o']
"Hello"
```

The advantage of the strings-as-lists approach is that we don't need a separate set of functions to work on lists. We can simply reuse all the available list functions. For example, we can use head to get the first character of a string:

```
*Main> head "Hello"
'H'
```

The (++) operator is also useful to append strings:

```
*Main> "Hello" ++ " World!"
"Hello World!"
```

A disadvantage of using lists to represent strings is that the representation takes up more memory than a built-in representation. For this reason, Haskell also provides the Data.Text library for strings with an opaque, but memory-efficient, representation.

Now that we have a good idea of the main predefined functionality for lists, let us complement this by writing our own custom list functions.

## Custom list processing

We can write our own functions to process lists in very much the same style as we wrote functions over algebraic datatypes in the previous section.

As a first example, let us write evenLength. This function determines whether a given list has an even length:

```
evenLength :: [a] -> Bool
evenLength []     = True
evenLength (x:xs) = not (evenLength xs)
```

The empty list case is the base case – the empty list does have an even length. The non-empty list case is the recursive case. We determine whether the tail, xs, has an even length and then negate its result to determine whether (x:xs) has an even length.

It is instructive to see how a recursive function such as evenLength is evaluated:

```
  evenLength (1 : 2 : 3 : [])
= not (evenLength (2 : 3 : []))
= not (not (evenLength (3 : [])))
= not (not (not (evenLength [])))
= not (not (not True))
= False
```

The preceding snippet shows a sequence of simplification steps that starts from the evenLength [1,2,3] function call. Because it is easier to see how this works, we have, in fact, already desugared the call to the primitive list notation, evenLength (1 : 2 : 3 : []). In each step, we replace the function call with the matching equation in the definition of the evenLength function. We can see how the list gets smaller in every step while the result is built up.

A similar function, which we saw written with guards earlier, sums the elements of a list of integers:

```
Prelude
sum :: [Integer] -> Integer
sum []     = 0
sum (x:xs) = x + sum xs
```

Here is an example of derivation:

```
  sum (1 : 2 : 3 : [])
= 1 + sum (2 : 3 : [])
= 1 + 2 + sum (3 : [])
= 1 + 2 + 3 + sum []
= 1 + 2 + 3 + 0
= 6
```

We have now comprehensively covered lists as our first example of recursive datatypes. Let us move on to additional examples.

# Recursive datatypes

While the list type is predefined, we can also define our own recursive algebraic datatypes.

## Arithmetic expressions

The `Expr` datatype is a symbolic representation of arithmetic expressions:

```
data Expr = Lit Int | Add Expr Expr
```

The recursive datatype `Expr` has two constructors:

- The first, `Lit`, is the base case; it represents a trivial expression that is just an `Int` constant (aka literal)

- The second constructor, `Add`, is a recursive case; an addition is built out of two smaller expressions (also called subexpressions)

For example, we symbolically represent $2 + 5$ as `Add (Lit 2) (Lit 5)`.

Of course, a symbolic expression is just data; it does not compute. To actually evaluate expressions, we need to write an evaluation function:

```
eval :: Expr -> Int
eval (Lit n)     = n
eval (Add e1 e2) = eval e1 + eval e2
```

This function has a base case that returns the `Int` value of the literal and a recursive case for `Add` that sums the evaluation results of the two subexpressions. The function turns the `Expr` data into a computation with the expected behavior:

```
*Main> eval (Add (Lit 2) (Lit 5))
7
```

A second function turns an expression into the usual textual representation:

```
renderExpr :: Expr -> String
renderExpr (Lit n)     = show n
renderExpr (Add e1 e2) =   renderExpr e1 ++ " + " ++ renderExpr e2
```

Here is an example of a function call:

```
*Main> renderExpr (Add (Lit 2) (Lit 5))
"2 + 5"
```

## Parametric recursive datatypes

Recursive datatypes can be parametric too. The most prominent example is the built-in list type, [a], which is parametric in the type of elements. If we would write it ourselves as a custom ADT, it would look as follows:

```
data List a = Nil | Cons a (List a)
```

This List a definition makes it apparent that lists are recursive, with the empty list (Nil) as the base case and Cons as the recursive constructor that takes an element and the tail of the list as its parameter.

This is what the length function looks like on this ADT:

```
lengthList :: List a -> Int
lengthList Nil          = 0
lengthList (Cons x xs) = 1 + lengthList xs
```

Another common datatype that is both parametric and recursive is that of trees. Trees denote a generic hierarchical structure where the type of elements in the hierarchy is a parameter. There are many different possible definitions. Here is one:

```
data Tree a = Empty | Branch (Tree a) a (Tree a)
```

This definition states that a tree is either empty (the base case) or consists of a branch (the recursive case). A branch holds two subtrees and an element. The type of elements is a type parameter of the Tree type.

Here is an example tree with the elements 1, 2, and 3:

```
tree123 :: Tree Int
tree123 = Branch (Branch Empty 2 Empty)
                 1
                 (Branch Empty 3 Empty)
```

The treeToList function turns the branching structure of a tree into a list:

```
treeToList :: Tree a -> [a]
treeToList Empty         = []
treeToList (Branch l x r) = x : treeToList l ++ treeToList r
```

An empty tree yields an empty list. A branch yields a list where the element comes first, followed by, respectively, the elements of the left and right subtrees:

```
*Main> treeToList tree123
[1,2,3]
```

While the definition of recursive ADTs should now be clear, it is worthwhile diving deeper into the definition of recursive functions.

# Structural recursion

You may have noticed that the recursive functions we have written so far in this section show a great deal of commonality. This is no coincidence, as they are, in fact, all based on the same recipe for writing recursive functions, known as *structural recursion*. Structurally recursive functions are sometimes also called *catamorphisms*.

## Structural recursion on lists

Let us revisit two recursive functions on lists we wrote earlier and expose their common structure:

```
evenLength :: [a] -> Bool
evenLength []      = True
evenLength (x:xs) = not (evenLength xs)
Prelude
sum :: [Integer] -> Integer
sum []      = 0
sum (x:xs) = x + sum xs
```

These two definitions follow a standard recursion scheme to define functions over a list:

```
f :: [A] -> B
f []      = n
f (x:xs) = c x (f xs)
```

It features two equations, one for the empty list pattern, `[]`, and one for the non-empty list pattern, `(x:xs)`. The former is the base case of the recursion, while the latter is the recursive case. The recursive case features a recursive function call, `(f xs)`, in its body. This way, the function winds its way down to the base case. Of course, the recursive case can also refer to x, the first element of the list.

Besides the name of the function, which obviously varies from one function to the next, there are four elements in the recursion scheme, which we have underlined, that can be chosen by a concrete function:

1.  The first choice, in the signature of the function, is the type of elements, A, in the list. This is not specific for structural recursion, but a choice that has to be made for every function over lists. The `evenLength` function works for any type of element and, hence, uses a type variable, a, in its signature. In contrast, the `sum` function only works for `Integer` elements.

2.  The second choice, also in the signature, is the result type, B, of the function, which need not be the same type as that of the list elements. The `evenLength` function returns `Bool`, while the `sum` function returns an `Integer`.

3. Next, in the first equation of the function, which covers the empty list base case, we can choose the resulting value, n. This value, of course, has to be of the result type, B. The evenLength function returns the Bool value, True, for the empty list, while the sum function returns the Integer value, 0.

4. Finally, the second equation returns the result for the recursive case. This result is defined in terms of a c :: A -> B -> B function that combines the first element, x, and the result of the recursive call, (f xs), into the overall result. In the case of sum, this function, c, is clearly the operator, (+). In the case of evenLength, the c function is less explicit. It is, in fact, the following function:

```
cEL :: a -> Bool -> Bool
cEL x r = not r
```

However, instead of explicitly calling cEL x (evenLength xs), the reduced form, not (evenLength xs), is used.

Another application of this structural recursion scheme is the predefined and function that checks whether all Booleans in the given list are True:

```
Prelude
and :: [Bool] -> Bool
and []     = True
and (x:xs) = x && and xs
```

All elements of the empty list are indeed True. In the non-empty list, the first element has to be True, and all elements in the tail also have to be True.

## Structural recursion on other algebraic datatypes

The structural recursion scheme for lists can be adapted to any other algebraic datatype, following the same principles. Here it is for the expression datatype:

```
f :: Expr -> B
f (Lit n)     = l n
f (Add e1 e2) = a (f e1) (f e2)
```

It differs from that of lists in that it has equations for the two constructors of the Expr type. There is no choice of the A element type, as Expr is not a parametric type. There are just three choices to be made:

1. The first choice is result type B. In the case of the eval function this is Int.

2. The second choice is what to return in the base case – that is, the case of a literal, Lit n. This result can depend on the integer field, n, of the Lit constructor. Hence, in general, it can be expressed as l n, where l :: Int -> B. In the case of eval, this function is as follows:

```
lE :: Int -> Int
lE x = x
```

However, the function is not shown as `1E n` but in its already reduced form, `n`.

3.  The third choice is what to return in the recursive case of the `Add e1 e2` constructor. This
    is an `a :: B -> B -> B` function of the recursive calls, `(f e1)` and `(f e2)`, on the
    two subexpressions. In the case of `eval`, this is just the `(+)` operator.

Let us use this recursion to write another function, `literals`, on expressions, one that returns a list of
all the integer values that appear as literals in an expression. Here is an example of the intended behavior:

```
*Main> literals (Add (Lit 2) (Lit 5))
[2,5]
```

From the description, we can work out that the function should return a list of integers. Hence, the
result type, B, is `[Int]`:

```
literals :: Expr -> [Int]
```

In the case of `(Lit n)`, there is only one literal value, and that is n. The function that turns one
element into a (one-element) list is as follows:

```
singleton :: Int -> [Int]
singleton n = [n]
```

Hence, the base case of the function can be written thus:

```
literals (Lit n)      = singleton n
```

As the `singleton` function is so simple, it is natural to replace its call with the right-hand side of
its definition:

```
literals (Lit n)      = [n]
```

Lastly, in the case of `(Add e1 e2)`, we should combine the literals of `e1` and `e2` into a single list.
This can be accomplished with the `(++)` operator for appending lists:

```
literals (Add e1 e2) = literals e1 ++ literals e2
```

In summary, we end up with the following definition:

```
literals :: Expr -> [Int]
literals (Lit n)      = [n]
literals (Add e1 e2) = literals e1 ++ literals e2
```

Following the same recipe, you should now be able to work out the structural recursion scheme for
the `Tree` type.

Structural recursion is a very elegant template for writing recursive functions. Unfortunately, it doesn't
always apply.

# Variants on structural recursion

Not all recursive functions can be written in a basic structurally recursive manner on an algebraic datatype. Here, we will review a range of common variations and extensions.

## Primitive recursion

Structurally recursive functions only use the recursive occurrences of a datatype (e.g., the tail of a list or the subtrees of a tree) in recursive calls. Consider the following predefined function, which multiplies all the elements of a list:

```
Prelude
product :: [Integer] -> Integer
product []     = 1
product (x:xs) = x * product xs
```

The body of the recursive case only uses the tail of the list, xs, in the recursive call product, xs. This is an essential part of structural recursion; the tail cannot be used in any other way.

Primitive recursive functions (also called *paramorphisms*) relax this condition; the recursive occurrences can be used in other ways. For example, the following function computes all the tails of a list:

```
tails' :: [a] -> [[a]]
tails' []     = [[]]
tails' (_:xs) = xs : tails' xs
```

Observe that the recursive case uses the tail, xs, in two ways – in a recursive call, and as part of the output list:

```
*Main> tails' [1,2,3]
[[2,3],[3],[]]
```

There is an actual predefined function, which is defined as follows:

```
Data.List
tails :: [a] -> [[a]]
tails l = l : tails' l
```

It adds the input list to the other tails:

```
*Main> tails [1,2,3]
[[1,2,3],[2,3],[3],[]]
```

There is a fun idiom that uses `tails` in a list comprehension to generate all combinations of two elements from a given list:

```
allPairs :: [a] -> [(a,a)]
allPairs l = [ (x,y) | (x:xs) <- tails l, y <- xs ]
```

The list comprehension features two interdependent generators. The first generator draws a non-empty `(x:xs)` list from the tails of the input list. This will successively bind `x` to all the elements in `l`. The second generator draws `y` from the elements, `xs`, that appear after `x` in the list:

```
*Main> allPairs [1,2,3]
[(1,2),(1,3),(2,3)]
```

## Recursion on integers

While the two integer types of Haskell are built into the language and not proper ADTs, it can be convenient to recursively define functions on them that count down to a base case (usually 0):

```
fac :: Integer -> Integer
fac 0 = 1
fac n = n * fac (n - 1)
```

This factorial function computes the product, `n * (n-1) * ... * 2 * 1 * 1`, recursively. In each step, the integer becomes smaller until it reaches the base case, which accounts for the final factor, 1, in the product.

We have to be careful with such definitions because, when called with a negative number, the recursion moves away from the base case. This process does not terminate. A more robust definition could guard against that:

```
fac :: Integer -> Integer
fac n
  | n <= 0    = 1
  | otherwise = n * fac (n - 1)
```

Here, all negative numbers are incorporated into the base case.

## Additional parameters

Structurally recursive functions often require additional information beyond the data structure they recurse on. This additional information can be passed in as one or more parameters.

An interesting example of this pattern is the `(++)` operator, which appends two lists:

```
Prelude
(++) :: [a] -> [a] -> [a]
[]       ++ ys = ys
(x:xs) ++ ys = x : (xs ++ ys)
```

This operator performs structural recursion on the first list but also needs the second list to do its job. It basically rebuilds the first list but inserts the second list where `[]` was in the first list:

```
   (1 : 2 : 3 : []) ++ [4,5]
= 1 : (2 : 3 : []) ++ [4,5]
= 1 : 2 : (3 : []) ++ [4,5]
= 1 : 2 : 3 : [] ++ [4,5]
= 1 : 2 : 3 : [4,5]
```

The result can also be written `[1,2,3,4,5]`.

We obtain a second example by adding another case to the `Expr` datatype to represent a variable:

```
data Expr = X | Lit Int | Add Expr Expr
```

This allows us to present expressions with one variable. For instance, 2 + (x + 5) can be written as `Add (Lit 2) (Add X (Lit 5))`. In *Section 5.5.1*, we will see how to support an arbitrary number of variables, but for the time being, one is enough.

The additional constructor requires a new case in the `eval` function:

```
eval :: Expr -> Int -> Int
eval X          x = x
eval (Lit n)    x = n
eval (Add e1 e2) x = eval e1 x + eval e2 x
```

The new base case for the X variable causes some upheaval as it introduces a second parameter to the function. This `Int` parameter is the value that the variable takes. It not only appears in all the left-hand sides of the equations but is also recursively passed down in the body of the `Add` equation:

```
*Main> eval (Add (Lit 2) (Add X (Lit 5))) 3
10
```

## Varying parameters and the worker/wrapper structure

The parameter value need not remain the same throughout the recursion. It can actually be varied on the way down.

Let us illustrate this by adding a constructor for multiplication to the expression type:

```
data Expr = X | Lit Int | Add Expr Expr | Mul Expr Expr
```

The `Mul` constructor denotes the multiplication of its two subexpressions. Let us now revisit the `renderExpr` function and add support for X and `Mul`:

```
renderExpr :: Expr -> String
renderExpr X           = "x"
renderExpr (Lit n)     = show n
renderExpr (Add e1 e2) = renderExpr e1 ++ " + " ++ renderExpr e2
renderExpr (Mul e1 e2) = renderExpr e1 ++ " * " ++ renderExpr e2
```

This function does not do quite what we want:

```
*Main> renderExpr (Mul (Lit 2) (Add X (Lit 5)))
"2 * x + 5"
```

We would expect instead 2 * (x + 5), which has a rather different meaning. It is not x that is multiplied by 2 but x + 5. We can accomplish this by adding parentheses:

```
renderExpr :: Expr -> String
renderExpr X           = "x"
renderExpr (Lit n)     = show n
renderExpr (Add e1 e2) =
  parens (renderExpr e1 ++ " + " ++ renderExpr e2)
renderExpr (Mul e1 e2) = renderExpr e1 ++ " * " ++ renderExpr e2

parens :: String -> String
parens s = "(" ++ s ++ ")"
```

Now, we do get the expected result:

```
*Main> renderExpr (Mul (Lit 2) (Add X (Lit 5)))
"2 * (x + 5)"
```

Alas, we also get more parentheses than necessary:

```
*Main> renderExpr (Add (Lit 2) (Add X (Lit 5)))
"(2 + (x + 5))"
```

The preceding could just have been rendered as "2 + x + 5" without any parentheses. A more nuanced approach takes the precedence of the operators into account. We can model this precedence with an integer:

```
type Prec = Int
```

An operator with a higher value has precedence over one with a lower value:

```
basePrec, addPrec, mulPrec :: Prec
basePrec = 0
addPrec  = 6
mulPrec  = 7
```

Addition and multiplication respectively get the values 6 and 7 (which are the same precedence values they have in Haskell). Hence, multiplication has higher precedence than addition, as is conventional in mathematics.

We modify the rendering function to keep track of the precedence of the operator we are under. By comparing this to the precedence of the operator we are about to render, we can determine whether parentheses are needed:

```
renderExpr :: Expr -> String
renderExpr e = go e basePrec where
  go :: Expr -> Prec -> String
  go X           p = "x"
  go (Lit n)     p = show n
  go (Add e1 e2) p =
    parensP p addPrec
      (go e1 addPrec ++ " + " ++ go e2 addPrec)
  go (Mul e1 e2) p =
    go e1 mulPrec ++ " * " ++ go e2 mulPrec

  parensP :: Prec -> Prec -> String -> String
  parensP p1 p2 s
    | p1 <= p2  = s
    | otherwise = parens s
```

We have substantially changed the structure of renderPrec. Firstly, we have shifted the recursive definition to the auxiliary go function. This go function takes precedence over the operator we are under as an additional parameter. The main renderFunction calls go with the base precedence as the initial value; this denotes that we are not under any operator. The recursive calls in the bodies of the Add and Mul cases pass down the respective precedences of these two operators. Lastly, in the Add case, the use of parentheses is decided by the parensP function, which compares the precedences.

Such a setup of two functions is quite common – one is typically recursive and contains the main logic, and the other initializes some of the former's parameters and/or post-processes its result. The former is called the *worker* (here, go) for obvious reasons, and the latter is called the *wrapper* (here, renderExpr) because it tidies up the worker and makes it conveniently accessible. Usually, the worker is not meant to be accessed directly; we should always go through the wrapper. For that reason, we have opted to make the go worker a local definition of the renderExpr wrapper.

## Accumulation

The recursive functions we have seen so far build up a result in a bottom-up fashion – that is, the result of the recursive call is extended or modified in some way. For example, the base case of the sum function returns 0, and every recursive layer on top of the base case adds a value to it:

```
    sum [1,2,3]
  = 1 + (2 + (3 + 0))
```

Sometimes, it may be convenient to build up the result top-down. Here is a variant of the sum function that does this:

```
sumAcc :: [Integer] -> Integer
sumAcc l = go l 0 where
  go :: [Integer] -> Integer -> Integer
  go []       acc = acc
  go (x:xs) acc = go xs (acc + x)
```

This definition makes use of the worker/wrapper pattern:

- The worker takes an additional parameter, called the *accumulator*, that denotes the current value for the result. In the recursive case, the recursive call receives an updated accumulator that incorporates the first element. In the base case, the accumulator accounts for all the elements in the list and can be returned as the final result. This final result is recursively returned without further modifications.

- The wrapper takes care of initializing the accumulator. The initial value corresponds to the expected result for the base case – that is, 0 for the sum of an empty list.

It is instructive to see a derivation:

```
    sumAcc [1,2,3]
  = go [1,2,3] 0
  = go [2,3] 1
  = go [3] 3
  = go [] 6
  = 6
```

Reversing a list can also be done with an accumulator:

```
reverseAcc :: [a] -> [a]
reverseAcc l = go l [] where
  go :: [a] -> [a] -> [a]
  go []       acc = acc
  go (x:xs) acc = go xs (x:acc)
```

The structure of this definition is similar to that of sumAcc. The worker takes an additional accumulator, which is the reversal of the list processed so far. The wrapper sets its initial value to the empty list. The base case of the worker returns the accumulator, which by then is the reversal of the whole list. The recursive case extends the accumulator with the current element, which goes in front of the current reversal:

```
  reverseAcc [1,2,3]
= go [1,2,3] []
= go [2,3] [1]
= go [3] [2,1]
= go [] [3,2,1]
= [3,2,1]
```

Contrast this with a bottom-up strategy to reverse a list:

```
Prelude
reverse :: [a] -> [a]
reverse []     = []
reverse (x:xs) = reverse xs ++ [x]
```

While the definition looks simpler, it is actually more expensive because adding an element to the end of a list is more expensive than adding it to the front of the accumulator:

```
  reverse [1,2,3]
= reverse [2,3] ++ [1]
= (reverse [3] ++ [2]) ++ [1]
= ((reverse [] ++ [3]) ++ [2]) ++ [1]
= (([] ++ [3]) ++ [2]) ++ [1]
= ([3] ++ [2]) ++ [1]
= (3 : [] ++ [2]) ++ [1]
= [3,2] ++ [1]
= 3 : [2] ++ [1]
= 3 : 2 : [] ++ [1]
= [3,2,1]
```

Hence, the accumulator-based definition of reverse is more efficient. In contrast, we will see in *Chapter 7, Lazy Evaluation*, that the accumulator version of sum is actually a lot less efficient than the bottom-up approach.

## Recursion on nested datatypes

One recursive datatype can appear as the field of another. For instance, we can have a tree whose elements are lists. This has type Tree [a], where a is the type of list elements.

Let's suppose the list elements are integers and we want to double them:

```
doubleTree :: Tree [Integer] -> Tree [Integer]
doubleTree Empty
  = Empty
doubleTree (Branch l xs r)
  = Branch (doubleTree l) (doubleList xs) (doubleTree r)

doubleList :: [Integer] -> [Integer]
doubleList []     = []
doubleList (x:xs) = (2*x) : doubleList xs
```

This task is addressed with two functions. The first, doubleTree, recurses on the outer structure, that of the tree. In the Branch case, it processes the inner list structure with the second function, doubleList. This way, the two recursive functions resemble the nested recursive structure of the datatype.

A common occurrence of this pattern is lists of lists, [[a]], for some element type, a. These have many applications, such as modeling two-dimensional tables (rows of columns or columns of rows) of data, all kinds of grids, matrices, and partitions of lists.

One way of processing such nested lists is to write recursive functions that follow the nested structure. For example, a common task is to remove the nested structure by concatenating all the nested lists:

```
Prelude
concat :: [[a]] -> [a]
concat []       = []
concat (xs:xss) = xs ++ concat xss
```

Here, the concat function recurses on the structure of the outer lists, while the (++) operator recurses on the inner lists:

```
*Main> concat [[1,2],[],[3],[4,5]]
[1,2,3,4,5]
```

A more compact definition can be achieved with the help of a list comprehension:

```
Prelude
concat :: [[a]] -> [a]
concat xss = [ x | xs <- xss, x <- xs ]
```

Instead of two levels of recursion, this definition features two generators. The first generator selects the inner list, xs, and the second selects the element, x, within that inner list.

## Mutual recursion

All the examples of recursive functions (or datatypes) so far involve a single function (or datatype) that is defined in terms of itself. However, it is also possible to define two or more functions (or datatypes) in terms of each other.

A common example of two functions that can be defined mutually recursively is the even and odd functions, which determine whether a given positive integer is even or odd, respectively:

```
Prelude
even, odd :: Integer -> Bool

even 0 = True
even n = odd (n-1)

odd 0 = False
odd n = even (n-1)
```

A number, n, is even if its predecessor, n-1, is odd, and vice versa. The recursion alternatingly goes through the even and odd functions and has 0 as the base case:

```
  odd 5
= even 4
= odd 3
= even 2
= odd 1
= even 0
= True
```

An example of two mutually recursive datatypes is rose trees and forests:

```
data RoseTree a = Node a (Forest a)
data Forest a = Nil | Cons (RoseTree a) (Forest a)
```

A rose tree generalizes a binary tree. Instead of having exactly two subtrees, a node in a rose tree can have any number (i.e., a forest) of subtrees. The Nil constructor denotes a forest without trees, while the Cons constructor extends a given forest with one more rose tree. Many functions on these mutually recursive types will be recursive themselves, as shown here:

```
sumR :: RoseTree Int -> Int
sumR (Node x f) = x + sumF f

sumF :: Forest Int -> Int
sumF Nil        = 0
sumF (Cons r f) = sumR r + sumF f
```

Mutual recursion can also arise when the datatypes are nested. For example, here is an alternative mutually recursive definition of concat:

```
Prelude
concat :: [[a]] -> [a]
concat []        = []
concat (xs:xss) = concatAux xs xss where
  concatAux :: [a] -> [[a]] -> [a]
  concatAux []      xss = concat xss
  concatAux (x:xs) xss = x : concatAux xs xss
```

Instead of using the (++) operator, the concat function calls the auxiliary function, concatAux xs xss, which appends xs in front of the concatenation of xss. The base case of concatAux hands xss back to concat. This differs from our earlier definition of concat, where concat calls itself recursively on xss.

## Simultaneous recursion on multiple structures

All the preceding cases of recursion only process a single data structure. However, it is also possible to process multiple data structures simultaneously. The predefined zip function is a good example of this pattern:

```
Prelude
zip :: [a] -> [b] -> [(a,b)]
zip []       _       = []
zip _        []      = []
zip (x:xs) (y:ys) = (x,y) : zip xs ys
```

Like the zipper binds together the teeth on two sides of a coat, this function binds together two lists of elements into a single list. The elements in the resulting list are tuples whose elements come from the same positions in the two original lists:

```
*Main> zip [1,2,3,4] ['a','b','c','d','e']
[(1,'a'),(2,'b'),(3,'c'),(4,'d')]
```

As the example shows, the length of the resulting list is the minimum of that of the two input lists. The excess elements in the longer list are simply discarded.

## Combining variations

In practice, two or more variations on the structural recursion scheme can be combined.

The `insert` function combines both structural recursions with a parameter:

```
Data.List
insert :: [Int] -> Int -> [Int]
insert []     y = [y]
insert (x:xs) y
    | x <= y    = x : insert xs y
    | otherwise = y : x : xs
```

This inserts an element, y, at the appropriate position in an already sorted list of elements, as shown here:

```
*Main> insert [1,2,3] 4
[1,2,3,4]
*Main> insert [1,2,4] 3
[1,2,3,4]
```

The base case creates a singleton list with the new element. The recursive case distinguishes two scenarios. Firstly, the new element is larger than the first element of the list. Then, the new element is inserted in the tail by means of a recursive call on that tail. Secondly, the new element is smaller than the first element of the list. Then, the new element can be inserted at the front. No further recursive call is needed. The old list simply becomes part of the result.

Here, the additional parameter is used for the new element, and primitive recursion prevents us from having to traverse the remainder of the list when the new element's position is found.

As we just saw, there are a great many variations possible in the shape of recursive functions, even while they still essentially follow the structure of a recursive datatype. Yet, even that common aspect does not always apply.

## Non-structural recursion

You can write recursive functions that do not follow the structure of a datatype. Some of them are problematic and to be avoided, while others are legitimate. We will review several patterns here.

### Non-termination

Non-terminating functions are an important class of recursive functions that are non-structural. Here is a first, small example:

```
loop :: Integer -> Integer
loop x = loop x
```

Here is an example derivation:

```
    loop 5
=   loop 5
=   loop 5
=   ...
```

Clearly, this derivation never terminates; it just repeats itself endlessly. If you have inadvertently invoked such a non-terminating function call in GHCi, you can abort it with the *Ctrl + C* key combination.

While the `loop` function is blatantly non-terminating, the source of non-termination may often not be so apparent when it dresses up in a lot more code (such as mutually recursive functions).

A slightly different pattern of non-termination is the following:

```
diverge :: [Integer] -> Integer
diverge xs = diverge (1:xs)
```

Here is an example of a derivation:

```
    diverge []
=   diverge [1]
=   diverge [1,1]
=   ...
```

In every step of the recursion, the list parameter of the function grows longer. This too clearly goes on forever.

Most of these non-terminating functions are to be avoided, but we will see in *Chapter 7, Lazy Evaluation*, that some non-terminating functions are actually useful in Haskell.

## Unbounded search

A useful variation of the diverging example is when we look at ever-growing values to find one with a particular property. For example, the following function returns the first number larger than or equal to its input that is *perfect*:

```
nextPerfect :: Integer -> Integer
nextPerfect n
    | perfect n = n
    | otherwise = nextPerfect (n+1)
```

A number is perfect if it is equal to the sum of its divisors:

```
perfect :: Integer -> Bool
perfect n = sum (divisors n) == n
```

The divisors are those values smaller than n that leave no remainder after division:

```
divisors :: Integer -> [Integer]
divisors n = [ d | d <- [1..n-1], mod n d == 0 ]
```

The first two perfect numbers are found quickly:

```
*Main> nextPerfect 1
6
*Main> nextPerfect 7
28
```

However, subsequent perfect numbers are increasingly further apart. It is not known whether there is an infinite number of perfect numbers. Hence, once beyond the largest known perfect number, we do not know whether nextPerfect would terminate at all.

Here is another example of a recursive function that is not known to terminate for all inputs:

```
collatz :: Integer -> [Integer]
collatz n
   | n <= 1    = n : []
   | even n    = n : collatz (div n 2)
   | otherwise = n : collatz (3 * n + 1)
```

This function computes the so-called Collatz sequence, starting at a given positive integer. The sequence ends when it reaches the number 1. Otherwise, the sequence continues with the next number, which is determined in one of two ways. If the current number is even, it is halved. If the current number is odd, it is multiplied by three and then incremented by one.

Typically, the sequence goes up and down erratically:

```
*Main> collatz 5
[5,16,8,4,2,1]
*Main> collatz 6
[6,3,10,5,16,8,4,2,1]
*Main> collatz 7
[7,22,11,34,17,52,26,13,40,20,10,5,16,8,4,2,1]
```

Yet, there is no guarantee that it terminates for all starting points.

In cases like this, it may be hard to tell from a function's code whether it terminates. Termination may depend on the specific parameter values that are supplied or may require much deeper insight into the problem at hand.

# Summary

This chapter introduced the concept of recursive definitions for both functions and datatypes. We saw how recursive datatypes allow us to express values of an arbitrarily large size, with Haskell's built-in list type as a notable example. Functions that process such recursive datatypes are themselves naturally recursive. More specifically, when the recursive structure of a function aligns with that of the datatype it processes, we speak of structural recursion. We saw several common variations in structural recursion as well as a few examples of non-structural recursion.

In *Chapter 4, Higher-Order Functions*, we will see how repeated patterns in function definitions, such as the structural recursion scheme we used here, can themselves be captured as reusable code. The key mechanism that enables this is the ability to pass functions as parameters to other functions. Such functions with function parameters are called higher-order functions.

## Questions

1. How can we create lists and manipulate them with common predefined functions?
2. How can we write custom functions over lists?
3. How can we define and process custom recursive algebraic datatypes?
4. What is structural recursion?
5. How can we work with common variations on structured recursion?
6. What are examples of recursion that are not structural?

## Answers

1. Lists can be created with the syntax `[e1, ..., en]` where e1,...,en is a comma-separated list of elements. The empty list is just written `[]`. More primitive notation for constructing a composite list is `(e:es)`, where e is the first element of the new list and es is an existing list that becomes the tail (or remainder) of the new list.

   Lists can be processed with a range of predefined list functions, with list comprehensions and with custom functions (see the next question).

2. Functions over lists can be defined by pattern matching, just like for other ADTs. The typical form distinguishes two cases, that of the empty list `[]` and of the non-empty list `(x:xs)`.

3. ADT definitions are recursive when we mention the type we are defining in one or more of its constructors field types. They are processed, like ordinary ADTs, with pattern matching on the constructors. Usually the functions are recursive and make use of structural recursion (see the next question).

4.  In structural recursion the recursive structure of the function follows the recursive structure of the datatype it processes. The structural recursion scheme look as follows.

```
f :: [A] -> B
f []     = n
f (x:xs) = c x (f xs)
```

5.  We have covered a broad range of different possible variations:

    *   Adding parameters:

        *   That are unmodified throughout

        *   That change throughout

        *   That are accumulators for the result

    *   Using parts of the original data structure in the result (primitive recursion)

    *   Nested recursion on recursive ADTs that have other recursive ADTs in their fields

    *   Mutual recursion on mutually nested recursive ADTs

    *   Simultaneous recursion on two ADTs

    *   Combinations of them all.

6.  We have covered two examples. Firstly, looping and diverging definitions that definitely do not terminate. These are to be avoided. Secondly, functions that explore some infinite space or process that we do not know will terminate.

# 4
# Higher-Order Functions

One of the most important concepts in programming is the notion of **abstraction**. Abstraction is the ability to reuse a common code pattern without having to repeat its details and by referring to it by name. Functions themselves are a fundamental form of abstraction. For instance, in the expressions *1+2* and *1+40*, the common part is *(1+)*. We can abstract over this common pattern by defining a function:

```
inc :: Integer -> Integer
inc n = 1 + n
```

In this chapter, we go one step further by abstracting over these abstractions. Indeed, we allow functions to have other functions as parameters. Such functions are called **higher-order functions** (**HOF**). A HOF represents a whole family of different functions that have the same overall structure but differ in some of the details. Arguably, support for HOFs is one of the defining features of the functional programming paradigm. The typical concise nature of functional programs is often due to the judicious composition of HOFs, and a programmer who masters them can become highly productive.

We thus start this problem by comparing a number of similar functions and then capturing their similarity in a more general function. The generality comes from abstracting over a function parameter that is instantiated differently in each of the original functions. Because the generalized function abstracts over a function parameter, it is known as a HOF. Next, we move on to studying how the recursion schemes from the previous chapter can be captured in reusable HOF. We follow up with a range of predefined HOF that should be part of every Haskell programmer's vocabulary. Lastly, we will show how these well-known HOF can be used to quickly and compactly solve a number of tasks.

In short, this chapter asks the following questions:

- How do you write and use HOF?
- How do you capture and use structural recursion as a HOF?
- What are predefined and much-used HOF?
- How do you write compact code by assembling it out of HOF?

# Abstracting over functions

This section introduces HOF as a way to share code between similar functions. We will investigate two small case studies – dropping a prefix from a list or string and sorting a list.

## Dropping a prefix

A frequent data-cleaning task is to drop the leading spaces from a string. This is accomplished by the following function:

```
dropSpaces :: String -> String
dropSpaces []       = []
dropSpaces (c:cs)
    | c == ' '       = dropSpaces cs
    | otherwise      = c:cs
```

Recall that strings are just lists of characters. This function uses that fact to perform primitive recursion over the string. It does the job as required:

```
*Main> dropSpaces "   hello"
"hello"
```

This is usually not enough though, as we also want to drop other so-called whitespace characters such as tab and newline. The isSpace :: Char -> Bool function from the Data.Char library identifies all such whitespace characters. Hence, let us use it instead:

```
dropWhitespaces :: String -> String
dropWhitespaces []      = []
dropWhitespaces (c:cs)
    | isSpace c       = dropWhitespaces cs
    | otherwise       = c:cs
```

Another related task is to drop the leading 0 entries in a list of integers:

```
dropZeroes :: [Int] -> [Int]
dropZeroes []       = []
dropZeroes (c:cs)
    | c == 0         = dropZeroes cs
    | otherwise      = c:cs
```

This definition only differs in the type of list elements and the test performed on the elements:

```
*Main> dropZeroes [0,0,1,2,3]
[1,2,3]
```

We can abstract over these different variants with a HOF:

```
dropWhile :: (a -> Bool) -> [a] -> [a]
dropWhile p []      = []
dropWhile p (c:cs)
    | p c                = dropWhile p cs
    | otherwise          = c:cs
```

This generalized function takes an additional parameter of type function type (a -> Bool). The idea is that this function parameter decides whether the current element should still be dropped or whether all remaining elements should be returned.

We can recover the specific functions we defined earlier by calling dropWhile with an appropriate function parameter:

```
dropSpaces l = dropWhile isSpaceCharacter l where
  isSpaceCharacter :: Char -> Bool
  isSpaceCharacter c = c == ' '

dropWhiteSpaces l = dropWhile isSpace l

dropZeroes l = dropWhile isZero l where
  isZero :: Int -> Bool
  isZero n = n == 0
```

In general, functions of type a -> Bool are called predicates. In the preceding three cases, the type of the predicate is appropriately instantiated to Char -> Bool or Int -> Bool, depending on the element type.

Because dropWhile takes a function parameter, we call it a HOF. An ordinary function that does not take a function parameter has order 1; it is called a first-order function. A function that takes a first-order function as a parameter is called a second-order function, and so on. Any function with an order greater than 1 is called higher-order. Generally, we do not care about the specific order and only distinguish between first-order and higher-order.

## Sorting in ascending and descending order

Let us investigate a slightly larger example where a HOF provides for additional generality and code reuse. Recall the insert function that we introduced in the previous chapter:

```
insert :: [Int] -> Int -> [Int]
insert []       y = [y]
insert (x:xs) y
    | x <= y        = x : insert xs y
    | otherwise = y : x : xs
```

It is a key component of the insertion sort algorithm:

```
isort :: [Int] -> [Int]
isort l = insertAll l [] where
  insertAll []     sl = sl
  insertAll (x:xs) sl = insertAll xs (insert sl x)
```

This sorting algorithm uses the accumulator strategy to construct a sorted list from an unsorted one. Initially, the accumulator is empty, and one by one, the elements of the unsorted list are inserted into the appropriate positions:

```
*Main> isort [3,1,4,2]
[1,2,3,4]
```

As the example shows, isort sorts a list in ascending order. If we want to sort lists in descending order, we would have to create a variant of the insert function that uses >= instead of <= in its guard. On top of that, we'd need a variant of isort that calls the insert variant instead of the original:

```
insertDesc :: [Int] -> Int -> [Int]
insertDesc []     y = [y]
insertDesc (x:xs) y
  | x >= y      = x : insertDesc xs y
  | otherwise = y : x : xs

isortDesc :: [Int] -> [Int]
isortDesc l = insertAll l [] where
  insertAll []     sl = sl
  insertAll (x:xs) sl = insertAll xs (insertDesc sl x)
```

This amounts to a lot of code duplication, with only a single variation, to get sorting done in descending order:

```
*Main> isortDesc [3,1,4,2]
[4,3,2,1]
```

The only difference between the two versions is the use of one operator. If we turn insert into a HOF, we can avoid duplication. The idea is to turn the comparison operator into a parameter of the insertion function:

```
insertGen :: (Int -> Int -> Bool) -> [Int] -> Int -> [Int]
insertGen comp []     y = [y]
insertGen comp (x:xs) y
  | comp x y    = x : insertGen comp xs y
  | otherwise = y : x : xs
```

The type signature of this generalized function indicates that the additional comp parameter has type Int -> Int -> Bool. Hence, it is a function that takes two integers and returns a Boolean. This parameter is used in the guard of the second equation to determine whether or not to insert the new x element before the first element in the list.

When calling insertGen, we can pass it the appropriate operator:

```
*Main> insertGen (<=) [1,3] 2
[1,2,3]
*Main> insertGen (>=) [1,3] 2
[3,2,1]
```

To benefit from this new generality, we can likewise turn isort into a HOF:

```
isortGen :: (Int -> Int -> Bool) -> [Int] -> [Int]
isortGen comp l = insertAll l [] where
  insertAll []     sl = sl
  insertAll (x:xs) sl = insertAll xs (insertGen comp sl x)
```

This generalization takes the comparison operator as a parameter in order to pass it on to insertGen.

Based on this generalized sorting function, we can create two specialized functions to sort in ascending and descending order:

```
isortAsc :: [Int] -> [Int]
isortAsc l = isortGen (<=) l

isortDesc :: [Int] -> [Int]
isortDesc l = isortGen (>=) l
```

Now that we have the basics of HOF down, let us move on to a widespread use case.

# An abstraction for structural recursion

In the previous chapter, we studied recursive functions and presented structural recursion schemes as a useful template to write such functions. Thanks to HOF, we can capture these structural recursion schemes in reusable functions.

## Folding lists

The first structural recursion scheme we encountered in the previous chapter is that for lists:

```
f :: [A] -> B
f []     = n
f (x:xs) = c x (f xs)
```

By replacing the underlined elements in the preceding template with concrete names, we obtain different functions, such as sum and and:

```Prelude
sum :: [Integer] -> Integer
sum []     = 0
sum (x:xs) = x + sum xs

and :: [Bool] -> Bool
and []     = True
and (x:xs) = x && and xs
```

Thanks to the ability to parameterize over functions, we can actually do better than this. Indeed, we can capture the recursion scheme in a HOF called `foldr`:

```Prelude
foldr :: (a -> b -> b) -> b -> [a] -> b
foldr c n []     = n
foldr c n (x:xs) = c x (foldr c n xs)
```

Instead of types that need to be filled in, a and b are now type parameters. Likewise, c and n are now passed as parameters to `foldr` rather than being filled in.

The `foldr` function is, in fact, predefined, and using it gives rise to very concise definitions:

```Prelude
sum :: [Integer] -> Integer
sum l = foldr (+) 0 l

and :: [Bool] -> Bool
and l = foldr (&&) True l
```

Observe that sum and and are no longer defined in an explicitly recursive style. Instead, they defer the explicit recursion to `foldr`.

## Folds for other algebraic datatypes

The same idea can be applied to our own custom algebraic datatypes. Recall the recursion scheme for basic arithmetic expressions (without variables or multiplication):

```
f :: Expr -> B
f (Lit n)     = l n
f (Add e1 e2) = a (f e1) (f e2)
```

Again, we can write a HOF that abstracts over the parameters:

```
foldExpr :: (b -> b -> b) -> (Int -> b) -> Expr -> b
foldExpr a l (Lit n)     = l n
foldExpr a l (Add e1 e2) = a (foldExpr a l e1) (foldExpr a l e2)
```

This is an HOF with two function parameters. The first determines how to combine the two recursive results of an addition and the second how to treat the integer literals.

We can use this HOF to compactly write the `eval` function:

```
eval :: Expr -> Int
eval e = foldExpr (+) id e
```

This definition states that `eval` is a structurally recursive function that adds the recursive results (with the + operator) and returns the literal values as they are (using the identity function, `id`).

Similarly, we can rewrite the basic `renderExpr` function in terms of `foldExpr`:

```
renderExpr :: Expr -> String
renderExpr e = foldExpr a show e where
  a :: String -> String -> String
  a s1 s2 = s1 ++ " + " ++ s2
```

Now, the literals are converted to strings with the predefined `show` function. In contrast, because there is no predefined function that does what is required for addition, we have defined a local function called a to do the job.

Finally, we also show the `fold` function for trees:

```
foldTree :: (b -> a -> b -> b) -> b -> Tree a -> b
foldTree b e Empty         = e
foldTree b e (Branch l x r) =
  b (foldTree b e l) x (foldTree b e r)
```

This allows us to write the `treeToList` function concisely:

```
treeToList :: Tree a -> [a]
treeToList t = foldTree b [] t where
  b l1 x l2 = x : l1 ++ l2
```

While the `foldr` function for lists is used frequently, in practice developers often do not take the trouble to write a fold function for their own datatypes. Perhaps it is due to the fact that it constitutes an upfront effort, while the payoff comes when a sufficient number of structurally recursive datatypes have been written. Also, when a datatype has more than two constructors, the number of parameters to the corresponding fold function may become too unwieldy.

## Variations on structural recursion

Concerning the variations on structural recursion that we studied in the previous chapter, only accumulation is readily supported, namely by the `foldl` function explained in the next section. Some variants are available in more specialized and little-used libraries. Nevertheless, we can get quite far with `foldr` alone.

Consider, for example, primitive recursion in which `tails'` is an instance:

```
tails' :: [a] -> [[a]]
tails' []     = []
tails' (_:xs) = xs : tails' xs
```

We can write a recursion scheme that captures the pattern:

```
para :: (a -> [a] -> b -> b) -> b -> [a] -> b
para c n []     = n
para c n (x:xs) = c x xs (para c n xs)
```

The name `para` refers to *paramorphism*, a general name for primitive recursive functions. We can write `tails'` in terms of `para`:

```
tails' :: [a] -> [[a]]
tails' l = para c [] l where
  c _ xs r = xs : r
```

Yet, we can also write `tails'` in terms of `foldr` with a little trick:

```
tails' :: [a] -> [[a]]
tails' l = snd (foldr c ([],[]) l) where
  c x (xs,yss) = (x:xs,xs:yss)
```

The trick is to have `foldr` compute a tuple whose first component reconstructs the original list, and whose second component computes the result we are actually interested in. This way, the xs tail that c requires is available as part of the recursive result. After `foldr`, we need to project on the second component of the resulting tuple because that's what we are interested in. While reconstructing the original list is not as efficient as `para`, it will get the job done in a pinch. This trick is called *Kleene's dentist trick* because the mathematician Stephen Kleene came up with the idea while at the dentist.

We now know how to capture the key recursion schemes from the previous chapter in HOF. In the next chapter, we will see that `foldr` can also handle folds with parameters, but in this chapter, we will move on to other common HOF. Several of these can actually be defined in terms of `foldr`.

# Common HOFs

Besides `foldr` and `dropWhile`, Haskell's standard library contains a number of useful and frequently used HOF.

## Taking instead of dropping

The `dropWhile` function has an opposite that takes rather than drops elements from the front of a list:

```
Prelude
takeWhile :: (a -> Bool) -> [a] -> [a]
    takeWhile p []      = []
    takeWhile p (x:xs)
        | p x           = x : takeWhile p xs
        | otherwise     = []
```

As long as the elements satisfy the predicate, they are returned. Yet, as soon as a first element is found that does not satisfy the predicate, no more elements are returned.

For example, by passing `isDigit` from the `Data.Char` module to `takeWhile`, we can take the leading digits of a string:

```
*Main> takeWhile isDigit "123hello"
"123"
```

If we also want to get the remainder, we can use `dropWhile`:

```
*Main> dropWhile isDigit "123hello"
"hello"
```

The `span` function performs both tasks at the same time and is, thus, slightly more efficient:

```
Prelude
span :: (a -> Bool) -> [a] -> ([a],[a])
    span p []      = ([],[])
    span p (x:xs)
        | p x           = let (ys,zs) = span p xs
                          in (x:ys,zs)
        | otherwise     = ([],x:xs)
```

With `span`, we can separate the leading digits from the remainder in one go:

```
*Main> span isDigit "123hello"
("123","hello")
```

## Mapping

One of the most elementary and, thus, also most commonly used HOF is map:

```
Prelude
map :: (a -> b) -> [a] -> [b]
```

The type signature reveals that map converts a list with elements of type a into a list with elements of type b, by means of a given function from a to b.

Here are several example applications:

```
*Main> map show [1,2,3]
["1","2","3"]
*Main> map not [True,False]
[False,True]
```

The two examples show that map applies the given function to all elements in the list. The resulting list has the same shape as the original list but with transformed elements. In the first example, the integers have become strings. In the second example, the Booleans have remained Booleans, but their values have been negated.

Here is a simple one-line definition of map using a list comprehension:

```
Prelude
map f l = [ f x | x <- l ]
```

The list comprehension draws elements from the input list and returns them, transformed by f.

Alternatively, we can give an explicit recursive definition:

```
Prelude
map f []     = []
map f (x:xs) = f x : map f xs
```

This shows that the list structure itself (i.e., the constructors) is preserved and only the elements are transformed. If we preserve the elements, by transforming them with the identity function, we get the original list back:

```
*Main> map id [1,2,3]
[1,2,3]
```

The second definition shows that map is structurally recursive. Hence, we can give a third definition in terms of foldr:

```
Prelude
map f l = foldr c [] where
        c x r = f x : r
```

The map function has a powerful *fusion* property – we can combine two consecutive applications of map into a single one. Consider the following:

```
*Main> map length (map show [1,10,100])
[1,2,3]
```

The first application of map transforms list [1,10,100] into the intermediate result, ["1","10","100"], which is transformed into the final result, [1,2,3], by the second application of map.

We can accomplish the same with a single application of map:

```
*Main> map lengthOfShow [1,10,100]
[1,2,3]
```

Here, lengthOfShow is defined as the composition of length and show:

```
lengthOfShow :: Int -> Int
lengthOfShow n = length (show n)
```

Generally, the fused application of map will be more efficient because it does not create an intermediate list. The GHC compiler exploits this when optimizing code by automatically fusing any successive maps it encounters in program code.

## Filtering

The filter function selects particular elements out of a given list:

```
Prelude
filter :: (a -> Bool) -> [a] -> [a]
```

The (a -> Bool) function parameter, another use of a predicate, determines which elements are selected.

Here are two examples:

```
*Main> filter even [1..10]
[2,4,6,8,10]
*Main> filter isUpper "HwEoLrLlOd"
"HELLO"
*Main> filter isLower "HwEoLrLlOd"
"world"
```

Here, isUpper :: Char -> Bool and isLower :: Char -> Bool are predicates from the Data.Char library that identify uppercase and lowercase letters, respectively.

There also is a simple one-line definition of `filter` that uses a list comprehension:

```
Prelude
filter p l = [ x | x <- l, p x ]
```

The list comprehension draws elements from the input list and selects the appropriate ones by using the predicate as a guard.

Alternatively, we can write a directly recursive definition:

```
Prelude
filter p []      = []
filter p (x:xs)
  | p x          = x : filter p xs
  | otherwise    = filter p xs
```

Again, there also is a definition in terms of `foldr`:

```
Prelude
filter p l = foldr c [] l where
        c x r
          | p x          = x : r
          | otherwise = r
```

This version calls `foldr` with the `[]` result of the base case and the local `c` function, to check whether an x element should or should not be added to the recursive result, `r`.

## Any and all

The `any` and `all` functions also make use of a predicate:

```
Prelude
any :: (a -> Bool) -> [a] -> Bool
all :: (a -> Bool) -> [a] -> Bool
```

The `any` function checks whether at least one of the elements in the list satisfies the predicate, while `all` checks whether all elements do.

Here are several examples:

```
*Main> any even [1..10]
True
*Main> any even []
False
*Main> all even [1..10]
False
```

```
*Main> all even []
True
```

Both functions can be defined in terms of map, and, and or:

```
Prelude
any p l = or  (map p l)
all p l = and (map p l)
```

Consider the following:

```
Prelude
or, and :: [Bool] -> Bool
or  l = foldr (||) False l
and l = foldr (&&) True l
```

Here, the or function checks whether there is at least one True value in the list, while and checks that there are no False values.

While the composite definitions of any and all are quite neat and readable, we can also write each as a single recursive function:

```
Prelude
any p l  = foldr c False l where
  c x r = p x || r

all p l  = foldr c True l where
  c x r = p x && r
```

These two definitions fuse the foldr function of or/and with the preceding map. As they avoid creating an intermediate list, they are more efficient.

## Folding from the left

The foldl function captures the structural recursion scheme with an accumulator. Recall the example from the previous chapter to reverse a list in terms of an accumulator:

```
reverseAcc :: [a] -> [a]
reverseAcc l = go l [] where
  go :: [a] -> [a] -> [a]
  go []     acc = acc
  go (x:xs) acc = go xs (x:acc)
```

We can rewrite this example in terms of `foldl`:

```
Prelude
foldl :: (b -> a -> b) -> b -> [a] -> b
```

The first parameter of `foldl` is the function that updates the accumulator with the next element of the list. The second parameter is the initial value of the accumulator:

```
reverseAcc :: [a] -> [a]
reverseAcc l = foldl u [] l where
  u acc x = x:acc
```

Here, the initial value of the accumulator is the empty list, and the u function updates the accumulator by adding the next element in front of it.

Likewise, we can rewrite the accumulator-based sum function in terms of `foldl`:

```
sumAcc :: [Int] -> Int
sumAcc l = foldl (+) 0 l
```

Now, the initial value of the accumulator is 0, and the update function is simply (+).

The definition of `foldl` is as follows:

```
Prelude
foldl u acc []     = acc
foldl u acc (x:xs) = foldl u (u acc x) xs
```

The names `foldl` and `foldr` have been chosen to expose the close connection between the two functions. The *l* is short for *left* and the *r* is short for *right*. When a list is laid out from left to right, with the first element on the left and the empty list on the right, then `foldl` builds up the result in its accumulator from left to right. In contrast, `foldr` builds up the result from right to left.

We can, in fact, define `foldl` in terms of `foldr` by first reversing the list (which swaps left and right):

```
Prelude
foldl u acc l = foldr c acc (reverse l) where
  c x acc = u acc x
```

This definition reveals a subtle difference between `foldl` and `foldr` – their function parameter takes its input in the opposite order. Indeed, compare the two types:

```
u :: b -> a -> b
c :: a -> b -> b
```

The opposite, defining `foldr` in terms of `foldl`, is also possible.

Novice Haskell programmers tend to confuse `foldl` and `foldr` initially because of their similarity. My advice is to deliberately consider what direction of folding is desired.

## Scanning left and right

The difference between `foldr` and `foldl` is made clearer by the two scan functions. These two functions, `scanr` and `scanl`, perform the same computation as their fold counterpart but also return all the intermediate results.

For example, `foldr` only shows the final result:

```
*Main> foldr (+) 0 [1..5]
15
```

In contrast, `scanr` returns the list of all intermediate results:

```
*Main> scanr (+) 0 [1..5]
[15,14,12,9,5,0]
```

We can see that the sum is built up from right to left, while `scanl` does it in the opposite direction:

```
*Main> scanl (+) 0 [1..5]
[0,1,3,6,10,15]
```

While the two directions obtain the same outcome, 15, the difference in direction means that they get different intermediate results.

One way to understand and define `scanr` is in terms of the `tails` function, which we discussed in the *Structural recursion on lists* section of *Chapter 3, Recursion*:

```
Prelude
scanr :: (a -> b -> b) -> b -> [a] -> [b]
scanr c n l = map f (tails l) where
  f l = foldr c n l
```

This definition creates all the intermediate results of `foldr` by independently applying `foldr` to every tail of the list.

However, because the tails have many suffixes in common, the `foldr` applications will repeat the same computations over and over again. This can be prevented by a leaner, directly recursive definition:

```
Prelude
scanr :: (a -> b -> b) -> b -> [a] -> [b]
scanr c n []     = n : []
scanr c n (x:xs) = c x (head r) : r where
  r = scanr c n xs
```

Two similar definitions can be written for `scanl`. You may want to consider what they would look like.

This concludes our review of predefined HOF in Haskell's standard libraries. In the next section, we will show you how larger problems can be solved by combining several of the library functions.

# Writing compact code with HOF

Thanks to their function parameters, the behavior of HOF can be customized more extensively than that of similar first-order functions. This means they can be used in more circumstances. That is particularly true for the HOF of the previous sections because they cover highly general code patterns. In this section, we will show how some problems can be quickly and compactly solved by combining a number of HOF.

## Standard deviation

The standard deviation of a list of numbers is a well-known statistical value that characterizes the amount of variation among those numbers. It is defined in terms of the average of those numbers. Let us first work out how to implement this average and then move on to the actual standard deviation.

### *Average*

This average can easily be computed using predefined first-order functions:

```
average :: [Float] -> Float
average l = sum l / fromIntegral (length l)
```

Both sum and length are predefined functions that are themselves defined in terms of `foldr`. We can make the code slightly more efficient by merging the two structural traversals of the list into one:

```
average :: [Float] -> Float
average l = s / fromIntegral len where
  (s, len) = foldr c n l
  n = (0,0)
  c x (sr, lenr) = (sr + x, lenr + 1)
```

The idea of the merged traversal is to compute a tuple of the sum and the length of the list. For the base case, both components of the tuple are zero. A new x element is added to the tuple, by incrementing the length and adding x to the sum.

Now that we have implemented the average, let us move on to the standard deviation.

## Standard deviation

If μ is the average of a list of elements, $x_1,...,x_n$, then the standard deviation σ is defined with a mathematical formula as follows:

$$\sigma = \sqrt{\frac{\sum_{i=1}^{n}(x_i - \mu)^2}{n}}$$

We can implement this from the inside out:

1. Subtract the average from each element.
2. Square each result of *step 1*.
3. Sum the results of *step 2*.
4. Divide the result of *step 3* by the number of elements.
5. Take the square root of the result of *step 4*.

This results in the following code:

```
stdev :: [Float] -> Float
stdev l = sqrt (sum (map square (map diff l)) / fromIntegral n) where
    m         = average l
    n         = length l
    diff x    = x - m
    square x  = x^2
```

Here, the map function applies the computation on the individual elements across the list.

## Odds and evens

Consider a list of integer tuples. Our job is to check whether all the tuples with an odd first component have an even second component:

```
*Main> oddsAndEvens [(1,2),(3,8)]
True
*Main> oddsAndEvens [(1,2),(3,7)]
False
*Main> oddsAndEvens [(2,1),(4,6)]
True
```

Let us split up this job into a number of steps:

1. Select all tuples with an odd first component.
2. Extract the second component of the selected tuples.
3. Check that all values are even.

This results in the following code:

```
oddsAndEvens :: [(Int,Int)] -> Bool
oddsAndEvens l = all even (map snd (filter oddFst l)) where
    oddFst :: (Int,Int) -> Bool
    oddFst (x,_) = odd x
```

*Step 1* is implemented by `filter`, *step 2* by map, and *step 3* by the `all` function.

## All you can buy

Suppose we have a limited budget and a shopping list of products we want to buy:

```
data Product = MkP {name :: String, price :: Int}
    deriving Show
```

Because of the limited budget, we likely cannot buy all the products we want. Hence, we list the products in order of priority, with the more important ones coming first. Write a function that determines which products we can buy, given our budget and shopping list:

```
*Main> budgetBuy 10 [MkP "medicine" 8, MkP "rice" 1, MkP "sweets" 3]
[MkP {name = "medicine", price = 8},MkP {name = "rice", price = 1}]
```

This example calculates that we can afford medicine and rice but do not have enough money left to buy sweets.

Let us again break this down into a number of steps:

1.  Determine the price of each product.
2.  Determine the *cumulative price* of each product; this is the price of buying that product and all the higher-priority products.
3.  Pair up each product with its cumulative price.
4.  Take pairs of products with their cumulative price as long as the cumulative price does not exceed the budget.
5.  Extract the products out of the pairs.

These steps can be implemented as follows:

```
budgetBuy :: Int -> [Product] -> [Product]
budgetBuy budget ps =
  map fst (takeWhile inBudget (zip ps cprices))
  where
    cprices = tail (scanl (+) 0 (map price ps))
    inBudget (p,cprice) = cprice <= budget
```

Here, we use map to extract the prices of the products. Next, scanl computes the cumulative prices. Note that we use tail to drop the first cumulative price, which is 0 and corresponds with buying no products. Then, we pair up the products and cumulative prices, using zip, and take the leading pairs that are within budget, using takeWhile. Finally, we remove the cumulative prices and retain only the products, again using map.

## Summary

This chapter introduced HOF. We saw how we can generalize existing code by abstracting over function parameters and then reuse this generalization more widely. Next, we studied how this mechanism can be used to capture structural recursion in a reusable HOF. Then, we reviewed a range of commonly used predefined HOF and combined them to concisely solve tasks.

In *Chapter 5, First-Class Functions*, we will see how Haskell strongly encourages the use of HOFs with a range of language features that facilitate their use. In particular, they make it easy to write function parameters for HOFs and, more generally, write programs mostly in terms of functions, rather than in terms of the values they process.

## Questions

1.  How do you generalize functions by abstracting over function parameters?
2.  How do you capture structural recursion as a HOF?
3.  What are common predefined HOF?
4.  How do we solve problems by composing HOF?

## Answers

1.  You can make a function more general by replacing one of the (other) functions it calls with a parameter. The type of this function parameter will be the same as the type of the function abstracted over. Further generality is often possible at this point by generalizing the types by means of parametric polymorphism.
2.  The foldr function captures the structural recursion scheme for lists:

    ```
    foldr :: (a -> b -> b) -> b -> [a] -> b
    foldr c n []     = n
    foldr c n (x:xs) = c x (foldr c n xs)
    ```

    The n parameter abstracts over the result for the base constructor, [], and the c function parameter for the recursive constructor, (:). Similar fold functions can be written for other algebraic datatypes.

3.  Notable predefined HOF are as follows:

    - `map :: (a -> b) -> [a] -> [b]`
    - `filter :: (a -> Bool) -> [a] -> [a]`
    - `any :: (a -> Bool) -> [a] -> Bool`
    - `all :: (a -> Bool) -> [a] -> Bool`
    - `takeWhile :: (a -> Bool) -> [a] -> [a]`
    - `dropWhile :: (a -> Bool) -> [a] -> [a]`
    - `span :: (a -> Bool) -> [a] -> ([a],[a])`
    - `foldr :: (a -> b -> b) -> b -> [a] -> b`
    - `foldl :: (b -> a -> b) -> b -> [a] -> b`
    - `scanr :: (a -> b -> b) -> b -> [a] -> [b]`
    - `scanl :: (b -> a -> b) -> b -> [a] -> [b]`

4.  Split the problem up into a number of sub-tasks that match predefined HOF.

# Part 2:
# Haskell-Specific Features

In this part, you will get an overview of the key language features that Haskell provides on top of standard functional programming functionality. Firstly, you will learn a range of techniques that greatly increase the ergonomics of working with higher-order functions. Next, you will discover Haskell's unique mechanism for ad hoc overloading, type classes. Then, you will gain insight into Haskell's lazy execution mechanism and the daring programs it allows you to write. Finally, you will explore the unusual way in which Haskell programs interface with their environment.

This part has the following chapters:

- *Chapter 5, First-Class Functions*
- *Chapter 6, Type Classes*
- *Chapter 7, Lazy Evaluation*
- *Chapter 8, Input/Output*

# 5
# First-Class Functions

In the previous chapter, we studied **higher-order functions** (HOFs), one of the defining features of functional programming. This chapter explains how Haskell actively supports working with HOFs by providing a number of facilitating language features.

The ability of HOFs to abstract over functions means that they are more reusable than first-order functions. Indeed, often tasks can be concisely handled by assembling a number of predefined higher-order functions. Of course, HOFs are useless without the functions that we supply to them as parameters. Hence, part of the effectiveness of HOFs stems from being able to quickly and concisely supply the right function parameters to instantiate the HOFs.

In the previous chapter, we often did not have the right function at hand to supply as a parameter. Instead, we wrote a dedicated new function, often in the form of a local definition, to make up for this lack. Recall, for example, the isSpaceCharacter function that we wrote as a custom parameter for dropWhile:

```
dropSpaces l = dropWhile isSpaceCharacter l where
  isSpaceCharacter :: Char -> Bool
  isSpaceCharacter c = c == ' '
```

Writing such a local function may not seem like a huge burden, but it does slow us down a little and takes up one or more additional lines in a program.

Haskell reduces the friction of writing such functions in four different ways:

- Anonymous functions
- Currying
- Eta reduction
- The function composition operator

These four ways, when used individually or in combination, make it possible to quickly define new functions in terms of existing ones, usually without even giving them a name, and they use significantly less space in a program. In fact, Haskell did not invent these four ways; they have already shown their worth in other contexts. The fourth feature is an established operator from mathematics.

The first three features were borrowed from the very first functional programming language, the lambda calculus, which we mentioned in *Chapter 1, Functions*. Another way to look at it is that Haskell is, in fact, an extended version of the lambda calculus. This lambda calculus treats functions as values; in fact, as a minimal language, the lambda calculus has no other values. In contrast, Haskell is a language rich with various types of primitive values, to which programmers can add even more by defining algebraic data types. Still, Haskell too treats functions as values. We use the term **first-class** functions to indicate that functions are on the same footing as other values; they are not second-class citizens.

In this chapter, we will cover the following main topics:

- How to define and use anonymous (i.e., nameless) functions
- How to create new functions out of existing ones with the function composition operator
- What is currying, and how can it be used to specialize existing functions with partial application?
- What is eta reduction, and how does it lead to more compact function definitions?
- How to use functions to represent data structures

## Anonymous functions

The first feature we will study to facilitate writing custom functions, usually as parameters for HOFs, are **anonymous** functions. These are also called **lambda functions** or **lambda abstractions** after their origin in the lambda calculus.

We will illustrate the concept of an anonymous function using the `dropSpaces` example from this chapter's introduction. The local definition of its `isSpaceCharacter` function takes up two additional lines (or one if we omit the optional type signature). Moreover, it has to be given a name, which, while useful for documentation purposes, takes some effort. This effort has very little benefit, as the function is only called once, right where it is defined. Hence, the effort cannot be amortized over multiple call sites.

### Anonymous function syntax

An anonymous function is a function that is not given a name. Hence, when referring to such a nameless function, we have to supply its definition instead. The nameless version of `isSpaceCharacter` is written as follows:

```
\c -> c == ' '
```

Instead of using an equation, it is written with a backslash and an arrow. The c parameter of the function is written between the backslash and the arrow. After the arrow comes the function body, c == ' '. This notation mimics that of the lambda calculus, which uses the Greek letter *lambda*, written as λ, instead of the backslash. The lambda calculus also uses a dot instead of an arrow. As we will see shortly, the dot already serves a different purpose in Haskell – hence, the arrow.

## Anonymous function use

An anonymous function does not have the syntactic status of a definition or a declaration. It is an expression. It is usually written as part of a larger expression and in the position where we would otherwise write the name of a function.

A function call, such as `isSpaceCharacter 'a'`, is perhaps the simplest kind of expression where a function name is used. Instead, we can now use an anonymous function:

```
*Main> (\c -> c == ' ') 'a'
False
```

While this works, it is generally not a typical use case for an anonymous function. The reason for that is that, if we have the definition of the function available, we can write the expression more directly by filling in the actual parameter in the function body:

```
*Main> 'a' == ' '
False
```

The main use case of anonymous functions is where functions are not directly applied – when passed as parameters to higher-order functions. For instance, here is `dropSpaces` written in terms of an anonymous function:

```
dropSpaces l = dropWhile (\c -> c == ' ') l
```

Thanks to the use of an anonymous function, the definition fits on a single line and can arguably be understood more quickly than the original.

## Multi-parameter anonymous functions

Anonymous functions are not restricted to single-parameter functions. Take, for instance, the definition of map in terms of `foldr`:

```
Prelude
map f l = foldr c [] l where
        c x r = f x : r
```

Here, the auxiliary `c` function takes two parameters. It can easily be replaced by an equivalent anonymous function:

```
Prelude
map f l = foldr (\x r -> f x : r) [] l
```

As in the single-parameter case, the two parameters here are written between the backslash and the arrow, separated by a space. This generalizes to any number of parameters.

## Pattern matching without equations

Just like functions defined by equations, anonymous functions can also make use of pattern matching. Recall, for example, the `fst` function:

```
Prelude
fst :: (a,b) -> a
fst (x,y) = x
```

We can write an anonymous function that features the same pattern matching on the tuple data constructor:

```
\(x,y) -> x
```

Instead of writing to pattern in the left-hand side of the equation, we write the function to the left of the arrow.

This kind of pattern matching should only be used when the data type we match on has only a single constructor. If there are multiple constructors, we would normally define a named function by means of multiple equations. Haskell has an expression-level feature for pattern matching that is not tied to equations; nor is it tied to anonymous functions. Consider a simple function to check whether a list is empty or not:

```
Prelude
null :: [a] -> Bool
null []     = True
null (x:xs) = False
```

The two patterns that are covered by two equations can also be captured in the body of a single equation, as follows:

```
Prelude
null :: [a] -> Bool
null l = case l of
                []     -> True
                (x:xs) -> False
```

This form of expression is known as a `case` expression. It matches the result of a particular expression, which is also known as the **scrutinee**, against a number of patterns and then returns the corresponding result. The scrutinee here is the list, `l`, which is matched in turn against the empty and non-empty list patterns, respectively. The first pattern that matches is selected and determines the result.

A case expression can also be used inside an anonymous function:

```
\ l -> case l of
          []      -> True
          (x:xs) -> False
```

Generally, however, anonymous functions are at their best when they are relatively short and do not stretch out over more than one line. Another use case where anonymous functions should generally not be used is recursion, as there is no built-in mechanism for recursive anonymous functions.

While anonymous functions allow us to define arbitrary new functions, the next feature allows us to create specialized versions of existing functions.

# Currying and partial application

The second feature that aids in creating new functions as parameters to HOFs is currying. Currying is named after Haskell B. Curry, the logician after whom the Haskell language is named, even though Curry attributed the concept of currying to the logician Moses Schönfinkel; in fact, the first known application predates both and is credited to a third logician, Gottlob Frege. It is based on an idea that greatly simplifies the design and mechanics of a functional programming language, possibly requiring a revision of your current mental model of Haskell. The idea is that functions need not have more than one parameter. Whenever we want to write a multi-parameter function, we can simulate it instead by means of single-parameter functions. This idea features in the lambda calculus, as it serves its minimality objective. As we will now see, Haskell too has currying built in.

## One parameter is enough

Let us revisit the very first two-parameter function we wrote back in *A Two-Parameter Function section in Chapter1, Functions:*

```
average :: Float -> Float -> Float
average a b = (a + b) / 2
```

The type signature of this function expresses that it is not actually a two-parameter function. The function arrow, `->`, is a binary operator that acts on types; it creates a function type out of an input type and an output type. As an operator, it implicitly associates with the right. If we add parentheses to the type signature to make this association explicit, we get the following:

```
average :: Float -> (Float -> Float)
```

This reveals that `average` is, in fact, a function that takes a Float and returns a Float-to-Float function. In other words, `average` is a single-parameter, HOF. Indeed, the term *HOF* is not exclusively reserved for functions that take function parameters but is also attributed to functions that return functions. We can rewrite the definition of `average` to explicitly reveal this fact:

```
average a = \b -> (a + b) / 2
```

Now, we see that `average` takes its "first" parameter and returns an anonymous function that takes the "second" parameter.

What is important to realize is that it does not actually matter which of the two definitions we give. They both behave in the same way as curried (i.e., single-parameter) functions. In fact, a third, equivalent definition is as follows:

```
average = \a -> (\b -> (a + b) / 2)
```

This third form decouples the naming of the function from its behavior.

Currying also has an impact on calling the average function. Consider the following:

```
*Main> average 4 6
```

This has the same meaning as the following:

```
*Main> (average 4) 6
```

In other words, calling `average` with the parameter 4 yields a new function: `(\b -> (4 + b) / 2)`. This new function is subsequently called with the parameter 6 and yields the result 5.

## Partial application

We did not need to know that Haskell curries all its functions in order to be able to use multi-parameter functions. Haskell performs the currying implicitly. Yet, armed with the awareness of currying, we can actually exploit it. That is to say, we can *partially apply* a multi-parameter function. Partial application means that, when calling a function, we do not supply its full number of parameters.

Continuing the previous example, `average  4` is a partial application. While `average` expects two parameters, we only supply the first and do not give it a second. As we already pointed out, this yields a new function, `(\b -> (4 + b) / 2)`, which can be seen as a specialized version of `average` and already has the first parameter filled in.

While `average` is useless if we don't fully apply it, the point of partial application is to defer its full application to a *later time* or a *different location* in the code. A good example is its use in combination with the map function:

```
*Main> map (average 4) [1,2,3]
[2.5,3.0,3.5]
```

Here, the specialized function that results from the partial application is used three times by map to compute three different averages.

Partial application also works for functions with more than two parameters. Recall that the `foldr` function takes three parameters. Here, we partially apply it to its first two:

```
*Main> map (foldr (*) 1) [[],[1,2,3],[4,5]]
[1,6,20]
```

This example computes the products of the elements in the inner lists, for which it uses the partially applied `foldr (*) 1`. If we want to fill in, say, the second and third parameters but not the first, that is not possible with partial application. Instead, we have to resort to an anonymous function (or even a named function), such as (`\op -> foldr op 1 [1,2,3]`).

## Operator sections

When it comes to partial application, there is separate support for infix operators. We can partially apply an operator to either its left or its right operand. These are known respectively as the left (operator) section and the right (operator) section. For example, the left section (`1+`) is equivalent to `\x -> 1 + x`, and the right section (`+1`) is equivalent to `\x -> x + 1`. Of course, for +, the two sections do not matter (we say that the + operator is *commutative*), as shown here:

```
*Main> (1+) 2
3
*Main> (+1) 2
3
```

In contrast, for non-commutative operators, the difference matters very much:

```
*Main> (1/) 2
0.5
*Main> (/1) 2
2.0
```

One special gotcha is the binary minus operator. It only supports the left section (e.g., (`1-`)). The form (`-1`) is interpreted by Haskell as the unary minus applied to 1. This yields the negative number -1. The binary minus has no right section. Instead, you have to write `\x -> x - 1`.

An interesting operator to use in a section is the list constructor (`:`). Its two sections have different types:

```
*Main> :type (True:)
[Bool] -> [Bool]
*Main> :type (:[True])
Bool -> [Bool]
```

Here, the left section creates a function that adds the `True` element in front of an existing list of Booleans. The right section creates a function that adds an element in front of the singleton list containing `True`.

Besides operator sections, we can still use the regular partial application when writing operators in prefix form. For instance, we can write `(+)` `1` instead of the `(1+)` section or the anonymous function. The added benefit of operator sections is that we can also partially apply the second operand, which has no (direct) counterpart in the partial application of ordinary functions.

## Flipping function parameters

Part of the challenge of writing a good signature is to anticipate which parameter we will want to partially apply the most and to put that parameter first. Yet, even if we do a good job, we won't be able to accommodate all use cases. Sometimes, the parameter we want to partially apply comes second. For that purpose, the standard library contains the `flip` function:

```
Prelude
flip :: (a -> b -> c) -> (b -> a -> c)
flip f = \b a -> f a b
```

What the `flip` function does is take a two-parameter function, f, and create a new function flip, f, that behaves like f but has its parameters in the opposite (or *flipped*) order. This way, we can effectively partially apply the second parameter.

For example, the map function has the signature map `:: (a -> b) -> [a] -> [b]` because we most often want to partially apply its function parameter. This is, for instance, useful when modifying elements in a nested list:

```
*Main> map (map show) [[1,2],[],[4]]
[["1","2"],[],["4"]]
```

Yet, when we want to partially apply map to a given list, we can use `flip`:

```
*Main> flip map [1,2,3] (1+)
[2,3,4]
*Main> map (flip map [1,2,3]) [(1+),(2*),(/2)]
[[2.0,3.0,4.0],[2.0,4.0,6.0],[0.5,1.0,1.5]]
```

This last example creates a list of functions (operator sections) and uses each, in turn, to map over the list of numbers, `[1,2,3]`.

My advice is to use the `flip` function very sparingly, as it generally does not contribute to the comprehensibility of the code.

Through partial application, currying allows us to create specialized versions of functions. The next feature, eta reduction, is complementary and provides a more compact notation.

# Eta reduction

The third feature that Haskell has borrowed from the lambda calculus is *eta reduction*. Eta reduction is named after the Greek letter *eta*, written as $\eta$. It allows us to shorten function definitions of a particular form. Its inverse is known as *eta expansion*, and collectively, they are known as *eta conversion*.

## Basic eta reduction

We will illustrate the idea using a basic anonymous function:

```
\x -> sin x
```

This function takes a parameter, x, and computes its sine by calling the sin function on it. The observation that eta reduction makes is that this anonymous function behaves in exactly the same way as the sin function itself; both functions produce the same output given the same input. In other words, this anonymous function is indistinguishable from sin and, therefore, equal to it. For example, consider the following:

```
map (\x -> sin x) [1.0, 2.0, 3.0]
```

We can rewrite that as the following:

```
map sin [1.0, 2.0, 3.0]
```

This idea also works at the level of equations. For instance, consider the following:

```
f :: Float -> Float
f x = sin x
```

Recall that this is equivalent to the following:

```
f :: Float -> Float
f = \x -> sin x
```

After eta conversion, we end up with a shorter definition than the original:

```
f :: Float -> Float
f = sin
```

Where the original definition reads "the f function takes a floating point value and returns its sine," we can read this definition as "the f function is the sine function." This form is quite appealing because it shifts the focus away from the values (x) that are processed by functions toward the functions themselves.

## Eta reduction with partial application

Eta reduction is particularly useful in combination with partial application. Consider the following function:

```
squareList :: [Int] -> [Int]
squareList l = map (\x -> x * x) l
```

Let us rewrite this to use an anonymous function:

```
squareList :: [Int] -> [Int]
squareList = \l -> map (\x -> x * x) l
```

The way we can read this code is that, because of currying, `map (\x -> x * x)` yields a function that is applied to the list, `l`. We can apply eta reduction to this:

```
squareList :: [Int] -> [Int]
squareList = map (\x -> x * x)
```

The result is a definition of `squareList` as a partially applied HOF.

## Eta reduction of two-parameter functions

Thanks to currying, eta reduction also works in the context of multi-parameter functions. Consider this example:

```
\x y -> average x y
```

With currying in mind, we can write this equivalently as follows:

```
\x -> (\y -> (average x) y)
```

Now, we can apply eta reduction to the inner lambda function. That lambda function behaves exactly like the function produced by the partial application, `(average x)`. Hence, we can simplify the whole expression:

```
\x -> average x
```

Here, we can apply another eta reduction:

```
average
```

Finally, we can see that the anonymous two-parameter function was just the `average` function.

## Irreducible cases

Eta reduction is not always possible, even in cases that at first sight might seem to allow it. Our first example is one where the anonymous function switches the order of the parameters to `average`:

```
\y x -> average x y
```

It is, of course, not valid to replace this with `average` because it takes its parameters in a different order. A way around the problem is to use the `flip` function from *Chapter 5, First-Class Functions*:

```
\y x -> flip average y x
```

Now, `flip average` takes its parameters in the same order as the anonymous function, and eta reduction becomes possible (twice). The result is the following:

```
flip average
```

Indeed, the original function is equivalent to `flip average`. Another case where eta reduction is not possible is the following:

```
\x -> average x x
```

If we were to reduce this expression once, we would get the invalid `average x` expression, where x is no longer bound anywhere.

We can address the situation by writing a HOF that captures the parameter pattern, in a similar way that `flip` did in the previous example:

```
doubleApply :: (a -> a -> b) -> (a -> b)
doubleApply f x = f x x
```

This function captures the pattern of applying a function to two copies of a value. Now, we can write the anonymous function as follows:

```
\x -> doubleApply average x
```

Alternatively, after eta reduction, we can write it as follows:

```
doubleApply average .
```

Of course, you should assess whether it is worthwhile introducing a new non-standard HOF for this purpose. The larger the required vocabulary of higher-order functions, the more effort it will require to read the code. If this pattern appears only once or twice in a code base, it does not seem worth it.

Next, we will see a particularly common case where eta reduction is blocked, and where a commonly used operator comes to the rescue to recover a compact notation.

# Function composition

Function composition is a well-known operator from mathematics, written as ∘, that combines two functions into a new one.

## Basic function composition

Consider the following anonymous function:

```
\l -> show (length l)
```

This function returns the length of a list rendered as a string. It is not in the right shape to apply eta reduction to because, in its current form, we cannot identify one function that is applied to l.

The function composition operator captures this particular pattern in a general way:

```
Prelude
(.) :: (b -> c) -> (a -> b) -> (a -> c)
f . g = \x -> f (g x)
```

This higher-order operator takes two functions and returns a new function that applies the first to the output of the second. We can use this to replace our preceding example with the following:

```
show . length
```

This can be read as "show composed with length" or, better, "show after length".

## Pipelines

The function composition operator can also be used in pile-ups of more than two functions. For example, consider this anonymous function:

```
\l -> show (1 + length l)
```

It computes a string representation of one more than the length of the given list. If we replace the addition with an operator section, we can more clearly see that it involves a pile-up of three functions – show, (1+), and length:

```
\l -> show ((1 +) (length l))
```

We can combine the outer two by means of function composition:

```
\l -> (show . (1 +)) (length l)
```

Next, we can do the same with the combined outer function and the remaining inner one:

```
\l -> ((show . (1 +)) . length) l
```

Finally, we can eta reduce this and drop the outer parentheses:

```
(show . (1 +)) . length
```

If we had started by composing the two inner functions, we would have arrived at the following:

```
show . ((1 +) . length)
```

In fact, it does not matter which way we group the compositions; they all mean the same thing. Hence, we usually drop the parentheses altogether (just as we would do for (+) ):

```
show . (1 +) . length
```

Such a function composition sequence is sometimes called a *(function) pipeline*. The data travels through such a pipeline from right to left and is transformed at each stage.

Both function composition and eta reduction promote the definition of new functions in terms of existing functions, without referring explicitly to the values they process. This is known as the point-free programming style, where the word point refers to values. Ironically, point-free code is full of points, namely those of the function composition operator ( . ).

Now that we have seen the extent of Haskell's support for programming with higher-order functions, we will finish with an illustration of the first-class nature of functions.

# Functions as data structures

In this last section, we will aim to further shift our perspective away from functions as a mechanism to perform computations on functions as data, or, more specifically, on functions as data structures.

## Evaluation with many variables

In *Chapter 3*, *Recursion*, we looked at an interpreter for a small expression language that features one variable. Let us generalize this now to expressions that can contain many different variables:

```
data Expr = Var String | Lit Int | Add Expr Expr
```

This data type has a constructor, Var, to denote a variable expression. The constructor's String field identifies which of the possibly many variables is referenced. For example, the expression x + (y + 3) would be written as follows:

```
expr :: Expr
expr = Add (Var "x") (Add (Var "y") (Lit 3))
```

When evaluating an expression like this, we need to know what values the "x" and "y" variables take. This was easy in *Chapter 3, Recursion* when we had only a single variable and, thus, only one value had to be supplied. Now, we need an arbitrary number of values and a data structure that tells us which value corresponds to which variable. Such a data structure is known as an **environment**. We provisionally assign it the Env type and require that it supports one operation, lookupEnv :: Env -> String -> Int, which, given an environment and a variable name, returns the value associated with that variable.

Given the preceding environment interface, we can write the evaluation function as follows:

```
eval :: Expr -> Env -> Int
eval (Var v) env = lookupEnv env v
eval (Lit n) env = n
eval (Add e1 e2) env = eval e1 env + eval e2 env
```

The environment is recursively passed down and then used in the variable case to look up the value.

We now compare two different ways to realize environments.

## Association list

A conventional representation of an environment is as an association list:

```
type Env = [(String,Int)]
```

This is a list of pairs, a variable name, and its associated value. In this context, the two entries of a pair are also known as the key and the value. The key is used in the lookup to find the corresponding value:

```
lookupEnv :: Env -> String -> Int
lookupEnv [] _ = 0
lookupEnv ((v,n):env) w
  | v == w    = n
  | otherwise = lookupEnv env w
```

The lookup proceeds recursively through the list. Every entry's key is compared to the variable name we look for. If they are equal, the associated value is returned. If not, the search continues. Finally, in the base case, if the key has not been found, we return a default value of 0.

With this representation, we can evaluate the example expression as follows:

```
*Main> eval expr [("x",5),("y",2)]
10
```

Here, the x variable takes the value 5, and y takes the value 2.

## Functional environments

Alternatively, we can represent environments with a more lightweight function-based representation:

```
type Env = String -> Int
```

This expresses an environment as its *characteristic function* – the function that maps a variable name to its value. This function contains all the data that we need from an environment. Moreover, it also contains all the functionality we need from an environment, as the definition of `lookupEnv` becomes trivial:

```
lookupEnv :: Env -> String -> Int
lookupEnv env = env
```

In other words, the environment is its own lookup function; we find a variable's associated value by applying the environment to it.

We evaluate an expression as follows:

```
*Main> :{
*Main| let env "x" = 5
*Main|     env "y" = 3
*Main|     env _   = 0
*Main| in eval expr env
*Main| :}
10
```

Here, the : { and : } markers allow us to write a multiline GHCi expression. We use this to define an environment, env, that we can pass to `eval`.

We can facilitate defining new environments by providing two building blocks:

```
nil :: Env
nil = \ w -> 0

infixr 5 +:

(+:) :: (String, Int) -> Env -> Env
(v,n) +: env = \w -> if v == w then n else env w
```

Here, `nil` defines an empty environment that associates the default value, 0, with every variable, and the custom operator, (+:), extends an environment with an additional variable–value association. The *fixity declaration*, `infixr 5 +:`, is the same as that for the list constructor ( : ); it expresses that (+:) associates to the right and has precedence 5.

The two environment building blocks are used as follows:

```
*Main> eval expr (("x",5) +: ("y",2) +: nil)
10
```

This illustrates that we can build a data structure out of functions in much the same way as building a data structure using algebraic data types. The function-based approach can be very lightweight, especially when it comes to extracting data, although defining the "constructor" functions requires a bit more effort than for algebraic data types. The main weakness of functions is that we can do only one thing with them – apply them. In contrast, there are many different ways in which we can extract data from a list data structure.

## Summary

This chapter introduced a number of language features that facilitate the creation of new functions out of existing ones, which is particularly useful when working with higher-order functions. Three of these features originate in the lambda calculus – anonymous functions, currying, and eta reduction. The fourth feature, function composition, is a common operator used in mathematics. Function composition and eta reduction both promote the point-free programming style that focuses on functions, rather than on the values they process. Finally, to illustrate the first-class nature of functions, we saw how they can be used to represent data structures.

In *Chapter 6*, *Type Classes*, we will learn about Haskell's mechanism for overloading functions called *type classes*. While we expect that predefined operators such as (+) and (<) work for different built-in types, type classes also allow us to define these operators for our own algebraic data types. Moreover, with type classes, we can introduce new overloaded functions. Because it is a powerful abstraction mechanism, it is used pervasively throughout Haskell libraries.

## Questions

1.  What are anonymous functions?
2.  What is currying?
3.  What is eta reduction?
4.  What is function composition?
5.  What are first-class functions?

# Answers

1. Anonymous functions are functions that are not given by name but by their definition. They are used where an expression is expected – for example, as a parameter to a HOF. Syntactically, they take the form `\x1 ... x2n -> e`, where `x1,...,xn` are the function parameters and `e` is the function body.

2. Currying is the technique of encoding a multi-parameter function in terms of single-parameter functions. In Haskell, all functions are curried. For example, the `\x y -> x + y` function is encoded as `\x -> (\y -> x + y)`. Currying allows partial application – a multi-parameter function is not applied to all of its parameters. The result is a function that expects the remaining parameters. For example, `map not` is a partial application of `map`; it is a function that turns a list of Booleans into a list of the negation of them.

3. Eta reduction is the simplification of a function of the form `(\x -> f x)` to just `f`. The idea is that both functions are indistinguishable and, thus, equivalent.

4. Function composition is a higher-order operator that takes two functions and returns a new one. It is defined as follows:

```
(.) :: (b -> c) -> (a -> b) -> (a -> c)
f . g = \x -> f (g x)
```

The input, `x`, is passed to `g`, and `g`'s output is passed to `f`.

5. Functions are called first-class in a programming language when that language puts functions on equal footing with other data types. Specifically, functions can be passed to and returned from other (higher-order) functions. They can be stored in data structures and even treated as data structures themselves.

# 6
# Type Classes

Like most other programming languages, Haskell features a number of overloaded operators and functions, such as (+), that work at different types. For instance, (+) has the following four types:

```
(+) :: Int -> Int -> Int
(+) :: Integer -> Integer -> Integer
(+) :: Float -> Float -> Float
(+) :: Double -> Double -> Double
```

Overloading is not the same as (parametric) polymorphism: (+) does not have the type a -> a -> a and does not work on all possible types. Overloading means that the operator only works for a specific set of types and that the operator's behavior is different for each type.

In many languages, overloading is ad hoc: it exists for a fixed number of operators and functions and a fixed set of types. Moreover, a function that uses an overloaded operator often has to be written once for each type. For example, see the following:

```
plusInt :: Int -> Int -> Int
plusInt x y = x + y
plusFloat :: Float -> Float -> Float
plusFloat x y = x + y
```

Haskell has introduced a new language feature, called type classes, to address the shortcomings of ad hoc overloading and make the approach more systematic. With type classes, we can extend the overloaded methods to cover new types and decide what the methods do for those types. Moreover, we can introduce new overloaded methods to help structure our programs. Finally, type classes give us a mechanism to abstract over the family of types that implements the overloaded method. This allows us, for example, to write only a single definition:

```
plus :: Num a => a -> a -> a
plus x y = x + y
```

In short, this chapter covers the following main topics:

- What is ad hoc polymorphism with type classes and how do you use it?
- How do you implement overloaded functions and operators for new types?
- What are the main predefined type classes and what are they used for?
- What are several prominent applications of type classes in the standard libraries?
- How do custom-type classes help with setting up extensible infrastructure?

# Ad hoc polymorphism

We will start this chapter by exploring the concept of ad hoc polymorphism. We will learn that Haskell uses type classes to declare which operators and functions are overloaded, and uses type class constraints in function signatures to limit how type variables can be instantiated.

## What is ad hoc polymorphism?

Haskell provides several operators that work on values of multiple types, such as the equality test (==). We can, for instance, check whether two integer values are equal, two Boolean values, or two strings:

```
*Main> 1 == 2
False
*Main> True == True
True
*Main> "hello" == "world"
False
```

However, the operator does not work for all types. Notably, it does not work on functions. For example, we can't compare the not :: Bool -> Bool function to itself:

```
*Main> not == not

<interactive>:2:1: error:
    • No instance for (Eq (Bool -> Bool)) arising from a use of '=='
      (maybe you haven't applied a function to enough arguments?)
    • In the expression: not == not
      In an equation for 'it': it = not == not
```

Likewise, it does not work on custom algebraic data types. Recall the Suit type:

```
data Suit = Hearts | Diamonds | Clubs | Spades
```

We cannot compare these suits:

```
*Main> Hearts == Clubs

<interactive>:2:1: error:
    • No instance for (Eq Suit) arising from a use of '=='
    • In the expression: Hearts == Clubs
      In an equation for 'it': it = Hearts == Clubs
```

This mechanism, whereby certain operators work for some types but not others, is known as **ad hoc polymorphism**; it also goes by the name **(operator) overloading**. It means that different types of the same function or operator are available. Here, (==) has the following types:

```
(==) :: Int      -> Int      -> Bool
(==) :: Bool     -> Bool     -> Bool
(==) :: String   -> String   -> Bool
...
```

It differs from parametric polymorphism in two ways. Firstly, as we have seen, (==) does not have the type (==) :: a -> a -> Bool because it is not available as all types. Secondly, it does not have one definition that works uniformly across all types. Instead, there is a separate definition for each type that is specific to that type. This special casing is what the term *ad hoc* refers to.

## Type classes

To indicate which types support the (==) operator, Haskell uses the *type class mechanism*. The type class associated with (==) is called **Eq**, which is short for **Equality**. A type class like Eq acts as a *predicate* or a *constraint* on types. To assert or require that a particular type, say Int, supports (==), we write Eq Int. Indeed, the most general type of (==) is written as follows:

```
(==) :: Eq a => a -> a -> Bool
```

This type signature contains a part we have not seen yet. The actual type, a -> a -> Bool, is preceded by a double arrow, =>, and before that double arrow, we see a type class constraint. This constraint restricts the possible choices for the type variable a; we can only choose types that have an implementation for (==). That sounds a bit self-referential, but we will shortly see that a constraint such as Eq a can also appear in the signatures of other functions.

There is one other primitive operator that comes with the Eq a type class constraint – not equal:

```
(/=) :: Eq a => a -> a -> Bool
```

It is the obvious opposite of (==). For example, see the following:

```
*Main> 1 /= 2
True
*Main> 1 /= 1
False
```

Hence, the Eq-type class brings together two operators. This is declared as follows:

```
Prelude
class Eq a where
   (==) :: a -> a -> Bool
   (/=) :: a -> a -> Bool
```

The class keyword is followed by the name of the type class, Eq, and a type parameter, a. Next, following the where keyword is an indented list of overloaded operators (and, more generally, functions) with their signatures. These overloaded operators and functions are known as the *methods* of the type class.

Types that implement the (methods of the) type class are known as *instances* of that type class. In GHCi, we can query what instances a type class has with the :info command:

```
*Main> :info Eq
type Eq :: * -> Constraint
class Eq a where
   (==) :: a -> a -> Bool
   (/=) :: a -> a -> Bool
   {-# MINIMAL (==) | (/=) #-}
        -- Defined in 'GHC.Classes'
instance (Eq a, Eq b) => Eq (Either a b)
   -- Defined in 'Data.Either'
instance Eq a => Eq (Maybe a) -- Defined in 'GHC.Maybe'
instance Eq a => Eq [a] -- Defined in 'GHC.Classes'
instance Eq Word -- Defined in 'GHC.Classes'
instance Eq Ordering -- Defined in 'GHC.Classes'
instance Eq Int -- Defined in 'GHC.Classes'
instance Eq Float -- Defined in 'GHC.Classes'
instance Eq Double -- Defined in 'GHC.Classes'
instance Eq Char -- Defined in 'GHC.Classes'
instance Eq Bool -- Defined in 'GHC.Classes'
...
```

Besides the type class declaration, this shows a long list of its instances. Not all of these make sense yet, but most should by the end of this chapter. We should already recognize several familiar ones at least, such as those for Int, Float, Double, Char, and Bool.

Likewise, we can ask GHCi which type class a given type instantiates with the : instances command:

```
*Main> :instances Int
instance Eq Int -- Defined in 'GHC.Classes'
instance Ord Int -- Defined in 'GHC.Classes'
instance Enum Int -- Defined in 'GHC.Enum'
instance Num Int -- Defined in 'GHC.Num'
instance Real Int -- Defined in 'GHC.Real'
instance Show Int -- Defined in 'GHC.Show'
instance Read Int -- Defined in 'GHC.Read'
instance Bounded Int -- Defined in 'GHC.Enum'
instance Integral Int -- Defined in 'GHC.Real'
instance GHC.Ix.Ix Int -- Defined in 'GHC.Ix'
instance Data.Bits.Bits Int -- Defined in 'Data.Bits'
instance Data.Bits.FiniteBits Int -- Defined in 'Data.Bits'
instance Foreign.Storable.Storable Int
   -- Defined in 'Foreign.Storable'
```

At this point, we only recognize the Eq type class, but by the end of this chapter, we will understand what many of the others are.

## Type class constraints are contagious

Let us write a function that makes use of (==) to delete all the occurrences of a given element in a list:

```
*Main> deleteAll 1 [1,2,3,1]
[2,3]
```

This function can be defined as follows:

```
deleteAll x []       = []
deleteAll x (y:ys)
  | x == y          = deleteAll x ys
  | otherwise       = y : deleteAll x ys
```

It recurses on the list and along the way drops all the elements that are equal to x. An alternative, more concise definition makes use of filter:

```
deleteAll x ys = filter (/= x) ys
```

This definition selects all the elements from the list that are not equal to x.

We can assign the `deleteAll` function a type signature for a specific type of element such as the following:

```
deleteAll :: Int -> [Int] -> [Int]
deleteAll :: Char -> [Char] -> [Char]
...
```

However, ideally, we pick the most general type that covers all the preceding possibilities. This most general type is also called the *principal type*. It is the following:

```
deleteAll :: Eq a => a -> [a] -> [a]
```

This is a polymorphic type with a type class constraint `Eq a` on the type variable a. While the type variable indicates that this type can be freely chosen, the constraint stipulates that the choice is not entirely free, but subject to the constraint that it is an instance of the `Eq` type class. For this reason, we sometimes speak of *constraint polymorphism*.

The reason that the `Eq a` constraint appears in the type signature is of course that the definition of `deleteAll` makes use of an `Eq` method, the `(==)` or `(/=)` operator. We already saw that the `Eq a` constraint appears in the type signature of these operators. Hence, we can think of this constraint as being "contagious." Any function that uses a constraint polymorphic function may be infected and become constraint-polymorphic itself. A further example of that is the `nub` function, which uses `deleteAll`:

```
Data.List
nub :: Eq a => [a] -> [a]
nub []     = []
nub (x:xs) = x : nub (deleteAll x xs)
```

The word nub means the essence of something. This function extracts the essence from a list: a list of all its distinct elements. It does so by deleting all the repeated occurrences of elements in the list. Its type signature mentions `Eq a` because it gets infected by `deleteAll`, which requires that constraint.

The spread of a type class constraint is only stopped when the type variable is instantiated to a concrete type that is an instance of the type class. For example, we can apply nub to a list of integers:

```
example :: [Integer]
example = nub [1,2,3,1]
```

Here the type variable a of nub is instantiated to the type `Integer`. Because this type is an instance of Eq, it discharges the type class constraint.

Now that we understand how type classes enable ad hoc polymorphism, let us investigate how we can extend overloaded operations to additional types.

# Type class instances

The set of types that instantiates the Eq type class is not fixed. As programmers, we can extend it with additional types.

## Type class instantiation

As we saw in the *What is ad hoc polymorphism?* section, the Suit data type does not instantiate the Eq type class and therefore does not support (==) and (/=). We can remedy that by writing our own instance for it:

```
instance Eq Suit where

    Hearts   == Hearts   = True
    Diamonds == Diamonds = True
    Spades   == Spades   = True
    Clubs    == Clubs    = True
    _        == _        = False

    Hearts   /= Hearts   = False
    Diamonds /= Diamonds = False
    Spades   /= Spades   = False
    Clubs    /= Clubs    = False
    _        /= _        = True
```

This declaration states on the first line that Suit is an instance of Eq. The following, indented lines then provide definitions for the two methods of Eq. Two suits are equal when they match the same constructor and not equal when they match different constructors.

With this instance declaration in play, our earlier example now does work:

```
*Main> Hearts == Clubs
False
```

Hence, unlike many existing languages, Haskell allows us to extend the overloading of existing operators, such as (==), for any new types we define.

## Default implementations and minimal complete definitions

Before we move on to defining additional instances, let us do something about their size. Firstly, since (/=) should be the negation of (==), we can write the Eq Suit instance more concisely as follows:

```
instance Eq Suit where

    Hearts   == Hearts   = True
```

```
Diamonds == Diamonds = True
Spades   == Spades   = True
Clubs    == Clubs    = True
_        == _        = False

s1 /= s2 = not (s1 == s2)
```

This shows that the two methods do not have to be defined independently. We can define one in terms of the other. In fact, the definition we have used here for ( /= ) is not really specific to Suit. It works for any other type as well. Yet, as it would be quite annoying to have to repeat the same generic definition in every instance, type classes can provide *default implementations*. In fact, the Eq type class actually provides two default implementations:

```
Prelude
class Eq a where
  (==) :: a -> a -> Bool
  x == y = not (x /= y)
  (/=) :: a -> a -> Bool
  x /= y = not (x == y)
```

The default implementations define the two methods in terms of each other. This way, we can write an instance and implement only one of the two methods:

```
instance Eq Suit where

  Hearts   == Hearts   = True
  Diamonds == Diamonds = True
  Spades   == Spades   = True
  Clubs    == Clubs    = True
  _        == _        = False
```

Because we do not implement ( /= ) in this instance, we automatically get its default implementation. Hence, we can still write the following:

```
*Main> Hearts /= Clubs
True
```

As ( == ) also has a default implementation, we might be tempted to write an empty instance:

```
instance Eq Suit where
     -- no methods defined
```

Yet, this would be a mistake. We now get the two default implementations, which define the two methods in terms of each other. This leads to an infinite loop where each operator calls the other, which is certainly not what we want. (If you try this, remember that *Ctrl + C* aborts the infinite loop.) The only way this works is if we implement at least one of the two operators independently from the other.

The documentation of the Eq type class indicates this by saying that the minimal complete definition comprises either `(==)` or `(/=)`. In the output of `:info Eq`, we see this in the following form:

```
{-# MINIMAL (==) | (/=) #-}
```

Here, the bar (`|`) means `or`.

## Instances for composite values

Consider a data type for points in a two-dimensional space:

```
data Point = MkPoint Int Int
```

Each point has two coordinates and two points are equal when their corresponding coordinates are equal. The latter is captured in the following instance.

```
instance Eq Point where
  MkPoint x1 y1 == MkPoint x2 y2 = x1 == x2 && y1 == y2
```

This definition of `(==)` looks recursive, but it is not. It defines the equality for points (on the left of the equation) in terms of the equality for integers (on the right in the equation). Because of overloading, the two equality functions have the same name, but they are still different functions.

Contrast this with an instance for the `Expr` data type of arithmetic expressions:

```
data Expr = Lit Int | Add Expr Expr
```

The following instance checks whether two arithmetic expressions are structurally equal:

```
instance Eq Expr where
  Lit n      == Lit m    = n == m
  Add e1 e2 == Add e3 e4 = e1 == e3 && e2 == e4
  _          == _        = False
```

The first equation says that two literals are equal if their integer values are equal. This defines equality of expressions in terms of equality on integers. The second equation, however, states that two additions are equal if their subexpressions are equal pairwise. This is a genuine example of recursion because it defines the equality of expressions in terms of the equality of expressions. Finally, the third equation catches the remaining cases, comparing an addition with a literal or vice versa.

An equivalent but more roundabout instance declaration shows better where the actual recursion is. We first define an independent function that checks the equality of expressions:

```
eqExpr :: Expr -> Expr -> Bool
eqExpr (Lit n)     (Lit m)     = n == m
eqExpr (Add e1 e2) (Add e3 e4) = eqExpr e1 e3 && eqExpr e2 e4
eqExpr _           _           = False
```

Here, `(==)` is only used for equality on integers, while `eqExpr` is used for the recursive calls. With this function already given, we can write a concise instance declaration:

```
instance Eq Expr where
   (==) = eqExpr
```

Following the style of *Chapter 5*, *First-Class Functions*, this defines the `(==)` operator as equal to the `eqExpr` function.

## Equality of functions

By default, new Haskell types do not have an `Eq` instance. Yet, based on the examples we have seen so far, this seems to be a matter of choice. However, for some types, we cannot sensibly write an equality check.

The core example for which an equality check does not exist is function types whose domain is infinitely large, such as `Integer -> Bool` or `[Bool] -> Int`. Following Haskell's mathematically inspired notion of functions, two functions `f1` and `f2` are equal if and only if `f1 x == f2 x` for every value `x` in their domain. If the domain is infinitely large, this property is undecidable. Obviously, we cannot possibly check every value in the domain, and thus we can never be sure that the two functions are equal.

Even in cases where the domain of the functions is finite, but prohibitively large, for example, of type `Int` or `Float`, it would be impractical to check all possible inputs. Hence, as a general rule, Haskell does not supply an `Eq` instance for function types.

Moreover, the problem is contagious. Consider the following type declaration:

```
data T = MkT String (Integer -> Bool)
```

Because the values of this algebraic data type contain a function, we likely won't be able to write an `Eq` instance for it, as we cannot compare the function field.

## Recursive instances

The instances of polymorphic data types are typically conditional. Consider for instance the predefined `Maybe` data type.

```
Prelude
data Maybe a = Nothing | Just a
```

It has the following `Eq` instance:

```
Prelude
instance Eq a => Eq (Maybe a) where
  Nothing == Nothing = True
```

```
Just x  == Just y  = x == y
        == _       = False
```

This instance performs the obvious structural comparison of the two values. If both are constructed with `Just`, their fields `x` and `y` are compared as well. Because of the polymorphism, the type of these fields could be anything. Actually, not every type would work as we want to check the fields for equality. This is only possible when the type a is itself an instance of `Eq`. For that reason, the instance has a constraint `Eq a =>` in its first line. This constraint is also called the *(instance) context*; just as in type signatures of polymorphic functions, it restricts the possible choices for a type variable.

The preceding instance enables the following comparison:

```
*Main> Just 'a' == Just 'b'
False
```

The two values are of type `Maybe Char`. Hence, `(==)` uses the `Eq (Maybe Char)` instance. This in turn requires the `Eq Char` instance, which is also available.

In fact, with a polymorphic instance like that of `Maybe`, we get equality for arbitrarily many nestings of `Maybe`. For example, the instance also establishes that we have `Eq (Maybe (Maybe Char))` because we have `Eq (Maybe Char)` because we have `Eq Char`. Hence, checking whether an instance exists becomes a recursive process and the instances that require recursive checks are called *recursive instances*.

When a data type has multiple parameters, the instance context may contain multiple type class constraints. For example, this is the `Eq` instance for tuples:

```
Prelude
instance (Eq a, Eq b) => Eq (a,b) where
  (x1,y1) == (x2,y2) = x1 == x2 && y1 == y2
```

The tuple type `(a,b)` has two type parameters a and b for the types of its two fields. To compare two tuples, we compare these fields pairwise and thus require that both a and b support equality. This is expressed with the instance context `(Eq a, Eq b) =>`, which is a pair of two equality constraints.

## Deriving structural instances

All the `Eq` instances we have written here are structural in nature. Take the `Eq Suit` instance as an example. If two suits have been created with the same constructor, they are equal. If they have different constructors, they are not. This idea of structural equality is applied recursively in the `Expr` instance, and in the others we have seen.

Once you have written a few of these structural equality instances, writing more of them becomes tedious and gets in the way of writing other, more interesting code. Fortunately, Haskell helps us out with its `deriving` mechanism. For a number of type classes, including `Eq`, the language has a standard recipe for writing instances. Hence, instead of manually writing an instance, we can ask Haskell to use the standard recipe and derive an instance for us. This is done by adding a `deriving` clause to the data type declaration:

```haskell
data Suit = Hearts | Diamonds | Clubs | Spades
  deriving Eq
```

Here, the clause is written on the second line but indented to indicate it is still part of the data declaration. It could also have been written at the end of the first line.

If you are interested in seeing the code of the derived instance, you can pass the `-ddump-deriv` flag to GHCi:

```
$ ghci -ddump-deriv TypeClasses.hs
GHCi, version 8.10.2: https://www.haskell.org/ghc/  :? for help
Loaded GHCi configuration from /Users/toms/.ghci
[1 of 1] Compiling Main              ( TypeClasses.hs, interpreted )


==================== Derived instances ====================
Derived class instances:
  instance GHC.Classes.Eq Main.Suit where
    (GHC.Classes.==) (Main.Hearts) (Main.Hearts) = GHC.Types.True
    (GHC.Classes.==) (Main.Diamonds) (Main.Diamonds) = GHC.Types.True
    (GHC.Classes.==) (Main.Clubs) (Main.Clubs) = GHC.Types.True
    (GHC.Classes.==) (Main.Spades) (Main.Spades) = GHC.Types.True
    (GHC.Classes.==) _ _ = GHC.Types.False

Derived type family instances:


==================== Filling in method body ====================
GHC.Classes.Eq [Main.Suit]
  GHC.Classes./= = GHC.Classes.$dm/= @(Main.Suit)

Ok, one module loaded.
```

Now GHCi shows us the code of the derived instance for `Suit`. The code is much noisier than what we would write ourselves because all names have been qualified by their module, `GHC.Classes`, for all names related to the `Eq` type class and `Main` for our own code. The last part of the output also shows that the default implementation is used for `(/=)`.

The `deriving` mechanism also works for polymorphic data types, like the following `Tree` type:

```haskell
data Tree a = Leaf a | Fork (Tree a) (Tree a)
  deriving Eq
```

In this case, it does equip the instance with the appropriate Eq a instance context:

```
instance Eq a => Eq (Tree a) where …
```

## Semantic equality instances

While the `deriving` mechanism relieves us from writing structural equality instances, that is not always what we want. Often, we want a different kind of instance for Eq that looks beyond the structure and considers the meaning (also called **semantics**) of the data that is compared.

We illustrate this on the `Expr` data type of arithmetic expressions. The earlier instance we saw was purely structural; two arithmetic expressions that have the same structure should be considered the same. However, in practice, we sometimes also want to consider two expressions equal that have a different structure. For instance, Lit 3 and Add (Lit 1) (Lit 2) are two expressions that have a different structure but have the same meaning. For that reason, we would like to consider them equal as well. In fact, there are infinitely many more expressions equal to these two: Add 0 (Lit 3), Add (Lit (-1)) (Lit 4), and so on.

The way to tackle this situation is to spell out what we mean by the semantics of an expression. The reason we consider the preceding expressions equal is that they generate the same result. Hence, the evaluation function, `eval`, gives us the meaning of expressions:

```
eval :: Expr -> Int
eval (Lit n)     = n
eval (Add e1 e2) = eval e1 + eval e2
```

From this, the Eq Expr instance follows naturally:

```
instance Eq Expr where
  e1 == e2 = eval e1 == eval e2
```

This instance defines the equality of expressions (the occurrence of == on the left) in terms of the equality defined for integers (the == on the right). Two expressions e1 and e2 are deemed equal if they evaluate to equal integers. Hence, because Lit 3 and Add (Lit 1) (Lit 2) both come to the same integer 3, they are considered equal by this instance.

We have now seen two different Eq instances for Expr, one structural and one semantic. Each may be appropriate for different purposes. Nevertheless, Haskell only allows a type to have one instance of a given type class. Hence, we must decide what the canonical notion of equality is.

## Lawful instances

As the previous example of semantic equality has shown, there is great freedom in defining instances of the Eq type classes. Even so, not any well-typed definition of equality is sensible. There are certain expectations of how instances should behave. These expectations are formulated in the form of properties that are called **laws**. For Eq, there are five laws. These laws are given in the form of equations that must hold.

### Reflexivity

The first law states that any value x should be equal to itself:

```
x == x = True
```

### Symmetry

The second law states that it should not matter which way around we have written the parameters. If x equals y, then y should equal x:

```
x == y = y == x
```

### Transitivity

The third law is conditional. It establishes that two elements x and z are equal if they are both equal to a common third element y:

```
if x == y && y == z = True, then x == z = True
```

### Extensionality

The fourth law states that equality should be respected by functions. Any function f :: A -> B where the types A and B are instances of Eq should map equal inputs to equal outputs:

```
if x == y = True, then f x == f y = True
```

Notice that the opposite need not be true: f may map unequal inputs to either equal or unequal outputs.

### Negation

The fifth and final law relates equality and inequality in the way we have observed before:

```
x /= y = not (x == y)
```

This law is captured in the default implementation of (/=) and thus is automatically satisfied when that default implementation is used.

These five laws are part of the documentation of the type class and libraries do rely on them. Hence, while the language does not enforce these laws, not following them may lead to unexpected and undefined results.

So, while unlawful instances are to be avoided, we do run into them on occasion. A notorious example is the Float and Double instances of Eq. Here, Haskell follows the *IEEE Standard for Floating-Point Arithmetic* (*IEEE 754*). This standard defines a special value called not-a-number, NaN for short, which is obtained from 0/0 for example. This NaN is not equal to itself, thus violating the reflexivity law.

Another law that is regularly violated is that of extensionality. The reason for the violation is simple: the law does not so much govern the type class instances themselves, as it does the definition of arbitrary functions. When writing functions, we are much less (or even not) aware that we should respect this law. Moreover, when non-structural equality is involved, it is very easy and often also useful to violate extensionality. Consider writing a function that computes the size of an arithmetic expression as its number of constructors:

```
size :: Expr -> Int
size (Lit n) = 1
size (Add e1 e2) = 1 + size e1 + size e2
```

We might want to use this function to order a list of expressions from small to large. Yet, it clearly violates the extensionality law as Lit 3 and Add (Lit 1) (Lit 2) are equal, yet have different sizes.

As we now have a thorough understanding of the Eq type class, let us learn about other key type classes.

## Common type classes

The Haskell standard library features a range of other type classes that are frequently used in Haskell applications. We provide an overview here.

### Ord

The Ord type class captures types that have a *total ordering*. This means that for any two values of the type, we can determine which one is *less than* the other. The type class itself comes with a slew of methods based on this ordering:

```
Prelude
class Eq a => Ord a where
  compare :: a -> a -> Ordering
  (<)     :: a -> a -> Bool
  (<=)    :: a -> a -> Bool
  (>)     :: a -> a -> Bool
  (>=)    :: a -> a -> Bool
  max     :: a -> a -> a
  min     :: a -> a -> a
```

Besides the four well-known comparison operators, we see three additional methods. The `max` and `min` functions select the largest and smallest of two given values respectively. Finally, the `compare` method is perhaps the most primitive of all. While the comparison operators return one of two possible results, `True` and `False`, `compare` has three possible outcomes, of the enumeration type `Ordering`:

```
Prelude
data Ordering = LT | EQ | GT
```

When comparing two values x and y with `compare  x  y`, we learn whether x is less than (`LT`), equal to (`EQ`), or greater than (`GT`) y.

Because a total ordering only makes sense for types that already have a notion of equality, the `Ord` type class is declared to be a *subclass* of `Eq` or, conversely, `Eq` to be a *superclass* of `Ord`. We see this in the header of the class declaration where the class context `Eq  a  =>` imposes the constraint that a must already be an instance of `Eq` in order to be an instance of `Ord`.

The minimal complete definition of `Ord` is `compare  or  (<=)`; we only need to implement one of these. While we do not have to define any of the other `Ord` methods, we still have to provide an instance of the `Eq` superclass as well.

Here is an example for the `Suit` type:

```
instance Ord Suit where
  Diamonds <= _          = True
  Clubs    <= Clubs  = True
  Clubs    <= Hearts = True
  Hearts   <= Hearts = True
  _        <= Spades = True
  _        <= _          = False
```

This implements the ordering used in the game of bridge, where diamonds is less than clubs, clubs less than hearts, and hearts less than spades.

The `Ord` type class instance can be automatically derived. This derivation assumes that the constructors of the type are listed from small to large. For example, to accomplish the ordering just given, we should write the following:

```
data Suit = Diamonds | Clubs | Hearts | Spades
  deriving (Eq, Ord)
```

Here the first constructor, `Diamonds`, is assumed to be the smallest, and the last `Spades` to the largest. This also shows that we can derive two type classes, `Eq` and `Ord`.

The `Ord` instances are subject to four laws.

## Comparability

Given two elements x and y, one of them should be less than or equal to the other. They can't be both greater than the other:

```
x <= y || y <= x = True
```

## Transitivity

An alternative term for total ordering is linear ordering. This means we can put all values in a line, say from left to right, where smaller values are to the left of larger values. This is captured by the transitivity property: if x is to the left of y and y is to the left of z, then x is to the left of z:

```
if x <= y && y <= z = True, then x <= z = True
```

## Reflexivity

Because any value x should be equal to itself, it is also less than or equal to itself:

```
x <= x = True
```

## Antisymmetry

The only way two elements can be less than or equal to each other is if they are equal:

```
if x <= y && y <= x = True, then x == y = True
```

# Show

The Show type class is used by GHCi to display results. It is defined as follows:

```
Prelude
class Show a where
  show :: a -> String
  showsPrec :: Int -> a -> ShowS
  showList :: [a] -> ShowS
```

The core method of this type class is show, which converts a value of type a into a String, which can be displayed. Derived instances display values as valid source code text that can be copied into a program to generate the value shown. We already saw an example of this in section Showing Cards.

Deriving a Show instance is convenient and adequate in most situations. In those cases, the other two methods of the type class can be safely ignored as they constitute internal details. Yet, because they embody several clever ideas, they are worth delving into anyway.

## The *showsPrec method*

Let us unpack what is going on with `showsPrec`:

- Firstly, `showsPrec` takes integer precedence as an additional parameter. We have already explored this approach in the Varying parameters and the worker/wrapper structure: the idea of `showsPrec p x` is that x has to be shown as a parameter of an operator with precedence p. The default precedence is 0 – for example, when x does not appear under an operator. The idea is that it influences whether x is shown surrounded by parentheses or not.

- The result type of `showsPrec` is the type synonym `ShowS`, which is defined as follows:

```
type ShowS = String -> String
```

  If we inline this definition in the type of `showsPrec`, we get the following:

```
showsPrec :: Int -> a -> String -> String
```

  Hence, `showsPrec` takes an additional string as a parameter. The idea is that `showsPrec p x s` adds the string representation of x in front of s. In the right circumstances, this can be done more efficiently than using `(++)`. We will study those circumstances in *Chapter 9, Monoids and Foldables*.

Let us look at a few examples to see these two ideas in action:

```
*Main> showsPrec 0 (Just 5) ""
"Just 5"
```

This first example illustrates that we get back a string that is valid Haskell code for creating the shown value:

```
*Main> showsPrec 11 (Just 5) ""
"(Just 5)"
```

Here, we pretend that the value `Just 5` appears under an operator with precedence 11. Because 11 is greater than the precedence of applying `Just` to 5, which is 10, parentheses are added to protect the latter:

```
*Main> showsPrec 0 (Just 5) "abc"
"Just 5abc"
```

In this last example, we see that the string representation of `Just 5` is appended in front of the given string.

The minimal complete definition of `Show` is either `show` or `showsPrec`. The default implementation of `show` in terms of `showsPrec` is as follows:

```
show x = showsPrec 0 x ""
```

Hence, we use the default precedence and append the empty string at the end. Conversely, by default, showsPrec behaves as follows:

```
showsPrec _ x s = show x ++ s
```

This ignores the precedence and explicitly appends the given string with (++).

The one law imposed on Show actually governs shows:

```
showsPrec p x s1 ++ s2 = showsPrec p x (s1 ++ s2)
```

This states that when we append a string, s2, to the result of showsPrec, we can instead incorporate it into the string parameter. The following is a special case where s1 is empty:

```
showsPrec p x "" ++ s2 = showsPrec p x s2
```

This indicates that the parameter of showsPrec should be appended to whatever string is produced from x.

### The showList method

Recall that lists are generally shown as a comma-separated list of elements between square brackets:

```
*Main> 1 : 2 : 3 : []
[1,2,3]
*Main> True : False : False : []
[True,False,False]
```

Yet, in the special case of lists of characters (i.e., strings), the list is shown as the consecutive elements between double quotes:

```
*Main> 'a' : 'b' : 'c' : []
"abc"
```

Even though the formats of the output differ, they both follow from the same Show instance for lists. This is possible because that list instance simply delegates to the showList method of its element type:

```
Prelude
instance Show a => Show [a] where
   showsPrec _ l = showList l
```

Hence, the whole point of the showList method is to customize how a list is shown for a specific element type. The default implementation uses square brackets and commas, while that of Char is a custom definition.

## Read

The purpose of the Read type class is the dual of that of Show: it is to turn a textual representation back into a value of some type.

We will not go into the methods of the type class. Most programmers are never confronted with them and always derive the instances automatically. For that reason, we will instead only consider the three functions that are actually used, functions that have been defined in terms of Read's methods.

The best-known function is read :: Read a => String -> a, which turns a string into a value:

```
*Main> read "True" :: Bool
True
```

Because read is (constraint-)polymorphic in its result type, we have added a type annotation here that indicates what type of result we expect.

In general, read should be the inverse of show, and together they should satisfy the following round-trip property:

```
x = read (show x)
```

This property expresses that when reading a shown value, we should get back the value we started from. The opposite need not be true: when reading a string and then showing the value, we need not get back exactly the same string. The reason for that is that read typically accepts redundant parentheses and whitespace in its input that would not be generated by show:

```
*Main> read "(True )" :: Bool
True
*Main> show True
"True"
```

When the input is malformed, read generates a runtime error:

```
*Main> read "Tru" :: Bool
*** Exception: Prelude.read: no parse
```

Because such an error makes your code quite fragile, there are two more robust alternatives to read, which can be imported from Text.Read:

```
Text.Read
readMaybe  :: Read a => String -> Maybe a
readEither :: Read a => String -> Either String a
```

The former returns Nothing when read fails, while the latter returns a human-readable error message:

```
*Main> readMaybe "Tru" :: Maybe Bool
Nothing
*Main> readEither "Tru" :: Either String Bool
Left "Prelude.read: no parse"
```

In *Chapter 14, Parser Combinators*, we will have a more in-depth look at how we can parse strings and turn them into values of other types.

## Bounded and Enum

Now we consider two type classes that both provide functionality for ranges of values.

### The Bounded class

This is a class for types with a minimal and maximal value:

```
Prelude
class Bounded a where
    minBound :: a
    maxBound :: a
```

Unfortunately, Bounded is not very well integrated into the rest of the standard library. It is not used by many functions. Also, the class does not have Ord as a superclass. The motivation is that a type does not require total ordering to have a maximal and minimal value. At the same time, there are no standard type classes for more general notions of ordering, such as partial ordering, which could have been used as a superclass instead. Hence, you will likely not have much use for Bounded. Still, I find it occasionally useful for getting the minimal or maximal Int value:

```
*Main> minBound :: Int
-9223372036854775808
*Main> maxBound :: Int
9223372036854775807
```

Let us move on to the more useful Enum class.

### The Enum class

The Enum type class provides support for enumerating the values of a type:

```
Prelude
class Enum a where
    succ :: a -> a
    pred :: a -> a
    toEnum :: Int -> a
```

```
fromEnum :: a -> Int
enumFrom :: a -> [a]
enumFromThen :: a -> a -> [a]
enumFromTo :: a -> a -> [a]
enumFromThenTo :: a -> a -> a -> [a]
```

The minimal complete definition consists of toEnum and fromEnum. Yet, the method that is used frequently is enumFromTo, albeit behind the scenes: the notation [x..y] is syntactic sugar for enumFromTo x y:

```
*Main> enumFromTo 1 5
[1,2,3,4,5]
```

Because this function is a type class method, it also works for types other than Int and Integer. Notably, Char is also an instance of Enum:

```
*Main> ['a'..'z']
"abcdefghijklmnopqrstuvwxyz"
```

With the deriving mechanism, we can easily get an instance for a custom algebraic data type:

```
data Day = Mon | Tue | Wed | Thu | Fri | Sat | Sun
  deriving (Show, Enum)
```

The enumerating order is that of the constructors in the data declaration:

```
*Main> > [Mon .. Fri]
[Mon,Tue,Wed,Thu,Fri]
```

Mind the space before the double dots. Without it, the Haskell Parser thinks that Mon is a module name that qualifies the (second) dot. The second space is optional but provides a pleasing symmetry.

## Numeric type classes

The last family of type classes from the standard library we will cover are those for different kinds of arithmetic operations.

### The Num class

The Num type class is the central type class for arithmetic:

```
Prelude
class Num a where
  (+)      :: a -> a -> a
  (-)      :: a -> a -> a
  (*)      :: a -> a -> a
```

```
negate :: a -> a
abs    :: a -> a
signum :: a -> a
fromInteger :: Integer -> a
```

Besides the three main binary arithmetic operators, Num also provides two functions that determine special syntax. Firstly, `negate` determines the behavior of the unary minus syntax. Secondly, the `fromInteger` function determines the meaning of integer literals.

Finally, `abs` and `signum` determine the absolute value and sign of a value. The sign is either -1, 0, or 1 depending on whether the value is negative, zero, or positive.

The binary minus and the unary negate have default implementations in terms of each other. All other methods have to be defined explicitly.

We can illustrate all of this with an extended type for arithmetic expressions:

```
data Expr = Lit Integer | Add Expr Expr | Mul Expr Expr
          | Negate Expr | Abs Expr | Sign Expr | Var String
     deriving Show
```

This type has one constructor for each of the Num methods (except the binary minus, which follows from `negate`) and one extra `Var` constructor to represent variables.

Now we can write this trivial Num instance where each method is implemented by a constructor:

```
instance Num Expr where
  (+) = Add
  (*) = Mul
  negate = Negate
  abs = Abs
  signum = Sign
  fromInteger = Lit
```

We can use this type to observe the abstract syntax tree structure of an arithmetic expression. For example, see the following:

```
anExpression :: Num a => a -> a -> a
anExpression x y = 2 * x - y
```

This function takes two parameters and performs an arithmetic computation with them. Because of its constraint-polymorphic type signature, it works for any numeric type. By supplying two `Expr` parameters, we can observe what computation it performs:

```
*Main> anExpression (Var "x") (Var "y")
Add (Mul (Lit 2) (Var "x")) (Negate (Var "y"))
```

This shows that the binary minus a - b is translated into a + negate b. We also see that the literal 2 is converted into an expression by means of the fromInteger function, which applies the Lit constructor to it.

In practice, the Num type class is used mainly for the predefined numeric types Int, Integer, Float, and Double.

### Other arithmetic classes

There are a number of additional arithmetic type classes that provide functionality for operations that are specific to particular kinds of numbers, such as real numbers or integral numbers: Real, Integral, Fractional, Floating, and RealFrac. They provide, among others, the operations we already saw in sections Int and Integer and Float and Double in *Chapter 1*, *Functions*. The following is one example:

```
Prelude
sin :: Floating a => a -> a
```

Also see this example:

```
Prelude
mod :: Integral a => a -> a -> a
```

As the approach in these type classes is similar to that of the Num class, we will not cover the methods here in detail – instead, refer to the documentation on Haskell's Prelude.

We have now covered several key type classes in the standard library. Several later chapters will be devoted to other important type classes that require substantially more explanation. In the remainder of this chapter, we will shift our focus to a few applications of type classes.

## Library uses of type classes

Many applications of type classes can be found in libraries rather than in application-specific code. While applications usually feature concrete types for a specific use case, libraries typically aim to cover as many use cases as they can. For that reason, they prefer regular polymorphic types where possible, or constraint polymorphic types when needed. We have seen various examples of the former before. Here, we will cover a number of basic library functions with constraint-polymorphic type signatures.

### List membership functions

The first three functions we consider can be found in the automatically imported Prelude library. They are all related to the presence of a particular element in a list. Firstly, elem checks whether an element appears in a list:

```
Prelude
elem :: Eq a => a -> [a] -> Bool
```

```
elem x []      = False
elem x (y:ys) = x == y || elem x ys
```

This returns True when the element is in the list and False if it is not. Because of the equality check on the elements, the signature features the Eq a constraint:

```
*Main> elem 3 [1..5]
True
*Main> elem 6 [1..5]
False
```

The notElem function gives the opposite answer to elem:

```
Prelude
notElem :: Eq a => a -> [a] -> Bool
notElem x ys = not (elem x ys)
```

The signatures we give here of the preceding two functions are specific to lists. In *Chapter 9*, *Monoids and Foldables*, we will see that the functions actually generalize to other types of collections.

The third function, lookup, is defined specifically for lists of pairs:

```
Prelude
lookup :: Eq k => k -> [(k,v)] -> Maybe v
lookup k []             = Nothing
lookup k ((k',v):kvs)
  | k' == k             = Just v
  | otherwise           = lookup k kvs
```

The first components of the pairs are called *keys* and the second components are called *values*. A list of such key-value pairs is also known as an *association* list; it associates a value with some keys. The purpose of the lookup function is to find in the list the value associated with a given key.

If the given key does not appear in the list, it has no associated value. For that reason, the result type is Maybe v rather than v.

The following example uses lookup to translate words from English into Dutch, where the association list is a simplified English-Dutch dictionary:

```
*Main> lookup "dog" [("cat","kat"),("dog","hond"),("fish","vis")]
Just "hond"
*Main> lookup "rabbit" [("cat","kat"),("dog","hond"),("fish","vis")]
Nothing
```

If there are two or more associated values for a given key, lookup always only returns the first:

```
*Main> lookup "hond" [("hond","dog"),("hond","canine")]
Just "dog"
```

The function works for different types of keys and values, as long as the keys can be checked for equality, hence the `Eq k` constraint in the signature.

## The Map library

Association lists are quick and easy data structures that support lookups. However, the lookups are not particularly efficient; when the key is absent, `lookup` has to go linearly through the whole list and check every entry.

The `Data.Map` library provides an alternative data type for associating keys with values called `Map k v`. This data type is based on a clever data structure (size-balanced binary trees) whose `lookup` function visits considerably fewer elements, proportional to the logarithm of the map's size. For medium-sized and heavy-duty applications, this will be noticeably faster.

To achieve this efficiency, `Map k v`'s `lookup` function does not just use a more sophisticated data structure; it also requires more from the key type:

```
Data.Map
lookup :: Ord k => k -> Map k v -> Maybe v
```

Indeed, the internal structure of the maps expects that the keys are totally ordered. This way, the `lookup` function can quickly skip over irrelevant parts of the map that contain only keys that are too large or too small.

Let us write a `frequency` function that uses a map to represent a so-called *frequency table*, which associates each element of a list with how often it appears in that list. For example, see the following:

```
*Main> frequency "banana"
fromList [('a',3),('b',1),('n',2)]
```

This shows that the word `banana` contains 3 letters a, 1 letter b, and 2 letters n. Observe that the `Show` instance of maps cleverly displays a map as a call to the function:

```
Data.Map
fromList :: Ord k => [(k, v)] -> Map k v
```

This turns an association list into a map.

We can write `frequency` as follows:

```
frequency :: Ord a => [a] -> Map a Int
frequency []     = empty
frequency (x:xs) = insertWith (+) x 1 (frequency xs)
```

The first equation states that an empty list has an `empty` map as its frequency table. The second equation inserts a new element in the recursively built frequency table using the following higher-order function:

```
Data.Map
insertWith
   :: Ord k => (v -> v -> v) -> k -> v -> Map k v -> Map k v
```

The function inserts the element x as a key with an associated value of 1 into the recursively constructed map. If that map does not yet contain that key, it adds the key with that value:

```
*Main> insertWith (+) 'a' 1 empty
fromList [('a',1)]
```

However, if the key is already present with some "old" value, it combines the old and the new value using the given `(+)` operator:

```
*Main> insertWith (+) 'a' 1 (fromList [('a',5)])
fromList [('a',6)]
```

In contrast, the `insert` function of maps overwrites the old value with the new value:

```
*Main> insert 'a' 1 (fromList [('a',5)])
fromList [('a',1)]
```

We will not go much further into the API of `Data.Map` here, but I recommend browsing its documentation as it provides a rich interface of functions for creating, inspecting, and modifying maps.

Type classes are not just useful within existing libraries; they can also be used to help structure application code and make it more reusable.

## Custom type class example

Having studied a range of predefined type classes, we will finish this chapter with a worked example that declares a custom type class. This example builds on the `frequency` function defined previously. The goal is, for a call such as `frequency "banana"`, to not get the standard but boring `Show` behavior. Instead, we want to get a more pleasant, human-readable format in tabular form, as follows:

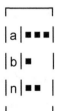

To make our solution work for different types of keys, we will introduce a custom type class.

## Text boxes

Our solution is based on a custom representation of text as rectangular boxes:

```
data Box = MkBox { content :: [String]
                 , width    :: Int
                 , height   :: Int }
```

The `content` of a box is a list of strings, the lines of text in the box. Its `height` separately captures how many lines there are; it should be equal to the length of the content. Each line should be equally long and be equal to the `width` should be equal to the width of the box.

Here is an example box:

```
exampleBox :: Box
exampleBox = MkBox ["abcd","efgh","ijkl"] 4 3
```

It contains the first twelve letters of the alphabet spread over 3 lines of 4 characters each.

The empty box is a box with no content:

```
emptyBox :: Box
emptyBox = MkBox [] 0 0
```

With the following `Show` instance, we display a box's content:

```
instance Show Box where
   show = unlines . content
```

Here, the Prelude function `unlines :: [String] -> String` turns a list of lines into a single string with newline characters separating the lines. Thanks to this instance, we get the following output in GHCi:

```
*Main> exampleBox
abcd
efgh
ijkl
```

Now that we have the basic definition of boxes in place, let us add additional convenience functions.

## Box combinators

We define a number of *combinators*; these are functions that transform existing boxes into new ones.

Our first combinator adds a frame around a given box:

```
*Main> frame exampleBox
┌────┐
│abcd│
│efgh│
│ijkl│
└────┘
```

It is defined as follows:

```
frame :: Box -> Box
frame (MkBox c w h)
  = MkBox ([tline] ++ map vline c ++ [bline]) (w+2) (h+2)
    where
      tline = "┌" ++ replicate w '─' ++ "┐"
      bline = "└" ++ replicate w '─' ++ "┘"
      vline l = "│" ++ l ++ "│"
```

The new box is two characters wider and higher to account for the added frame on all sides. Its content consists of the original lines, transformed to have a bar on the left and the right, as well as an additional top and bottom line.

The next combinator puts two boxes on top of each other:

```
*Main> vcomp exampleBox exampleBox
abcd
efgh
ijkl
abcd
efgh
ijkl
```

Here is the definition of this *vertical composition* combinator:

```
vcomp :: Box -> Box -> Box
vcomp (MkBox c1 w1 h1) (MkBox c2 w2 h2)
  = MkBox (c1' ++ c2') w h
  where
    w = max w1 w2
    h = h1 + h2
    pad n l = l ++ replicate n ' '
    c1' = map (pad (w - w1)) c1
    c2' = map (pad (w - w2)) c2
```

The new box combines the lines of the two original boxes. To make up for a possible difference in width between the two boxes, it pads the shorter lines with spaces. This is done using the Prelude function `replicate :: Int -> a -> [a]`, which creates a list with the given number of copies of an element.

We can extend this to a combinator that takes a list of boxes and vertically composes them:

```
vcompList :: [Box] -> Box
vcompList bs = foldr vcomp emptyBox bs
```

This returns the empty box when the list is empty.

Our last combinator is the horizontal counterpart to `vcomp`. It adds an embellishment, a separator string, which is placed on the lines between the two boxes:

```
*Main> hcomp "<->" exampleBox exampleBox
abcd<->abcd
efgh<->efgh
ijkl<->ijkl
```

The definition is similar to that of `vcomp`:

```
hcomp :: String -> Box -> Box -> Box
hcomp sep (MkBox c1 w1 h1) (MkBox c2 w2 h2)
  = MkBox (zipWith (\l1 l2 -> l1 ++ sep ++ l2) c1' c2') w h
  where
    w = w1 + length sep + w2
    h = max h1 h2
    pad n m l = l ++ replicate n (replicate m ' ')
    c1' = pad (h - h1) w1 c1
    c2' = pad (h - h2) w2 c2
```

The lines here are combined with the Prelude function, `zipWith :: (a -> b -> c) -> [a] -> [b] -> [c]`. It combines elements (which are lines here) pairwise using the given function.

## Boxable things

Finally, to meet our goal of displaying pretty frequency tables, we want to get an appropriate box for a given `Map k Int` structure. Following a compositional approach, that means we should also get boxes for the keys and the values in the map. However, because of the (constraint) polymorphism, we don't know what the type of the keys is going to be. We could fix the type of keys to some known type, such as `Char`, but that is not desirable.

Instead, we create a new type class, `Boxable`, for types whose values can be turned into a box:

```
class Boxable a where
  toBox :: a -> Box
```

A trivial instance is for characters where the box contains only one character:

```
instance Boxable Char where
  toBox c = MkBox [[c]] 1 1
```

A fancier instance for `Int` creates a line of little *box* characters:

```
instance Boxable Int where
  toBox n = MkBox [s] n 1
    where s = replicate n '■'
```

Finally, the instance for maps produces the tabular format:

```
instance (Boxable k, Boxable v) => Boxable (Map k v) where
  toBox m = frame (hcomp "|" col1 col2)
    where (ks, vs) = unzip (toList m)
          col1 = vcompList (map toBox ks)
          col2 = vcompList (map toBox vs)
```

This uses `toList :: Map k v -> [(k,v)]` from `Data.Map` to turn the map into an association list, and then `unzip :: [(k,v)] -> ([k],[v])` from the Prelude to separate it into one list of keys and one of values. The keys and values are turned into boxes and then combined appropriately into a big box. We have made one simplifying assumption in this code; we expect that each key and its corresponding value take the same number of lines. If you feel up to it, you can generalize this code by adding padding when needed.

Now, let us box the frequency result:

```
frequencyBox :: (Ord a, Boxable a) => [a] -> Box
frequencyBox = toBox . frequency
```

This accomplishes our goal:

```
*Main> frequencyBox "banana"
 ┌───┐
 │a│■■■│
 │b│■  │
 │n│■■ │
 └───┘
```

Thanks to the `Boxable` type class, this tabular formatting can easily be extended to other types.

For instance, we can obtain the following output:

```
*Main> frequencyBox [Hearts,Diamonds,Hearts,Hearts,Clubs,Clubs,Clubs]
 ┌─────────┐
 |♥|■ ■ ■|
 |♦|■    |
 |♣|■ ■ ■|
 └─────────┘
```

This only requires an appropriate `Boxable` instance for the `Suit` type.

## Summary

In this chapter, we saw how type classes provide a powerful mechanism for ad hoc overloading. We learned how to instantiate existing type classes with new types, and what key type classes in the standard library are. In addition, we studied several uses of type classes, both in the standard library and in a small case study.

*Chapter 7, Lazy Evaluation*, moves on to another remarkable feature of Haskell, its lazy evaluation strategy. A language's evaluation strategy determines the order in which different parts of a program are executed. We will learn how Haskell's approach works, how it deviates from that of most other languages, and what its benefits and gotchas are.

## Questions

1. *What are ad hoc overloaded functions?*
2. *How do you implement an overloaded method for a new type?*
3. *What are some key type classes in the standard libraries?*
4. *What are some key functions in the libraries that impose type class constraints?*
5. *Why would you introduce a new type class?*

## Further reading

- The Prelude library documentation: `https://hackage.haskell.org/package/base-4.18.0.0/docs/Prelude.html`
- The `Data.Map` library documentation: `https://hackage.haskell.org/package/containers-0.4.0.0/docs/Data-Map.html`

# Answers

1.  An ad hoc overloaded function (or operator) is similar to a polymorphic function in that it works for different types. Yet, it differs in two ways from a polymorphic function: 1) it does not work for all types, and 2) it has a different implementation per type. Haskell groups ad hoc overloaded functions into type classes, such as Eq with its `(==)` and `(/=)` methods. To indicate that a polymorphic function makes use of ad hoc overloaded operations, its type signature lists type class constraints on the type variables. For example, `sort :: Ord a => [a] -> [a]` lists the `Ord a` constraint to indicate that it works for all element types that provide total ordering.

2.  You write a type class instance that provides implementations for the methods of the type class. Not all methods need to be implemented, only those that provide a minimal complete definition. For example, only `(==)` or `(/=)` needs to be implemented for Eq. An instance is expected to satisfy the laws of the type class, if any are provided. These laws are the expected properties of the methods, such as reflexivity, symmetry, transitivity, extensionality, and negation for Eq.

3.  Important type classes in the Prelude are as follows:

    *   Eq for equality

    *   Ord for total ordering

    *   Show for generating a string representation

    *   Read for parsing values from their string representation

    *   Bounded for types that have a minimum and maximum value

    *   Enum for types whose values can be enumerated

    *   Num for basic arithmetic operations

4.  Introducing a new type class is useful for making code that is tied to a particular type work for other types as well. The type class methods abstract over the type-specific functionality and allow different types to each provide a custom implementation. For this reason, type classes are often employed by libraries to enable algorithms that involve type-specific components.

5.  Prelude features several functions for checking elements of lists:

    *   `elem    :: Eq a => a -> [a] -> Bool`
    *   `notElem :: Eq a => a -> [a] -> Bool`
    *   `lookup  :: Eq k => k -> [(k,v)] -> Maybe v`

    The `Data.Map` library is devoted to an efficient map data structure of type `Map k v` that associates keys with values. Its efficiency stems from the requirement that the keys have total ordering – for example, `Ord k`.

# 7
# Lazy Evaluation

So far, we have not paid much attention to how Haskell programs are evaluated. Perhaps you have not seen anything out of the ordinary, but then we have really only scratched the surface. When we dig a little deeper, it turns out that Haskell's evaluation strategy is quite different from that of other languages.

While other languages eagerly evaluate the program, Haskell has a much *lazier* attitude. Why should it do any work when it's not clear that work is actually necessary? That's why Haskell puts off evaluating any part of the program until it becomes clear that no result can be produced without doing that work.

This chapter gives a good idea of how evaluation works and why there is room for different strategies. It briefly covers the most popular evaluation strategy among programming languages, Call by Value, and its opposite, Call by Name. We will learn that neither is ideal and that Haskell's lazy evaluation strategy combines the best of both.

This strategy has a marked impact on the programming language, giving rise to new programming techniques, pitfalls, and supporting language features. Notable are the streaming behavior of lists and the generation of infinite data structures.

In short, this chapter covers the following main topics:

- What is an evaluation strategy and how can strategies differ?
- What is Haskell's lazy evaluation strategy and how does it work?
- What programming approaches exploit lazy evaluation?
- What are the main pitfalls of lazy evaluation and how do we deal with them?

As a gentle heads-up, I want to point out that from this chapter onwards, things will be getting a bit more challenging. We are starting to tackle the more advanced Haskell topics that do not have familiar counterparts in other programming languages you may already know. It is therefore perfectly normal to dwell a bit longer on this and the coming chapters, perhaps revisiting parts multiple times.

# Evaluation strategies

Before we delve into Haskell's evaluation strategy, let us first consider what an evaluation strategy is. This is an aspect of a programming language that is usually not questioned or mentioned because most languages adopt the same strategy and act alike. This section shows that there is room for variation and that there are good reasons for deviating from the mainstream strategy.

## Beta reduction

The mechanism at the core of program evaluation in function programming is called **beta reduction**. It defines how a function call should be evaluated. Let us take a small example of a function call (also called a **function application**):

```
(\ x -> sin x) 1.0
```

Here the (anonymous) `(\ x -> sin x)` function maps its formal parameter x to the function body `sin x`. This function is applied to the actual parameter `1.0`.

Conceptually, the function call is evaluated, or *reduced*, by replacing it with a *simpler* expression. That simpler expression is the function body in which the formal parameter is replaced by the actual parameter. In our example, the x in `sin x` is replaced with `1.0` that yields the following:

```
sin 1.0
```

We will use a special arrow ⤜ to denote such a reduction step:

```
(\ x -> sin x) 1.0  ⤜   sin 1.0
```

## Evaluation

In general, reducing one function call may reveal another. Program evaluation strings together beta reductions as long as there is a function call to reduce. Take this, for instance:

```
((\ f -> f) (\ x -> sin x)) 1.0
```

There are two functions called here:

- The function `(\ f -> f)` is called on `(\ x -> sin x)`
- The function `((\ f -> f) (\ x -> sin x))` is called on `1.0`

However, only the first call can be reduced. The reason for that is that its function `(\ f -> f)` is directly given, whereas the function in the second call is a complex expression that first has to be reduced to reveal what its definition is. Hence, the only call that can at first be reduced is the first one. We have the following:

```
(\ f -> f) (\ x -> sin x)  ⤜  (\ x -> sin x)
```

Reduction is compositional; if we can reduce a part of a larger expression, the whole expression reduces accordingly. Hence, we have this:

```
((\ f -> f) (\ x -> sin x)) 1.0 ↦ (\ x -> sin x) 1.0
```

Here, we have underlined the function call that we have reduced. This is a useful convention when there is more than one function call in the expression.

If we combine this with the next reduction step, we get this:

```
  ((\ f -> f) (\ x -> sin x)) 1.0
↦ (\ x -> sin x) 1.0
↦ sin 1.0
↦ 0.8414709848078965
```

The third step is special because `sin` is a built-in function not defined in Haskell itself. Hence, we (pretend to) immediately step to its result. The last expression does not contain any further function calls and is thus the overall result of the program.

## Evaluation strategies

It may be the case that an expression contains multiple function calls that can be reduced. Take this, for instance:

```
(\x -> x) ((\y -> sin y) 1.0)
```

This contains calls to two functions, `(\x -> x)` and `(\y -> sin y)`, that can both be reduced. Hence, there is room to choose which call to reduce first. If we choose the first call, we get this:

```
  (\x -> x) ((\y -> sin y) 1.0)
↦ (\y -> sin y) 1.0
↦ sin 1.0
↦ 0.8414709848078965
```

Alternatively, we reduce the second call first:

```
  (\x -> x) ((\y -> sin y) 1.0)
↦ (\x -> x) (sin 1.0)
```

At this point, we can again choose which call to reduce first:

```
  (\x -> x) (sin 1.0)              (\x -> x) (sin 1.0)
↦ sin 1.0                        ↦ (\x -> x) 0.8414709848078965
↦ 0.8414709848078965             ↦ 0.8414709848078965
```

As we can see, there are already three ways to evaluate this small example expression. For larger programs, the number of possibilities can be huge. Of course, in practice, a compiler or interpreter wants to use a systematic approach to choose among the possibilities. Such a systematic approach is called an **evaluation strategy**. Does it matter what evaluation strategy is used? Yes and no:

- No, it does not matter, because all choices eventually yield the same result. We can see this clearly in the example; all three evaluation approaches yield the result 0.8414709848078965.

- Yes, it does, because the strategy affects the efficiency of evaluation. Some approaches require more reduction steps than others for particular programs. In an extreme case, some approaches may fail to terminate with a result, while others don't.

Let us investigate what the impact of the evaluation strategy is by comparing two extreme choices before appreciating the middle ground that Haskell chooses.

## Call by Value

The **Call by Value** evaluation strategy is the one most commonly found in programming languages. Hence, you are most likely already familiar with this strategy and may have expected that Haskell would behave accordingly (but it does not).

The idea of Call by Value is that a function call should only be reduced when its parameter is already fully reduced—a fully reduced expression is called a **value**. A practical consequence of this choice is that the innermost function call is reduced first.

This is the call-by-value reduction of our example expression:

```
    (\x -> x) ((\y -> sin y) 1.0)
 ↦  (\x -> x) (sin 1.0)
 ↦  (\x -> x) 0.8414709848078965
 ↦  0.8414709848078965
```

What is good about Call by Value is that it is a steady and predictable strategy, which is easy to replicate in one's mind. It can also be implemented efficiently.

A downside of Call by Value is that it may do unnecessary work. The following variation on the earlier example illustrates this:

```
    (\x -> 5) ((\y -> sin y) 1.0)
 ↦  (\x -> 5) (sin 1.0)
 ↦  (\x -> 5) 0.8414709848078965
 ↦  5
```

Here, we reduce the inner function call and compute the sine that follows from it. Yet, the outer function is not interested in the result; it discards the sine's value and simply returns 5. Hence, we have performed two unnecessary reduction steps.

We can easily make the redundant work arbitrarily large. In the extreme case, the redundant work runs forever and causes overall non-termination. Consider this looping example:

```
    (\x -> 5) (loop 1.0)
 ↦  (\x -> 5) (loop 1.0)
 ↦  (\x -> 5) (loop 1.0)
 ↦  ...
where
loop :: a -> a
loop x = loop x
```

Another issue may be that the redundant work causes a runtime error:

```
    (\x -> 5) (div 1 0)
 ↦  *** Exception: divide by zero
```

A smarter evaluation strategy can avoid doing redundant work and thus be more efficient for some programs.

## Call by Name

The opposite extreme of Call by Value is **Call by Name**. Call by Name reduces the outermost function call first. This avoids the redundant work that Call by Value takes on:

```
    (\x -> 5) ((\y -> sin y) 1.0)
 ↦  5
```

As the outer function is not using its parameter, Call by Name yields the result in a single reduction step. Likewise, in the cases where the parameter is looping or raising a runtime error, Call by Name simply sidesteps those issues. Hence, it can be arbitrarily more efficient than Call by Value. Unfortunately, the opposite is also true. A big flaw of Call by Name is that it may duplicate work. Consider the following:

```
    (\x -> x + x) (sin 1.0)
 ↦  sin 1.0 + sin 1.0
 ↦  0.8414709848078965 + sin 1.0
 ↦  0.8414709848078965 + 0.8414709848078965
 ↦  1.682941969615793
```

Because the outer function mentions its formal parameter x twice in the body, Call by Name creates two copies of the actual parameter sin 1.0. These two copies both need to be reduced to produce the overall result. That is of course a pointless duplication of work. Moreover, it can get arbitrarily worse if the function references its formal parameter an arbitrary number of times.

Further downsides of Call by Name are that its reduction steps are more expensive to implement and that it is harder for programmers to reason about its order of evaluation. Overall, this makes Call by Name simply not useful enough to be used in practice. Nevertheless, Call by Name is a useful reference for Haskell's evaluation strategy, which adopts the main advantage of Call by Name but not its main weakness. We will see next how this is achieved.

# Call by Need

Haskell's evaluation strategy is called **Call by Need** or **lazy evaluation**. It is quite similar to Call by Name in that it only evaluates work that is needed for the result of the computation. At the same time, it avoids the main problem of Call by Name: it does not duplicate any work.

## Sharing

The way in which lazy evaluation avoids duplication is known as **sharing**, or sometimes also as **memoization**. Instead of duplicating work, the work is shared, and when the work is performed once, all who share it can use the work's results without redoing them.

Conceptually, we model sharing the work by using `let` binding:

```
   (\x -> x + x) (sin 1.0)
↦ let w = sin 1.0
   in w + w
```

To evaluate the sum in the body of the `let` binding, we first have to evaluate its left operand. As this operand is a `let` bound variable w, we consult the binding. The binding shows that the variable is bound to a reducible expression. Hence, we reduce that expression to a value, replace the binding with that value, and use that value in the sum:

```
↦ let w = 0.8414709848078965
   in 0.8414709848078965 + w
```

Because we have overwritten the binding, the evaluation of the second operand goes more quickly. It can look up the value of w without recomputing `sin 1.0`:

```
↦ let w = 0.8414709848078965
   in 0.8414709848078965 + 0.8414709848078965
↦ let w = 0.8414709848078965
   in 1.682941969615793
```

In contrast to the Call by Value or Call by Name derivations, there is a `let` binding present in the final result. Yet, this is immaterial, as there is no more reference to w that could use it and thus it can be dropped. In practice, this dropping is implemented by the garbage collector, which reclaims the memory allocated for w.

Thanks to the sharing, Call by Need is more economical than either Call by Name or Call by Value; it will do any work at most once.

## Thunks

The Call by Need evaluation mechanism does incur some overhead. As a consequence, the reduction steps are more costly than those in Call by Value. Indeed, to represent shared values, GHC makes use of a data structure that is called a **thunk**.

Consider the following small function:

```
f :: Int -> Int
f x = x + 1
```

The function's signature claims that the function takes and returns a value of type Int. At runtime, however, *pointers to thunks of integers* are passed around rather than plain integers. A thunk data structure is in one of two states: *not yet evaluated* or *already evaluated*. It starts out in the former state. For example, when we call f (2 * 3), a thunk is allocated for the actual parameter 2 * 3. This thunk is initially in the *not yet evaluated* state, and its payload is a pointer to the code that performs the 2 * 3 computation. At some point, the content of the thunk can be demanded, e.g., to be able to perform the x + 1 computation. Because the thunk is *not yet evaluated*, we say that it is forced by this demand: its 2 * 3 code is executed to produce the value 6. Before returning this value, the thunk's state is modified to *already evaluated* and its payload is replaced by the value 6. Further demands of the thunk will not have to force it again; because the thunk *is already evaluated*, the value in the payload can be used directly.

Forcing a thunk can set off a chain reaction of forcing other thunks. For instance, if we call f on the thunk of 2 * 3, its result will be a new thunk. Forcing that resulting thunk will result in forcing the 2 * 3 thunk to get its value 6 and produce the result 7.

In fact, the whole execution of a Haskell program is driven by forcing the result of the main expression. For example, say you write this:

```
*Main> 1 + 2
```

GHCi calls show (1 + 2) and demands its result. This demand kicks off the computation.

## Bottom

A consequence of lazy evaluation is that the performance characteristics are quite different than in Call by Value languages. A function that seems to involve a lot of computation may return immediately after having merely thunked that computation. Conversely, scrutinizing a simple value of type Int may unexpectedly kick off a lengthy computation.

In the worst case, a value of type `Int` may simply not be there because, when forced, its thunk starts an infinite computation or a computation that ends in a runtime error. For that reason, we say that conceptually, every type in Haskell is equipped with a special value, called a bottom, and is often written using the ⊥ symbol. For example, while a Call by Value language would have only two values of type Bool, namely `True` and `False`, in Haskell, we also have to take into account a third value: ⊥. Of course, ⊥ is not like ordinary values; as soon as we force it, the program gets stuck or aborted. Still, it is a useful conceptual device.

Besides accidental ways to produce the bottom value, with inadvertent non-termination or runtime errors, the standard library provides two explicit ways:

1. The first bottom is meant for testing incomplete programs, often during rapid prototyping:

   ```
   undefined :: a
   ```

   This special value promises to be of any type. The only way this is possible is that it is a bottom:

   ```
   *Main> undefined
   *** Exception: Prelude.undefined
   ```

   When quickly sketching a program, it is used as a placeholder for function definitions that have not yet been worked out:

   ```
   process :: String -> Float
   process = step3 . step2 . step1

   step1 :: String -> Int
   step1 = undefined

   step2 :: Int -> Int
   step2 = undefined

   step3 :: Int -> Float
   step3 = undefined
   ```

   While such a program sketch cannot be run, at least it can be type-checked. Also, its parts can be gradually filled in and tested before the whole program is ready. The type checking comes in handy to point out flaws in the design early on and helps uncover new problems when the design is changed midway through.

2. The second bottom is a generic mechanism to raise a runtime error:

   ```
   error :: String -> a
   ```

3. The function takes a string that is used as the error message of the runtime error:

   ```
   *Main> error "This is the error message."
   *** Exception: This is the error message.
   ```

This error function is, for instance, used in the head function to signal that the empty list has no head:

```
Prelude
head :: [a] -> a
head []     = error "Prelude.head: empty list"
head (x:_) = x
```

The key with bottoms is that of course nothing goes wrong if we don't force them.

## Structured data

When using structured data, there can be bottoms at different levels. Consider the type Maybe Bool. It has five different values, of which two involve a bottom:

```
⊥, Nothing, Just ⊥, Just True, Just False
```

The basic idea is that every value could either be a bottom or could have an actual constructor. Hence, for Maybe Bool, we can have either ⊥, Nothing, or Just. Furthermore, Just has a field of type Bool, which can be either ⊥, True, or False.

### Newtypes

There is one special case that deviates from this principle, namely the special newtype alternative to data for defining a datatype. Compare the following two:

```
data D = MkD Bool
newtype N = MkN Bool
```

Both define a new datatype with one constructor that has a Bool field. The difference is that D has one more value that N has not.

```
values of D: ⊥, MkD ⊥, MkD True, MkD False
values of N: ⊥,         MkN True, MkN False
```

With the newtype keyword, we can only define datatypes that have one constructor, and that one constructor must have exactly one field. At runtime, the new datatype simply uses the representation of its field. Hence, MkN True is just represented by True at runtime. In other words, the MkN constructor is not represented at runtime. For that reason, we cannot distinguish between ⊥ and MkN ⊥.

The motivation for newtype is performance: its constructor does not take up any memory, nor does it require the double indirection of a nested thunk. Also, pattern matching against its constructor is a **no-op** at runtime. The idea is that, as far as Haskell's type checker is concerned, we are dealing with a new type, but as far as the runtime system is concerned, we are dealing with the existing type of the field.

Newtypes are often used to work around a key limitation of type classes: every type can have at most one instance. If there were, say, two or more Ord  Integer instances, the type system would not know which one to use for 1  <  2. A consequence is that constraint polymorphic functions, such as sort  ::  Ord  a  =>  [a]  ->  [a], always work the same way for a given type, following their one instance. For integers, it always sorts in ascending order. We cannot provide a second Ord Integer instance to make it sort in descending order. Yet, there is a workaround. We can package the integers in a newtype that has the desired Ord instance. To obtain a descending ordering, we can use the Down type:

```
Data.Ord
newtype Down a = Down { getDown :: a }
```

The Down  a newtype wraps around an underlying type a, and its Ord instance depends on that of a:

```
Data.Ord
instance Ord a => Ord (Down a) where
  compare (Down x) (Down y) = compare y x
```

We see that Down  a uses the opposite ordering of that of its underlying type a. This can be used to sort integers in descending order:

```
*Main> sort [3,5,2,4,1]
[1,2,3,4,5]
*Main> map getDown (sort (map Down [3,5,2,4,1]))
[5,4,3,2,1]
```

The Down datatype is defined as a newtype in order to not introduce any runtime overhead. Indeed, a Down  Integer adds no memory overhead to the underlying integer. Also, Down and getDown are *no-ops*; they simply return their input at a different type. Even so, the preceding code with Down is a bit more expensive than without it because it uses map twice, and map is not free.

If we want zero overhead in the preceding example, we can use the coerce  ::  Coercible  a b  ->  a  ->  b method. The Coercible type class is managed automatically by the compiler and provides zero cost conversion between newtypes and their underlying type, even inside data structures such as lists:

```
*Main> coerce (sort (coerce [3,5,2,4,1] :: [Down Integer]))
             :: [Integer]
[5,4,3,2,1]
```

The type annotations here are necessary to help the type checker in figuring out between what two types it should coerce. After type checking these coercions are removed by the compiler; they truly have zero cost at runtime.

## Lazy and stricter functions

Inspecting a value happens by means of pattern matching and only triggers the bottoms that are matched against constructors. Consider the following function:

```
Data.Maybe
isJust :: Maybe a -> Bool
isJust Nothing  = False
isJust (Just _) = True
```

This function-only pattern matches against the outer constructor. Hence, we get this:

```
*Main> isJust undefined
*** Exception: Prelude.undefined
*Main> isJust (Just undefined)
True
*Main> isJust (Just 42)
True
```

The way a function is defined can affect how lazy it is. Compare the boolean or operator defined with its full truth table:

```
Prelude
(||) :: Bool -> Bool -> Bool
True  || False  =  True
True  || True   =  True
False || True   =  True
False || False  =  False
```

Contrast this with a definition that coalesces overlapping cases by means of don't-care patterns:

```
Prelude
(||) :: Bool -> Bool -> Bool
True  || _      =  True
_     || True   =  True
_     || _      =  False
```

The first definition always matches against both parameters and thereby forces both. In contrast, in the second definition, the first equation forces the first parameter only. If that is true, the second parameter is not forced. Only if the first parameter is false does it move on to the second equation and force the second parameter. Hence, in the second definition, we get away with `True || undefined`, whereas in the first definition, we do not. We say that the second definition is *lazier* than the first, or, conversely, that the first definition is *stricter* than the second.

Now that we have a good idea of how lazy evaluation works, let us investigate how it can be exploited.

# Programming with lazy evaluation

The key benefit of lazy evaluation is that it allows for a much more compositional style of programming. Instead of writing large blocks of code from scratch, we can frequently assemble functionality out of highly reusable functions. Many key use cases of that revolve around lists.

## Streaming

Let us consider what happens in the following scenario:

```
*Main> [1..5]
```

Behind the scenes, GHCi calls show on [1..5] to display the resulting list. As a reminder, we show the definitions of the key functions involved. First, the enumeration [1..5] is generated by the enumFromTo method of the Enum class:

```
Prelude
enumFromTo :: Integer -> Integer -> Integer
enumFromTo l h
  | l <= h = l : enumFromTo (l+1) h
  | otherwise = []
```

Secondly, show l is defined as showList l "":

```
Prelude
showList :: [Integer] -> String -> String
showList []     s = "[]" ++ s
showList (x:xs) s = '[' : showsPrec 0 x (showl xs)
  where
    showl []     = ']' : s
    showl (y:ys) = ',' : showsPrec 0 y (showl ys)
```

What does not happen is this:

1.  The list [1,2,3,4,5] is created.

2.  Then the string [1,2,3,4,5] is created from the list.

3.  Finally, the string is shown.

Instead of this strict sequential order, the steps are interleaved and driven by the demand in the last step. We start essentially from this:

```
showList (enumFromTo 1 5) ""
```

To display the output, we reduce the `showList` call. This requires first reducing `enumFromTo 1 5` in order to know which of the two equations of is `showList` matched:

```
↦ showList (1 : enumFromTo (1+1) 5) ""
```

Now we can tell that the second equation of `showList` should be used:

```
↦ '[' : showsPrec 0 1 (showl (enumFromTo (1+1) 5))
```

Now the first character in the output string is available and can be displayed:

```
[
```

To show the next character, the remainder of the string is reduced until one becomes available:

```
↦ '1' : (showl (enumFromTo (1+1) 5))
```

This second character can now be shown:

```
[1
```

We continue the reduction to get more characters. Again, we need to reduce `enumFromTo` to know which equation to pick for `showl`, and we need to reduce `1+1` to know which equation to pick for `enumFromTo`:

```
↦ showl (enumFromTo 2 5)
↦ showl (2 : enumFromTo (2+1) 5)
↦ ',' : showsPrec 0 2 (showl (enumFromTo (2+1) 5))
```

Now the third character can be shown:

```
[1,
```

This continues in the same fashion until the whole output is shown. As we can see, the reduction jumps around in the expression, driven by the need to display characters. At no time do we actually require the whole list, or even the whole string, to be available in memory. Instead, the list (and the string) can be generated element by element. Each element can be consumed before the next is produced and its memory can again be reclaimed by the garbage collector. This approach is known as **streaming** and another word for a lazy evaluated list is a **stream**. Streams and streaming are very useful for processing large lists that would not otherwise require large amounts of memory (or that would simply not fit).

While other languages have special libraries and data structures to allow for streaming, in Haskell we do not require such. The humble list already does the job.

## Infinite lists

As we have already seen, lazy evaluation only evaluates what is needed for the result. Consider this, for instance:

```
*Main> take 5 [1..5]
[1,2,3,4,5]
*Main> take 5 [1..9999999999]
[1,2,3,4,5]
```

These two expressions take the same amount of time to evaluate. Indeed, both compute the list only up to the fifth element and do not evaluate anything beyond that. Hence, it is immaterial how much more there is. For this reason, Haskell can provide infinite lists. Here's an example:

```
*Main> take 5 [1..]
[1,2,3,4,5]
```

Here, [1..] is the infinite list of integers that starts at 1. It always has enough elements to give, as many as we want, without having to determine that up front.

The point of an infinite list is not to use it on its own; obviously that's not practical.

```
*Main> [1..]
[1,2,3,4,5,6,7,8,9,10,11,12,13,14,15,16,17,18,19,20,21,22,23,24,25,26,
27,28,29,30,31,32,33,34,35,36,37,38,39,40,41,42,43,44,45,46,47,48,49,
50,51,52,53,54,55,56,57,58,59,60,61,62,63,64,65,66,67,68,69,70,71,72,
73,74,75,76,77,78,79,80,81,82,83,84,85,86,87,88,89,90,91,92,93,94,95,
96,97,98,99,100,101,102,103,104,105,106,107,108,109,110,111,112,113,
114,115,116,117,Interrupted.
```

(I had to abort the evaluation with *Ctrl+C*.)

The idea is to use it in a context where it is curtailed to a finite length, such as by take as we have just seen. Another example is zipping with a finite list:

```
*Main> zip [1..] ["apple","banana","cherry","date"]
[(1,"apple"),(2,"banana"),(3,"cherry"),(4,"date")]
```

While the same result can be accomplished in other ways, we would have to sacrifice the conceptual elegance of this solution.

## Corecursive programs

In *Chapter 3*, *Recursion*, we emphasized the use of structural recursion as a good pattern for guaranteeing program termination. Such termination is of course not guaranteed anymore with infinite lists and other infinite data structures. For instance, sum [1..] clearly never produces a result, as we can't tell anything about the result before we have seen the last element.

Yet, lazy evaluation actively encourages writing so-called *co-recursive* functions, which are functions that construct infinite data structures. These do not use structural recursion at all. A first example is the function enumFrom from the enum type class, which is what the [1..] notation desugars to. The enum Integer instance has the following implementation:

```
Prelude
enumFrom :: Integer -> [Integer]
enumFrom n = n : enumFrom (n+1)
```

The parameter to this function steadily grows, and as there is no base case, this function never terminates. Still, it is a useful producer of an infinite list as in every step of the recursion it generates one element of the list. This means that it can be used in a streaming context.

A variation of this is *cyclic* programs. A simple example is an infinite list where all elements are 1:

```
ones :: [Integer]
ones = 1 : ones
```

This is again a co-recursive definition that produces one element in every step of the recursion. Unlike in the previous example, the recursive call does not grow; it cycles back on itself. Thanks to the thunk mechanism, ones also gets a cyclic memory layout. Namely, the thunk of ones refers to a list whose first element is 1 and whose tail refers back to the thunk.

The Prelude provides a generalization of ones that creates an infinite repetition of any given element:

```
Prelude
repeat :: a -> [a]
repeat x = let r = x : r in r
```

This is written carefully to obtain a cyclic memory layout just like that of ones. Compare this to a more native definition:

```
Prelude
repeat :: a -> [a]
repeat x = x : repeat x
```

Here, the compiler does reuse the thunk of x : repeat x for the recursive call, and as a consequence, each recursive step allocates more memory.

Indeed, while we have now seen several new programming techniques enabled by lazy evaluation, we should also be aware of possible pitfalls, especially related to memory allocation.

# Lazy memory leaks

One of the main issues with laziness is that it becomes much harder to reason about the order in which different parts of the program are executed. That in itself is not necessarily a problem, but a side effect can be. When a program does not need the result of a computation immediately but may need it later, it holds onto that computation in the form of a thunk. Over time, a build-up of such thunks can arise, and the program may start using excessive amounts of memory for them. In that case, we speak of a **memory leak**.

## The leaking accumulator

In *Chapter 3, Recursion*, we saw the accumulator-based approach to summing a list:

```
sumAcc :: [Integer] -> Integer
sumAcc l = go l 0 where
  go :: [Integer] -> Integer -> Integer
  go []     acc = acc
  go (x:xs) acc = go xs (acc + x)
```

This can also be written using the `foldl` recursion scheme from *Chapter 4, Higher-Order Functions*:

```
sumAcc' :: [Integer] -> Integer
sumAcc' l = foldl (+) 0 l
```

From the point of view of memory use, these two definitions are to be avoided. Here is a short reduction derivation that illustrates what the problem is:

```
    sumAcc [1,2,3,4]
 ↦ go [1,2,3,4] 0
 ↦ go [2,3,4] (0+1)
 ↦ go [3,4] ((0+1)+2)
 ↦ go [4] (((0+1)+2)+3)
 ↦ go [] ((((0+1)+2)+3)+4)
 ↦ ((((0+1)+2)+3)+4
 ↦ (((1+2)+3)+4
 ↦ (3+3)+4
 ↦ 6+4
 ↦ 10
```

As we can see, the accumulator parameter steadily grows as the recursion proceeds. In every recursive step, another thunk is allocated and layered on top of the previous thunk. These thunks represent a sum whose evaluation is deferred until the end. The amount of memory that is allocated for the thunks is proportional to the length of the input list, and thus arbitrarily much larger than the amount of memory needed to represent the result of the function: a single integer.

## Strictness annotations

The problem in the preceding program can be redressed by adding a so-called strictness annotation to the program. A strictness annotation tells Haskell to force a particular thunk ahead of time in order to avoid a build-up. For that, we use a special built-in function:

```
seq :: a -> b -> b
```

This function forces its first parameter before returning its second parameter. Hence, it imposes a sequential evaluation order. We can use it as follows in sumAcc:

```
sumAcc :: [Integer] -> Integer
sumAcc l = go l 0 where
  go :: [Integer] -> Integer -> Integer
  go []     acc = acc
  go (x:xs) acc = let acc' = acc + x
                  in  acc' `seq` go xs acc'
```

In the recursive case, we bind the updated accumulator to the name acc' and then force it with seq before returning the recursive call with acc'. This causes the recursive call to receive an already-evaluated thunk, and thunk build-up is avoided:

```
   sumAcc [1,2,3,4]
↦  go [1,2,3,4] 0
↦  let acc1 = 0+1
   in acc1 `seq` go [2,3,4] acc1
↦  let acc1 = 1
   in go [2,3,4] acc1
↦  let acc1 = 1
       acc2 = acc1 + 2
   in acc2 `seq` go [3,4] acc2
↦  let acc1 = 1
       acc2 = 3
   in go [3,4] acc2
↦  ...
```

The Prelude captures this approach in a variant of foldl that uses a strict accumulator:

```
Data.List
foldl' :: (b -> a -> b) -> b -> [a] -> b
foldl' f acc []     = acc
foldl' f acc (x:xs) = let acc' = f acc x
                      in acc' `seq` foldl' f acc xs
```

This allows us to write the efficient sum concisely, as follows:

```
sumAcc' :: [Integer] -> Integer
sumAcc' l = foldl' (+) 0 l
```

## Bang patterns

Bang patterns can provide a convenient variation on the explicit use of `seq`. Here is an example:

```
sumAcc :: [Integer] -> Integer
sumAcc l = go l 0 where
  go :: [Integer] -> Integer -> Integer
  go []        acc = acc
  go (x:xs) !acc = go xs (acc + x)
```

The exclamation mark (bang) in front of the `acc` parameter in the last equation indicates that this parameter should be forced before evaluation of the right-hand side. It desugars to the following code:

```
  go (x:xs) acc = acc `seq` go xs (acc + x)
```

While not exactly the same as our previous version, it also provides a build-up of thunks. The difference is that the accumulator is forced immediately in the call rather than right before the call.

## Strict fields

Fields of datatypes also take strictness annotations. Here's an example:

```
data Point = MkPoint !Int !Int
```

Like bang patterns, such annotations also desugar to invocations of `seq`. In particular, let's say we create a point such as this:

```
MkPoint x y
```

The compiler replaces this with:

```
x `seq` y `seq` MkPoint x y
```

This ensures that the values of the fields are forced before they are placed in the datatype.

## Strictness analysis and optimization

The GHC compiler contains a sophisticated **strictness analysis** that can often figure out when thunks are unnecessary, especially when aided by strictness annotations. In those cases, it optimizes the compiler output to never allocate thunks in the first place. In that case, it uses so-called *unboxed* representations of primitive types such as `Int#` (instead of `Int`) and primitive operations that work directly on unboxed operations such as `(+#) :: Int# -> Int# -> Int#`.

## Increased laziness

More strictness is not always the right answer. Especially in a streaming context, producing output more quickly is the better way. Various functions in the standard libraries have been written with this in mind. Consider, for instance, this straightforward definition of `tails`:

```
Data.List
tails :: [a] -> [[a]]
tails []     = [] : []
tails (x:xs) = (x:xs) : tails xs
```

This definition does not produce any output before forcing its parameter to pick the appropriate equation. In the library, we find a lazier definition that produces the first element before forcing its input:

```
Data.List
tails :: [a] -> [[a]]
tails l = l : case l of
                []      -> []
                (_:xs) -> tails xs
```

This definition is not only lazier; it also does not recreate (x:xs), which allocates new memory, but simply reuses l.

Laziness is also important when processing infinite structures. Suppose we want to split a list into two parts—the sublist of elements at odd positions and the sublist of elements at even positions—like so:

```
*Main> splitList [1..5]
([1,3,5],(2,4))
```

We can do this as follows using `foldr`:

```
splitList :: [a] -> ([a],[a])
splitList l = foldr c ([],[]) l
  where
    c x (ys,zs) = (x:zs, ys)
```

In the base case, the two sublists are empty. In the recursive case, we swap the roles of the recursive sublists (evens become odds and vice versa) and stick x in front of the odds.

This works well on short lists, but it takes gradually more time to return a result for longer lists and never produces anything for infinite lists. The problem is that the auxiliary function c matches, and thereby forces, the recursive result. This sets off a cascade that forces all recursive calls of `foldr` before producing the result.

We can prevent this problem by making c lazier:

```
splitList :: [a] -> ([a],[a])
splitList l = foldr c ([],[]) l
  where
    c x r = (x : fst r, snd r)
```

Instead of using pattern matching, and thus forcing, the second parameter, we use the projection fst and snd functions in the body. This way, we return the tuple and the first element of the odds list without forcing r.

Haskell produces syntactic sugar for the preceding code, which looks as follows:

```
splitList :: [a] -> ([a],[a])
splitList l = foldr c ([],[]) l
  where
    c x ~(ys,zs) = (x:zs, ys)
```

Here, ~(ys,zs) is called a lazy pattern or an irrefutable pattern. Patterns are implicitly irrefutable in so-called *pattern bindings*. A pattern binding is an equation whose whole left-hand side is one pattern. For example, the preceding code can be written as follows with a pattern binding:

```
splitList :: [a] -> ([a],[a])
splitList []     = ([],[])
splitList (x:xs) = (x:zs,ys)
  where (ys,zs) = splitList xs
```

The implicit irrefutability of pattern bindings is quite convenient, as it yields arguably the most natural definition of splitList.

## Summary

In this chapter, we have covered the basic evaluation mechanism of functional programs, beta reduction, and evaluation strategies that decide in which order reductions are performed. The common Call by Value strategy may perform unnecessary reductions. This is prevented by Call by Name but at the cost of sometimes duplicating work. Haskell's Call by Need (or lazy evaluation) mechanism combines the best of both: it only performs necessary reductions and never duplicates work. We can exploit this strategy for the purpose of streaming, often aided by infinite datatypes and corecursive functions. At the same time, we need to be careful about the memory allocations that arise from deferred reductions.

*The* next chapter explains how Haskell programs interface with their environment: the user, the file system, the operating system, and any other party outside of the program. This is particularly challenging due to lazy evaluation. Yet, Haskell has found a unique solution to make it work.

# Questions

1.  What is beta reduction?

2.  What is Call by Need/lazy evaluation?

3.  What is streaming?

4.  What are strictness annotations?

# Answers

1.  Beta reduction is the core mechanism of program evaluation in functional programs. It acts on a function application such as `(\ x -> sin x) 1.0` and simplifies it to the body of that function `sin x`, in which it replaces the formal parameter x with the actual parameter `1.0`.

2.  Call by Need is an evaluation strategy. An evaluation strategy decides which functional application to reduce in the current expression. Call by Need only reduces the top-level expression, provided it is a function application. Unlike the commonly used Call by Value strategy, this defers evaluating the function parameters and may eventually not evaluate them at all when this is not needed. At the same time, it employs a sharing mechanism known as thunks to avoid duplicating subexpressions and performing the same reduction repeatedly. In this sense, it is an improvement upon Call by Name.

3.  Streaming is an approach to data processing whereby a composite data structure (e.g., a list) is not first produced in one go and then consumed in one go. Instead, production and consumption are interleaved. Data is produced piecemeal (e.g., a list is produced one element at a time), and the pieces can be processed separately. Streaming arises naturally under the Call by Need strategy.

4.  Strictness annotations are annotations in a program that make Haskell deviate from the standard Call by Need strategy. They force certain subexpressions to be evaluated earlier. The most primitive strictness annotation is the built-in function `seq x y`, which forces x to be evaluated before y and then returns the result of y. Higher-level strictness annotations are as follows:

    -   Bang patterns, such as `!acc` in `go (x:xs) !acc = go xs (acc + x)`, force parameters to be evaluated before the function body

    -   Strict fields force the fields of data constructors to be evaluated when the constructor is, for example, the two fields of `data Point = MkPoint !Int !Int`

# 8

# Input/Output

This chapter explains Haskell's unique way of communicating with the *outside world*. The outside world is defined as any entities outside of the Haskell program, such as the user, the filesystem, the network, and the operating system. It's used to display text to a user and get their input, read and write files, access and provide web services, get the current time and date, and so on.

The reason Haskell has a unique approach is twofold:

- Firstly, lazy evaluation makes working with plain functions for communication purposes impossible from a practical point of view. The order of execution is too unpredictable to have a sensible interaction with a third party.

- Secondly, a strong principle of the Haskell language is that its functions resemble as closely as possible the mathematical definition of what a function is. For one, this means that functions should be predictable in a very precise sense – for the same input, a function should always give the same output. This is, of course, not the case with communication – when we ask the same question of a party, we may get a different answer each time.

To overcome these two problems and reconcile communication with both lazy evaluation and the mathematical notion of function, Haskell has found a unique type-driven approach. All computations that communicate are marked by a special type, called IO, which refers to **input/output**, or **I/O** for short. The standard library provides a number of primitive IO computations as well as combinators to compose them into larger programs. On top of that, the language provides special syntax to facilitate compositions and make them look somewhat like imperative programs.

This chapter will first explain why the existing approach of other languages is problematic, due to the lazy evaluation strategy and the language's purity principle.

Then, we will present the Haskell solution, using the IO type and `>>=`/`return` operators. Then, we will introduce the `do` notation as a more user-friendly notation for IO steps. Finally, we will cover common IO operations.

In this chapter, we will ask the following questions:

- Why does Haskell need a non-standard approach to I/O?
- How do we perform I/O in Haskell programs?
- How do we use the do notation to write I/O programs?
- What are the common I/O functions provided by the standard library?

## Technical requirements

Up to now, we have only used modules from Haskell's standard library. In this chapter, we will briefly touch upon two additional libraries that have to be installed separately, called random and time. Such libraries, which provide a number of modules, are called **packages**.

You can use the *cabal* build tool for Haskell to install packages where the ghc compiler can find them. Cabal draws its packages from *Hackage*, which is a large repository of publicly available Haskell packages. You can browse Hackage at https://hackage.haskell.org/.

To install the two relevant packages, you need to run the following two commands:

```
$ cabal install random
$ cabal install time
```

These will download and compile the two packages, and then make sure the ghc compiler can find them for use in the programs you write. For example, after the installation of the random package, we can simply access its System.Random module in our program by writing an import declaration at the top of our file:

```
import System.Random
```

Now, we are good to go and use the randomRIO function it exposes.

## Haskell versus I/O – a thought experiment

Most programming languages provide a similar approach to deal with I/O-related tasks. They provide functions, procedures, or methods that are essentially indistinguishable from other functions, procedures, or methods in the language. Not so in Haskell, where both lazy evaluation and Haskell's principled approach toward functions mean that I/O should not be treated in the same way.

Before diving into Haskell's approach toward I/O, this section explains why the conventional approach does not work. As a thought experiment, we will use two minimal I/O functions – getChar, which reads a single character from the standard input, and putChar, which writes a single character to the standard output. Following other languages, the types of these functions could be getChar :: () -> Char and putChar :: Char -> ().

Let us proceed with a hypothetical world where Haskell has the aforementioned two functions with those signatures. By writing imaginary code in this world and running it in our imagination, we will explore the two reasons why this hypothetical world makes no sense.

## Lazy evaluation versus I/O

Lazy evaluation makes the order of evaluation highly unpredictable and dependent on the need of the code context in which an expression appears.

Consider, for instance, the following expression:

```
-- imaginary code
t1 :: (Char, Char)
t1 = (getChar (), getChar ())
```

Given a standard input that contains the 'a' and 'b' characters, we would expect the following behavior:

```
*Imaginary> t1
('a','b')
```

Yet, when we use t1 as part of a larger expression, snd t1, which selects the second component of the tuple, we do not get 'b':

```
*Imaginary> snd t1
'a'
```

The reason is that lazy evaluation never evaluates the first component of the tuple. Hence, the second getChar () is the first and only one that is executed. As a consequence, it gets the first available character, 'a'. This shows that our compositional reasoning fails. Even though we know that t1 evaluates to ('a','b'), we cannot conclude that snd t1 evaluates to snd ('a','b'). We have to look at the expression as a whole and factor in lazy evaluation to predict what the outcome will be.

Besides dropping I/O computations, lazy evaluation may also change their order of execution. This is better illustrated with another example expression:

```
-- imaginary code
t2 :: ((),())
t2 = (putChar 'a', putChar 'b')
```

This expression produces a tuple of two unit values:

```
*Imaginary> t2
(a(),b())
```

Because of the laziness, GHCi's printing of the resulting tuple, ((),()), is interleaved with the output, ab, of the two putChar functions. To distinguish the latter from the former, we have underlined it.

Now, consider t2 being used in the following larger expression:

```
*Imaginary> (snd t2, fst t2)
(b(),a())
 —    —
```

This writes ba on the standard output. The reason is that lazy evaluation first needs the second component of t2 and then the first component.

We can see that the lazy evaluation makes the execution of I/O actions highly unpredictable. This is highly problematic because it makes it hard or impossible to predict how a program will behave. At the same time, the appropriate behavior of programs usually depends critically on I/O actions being performed in a particular order. Hence, the combination of lazy evaluation and I/O actions is unworkable, at least with the presented approach.

## Pure functions versus I/O

There is a second, more principled reason why I/O and Haskell do not work well together – namely, functions that perform I/O do not have the essential properties that Haskell wants to provide.

### Pure functions

A key property of mathematical functions, or *pure* functions as we like to call them, is that they are highly predictable. Given some input x, f  x should *always* yield the same result. It should not matter who is calling the function, what time of day it is, or any other aspect of the context in which the function is called. A pure function call should conversely also not have any impact on its context, other than returning its result. It should not turn on the lights, order a pizza, or do anything else that is observable.

This predictability and conceptual simplicity make pure functions relatively easy to reason about and reuse in new contexts. We do not have to scour their definitions for hidden dependencies or unexpected side effects on other parts of a system. They can be understood on their own terms and are relatively safe and easy to refactor and transplant to different settings.

There are also two ways in which a programmer or Haskell compiler can exploit this behavior in a program:

- We can avoid calling a pure function if we already know the result. For example, if our program contains the same function call twice, we can reuse the result of the first call in place of the second call. A trivial example would be to replace this:

```
(f x, f x)
```

by

```
let y = f x in (y,y)
```

Likewise, the compiler could decide to replace a function call by its result, which it could obtain by evaluating the function during the compilation process.

- We don't have to call a pure function if we are not interested in its result. We are not losing anything by dropping the function call, `f y`, because we are clearly not using its result, and as a pure function, `f` does nothing else than provide that result:

```
(\ x -> 5) (f y)
```

by

```
5
```

This, of course, also justifies lazy evaluation, which would not evaluate the function call.

## I/O functions are impure

I/O actions are quite the opposite of all this. Indeed, the `getChar` function's output is entirely determined by the context in which it is run – what characters are provided on the standard input. Different runs of the program could receive entirely different characters. Moreover, `getChar` also affects its context, as each call *consumes* a character from the standard input. Hence, successive calls in the same program will return different characters.

The program transformations that we are allowed to perform for pure functions are invalid for I/O functions. Consider, for instance, the following:

```
(getChar (), getChar ())
```

Compare that to this:

```
let y = getChar () in (y,y)
```

The former program would read the two characters from the standard input, while the latter reads only one. Hence, if the standard input consisted of `'a'` and `'b'`, then the first program would return `('a','b')` and the second `('a','a')`, which are clearly different results.

Also, consider the following:

```
(\ x -> getChar ()) (getChar ())
```

Compare that to this:

```
getChar ()
```

Assuming a call-by-value execution, the former program would read two characters and return the second, while the latter reads only one character. Hence, if the standard input consisted of `'a'` and `'b'`, then the first program would return `'b'` and the second `'a'`, which are, again, different results.

We can conclude that I/O functions do not have the nice properties of pure functions; they are *impure*. If our programming language combines both pure and impure functions, we often have to assume the worst of unknown functions – namely, that they could perform I/O. This is not Haskell's approach. Haskell wants us to be safe and allow us to assume the best of all functions – namely, that they are pure. We will see how this is actually possible in the following section.

# The IO approach

In this section, we will see how Haskell overcomes the challenges of performing I/O, by means of an approach based on a special type called IO. The solution to the I/O problem in Haskell is a conceptual one. We split I/O into two parts. First, we make a description of what I/O actions should be performed, and in what order. This is akin to, for example, writing a recipe for chocolate mousse. The second part is to perform the actions described. This corresponds to making chocolate mousse by following the recipe.

## Describing I/O

A description can be thought of as inert data; it just *is* and does not *do* anything itself. For example, a recipe is usually just text in a cookbook. We have seen an example of this already in the `Expr` datatype to describe arithmetic expressions:

```
data Expr = Lit Int | Add Expr Expr
```

When we write `Add (Lit 5) (Lit 3)`, we just construct a data structure. No computation happens, and we do not get the value 8.

We have already constructed data many times in the previous chapters. It works well with lazy evaluation and is not at odds with the mathematical definition of a function. Hence, this part works well with Haskell. Indeed, Haskell provides a built-in parameterized type `IO a`, which can be thought of as the type of I/O descriptions that, when performed, yield a result of type `a`.

The `IO` type is built into the language; there is no Haskell definition for it. We are only exposed to it through the library functions that use it. For example, the standard library provides the following function:

```
Prelude
putStrLn :: String -> IO ()
```

This function takes a string and constructs an I/O description that represents displaying that string on the standard output stream. The `Ln` part of the function's name refers to the fact that the string will be followed by a line terminator (a so-called newline). The I/O action described by `putStrLn`, when actually performed, yields a result of type `()`. This type signals that the result is of no interest. After all, as the `()` type has only one value, we already know in advance what the result will be. So, why perform this action then? For the side effect, it has to display the given string.

Now, we can write our first *proper* program in Haskell:

```
main :: IO ()
main = putStrLn "Hello, World!"
```

A proper program has a top-level function with the `main :: IO ()` signature. In other words, every Haskell program builds an I/O description that yields no result of interest but performs interesting side effects. Our little program here is the Haskell variant of one that is commonly the first shown for different programming languages, to illustrate their syntax.

## Performing I/O

Only when the I/O description is actually performed does something happen; this is the *doing*. Conceptually, we can place the performance outside of the Haskell program. An external entity, the runtime system, takes the description created by the `main` function and executes it.

We will compile a Haskell program as follows, where `Hello.hs` contains the aforementioned `main` function:

```
$ ghc --make Hello.hs
[1 of 1] Compiling Main              ( Hello.hs, Hello.o )
Linking Hello ...
```

This compilation proceeds in two steps. First, the source file, `Hello.hs`, is compiled into an object file, `Hello.o`. (This also produces an interface, `Hello.hi`, which is not needed here but is relevant when the program contains other modules that depend on `Hello.hs`.) In the following step, the object files are linked with the standard libraries and runtime system to produce an executable file, `Hello`.

Here is what happens when we run the executable:

```
$ ./Hello
Hello, World!
```

The runtime gets the `putStrLn "Hello, World!"` I/O description from the `main` function and performs it, which results in the string being displayed.

Recall from the previous chapter that Haskell's lazy evaluation does not evaluate anything until it is needed. This is the process of the runtime system, which wants to perform the main I/O description, driving the evaluation process. It creates the *need* in Call by Need.

## Composing I/O

In order to write larger I/O programs, Haskell provides a combinator that allows us to compose different I/O actions:

```
Prelude
(>>=) :: IO a -> (a -> IO b) -> IO b
```

This operator is called `bind`. It creates a composite I/O action out of two ingredients:

- A given I/O action that yields a result of some type a

- A function that, given that result, determines a second I/O action with a result of type b

The composite action performs the two actions, one after the other, and returns the result of the second action. For example, we can combine `putStrLn` with `getLine`, as follows:

```
*Main> getLine >>= \name -> putStrLn ("Hello, " ++ name ++ "!")
Tom
Hello, Tom!
```

The first action in the composition, `getLine :: IO String`, reads a string from the standard input. Here, I have entered my name. Based on this name, the second function creates an I/O action that displays a greeting. This example shows that we don't need to write a main function to experiment with I/O; GHCi conveniently executes any actions we give it.

It would be more helpful if the program first asked for my name. This can be accomplished by extending the composition:

```
main :: IO ()
main = putStrLn "What is your name?"      >>= (\_      ->
       getLine                            >>= (\name ->
       putStrLn ("Hello, " ++ name ++ "!")))
```

This program consists of three steps, written on consecutive lines:

1. Display the question.

2. Get the answer.

3. Display the greeting:

   ```
   *Main> main
   What is your name?
   Tom
   Hello, Tom!
   ```

We can write the program a little bit more compactly, as follows:

```
main :: IO ()
main = putStrLn "What is your name?"      >>
       getLine                            >>= \name ->
       putStrLn ("Hello, " ++ name ++ "!")
```

This formulation drops the redundant parentheses and replaces the first use of (>>=) with the derived (>>) operator:

```
Prelude
(>>) :: IO a -> IO b -> IO b
p >> q = p >>= \_ -> q
```

This operator sequentially composes two I/O actions, where the second action does not depend on the result of the first action. This is typically used in cases such as the preceding program, where the first action has a result of type ().

## Mixing I/O and control flow

The (>>=) operator takes a function as its second parameter. In that function, we can, of course, use Haskell's control flow mechanisms, such as case expressions and (recursive) function calls.

The following function asks the user for a single character and converts it to its character code:

```
getCharCode :: IO Int
getCharCode =
  putStrLn "Please enter a single character." >>
  getLine                                      >>= \l ->
  case l of
    [c] -> return (ord c)
    _   -> putStrLn "That is not a single character." >>
           getCharCode
```

This function uses a case expression to check whether the input entered by the user is indeed a single character. If not, the function invokes itself recursively to give the user another chance. If the input is indeed a single character, c, then the ord :: Char -> Int function of the Data.Char library is used to convert it to its character code.

This last step is not as straightforward as it might seem at first because there is a discrepancy between the type getCharCode, which obviously produces an I/O description, and ord, which produces a plain integer. Functions such as ord that do not produce an I/O description (basically, all the functions we've encountered in the previous chapters) are also called *pure* functions; conversely, functions that do produce an I/O description are called *impure*. Pure and impure functions do not compose naturally with either (.) or (>>=).

To address the problem, Haskell provides a special function that allows us to embed pure functions – or, more accurately, pure expressions – in IO:

```
Prelude
return :: a -> IO a
```

This function builds a trivial I/O description, which says to simply return the given value without performing any actual I/O. It is available by another name, `pure`, which has recently become more popular. The following two chapters will explain why there are two names for the same function.

As the `getCharCode` example shows, using the (>>=) operator becomes a little bit clumsy when more than two actions are composed. In the following section, we will see that Haskell provides syntactic sugar to mitigate this.

# The do notation

The so-called `do` notation is syntactic sugar that unclutters the use of I/O and makes Haskell code somewhat resemble that of imperative languages.

## Imperative Style

The `do` notation mimics the typical imperative programming style of writing sequential statements on consecutive lines. For example, here is the earlier greeting example, now with the `do` notation:

```
main :: IO ()
main = do putStrLn "What is your name?"
          name <- getLine
          putStrLn ("Hello, " ++ name ++ "!")
```

This program contains one do block. The block is started by the `do` keyword and features one I/O action per line. The result of the do block is the result of the last I/O action.

A do block can be systematically desugared as follows:

- When the block consists of multiple lines, we can extract the first line and recursively desugar the remaining block. How to extract the first line depends on its shape:

    - If the first line is just an I/O action, then we combine it with the (>>) operator. For example, if we extract the first line from the block in the preceding program, we get the following:

    ```
    putStrLn "What is your name?" >>
    do   name <- getLine
         putStrLn ("Hello, " ++ name ++ "!")
    ```

    - If the first line is a generator that binds the result of an I/O action to a name, we combine it with the (>>=) operator instead. Take the following example:

    ```
    do   name <- getLine
         putStrLn ("Hello, " ++ name ++ "!")
    ```

That becomes the following:

```
getLine >>= \name ->
do  putStrLn ("Hello, " ++ name ++ "!")
```

- When the block consists of a single I/O action, we can simply drop the keyword and obtain an ordinary expression. Take the following block, for instance:

```
do putStrLn ("Hello, " ++ name ++ "!")
```

That can be desugared as the following expression:

```
putStrLn ("Hello, " ++ name ++ "!")
```

This desugaring approach essentially explains the meaning of the do notation in terms of (>>=). Yet, in most cases, Haskell programmers prefer to use the do notation and consider (>>=) to be more low-level. It is mostly used for very small expressions and special cases, such as partial applications.

The do notation also provides a variation on let expressions. Consider the following program, which reads a line and then prints that line twice in all caps, using toUpper :: Char -> Char from the Data.Char library:

```
main :: IO ()
main = do l <- getLine
          (let ul = map toUpper l
           in do putStrLn ul
                 putStrLn ul)
```

Instead of using the let-in syntax with a nested do block, we can use the following more compact syntax where all lines become part of the same do block:

```
main :: IO ()
main = do l <- getLine
          let ul = map toUpper l
          putStrLn ul
          putStrLn ul
```

Here, the in keyword is dropped, and we don't need a second do block. This allows us to mix pure and impure steps more uniformly.

## Common syntax errors

The do notation takes some getting used to. The syntax and layout are quite sensitive, and mistakes can lead to sometimes puzzling error messages. To prepare you for that, we will look at two errors you are likely to encounter.

### The last statement in a do block must be an expression

The generator notation, `x <- action`, only makes sense if there is something that comes after it and possibly uses `x`. It makes no sense as the last line. The following small program violates this:

```
askName :: IO String
askName = do putStrLn "What is your name?"
             name <- getLine
```

This gives rise to the following syntax error:

```
Errors.hs:3:12: error:
    The last statement in a 'do' block must be an expression
      name <- getLine

  |
3 |              name <- getLine
  |              ^^^^^^^^^^^^^^^
Failed, no modules loaded.
```

If the name is meant to be returned, then we can fix the program by adding an explicit `return`:

```
askName :: IO String
askName = do putStrLn "What is your name?"
             name <- getLine
             return name
```

However, the preferred solution would be to shorten, rather than lengthen, the program by not binding the result of `getLine` at all:

```
askName :: IO String
askName = do putStrLn "What is your name?"
             getLine
```

Indeed, the general rule is that the result of the last line is the overall result, and as a consequence, the type of the last line is also the overall type. This does not require an explicit `return`.

### Indentation sensitivity

It is important that the lines in a do block all start in the same column. If not, the compiler gets confused and produces incomprehensible error messages. Consider this variant of the preceding program, where the last line is indented by one more space:

```
askName :: IO String
askName = do putStrLn "What is your name?"
              getLine
```

This produces the following error:

```
Errors.hs:18:15: error:
    • Couldn't match expected type 'IO String -> IO String'
                  with actual type 'IO ()'
    • The function 'putStrLn' is applied to two arguments,
      but its type 'String -> IO ()' has only one
      In a stmt of a 'do' block: putStrLn "What is your name?" getLine
      In the expression: do putStrLn "What is your name?" getLine
    |
18  | askName = do putStrLn "What is your name?"
    |              ^^^^^^^^^^^^^^^^^^^^^^^^^^^^^^ ...
Failed, no modules loaded.
```

This error message does not hint at the indentation mistake. It complains about a type error instead. This is due to the fact that the parser believes the second line is part of the first and, hence, that getLine is the second parameter passed to putStrLn. As putStrLn only takes one parameter, we get the resulting error message.

Conversely, let's say we indent the last line by too little:

```
askName :: IO String
askName = do putStrLn "What is your name?"
                getLine
```

Then, we get an entirely different error message:

```
Errors.hs:24:12: error:
    Unexpected do block in function application:
        do putStrLn "What is your name?"
    You could write it with parentheses
    Or perhaps you meant to enable BlockArguments?
    |
24  | askName = do putStrLn "What is your name?"
    |              ^^^^^^^^^^^^^^^^^^^^^^^^^^^^^^
Failed, no modules loaded.
```

Here, the erroneous indentation makes the compiler think the intention was to write a function application, when that is obviously not what we want.

As a general rule, whenever you get an error message that does not make sense to you in or near a do block that does not seem to make sense, I recommend that you check the indentation.

## A more flexible layout

Instead of the preceding minimal syntax, we can use the slightly more verbose layout-insensitive variant. Here is an earlier example of this style:

```
main :: IO ()
main = do { putStrLn "What is your name?";
            name <- getLine;
            putStrLn ("Hello, " ++ name ++ "!")
          }
```

The do block is delineated by curly braces, and the successive actions are separated by semicolons. The semicolons allow you to write multiple actions on the same line:

```
main :: IO ()
main = do { putStrLn "What is your name?";
            name <- getLine; putStrLn ("Hello, " ++ name ++ "!")
          }
```

The curly braces allow you to disregard the indentation requirements:

```
main :: IO ()
main = do { putStrLn "What is your name?";
        name <- getLine;
        putStrLn ("Hello, " ++ name ++ "!")
        }
```

Such a messy layout is, of course, not recommended.

Now that we have the principle of I/O in Haskell down, let us write a few small programs that involve several I/O tasks.

# Library functions by example

In this section, we will write two slightly larger I/O programs that combine several tasks. This gives us the opportunity to introduce several often-used library functions.

## Summing numbers

As a worked example, we will write a program that does the following:

- Reads an integer, $n$, from a line on the standard input
- Reads $n$ more integers
- Displays the sum of those $n$ integers

## Reading an integer

We can accomplish the first sub-task by combining the `getLine :: IO String` function with the parsing function, `read :: Read a => String -> a`, as follows:

```
readInteger :: IO Int
readInteger = do l <- getLine
                 return (read l)
```

This small function has to reconcile the discrepancy of `getLine` returning `IO String` and `read` taking `String`. Haskell novices often try to convert `IO String` to `String`. However, this does not make sense. The idea is that `IO String` is a description of an I/O action, and the action itself is not performed within Haskell. Hence, the only way is to change the type of `read` from `Read a => String -> a` to `Read a => String -> IO a`, using `return`, and then compose with `(>>=)`.

In fact, the standard library already contains this definition, with a more general type:

```
Prelude
readLn :: Read a => IO a
```

Therefore, we may as well use it.

## Summing a number of integers

Now, we will read and sum a given number of integers. This is easily accomplished by a function that recurses on the given number:

```
readSum :: Int -> IO Int
readSum 0 = return 0
readSum n = do x <- readLn
               s <- readSum (n-1)
               return (x + s)
```

While this approach of simultaneously reading and summing numbers is often followed by Haskell novices, it is not very idiomatic, especially not when rapid prototyping. Instead, a more compositional style is possible that separates concerns. Indeed, we can split the job into two parts – reading the numbers and summing the numbers. The latter job has already been solved for us by the `sum :: Num a => [a] -> a` library function. Hence, we only need to write a function for the former:

```
readInts :: Int -> IO [Int]
readInts 0 = return []
readInts n = do x <- readLn
                xs <- readInts (n-1)
                return (x:xs)
```

In fact, we do not have to write this ourselves. The `Control.Monad` library already contains a more general function that does the job:

```
Control.Monad
replicateM :: Int -> IO a -> IO [a]
```

This function replicates the given I/O action several times and collects their results in a list. Hence, we can write the following:

```
readSum :: Int -> IO Int
readSum n = do xs <- replicateM n readLn
               return (sum xs)
```

## Displaying an integer

Our last task is to display the resulting sum:

```
putInt :: Int -> IO ()
putInt n = putStrLn (show n)
```

Here, we first convert the integer to a string with `show` before displaying it with `putStrLn`. Because this is such a common task, it already exists as a library function:

```
Prelude
print :: Show a => a -> IO ()
```

This works for any type that has an instance of the `Show` type class.

## Putting everything together

If we put everything together as a single program, we can directly write a concise program that combines different library functions:

```
main :: IO ()
main = do n <- readLn
          xs <- replicateM n readLn
          print (sum xs :: Int)
```

We have to add an `Int` type annotation because there is no other clue in the program that forces the numbers that are read and summed to be of that type. They could otherwise easily be `Integer`, `Float`, `Double`, and so on.

This program is quick and easy to write and, unless the number of integers is really large, does the job. In the case of a larger number of integers, it would be better to use the original definition of `readSum`, augmented to force the sum at every step, to avoid the build-up of a larger number of thunks.

## Changing requirements

A distinct advantage of the separation of concerns is that we can easily replace different subparts to address changed requirements. For example, suppose we are instead expected to read the input from a file and write the result to another file.

A simple approach to read the contents of a file is the `readFile :: FilePath -> IO String` function. Here, `FilePath` is a type synonym that is meant to denote the path to a file:

```
Prelude
type FilePath = String
```

Likewise, we can use `writeFile :: FilePath -> String -> IO ()` to write a string to a file.

Suppose the input is in the `input.txt` file and the result should go to the `output.txt` file. Then, we can modify the program as follows:

```
main :: IO ()
main = do contents <- readFile "input.txt"
          let (l:ls) = lines contents
          let n  = read l
          let xs = map read (take n ls)
          writeFile "output.txt" (show (sum xs :: Int))
```

After getting the whole contents of the `input.txt` file, we process the string with the `lines` function to get a list of lines. Then, we parse the first line to an integer. This tells us how many further lines to take and parse. Finally, we use `show` to create the string that we write to `output.txt`.

For example, let's say that the following is the content of `input.txt`:

```
5
10
7
3
14
6
```

Then, after running the program, `output.txt` contains 40.

If we want to stay a bit closer to the original structure and get the lines of the file one by one, we can use the functionality of the `System.IO` library. It provides generalizations of `getLine` and `print` that take a *file handle* as a parameter:

```
System.IO
hGetLine :: Handle -> IO String
hPrint   :: Show a => Handle -> a -> IO ()
```

A file handle of type `Handle` is a representation of a particular open file. We can get a handle from a file path using `withFile`:

```
System.IO
withFile :: FilePath -> IOMode -> (Handle -> IO r) -> IO r
```

This takes the file path, a "mode" of use, and a function that captures what we want to do with the file handle. The mode can be one of four options:

```
System.IO
data IOMode = ReadMode | WriteMode | AppendMode | ReadWriteMode
```

`ReadMode` only allows you to read the contents of a file and starts at the beginning. `WriteMode` creates a file or empties it if it already exists and then allows you to write to it. `AppendMode` allows you to write to the end of the file. Finally, `ReadWriteMode` allows you to both read and write at arbitrary positions in the file.

Here, we need `ReadMode` for `input.txt`, and `WriteMode` for `output.txt`:

```
main :: IO ()
main = do xs <- withFile "input.txt" ReadMode (\hIn ->
                    do n <- hReadLn hIn
                       replicateM n (hReadLn hIn)
                  )
          withFile "output.txt" WriteMode (\hOut ->
                 hPrint hOut (sum xs :: Int)
                )
```

As you can see, the reading and writing phases of the program have each been wrapped in a call to `withFile`, to supply the corresponding file handle. That handle is used in the `hReadLn` and `hPrint` calls:

```
hReadLn :: Read a => Handle -> IO a
hReadLn h = do l <- hGetLine h
               return (read l)
```

This file handle-based approach is a bit more heavy-handed than the `readFile`/`writeFile` version, and it's best left to cases where reading and writing have to happen incrementally.

## Guessing game

Our second program is a little guessing game. The program randomly determines a number between 1 and 100, lets the user guess the number in as many attempts as necessary, and finally, says how long it took.

Here is a possible interaction:

```
Guess my number: 50
Guess again, but lower: 25
Guess again, but higher: 37
Guess again, but lower: 31
Guess again, but lower: 28
Guess again, but higher: 30
Guess again, but lower: 29
Congratulations, you have guessed my number.
It took you 29.048295s
```

This is accomplished by the following code:

```
main :: IO ()
main =
  do n <- randomRIO (1,100)
     putStr "Guess my number: "
     start <- getCurrentTime
     guess n
     end   <- getCurrentTime
     putStrLn "Congratulations, you have guessed my number."
     putStrLn ("It took you " ++ show (diffUTCTime end start))
```

We use randomRIO :: Random a => (a,a) -> IO a from the System.Random module
to generate a random integer in the given range. The Random type class specifies how random values
can be generated for a particular type. Since we use the available definition for the type Int, we need
not concern ourselves with its definition here.

To compute the elapsed time, we use the getCurrentTime :: IO UTCTime function
from the Data.Time module. With the diffUTCTime :: UTCTime -> UTCTime ->
NominalDiffTime pure function, we subtract the start time from the end time and get a time
difference that can be printed.

The repeated user interaction is encapsulated in the guess function, which recurses until the number
is correctly guessed:

```
guess :: Int -> IO ()
guess n = do m <- readLn
             case compare n m of
               LT -> do putStr "Guess again, but lower: "
                        guess n
               GT -> do putStr "Guess again, but higher: "
                        guess n
               EQ -> return ()
```

Here, we use `putStr :: String -> IO ()`, which is a variant of `putStrLn` that does not add a newline. This way, the prompt to enter a number, due to the subsequent `getLine`, appears on the same line.

## Summary

In this chapter, we explained why Haskell needs an unusual approach toward I/O – namely, to reconcile I/O with lazy evaluation and the mathematical notion of functions, Haskell separates the tasks of describing I/O and performing it. A Haskell program assembles an I/O description out of primitive functions and the bind operator, `(>>=)`, which is then performed by the runtime system. Writing I/O programs is facilitated by the imperative-style do notation and the availability of a convenient range of primitive I/O functions in the standard library.

Now that we have concluded our overview of the key functional programming and Haskell-specific language features, we will shift our focus to the more advanced programming patterns that are captured as reusable abstractions in the Haskell libraries. *Chapter 9, Monoids and Foldables*, introduces us to the first two abstractions – a generalization of lists to other collections whose content can also be processed in a fold-like fashion, and a minimal interface for the results produced by these folds. At this point, it is also useful to mention that *Chapter 11, Monads*, will generalize several of the concepts that we have introduced in this chapter.

## Questions

1.  Why does Haskell need a non-standard approach to I/O?
2.  How do we perform I/O in Haskell programs?
3.  How do we use the do notation to write I/O programs?
4.  What are some key I/O functions from the standard library?

## Further reading

- *The Prelude library documentation*: https://hackage.haskell.org/package/base-4.18.0.0/docs/Prelude.html

- *The System.IO library documentation*: https://hackage.haskell.org/package/base-4.18.0.0/docs/System-IO.html

- *The System.Random library documentation*: https://hackage.haskell.org/package/random-1.2.1.1/docs/System-Random.html

- *The Data.Time library documentation*: https://hackage.haskell.org/package/time-1.12.2/docs/Data-Time.html

# Answers

1.  There are two reasons, one more practical and the other more principled:

    - Firstly, lazy evaluation makes modeling I/O with ordinary functions practically unworkable. We lose the ability to reason compositionally about programs. Moreover, it is hard to figure out in what order I/O actions will happen, and this is crucial for program correctness.

    - Secondly, pure functions (i.e., without I/O) have a number of essential properties (e.g., predictability and ease of reasoning) that Haskell wants to preserve. Adding I/O in the standard way would destroy that.

2.  Conceptually, we separate describing I/O actions from performing them. Haskell provides a type, `IO a`, that describes I/O actions that, when performed, yield a result of type a. It's the job of the Haskell program's `main :: IO ()` function to construct such an I/O description, and the job of the runtime system to perform the I/O actions described.

    To create the `IO ()` description that `main` should produce, the Haskell standard library provides a number of primitive I/O actions, such as `getLine :: IO String` and `putStrLn :: String -> IO ()`. These can be composed into composite descriptions using the `(>>=) :: IO a -> (a -> IO b) -> IO b` operator and Haskell's existing control flow mechanisms (functions, recursion, pattern matching, and `if then else`).

3.  The do notation allows us to write sequential I/O actions on successive lines in a do block. These do blocks desugar to applications of the >>= operator and the derived >> operator, as follows:

| Original code | Desugared code |
|---|---|
| ```do line1```<br>```   line2```<br>```   line3``` | ```line1 >>```<br>```do line2```<br>```   line3``` |
| ```do x <- line1```<br>```   line2```<br>```   line3``` | ```line1 >>= \x ->```<br>```do line2```<br>```   line3``` |
| ```do let x = line1```<br>```   line2```<br>```   line3``` | ```let x = line1```<br>```in do line2```<br>```      line3``` |
| ```do line1``` | ```line1``` |

4.   We covered the following range of I/O functions:

```
Prelude
    return    :: a -> IO a
    (>>=)     :: IO a -> (a -> IO b) -> IO b
    putStr    :: String -> IO ()
    putStrLn  :: String -> IO ()
    print     :: Show a => a -> IO ()
    getLine   :: IO String
    readLn    :: Read a => IO a
    writeFile :: FilePath -> String -> IO ()
    readFile  :: FilePath -> IO String
System.IO
    withFile  :: FilePath -> IOMode -> (Handle -> IO r) -> IO r
    hPrint    :: Show a => Handle -> a -> IO ()
    hGetLine  :: Handle -> IO String
System.Random
    randomRIO :: Random a => (a,a) -> IO a
Data.Time
    getCurrentTime :: IO UTCTime
```

# Part 3:
# Functional Design Patterns

In this part, you will learn about several advanced functional design patterns that are organized around Haskell's type class mechanism and the powerful concept of type constructors. You will learn how these are used to structure programs, abstract over different kinds of loops, and model various control-flow and dataflow effects.

This part has the following chapters:

- *Chapter 9, Monoids and Foldables*
- *Chapter 10, Functors, Applicative Functors, and Traversables*
- *Chapter 11, Monads*
- *Chapter 12, Monad Transformers*

# 9

# Monoids and Foldables

In this and the coming chapters, we change gears from Haskell language features to Haskell programming/ design patterns. These patterns are ways of structuring commonly occurring programming problems or situations and communicating about them to other Haskell programmers. Although they show some similarities with the classical **object-oriented** (**OO**) design patterns that were introduced by the **Gang of Four** (**GoF**), there are many differences as well.

Firstly, while **OO programming** (**OOP**) design patterns were devised by software engineers for software engineers, Haskell's patterns are essentially concepts drawn from the mathematical fields of abstract algebra and category theory repurposed for (functional) programming. Besides being an astounding use of abstract mathematics in otherwise non-mathematical day-to-day programming, this has a number of consequences:

- OOP design patterns came about in a somewhat ad hoc fashion in the last 30-35 years. In contrast, the relevant mathematics has been under development since at least the 19th century. It provides a much more solid and integrated body of work, and their transfer from mathematics to programming demonstrates their universal nature.

- Most OOP design patterns are not well supported by programming languages. They often consist of boilerplate code that has to be repeated and instantiated for each particular use case. In contrast, Haskell's patterns are usually captured in type classes and polymorphic functions and made available through libraries.

- Because of this association with mathematics, Haskell is often perceived as a difficult language, only accessible to those who already have the underlying mathematical baggage. In particular, the use of established mathematical terminology is sometimes seen as alienating the common programmer.

This chapter takes the first steps on the path of mathematically inspired patterns. We study the notion of *foldables*. These are collections that support a range of frequently used operations to aggregate their contents into a summary of some form (for example, their length, their sum, or their maximum). To capture these summaries, we turn to the algebraic notion of monoids, which is an extension of semigroups. Along the way, we also learn that Haskell has a mechanism to abstract over parts of types called type constructors.

In short, this chapter covers the following main topics:

- What are semigroups and monoids?
- What are kinds and type constructors?
- What are foldables?
- What are common `Foldable` instances and which operations do they support?
- How do we solve problems with monoids and foldables?

## Semigroups and monoids

We start this chapter with two fairly elementary abstractions: **semigroups** and **monoids**. These are both standard concepts in the field of mathematics called *algebra*, and we are all familiar with examples of semigroups and monoids from primary school arithmetic (though not necessarily with the general concept). What is perhaps less well-known is that semigroups and monoids are also omnipresent in (functional) programming.

## Semigroups

A semigroup is an s type with a `(<>)` binary operator:

```
GHC.Base
class Semigroup s where
  (<>) :: s -> s -> s
```

The binary operator must obey one law: associativity.

### Associativity

This law states that when combining more than two values, the positioning of parentheses does not matter:

$$x <> (y <> z) == (x <> y) <> z$$

For this reason, the parentheses are usually omitted, and we simply write `x <> y <> z`.

### Instances

The `list` type forms a semigroup with the `(++)` operator:

```
GHC.Base
instance Semigroup [a] where
  (<>) = (++)
```

The following example demonstrates the associativity of this operator:

```
*Main> [1,2] <> ([3] <> [4,5])
[1,2,3,4,5]
*Main> ([1,2] <> [3]) <> [4,5]
[1,2,3,4,5]
```

Likewise, numeric types form a semigroup with addition (+) but also with multiplication (*). Indeed, we have this, for example:

```
*Main> (1 + 2) + 3
6
*Main> 1 + (2 + 3)
6
```

But we also have this:

```
*Main> (2 * 3) * 4
24
*Main> 2 * (3 * 4)
24
```

As we have already seen, in the *Structured data* section of *Chapter 7, Lazy Evaluation*, newtypes are used to provide two (or more) instances for the same type. In this case, Data.Monoid provides both the Sum and Product types:

```
Data.Semigroup
newtype Sum a = Sum { getSum :: a }
instance Num a => Semigroup (Sum a) where
   Sum x <> Sum y = Sum (x + y)
newtype Product a = Product { getProduct :: a }
instance Num a => Semigroup (Product a) where
   Product x <> Product y = Product (x * y)
```

The Num  a constraint in both instances means that they work for any numeric type, such as Int and Float.

Two semigroup instances for the Bool type are given by the Any and All newtype wrappers:

```
Data.Semigroup
newtype Any = Any { getAny :: Bool }
newtype All = All { getAll :: Bool }
```

The former uses the logical or binary operator, and the latter the logical and operator:

```
Data.Semigroup
instance Semigroup Any where
  Any x <> Any y = Any (x || y)
instance Semigroup All where
  All x <> All y = All (x && y)
```

The `Last` semigroup is a very simple one; it retains the last value provided:

```
Data.Semigroup
newtype Last a = Last { getLast :: a }
instance Semigroup (Last a) where
  x <> y = y
```

This is useful when some initial value is given, but it can be overridden by later values; the last one sticks. For example, bidding in an auction starts at an initial value and then later bids override earlier ones.

The opposite of `Last` is `First`, where the first value overrides later ones:

```
Data.Semigroup
newtype First a = First { getFirst :: a }
instance Semigroup (First a) where
  x <> y = x
```

The `First`/`Last` pair illustrates a particular construction known as *duality*. For every semigroup, there is a dual one where the binary operator of the second behaves as the flipped operator of the first. This pattern is captured in the `Dual` semigroup instance:

```
Data.Semigroup
newtype Dual a = Dual { getDual :: a }
instance Semigroup a => Semigroup (Dual a) where
  x <> y = Dual (getDual y <> getDual x)
```

For example, we can use `Dual [a]` to append lists in opposite order:

```
*Main> [1,2] <> [3,4]
[1,2,3,4]
*Main> Dual [1,2] <> Dual [3,4]
Dual {getDual = [3,4,1,2]}
```

This `Dual` construction is not interesting for `Sum` and `Product` because the binary operator of these two semigroups is not only associative but also commutative. This means that `x <> y = y <> x`.

Hence, flipping (<>) makes no difference:

```
*Main> Sum 2 <> Sum 3
Sum {getSum = 5}
*Main> Dual (Sum 2) <> Dual (Sum 3)
Dual {getDual = Sum {getSum = 5}}
```

Hence, in the case of so-called commutative semigroups, the Dual construction adds nothing.

Two final semigroups are formed by totally ordered types and, respectively, their Max and Min functions:

```
Data.Semigroup
newtype Max a = Max { getMax :: a }
newtype Min a = Min { getMin :: a }
```

The two instances require that the underlying a type has an Ord instance:

```
Data.Semigroup
instance Ord a => Semigroup (Max a) where
  Max x <> Max y = Max (max x y)
instance Ord a => Semigroup (Min a) where
  Min x <> Min y = Min (min x y)
```

Now that we have a basic understanding of semigroups and are aware of several examples, it makes sense to move on to the next structure: monoids. The reason is that the semigroup structure alone is not terribly useful. We need just a little bit more functionality and so much more becomes possible, which is what monoids provide. While there are several more examples of semigroups in the standard library, we return to them later when we also discuss their monoid structure.

## Monoids

m monoids extend semigroups with a distinguished element called mempty :: m. This element is the identity of the (<>) binary operator.

### Left identity

If we combine an element on the left with mempty, we get the element back:

$$\text{mempty <> y == y}$$

We also call mempty a left neutral element.

### Right identity

If we combine an element on the right with mempty, we get the element back:

$$\text{x <> mempty == x}$$

We also call `mempty` a right neutral element.

Because `mempty` is both a left and a right identity (or neutral element), we simply call it an identity (or a neutral element).

The first five semigroup examples we saw (`List`, `Sum`, `Product`, `Any`, and `All`) all have such an identity. In the case of lists and `(++)`, the identity is the empty list (`[]`). In the case of addition, it is 0, and in the case of multiplication, the identity is 1. For logical or (`Any`), it is `False`, and for logical and (`All`), it is `True`.

### The Monoid class

Here is the `Monoid` type class declaration in full:

```
GHC.Base
class Semigroup m => Monoid m where
  mempty   :: m
  mempty = mconcat []

  mappend :: m -> m -> m
  mappend = (<>)

  mconcat :: [m] -> m
  mconcat = foldr (<>) mempty
```

Besides the `mempty` method, the `Monoid` type class also contains a copy of the `(<>)` operator, called `mappend`. It is there for historical reasons: originally, the standard library did not contain a `Semigroup` class. This was only introduced later and made a superclass of `Monoid`, but the `mappend` method was kept to avoid breaking existing code.

Finally, the class provides the `mconcat` method to combine a list of values, which is defined by default in terms of `foldr`. While most instances simply rely on this default implementation, there are a few instances in the standard library that override this default for the sake of efficiency.

### Monoid instances

With the general notion of monoids in place, we now build up an arsenal of `Monoid` instances, which will prove valuable when we explore foldables later.

First, let us provide `Monoid` instances for the earlier semigroup examples that have a neutral element:

```
GHC.Base
instance Monoid [a] where
  mempty = []
```

```
Data.Semigroup
instance Num a => Monoid (Sum a) where
  mempty = Sum 0

instance Num a => Monoid (Product a) where
  mempty = Product 1

instance Monoid Any where
  mempty = Any False

instance Monoid All where
  mempty = All True
```

The other semigroup examples do not generally have a neutral element, but they may do for particular a types.

In the case of the Min a and Max a semigroups, there is only a neutral element if there is respectively a greatest and smallest value in the total ordering on a. This is fine for bounded types such as Int and Bool. Yet, the Integer type has neither. For this reason, the Monoid instances for Min and Max feature an additional Bounded constraint. This constraint allows us to refer to the greatest and smallest values of the type with maxBound and minBound, respectively (see *Chapter 6, Type Classes*):

```
Data.Semigroup
instance (Ord a, Bounded a) => Monoid (Min a) where
  mempty = maxBound

instance (Ord a, Bounded a) => Monoid (Max a) where
  mempty = minBound
```

For instance, First a and Last a only have a neutral element in the trivial case that the type a has only one value, which can then serve as the neutral element.

To remedy this situation, there is a construction that can systematically extend these and other semigroup a types with an artificial neutral element: Maybe a. The values of the original semigroup are wrapped in the Just constructor and the artificial neutral element is Nothing:

```
GHC.Base
instance Semigroup a => Semigroup (Maybe a) where
  Nothing <> y     = y
  x <> Nothing     = x
  Just a <> Just b = Just (a <> b)

instance Semigroup a => Monoid (Maybe a) where
  mempty = Nothing
```

For convenience, but perhaps somewhat confusingly, the `Data.Monoid` module provides alternative definitions of `First` and `Last`. These are essentially newtype wrappers around the `Maybe`-extended definitions of the same name in `Data.Semigroup`. Here's an example:

```
Data.Monoid
newtype First a = First { getFirst :: Maybe a }

instance Semigroup (First a) where
  First Nothing <> y = First y
  x             <> _ = x

instance Monoid (First a) where
  mempty = First Nothing
```

The implementation of `(<>)` is a bit more lazy than that of `Maybe` as it avoids forcing the second argument. The code for `Last` is the dual of this, with `(<>)` lazy in its first argument.

## Aggregation strategies

What makes monoids so interesting is that they give us great flexibility in the order of computation.

Suppose we have a list of monoid values, `[m1, ..., m8]`, that we want to aggregate to a single value. We can do that with `mconcat`, which we defined previously in terms of `foldr`:

$$\text{foldr } (<>) \text{ mempty } [m1, ..., m8]$$

This gives rise to a computation structure associated to the right:

```
m1 <> (m2 <> (m3 <> (m4 <> (m5 <> (m6 <> (m7 <> (m8 <> mempty)))))))
```

Because `(<>)` is associative, we are allowed to reassociate to the left:

```
(((((((m1 <> m2) <> m3) <> m4) <> m5) <> m6) <> m7) <> m8) <> mempty
```

Moreover, we can drop the neutral element on the right and we can add it on the left:

```
(((((((mempty <> m1) <> m2) <> m3) <> m4) <> m5) <> m6) <> m7) <> m8
```

This is the computation structure of `foldl`:

$$\text{foldl } (<>) \text{ mempty } [m1, ..., m8]$$

Hence, with monoids, `foldr` and `foldl` give the same result. In fact, they are only two options of many on a spectrum. Instead of associating all operators the same way (to the right or the left), we can have hybrid combinations. One compelling variant is the following tree-structured combination:

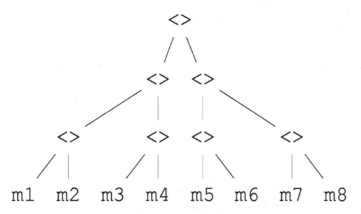

Figure 9.1 – Divide-and-conquer strategy for the aggregation of monoid values

This is a divide-and-conquer strategy that repeatedly splits up the work into two halves until only individual elements remain. Then, the values are repeatedly combined in a pairwise fashion until only one value remains.

If the number of initial values is not a power of two, we do not get a perfect binary tree, but one where some children are not at the lowest level.

The following code implements this strategy:

```
divideAndConquer :: Monoid m => [m] -> m
divideAndConquer ms = go ms (length ms) where
  go []  n = mempty
  go [m] n = m
  go ms  n = go ms1 n1 <> go ms2 n2
    where n1 = div n 2
          n2 = n - n1
          (ms1,ms2) = splitAt n1 ms
```

What is interesting about this strategy is that the two go ms1 n1 and go ms2 n2 subcomputations are independent of one another and can thus in principle be computed in parallel.

In principle, GHC will not actually introduce any parallelism in our program unless we explicitly ask for it. One way to do so is with the par :: a -> b -> b and pseq :: a -> b -> b special primitive functions in Control.Parallel. Here, par x y indicates that y produces the result we are interested in, but that x should be evaluated (that is, forced) *in parallel* because we may need its result later on. In contrast, pseq x y expresses that x should be evaluated before y, even though y produces the result we are interested in. Often, the two are used in combination:

```
pseq (par x y) (f x y)
```

This captures that we want to evaluate x and y first in parallel, and then combine them with some f function.

The following definition incorporates this parallelism in our divide-and-conquer strategy:

```
parallelDivideAndConquer :: Monoid m => [m] -> m
parallelDivideAndConquer ms = go ms (length ms) where
  go []  n = mempty
  go [m] n = m
  go ms  n = pseq (par x y) (x <> y)
    where n1 = div n 2
          n2 = n - n1
          (ms1,ms2) = splitAt n1 ms
          x = go ms1 n1
          y = go ms2 n2
```

In theory, this parallelism gives us an amazing speed-up: we only need time logarithmic in the number of elements rather than linear. In practice, it often does not work out that way for the following reasons:

- Firstly, the quadratic runtime from repeatedly invoking splitAt, which sets up the tree-shaped computation, may drown out any parallelism gains. This can be accommodated by replacing a data structure that is more cheaply split in two than a list, such as a binary tree.

- Secondly, the cost of firing off a separate thread is not insignificant. If it is larger than the actual cost of the work the thread performs, it will even cause a slowdown. A hybrid approach may be of aid here: evaluate the subtrees in parallel as long as they are above an experimentally determined threshold and switch to single-threaded evaluation once they go below it.

We now have a basic idea of the semigroup and monoid structures and covered plenty of examples. Before we move on to the concept of foldable containers that build on monoids, we first have to explain a fundamental concept of Haskell's type system: **kinds**.

# Kinds and type constructors

We have already studied and used types extensively. They allow us to distinguish between different forms of values in a way that can be used to document and automatically check our code. Kinds do the same thing *one level up*: they are a way of distinguishing different forms of types.

## Proper types

The simplest and most ubiquitous group of types are so-called **proper types**. These are what we meant when we used the word *type* earlier in this book. Probably all the types that come to your mind are proper types: Int, Bool, [Char], Float -> String, and so on.

The kind associated with proper types is written *. This kind is often pronounced *type*, and in recent years, GHC has provided `Type` as a synonym for * in the `Data.Kind` module.

We can check the kind of a type in GHCi with the `:kind` command (or `:k` for short):

```
*Main> :kind Int
Int :: *
*Main> :kind Bool -> (Char, Float)
Bool -> (Char, Float) :: *
```

Another term for proper types is *inhabited* types because these are the types that are *inhabited* by values. In other words, the type of a value is a proper type. For example, the type of `True` is `Bool`, and thus `Bool` is a proper type. Likewise, the type of the `not` function is `Bool -> Bool`, and thus `Bool -> Bool` is a proper type.

## Type constructors

The whole point of the concept of kinds is that some types are not proper types. We do not call them *improper* types, but type constructors as they are incomplete. Indeed, a type constructor is a type that has to be applied to other types to complete it.

A basic example of a type constructor is the `Maybe` type, which itself is not a proper type. Yes – `Maybe Int`, `Maybe Bool`, and even `Maybe a` are all proper types, but `Maybe` on its own (not applied to any parameter) is not. The `Maybe Int` type is inhabited by values such as `Nothing` and `Just 42`, but it does not even make sense to ask which values have the `Maybe` type.

We say that `Maybe` is a type constructor because, given a proper type, it constructs another proper type. This is captured in the kind of `Maybe`, namely * -> *. For example, given the `Int :: *` proper type, it constructs the `Maybe Int :: *` proper type. Another type constructor that has a kind of * -> * is the `[]` list type constructor:

```
*Main> :kind []
[] :: * -> *
*Main> :kind [] Bool
[] Bool :: *
```

Observe that `[] Bool` is simply another way to write `[Bool]`.

The general form of the kind for type constructors is `k1 -> k2` where `k1` and `k2` can be any two kinds. The case where `k1 = k2 = *` is only one possibility, albeit the most common one. The `First`, `Last`, `Sum`, and `Product` type constructors that we saw earlier in this chapter all have this kind.

A type constructor that has a different kind is `Either`, which takes two type parameters:

```
*Main> :kind Either
Either :: * -> * -> *
*Main> :kind Either Bool
Either Bool :: * -> *
*Main> :kind Either Bool Int
Either Bool Int :: *
```

As the interaction shows, `Either` has kind `* -> * -> *`. Syntactically, the arrow works in exactly the same way as the arrow for function types. Implicitly, it associates to the right. Hence, `* -> * -> *` can also be written `* -> (* -> *)`. Moreover, it enables partial application. For example, `Either Bool` is itself a type constructor of kind `* -> *`.

Two types with special syntax are the `a -> b` function type and the `(a, b)` tuple type. Both can be written with more regular syntax, a type constructor applied to some parameters – namely, `(->) a b` and `(,) a b`. Here `(->)` and `(,)` are both type constructors of kind `* -> * -> *`.

## Type constructor parameters

One of the key benefits of being able to talk about type constructors is that we can separately abstract over them. One small example is *generalized rose trees*. A (non-generalized) rose tree is a tree where every node contains a value and zero or more children:

```
data Rose a = RNode a [Rose a]
```

Here, we use a list to model zero or more children. In contrast, a trie (or prefix tree) is a tree where each child of a node is associated with a key in a map data structure:

```
data Trie k a = TNode a (Map k (Trie k a))
```

Clearly, both structures are very similar. The only difference is that they use a different data structure to hold the children. With a `c` type parameter that abstracts over the type constructor, we can capture the common pattern of both definitions, which is the so-called generalized rose tree:

```
data GRose c a = GNode a (c (GRose c a))
```

We can recover both rose trees and tries from `GRose` by choosing appropriate type constructors for the `c` parameter:

```
type Rose   = GRose []
type Trie k = GRose (Map k)
```

Let us figure out what kind the `c` type parameter has. Because it is applied to another type in the definition, we can tell that it is a type constructor of kind `k1 -> k2`. As the field of a data constructor must always be a proper type, we conclude that the resulting `k2` kind is `*`. Moreover, as a datatype,

GRose c a has kind *, and because c is applied to it, we have that k1 is also *. In short, c has kind * -> *. It follows that the GRose type has kind (* -> *) -> * -> * as it takes two parameters, a c type constructor of kind * -> * and a proper type a, and yields a proper type.

Besides the two preceding examples, we can also explore new instantiations of GRose. For example, with the Maybe type constructor, we get non-empty lists:

```
type NonEmptyList = GRose Maybe
```

The top-level node contains the first element. Because of the Maybe constructor, it has zero or one substructure, which provides possibly more elements. The following function helps to explain the list-like structure of NonEmptyList; it converts the structure to an ordinary list:

```
nonEmptyToList :: NonEmptyList a -> [a]
nonEmptyToList (GNode x xs) = x : go xs where
  go :: Maybe (NonEmptyList a) -> [a]
  go Nothing  = []
  go (Just l) = nonEmptyToList l
```

Rose trees, tries and non-empty lists are just three examples of collections of elements. One of the benefits of type constructor abstraction is that we can define common infrastructure for such collection types. This is exactly what we do next with the notion of foldables.

# Foldables

Foldables are type constructors of the * -> * kind that represent collections of elements and come equipped with particular functionality.

## The Foldable type class

The functionality that should be provided by a foldable is captured in the Foldable type class. This type class is a so-called **type constructor class** because it ranges over t type constructors rather than proper types:

```
Data.Foldable
class Foldable t where
  fold     :: Monoid m => t m -> m
  foldMap  :: Monoid m => (a -> m) -> t a -> m
  foldMap' :: Monoid m => (a -> m) -> t a -> m
  foldr    :: (a -> b -> b) -> b -> t a -> b
  foldr'   :: (a -> b -> b) -> b -> t a -> b
  foldl    :: (b -> a -> b) -> b -> t a -> b
  foldl'   :: (b -> a -> b) -> b -> t a -> b
```

```
foldr1    :: (a -> a -> a) -> t a -> a
foldl1    :: (a -> a -> a) -> t a -> a
toList    :: t a -> [a]
null      :: t a -> Bool
length    :: t a -> Int
elem      :: Eq a => a -> t a -> Bool
maximum   :: Ord a => t a -> a
minimum   :: Ord a => t a -> a
sum       :: Num a => t a -> a
product   :: Num a => t a -> a
```

The larger number of methods in the type class can be quite overwhelming at first. Yet, upon closer inspection, we are already familiar with these methods for the specific case of lists. Indeed, lists are the most obvious instance of this type class:

```
Data.Foldable
instance Foldable [] where
    elem        = List.elem
    foldl       = List.foldl
    foldl'      = List.foldl'
    foldl1      = List.foldl1
    foldr       = List.foldr
    foldr'      = List.foldr'
    foldr1      = List.foldr1
    foldMap f   = mconcat . map f
    fold        = mconcat
    length      = List.length
    maximum     = List.maximum
    minimum     = List.minimum
    null        = List.null
    product     = List.product
    sum         = List.sum
    toList      = id
```

We covered most of these methods when studying lists and recursive functions over lists. The main exception is mconcat, which came up earlier in this chapter when introducing monoids.

Minor exceptions are the fold' and foldr' primed versions, which are versions of foldl and foldr that are strict in their accumulator. Two other variants of these are foldl1 and foldr1, which take respectively the first and last element as the initial value of the accumulator and raise an error when the collection is empty.

## Listable collections

A good way to characterize foldables is as collections whose elements we can extract into a list. Take, for example, the following tree type:

```
data Tree a = Leaf a | Fork (Tree a) (Tree a)
```

We can easily extract the elements of a tree into a list:

```
treeToList :: Tree a -> [a]
treeToList (Leaf x)   = [x]
treeToList (Fork l r) = treeToList l ++ treeToList r
```

Now, we get a valid `Foldable` instance by performing this conversion and then calling the appropriate function on the resulting list:

```
instance Foldable Tree where
    toList      = treeToList
    sum         = List.sum . treeToList
    product     = List.product . treeToList
    foldr c n = List.foldr c n . treeToList
```

…and so on for the other methods.

As we can see, `toList` could in principle provide a minimum complete definition from which the implementation of all other methods can be derived. In essence, the laws governing the methods of `Foldable` also state the other methods should be consistent with `toList`.

### Minimum complete definition with foldr

The `Foldable` type class does not offer `toList` as a minimum complete definition. Instead, it can be provided through `foldr`. Indeed, all the functions in the list instance are (or can be) defined in terms of list `foldr`. For example, while `foldMap` is shown as the composition of `mconcat` and `map`, we can combine them into a single `foldr` definition:

```
foldMap f t = foldr (\x r -> f x <> r) mempty t
```

Instead of first mapping the elements of the collection to the monoid and then aggregating the monoid values, it does both simultaneously.

### Instances based on foldr

If `Foldable` instances for non-list collections provide a direct definition of `foldr` that avoids creating an intermediate list, that is going to be more efficient than the previous naive approach.

Setting up such a direct definition of `foldr` may take some getting used to, though. For example, here is a proper instance for `Tree` in terms of `foldr`:

```
instance Foldable Tree where
    foldr c n (Leaf x)   = c x n
    foldr c n (Fork l r) = foldr c (foldr c n r) l
```

To see where this definition comes from, we can actually systematically derive it from the previous naive specification as follows. Let us consider the base case of leaves first:

```
    foldr c n (Leaf x)
  = {- using our naive specification -}
    List.foldr c n (treeToList (Leaf x))
  = {- using the definition of treeToList -}
    List.foldr c n [x]
  = {- using the definition of List.foldr -}
    c x n
```

Now, on to the more complex recursive case of forks:

```
    foldr c n (Fork l r)
  = {- using our naive specification -}
    List.foldr c n (treeToList (Fork l r))
  = {- using the definition of treeToList -}
    List.foldr c n (treeToList l ++ treeToList r)
  = {- using a property of List.foldr/++ interaction -}
    List.foldr c (List.foldr c n (treeToList r)) (treeToList l)
  = {- tie recursive knot using naive specification in reverse -}
    foldr c (foldr c n r) l
```

The key step in the preceding derivation exploits a property of the interaction between `List.foldr` and `(++)`:

```
foldr c n (xs ++ ys) = foldr c (foldr c n ys) xs
```

This basically says that if we fold a `(xs ++ ys)` list, then we can first fold the second half, `ys`, and later resume from this intermediate result to fold over the first half, `xs`. An intuitive example is `sum = foldr (+) 0`. Suppose we sum over the `[1,2,3] ++ [4,5,6]` list.

We have the following:

```
foldr (+) 0 ([1,2,3] ++ [4,5,6])
```

Using the definitions of `foldr` and `++`, we simplify this to the following:

```
1 + (2 + (3 + (4 + (5 + (6 + 0)))))
```

The underlined part sums the second half of the list:

$$1 + (2 + (3 + \text{foldr } (+) \; 0 \; [4,5,6]))$$

Here, we have the sum of `[1,2,3]`, but starting from the sum of `[4,5,6]` rather than from `0`:

$$\text{foldr } (+) \; (\text{foldr } (+) \; 0 \; [4,5,6]) \; [1,2,3]$$

If a direct implementation of `foldr`, involving calculations and properties such as the previous one, is not your cup of tea, there is another way to provide a minimal complete definition.

## Aggregation into a monoid

The second way to provide a minimal complete definition is via `foldMap`, which is where monoids come into play:

```
foldMap  :: Monoid m => (a -> m) -> t a -> m
```

This method aggregates the elements of a foldable collection of type `t a` into a value of a `m` monoid. To accomplish this job, it takes a function of type `a -> m` to convert the elements to the monoid.

While it is often more challenging to express an accumulation in terms of a monoid, it also has an important benefit. Indeed, recall that the direction of monoid accumulation (left-to-right or right-to-left) does not matter. In fact, we have seen that the accumulation can even be parallelized and thus leverage multiple CPUs to speed up the process.

I do not expect you to get the knack of using `foldMap` upon a first reading, but I provide the next examples to offer you some insight into what is possible.

### Aggregation examples

It is now that our arsenal of `Monoid` instances comes in handy. For example, we can implement `sum` as follows in terms of `foldMap` and the `Sum` monoid:

```
sum = getSum . foldMap Sum
```

Here, `foldMap` uses the `Sum` constructor to turn every element into a value of the `Sum` monoid and then aggregates them into the overall sum. Finally, `getSum` extracts the value of that sum. The `length` function only requires a small variation:

```
length = getSum . foldMap (\_ -> Sum 1)
```

Now, every element is mapped to the value `1` in the `Sum` monoid.

Similarly, we can define `elem` in terms of the `Any` monoid:

```
elem x = getAny . foldMap (\y -> Any (x == y))
```

This maps every element to a Boolean that indicates whether it is the element we are looking for. The Any wrapper means that the Booleans are aggregated with ( | | ).

In contrast, the `null` method can be defined with the `All` monoid:

```
null = getAll . foldMap (\_ -> All False)
```

In the case of the empty collection, we get the `True` neutral element list. Yet, if there is any element in the collection, it is mapped to `False` and combined with (`&&`) to override any `True`.

The `maximum` method is, of course, based on the `Max` monoid:

```
maximum =  fromMaybe (error "maximum: empty structure") .
           getMax . foldMap (\x -> Max (Just x))
```

Unfortunately, `maximum` is partial. When the collection is empty, it raises an error. This happens in the last step of the preceding pipeline, where `Maybe a` is converted to `a`. This uses the `fromMaybe` function:

```
Data.Maybe
fromMaybe :: a -> Maybe a -> a
fromMaybe x Nothing  = x
fromMaybe x (Just y) = y
```

In this case, we have no way of giving a sensible value of type `a` when the collection is empty. Hence, instead, an error is raised.

### Minimal completeness

We have just seen that most other methods can be defined in terms of `foldMap` and an appropriate monoid. The encoding of one method in terms of `foldMap` that may not be so apparent is `foldr`. It requires the monoid of *endofunctions*. An endofunction is a function of type `r -> r` for any type `r`. To distinguish this from other function-based monoids, we use a newtype:

```
Data.Semigroup
newtype Endo r = Endo { appEndo :: r -> r}
```

Because the input and output types of endofunctions are the same, they can be composed both on the left and on the right:

```
Data.Semigroup
instance Semigroup (Endo r) where
  Endo f <> Endo g = Endo (f . g)
```

This composition is associative and has the `id :: r -> r` identity function as its neutral element:

```
Data.Semigroup
instance Monoid (Endo r) where
  mempty = Endo id
```

With this monoid of function composition, we can capture the computational structure of `foldr`. Indeed, `foldr c n [x1,x2,...,xm]` piles up function applications thus:

```
c x1 (c x2 … (c xm n))
```

However, we can, in fact, insert an identity function at the bottom of the pile-up:

```
c x1 (c x2 … (c xm (id n)))
```

Finally, we can shift from function application to function composition:

```
(c x1 . c x2 . … . c xm . id)
```

Now, we see the involvement of the Endo monoid in aggregating the `c xi :: r -> r` functions into a single function, which is applied at the end to n. This is written succinctly as follows:

```
foldr c n t = appEndo (foldMap (\x -> Endo (c x)) t) n
```

By changing the order of composition, using `Dual (Endo r)`, we can implement `foldl` as well:

```
foldl f a t =
  appEndo (getDual (foldMap (\x -> Dual (Endo (flip f x))) t)) a
```

One small wrinkle is that `foldl`'s `f :: r -> a -> r` function parameter takes its inputs in the opposite order from `foldr`'s `c :: a -> r -> r` parameter. By changing the order of composition, using `Dual (Endo r)`, we can implement `foldl` as well. That is easily rectified with `flip`.

### Instances based on foldMap

The implementation for lists is quite straightforward:

```
foldMap f = mconcat . map f
```

This first turns the list of type `[a]` into a list of type `[m]` with `map f` and then aggregates that intermediate list with `mconcat` to the single value of the m monoid.

With Tree, we can follow a divide-and-conquer strategy:

```
instance Foldable Tree where
    foldMap f (Leaf x)   = f x
    foldMap f (Fork l r) = foldMap f l <> foldMap f r
```

Here, we recursively aggregate the left and right subtrees of `Fork` and then combine their results. We bootstrap this process at the leaves where we turn the elements into monoid values.

A particularly small case of a foldable collection is `Maybe`, which has room for at most one element:

```
Data.Foldable
instance Foldable Maybe where
    foldMap f Nothing  = mempty
    foldMap f (Just x) = f x
```

The rose trees we defined earlier in this chapter require a nested treatment:

```
instance Foldable Rose where
    foldMap f (RNode x xs) = f x <> foldMap (foldMap f) xs
```

The nested `foldMap` call recursively aggregates all the subtrees (with the inner `foldMap` call) and then aggregates the resulting list (with the outer `foldMap` call). That result is merged with the monoid element for the value at the root of the tree.

We can extend this approach to generalized rose trees:

```
instance Foldable c => Foldable (GRose c) where
    foldMap f (GNode x xs) = f x <> foldMap (foldMap f) xs
```

If we require that the `c` collection is foldable, then the outer `foldMap` call can be generalized from lists to `c`.

## Deriving the Foldable instance

We don't actually have to write `Foldable` instances manually. The GHC Haskell compiler is able to derive them automatically for us. This is not one of the standard Haskell language features, but a GHC language extension. We have to explicitly enable it by putting the following line, a so-called pragma, at the top of our source file:

```
{-# LANGUAGE DeriveFoldable #-}
```

Now, we can add a `deriving` clause to the datatype definition:

```
data Tree a = Leaf a | Fork (Tree a) (Tree a)
    deriving Foldable
```

This gives us the behavior of the instance we have been writing ourselves before. In fact, in practice, there is little reason to ever write `Foldable` instances manually. The only exception is if you want to deviate from the automatically provided behavior.

For example, we can manually write an instance that only includes the left branches of forks:

```
instance Foldable Tree where
    foldMap f (Leaf x)   = f x
    foldMap f (Fork l r) = foldMap f l
```

This is perfectly valid as the `Foldable` type class does not actually come with any laws that require that all elements inside the collection should be declared. Nevertheless, hiding elements from the `Foldable` methods is not very likely to yield a sensible instance.

## Standard library instances

Besides the `Foldable` instance for lists, the `Set` and `Map k` type constructors both have useful instances that allow us to aggregate respectively the elements of a set and the values in a map.

In addition to those, there is an extensive number of instances for type constructors that we usually do not view as being collections. For example, all `Min`, `Max`, `Dual`, `Sum`, `Product`, `First`, and `Last` type constructors have `Foldable` instances. Indeed, with some goodwill, we see all of these as single-element collections. Similarly, `Maybe` is a foldable collection that contains zero or one element, depending on whether a `Nothing` or `Just` data constructor is used. This may lead to confusing situations. For instance, how long is the word associated with the key 2?

```
*Main> let r = lookup 2 [(1,"ant"),(2,"boa"),(3,"coon")]
*Main> length r
1
```

We get the surprising result 1 (instead of 3), because the type of `r` is of type `Maybe String`, and thus `length` uses `Maybe` instance of `Foldable`. As `r` is just `"boa"`, it is a collection that contains one element, namely `"boa"`.

With our new understanding of `Foldable`, we now investigate a small case study where we design a custom monoid to tackle an aggregation task.

# Case study – Sortedness

We now perform a small case study designing an algorithm to check whether a collection is sorted.

## Sorted lists

The more direct definition for checking whether a list is sorted makes use of explicit recursion and distinguishes three cases:

```
sorted :: Ord a => [a] -> Bool
sorted []       = True
sorted [x]      = True
sorted (x:y:zs) = x <= y && sorted (y:zs)
```

Empty and one-element lists are always sorted. A two-or-more-element list is sorted if the first two elements are in ascending order and if the tail is sorted.

We would like to carry this definition over to other `Foldable` collections. Unfortunately, it does not fit the structurally recursive pattern of `foldr` or `foldMap` that is supported by other foldables. The reason is that the definition distinguishes the one-element list from other non-empty lists.

## An attempt with structural recursion

Let us attempt to write sorted with structural recursion as follows:

```
sorted :: Ord a => [a] -> Bool
sorted l = foldr c n l where
  n :: Bool
  n = ?
  c :: Ord a => a -> Bool -> Bool
  c = ?
```

Using the `foldr` recursion scheme, we only have to fill in two parts:

- The n parameter says what the result should be for an empty list. We can read that from our initial definition: an empty list is always sorted. So, n = `True`.

- The c parameter defines how we combine an x element with the recursive result, r, to obtain the new result, c x r. There are two subcases here:

  - Suppose the remainder of the list is not sorted, so r = `False`. Then, it does not matter what the preceding element x is; the resulting list does not become sorted. Hence:

    ```
    c x False = False
    ```

  - Suppose the remainder of the list is sorted, so r = `True`. In this case, we cannot actually say whether the overall list is sorted or not. Consider x = 4. It could be that the sorted remainder of the list is [5,6,7]. Then, the overall list [4,5,6,7] is also sorted. However, if the sorted remainder is [1,2,3], then the overall list [4,1,2,3] is not sorted. In short, we cannot tell whether the result is sorted or not.

    ```
    c x True = error "cannot tell"
    ```

Our attempt to write sorted using `foldr` has hit a dead end, and we need to back up a little to get unstuck.

## A richer approach with structural recursion

When the remainder of the list was sorted, a Boolean did not give us enough information to decide whether the overall list would be sorted. So, let us add the information that we need to make that decision to the result: the first element of the list. We get the following, richer datatype in lieu of `Bool`:

```
data Sortedness a = NotSorted | Sorted a | EmptySorted
```

Here, NotSorted means that the list is not sorted, while Sorted x means that the list is sorted and that its first element is x. We need a third constructor, EmptySorted, which indicates that the list is sorted but does not have a first element, because it is empty.

With this new result type, we can define the function in terms of foldr:

```
sorted' :: Ord a => [a] -> Sortedness a
sorted' l = foldr c n l where

  n :: Sortedness a
  n = EmptySorted

  c :: Ord a => a -> Sortedness a -> Sortedness a
  c x NotSorted    = NotSorted
  c x EmptySorted = Sorted x
  c x (Sorted y)
    | x <= y       = Sorted x
    | otherwise    = NotSorted
```

At the end, we can convert the result to a Boolean as follows:

```
sorted :: Ord a => [a] -> Bool
sorted l = sortednessToBool (sorted' l)

sortednessToBool :: Sortedness a -> Bool
sortednessToBool NotSorted    = False
sortednessToBool (Sorted _)   = True
sortednessToBool EmptySorted = True
```

Thanks to the use of foldr, we can actually generalize the type signatures to work for any foldable:

```
sorted' :: (Foldable t, Ord a) => t a -> Sortedness a
sorted  :: (Foldable t, Ord a) => t a -> Bool
```

While this approach works for any Foldable instance, the use of foldr is unnecessarily biased toward right-to-left traversal. Some foldables might prefer left-to-right (foldl) or a divide-and-conquer style approach. Can we make our approach less biased in order to accommodate all preferences?

## The Sortedness monoid

The solution to make our approach unbiased is to turn Sortedness into a monoid. As a monoid, it can be extended on both sides and has a neutral element on either side. We only need to make one small modification to our existing datatype definition – in addition to the first element, the Sorted constructor should also carry the last element to support extension on that side:

```
data Sortedness a = NotSorted | Sorted a a | EmptySorted
```

With this extension, `Sortedness a` forms a semigroup:

```
instance Ord a => Semigroup (Sortedness a) where
  EmptySorted <> s = s
  s <> EmptySorted = s
  NotSorted <> s = NotSorted
  s <> NotSorted = NotSorted
  Sorted l1 u1 <> Sorted l2 u2
    | u1 <= l2   = Sorted l1 u2
    | otherwise  = NotSorted
```

From this definition of `(<>)`, we see that `EmptySorted` is the neutral element. Hence, `Sortedness a` also forms a monoid:

```
instance Ord a => Monoid (Sortedness a) where
  mempty = EmptySorted
```

Hence, we can define sorted in terms of `foldMap`, mapping the elements of the foldable collection to this monoid:

```
sorted :: (Foldable t, Ord a) => t a -> Bool
sorted l = sortednessToBool (foldMap (\x -> Sorted x x) l)
```

Here, the anonymous function expresses that every element is sorted on its own, and `foldMap` aggregates the sortedness of all elements. It is up to the particular implementation of the foldable how this aggregation happens: left-to-right, right-to-left, or divide-and-conquer.

## Summary

In this chapter, we have explored two basic algebraic structures that occur frequently in functional programs: semigroups and monoids. While these are interesting patterns on their own, they turn out to be particularly useful for aggregating the elements of collections. For that purpose, we have introduced the notion of type constructors, types of higher kinds that allow us to separate the collection type from its element type. Next, we have explored the `Foldable` constructor type class for collections whose elements can be extracted into a list. Its minimal complete definition based on `foldMap` turns out to be a Swiss Army knife that can be conveniently instantiated with different monoids to accomplish all manner of aggregation tasks. Finally, we have developed a custom monoid to tackle a new task, checking the sortedness of foldable collections.

*Chapter 10, Functors, Applicative Functors, and Traversables*, continues with a hierarchy of type classes for type constructors. Functors generalize the notion of the map function from lists to other type constructors. They allow transforming elements with a pure function. Applicative functors allow us to model a kind of impure functions, and traversables provide a notion of mapping for these impure functions.

# Questions

1.  What is a semigroup?

2.  What is a monoid?

3.  What are some examples of semigroups and monoids?

4.  What are type constructors?

5.  What is a foldable?

# Further reading

- The `Data.Semigroup` library documentation: `https://hackage.haskell.org/package/base-4.18.0.0/docs/Data-Semigroup.html`

- The `Data.Monoid` library documentation:

  `https://hackage.haskell.org/package/base-4.18.0.0/docs/Data-Monoid.html`

- The `Data.Foldable` library documentation: `https://hackage.haskell.org/package/base-4.18.0.0/docs/Data-Foldable.html`

# Answers

1.  A semigroup is an `s` type with a `(<>)` binary associative operator. In Haskell, it is modeled by the following type class:

    ```
    class Semigroup s where
        (<>) :: s -> s -> s
    ```

    This is subject to the following associativity law:

    $$(x <> y) <> z = x <> (y <> z)$$

2.  A monoid is a semigroup (that is, type `m` with a `(<>)` binary associate operator) that also has a neutral element (aka identity), `mempty`. In Haskell, it is modeled by the following subclass of `Semigroup`:

    ```
    class Semigroup m => Monoid m where
        mempty :: m
    ```

    This is subject to the two identity laws:

    $$x <> mempty = x$$
    $$mempty <> x = x$$

3.  The following table lists examples from the standard libraries we have covered. The first column gives the names of the types (possibly subject to type class constraints). The second column lists the names of the newtype wrappers, in case there are multiple possibilities for the same type. The third and fourth columns give a definition of the binary operator and neutral element. If an entry does not exist, this is indicated with a dash:

| Type | Newtype Name | (<>) | mempty |
|---|---|---|---|
| `[a]` | - | `(++)` | `[]` |
| `Num a => a` | `Sum a` | `(+)` | `0` |
| `Num a => a` | `Product a` | `(*)` | `1` |
| `Bool` | `Any` | `(||)` | `False` |
| `Bool` | `All` | `(&&)` | `True` |
| `A` | `First a` | `\x y -> x` | - |
| `A` | `Last a` | `\x y -> y` | - |
| `Ord a => a` | `Min a` | `min` | `maxBound` `(Bounded a)` |
| `Ord a => a` | `Max a` | `max` | `minBound` `(Bounded a)` |
| `Semigroup a => Maybe a` | - | `see chapter` | `Nothing` |
| `A` | `Dual a` | `flip (<>)` | `mempty` |
| `a -> a` | `Endo a` | `(.)` | `id` |

4.  Type constructors are types that have a higher kind. Whereas proper types, which have kind `*`, are the types of values, type constructors are incomplete and need to be applied to one or more type parameters before they form a proper type. The incompleteness is characterized by a higher kind of the form `k1 -> k2`, which denotes that after application to a type parameter of kind `k1`, a type of kind `k2` is obtained. The most common type constructors have kind `* -> *` or kind `* -> * -> *`; that is, they take respectively one or two parameters that are proper types.

Here are some examples of type constructors from the standard library:

```
[]          :: * -> *
Maybe    :: * -> *
Sum      :: * -> *
Product :: * -> *
First    :: * -> *
Last     :: * -> *

Either :: * -> * -> *
Map      :: * -> * -> *
(->)     :: * -> * -> *
(,)      :: * -> * -> *
```

5.  Foldables are t type constructors of kind `* -> *` that have an instance of the `Foldable` type class. In essence, they are collections whose elements can be enumerated, and thus aggregated. The minimal complete definition of `Foldable` is given by either `foldr :: (a -> b -> b) -> b -> t a -> b` or `foldMap :: Monoid m => (a -> m) -> t a -> m`.

The other methods in the type class are various forms of aggregations or variations on the preceding general recursion schemes for aggregation.

# 10

# Functors, Applicative Functors, and Traversables

This chapter leads us much further into Haskell's hierarchy of type classes for type constructors: functors, applicative functors, and traversables.

We will introduce the three abstractions in turn as a generalization of particular list-related functionality: mapping, zipping, and mapping with zipping. These list functions provide a good intuition for the mechanics of the generalizations. However, for applicative functors, the notion of *effectful computations* provides a much better and more important intuition.

Effectful computations are computations that do not only (or necessarily) produce a result. They also do or can do something additional (such as logging, failing, or changing a mutable state) that somehow interacts with the context in which the computation takes place. This is called the (side) effect of the computation.

It is quite paradoxical. On the one hand, Haskell is called a *purely* functional programming language and emphasizes that its functions do not have side effects. On the other hand, Haskell has a more sophisticated infrastructure (in the form of libraries) to model, classify, and structure effectful computations than most impure programming languages. In some sense, effects can be seen as one of the main *obsessions* of the language.

How do we reconcile these two opposites? Well, with its infrastructure, Haskell acknowledges that side effects are undeniably convenient for practical and pragmatic programming. At the same time, it aims to harness their use with a structured, type-based approach that prevents unbridled and unmanageable proliferation.

In short, this chapter covers the following main topics:

- What are functors?
- What are applicative functors?
- What computational effects can we model with applicative functors?
- How do we map over traversable functors with effectful functions?

# Functors

The first constructor type class we will encounter in this chapter is perhaps the simplest of all: `Functor`. This type class generalizes the higher-order `map :: (a -> b) -> ([a] -> [b])`.

Recall the definition of `map`:

```
Prelude
map :: (a -> b) -> ([a] -> [b])
map f [] = []
map f (x:xs) = f x : map f xs
```

The second pair of parentheses in the type signature of `map` can be dropped without changing the meaning. Nevertheless, I like to add them to emphasize that `map` lifts a function, `(a -> b)`, on elements to a function, `([a] -> [b])`, on lists.

The idea is that `map` transforms the elements of the list without changing the structure of the list itself:

```
*Main> map show [1,2,3,4]
["1","2","3","4"]
```

The `Functor` type class generalizes this idea from lists to other type constructors of the `* -> *` kind:

```
Prelude
class Functor f where
  fmap :: (a -> b) -> (f a -> f b)
  (<$) :: b -> (f a -> f b)
  x <$ t = fmap (\_ -> x) t
```

The generalized name of `map` is `fmap`, where `f` is short for functor; it is sometimes also called the **functorial** map. A type constructor that instantiates this type of class is also called a functor.

The `(<$)` operator is derived from `fmap`; it replaces every element in the collection with the same new value. It is a method in the type class that allows more efficient implementations than the default one.

The most obvious instance is that for lists:

```
Prelude
instance Functor [] where
  fmap = map
```

Hence, we can also write the following:

```
*Main> fmap show [1,2,3,4]
["1","2","3","4"]
*Main> '*' <$ "1234"
"****"
```

For convenience, the standard library also provides the infix operator, (<$>), as an alias for fmap:

```
*Main> show <$> [1,2,3,4]
["1","2","3","4"]
```

The laws of the type class are a guide for writing other instances.

# The functor laws

The idea is that fmap transforms the elements without changing the structure of the collection itself. This is captured in the two **Functor** laws.

## The identity law

The first law is called the **identity** law:

```
fmap id = id
```

This law expresses that if we don't change the elements (by using id :: a -> a), then we don't change anything (by using id :: f a -> f a).

Consider, for instance, the following collection type of pairs:

```
data Pair a = MkPair a a
  deriving Show
```

We could write the following unlawful instance:

```
instance Functor Pair where
  fmap f (MkPair x y) = MkPair (f y) (f x) -- invalid!
```

It violates the identity law because it swaps the order of the two elements. In this way, it twists the shape of the data structure:

```
*Main> fmap id (MkPair 1 2)
Pair 2 1
```

The only valid instance is as follows:

```
instance Functor Pair where
  fmap f (MkPair x y) = MkPair (f x) (f y)
```

This keeps the elements in their place.

## The fusion law

The second law is called the **fusion** law:

```
fmap f . fmap g = fmap (f . g)
```

This law is less important when writing an instance because it follows automatically from the identity law. However, for optimization purposes, this law is very interesting. When read from left to right, it allows us to combine (or fuse) two consecutive traversals of the collection into a single one. As a consequence, the intermediate data structure (the output of fmap  g) is never created, which can yield a noticeable speed-up of the program.

For example, if we increment and show the elements of a pair, we can do so with two fmap instances:

```
*Main> fmap show (fmap (+1) (Pair 1 2))
Pair "2" "3"
```

However, this creates the intermediate Pair "2" "3" value, which we can avoid with fusion:

```
*Main> fmap (show . (+1)) (Pair 1 2)
Pair "2" "3"
```

This does not create the intermediate pair.

## Functor instances

The Maybe :: * -> * type constructor is another example from the standard library that has a Functor instance:

```
Prelude
instance Functor Maybe where
  fmap f (Just x) = Just (f x)
  fmap f Nothing = Nothing
```

This instance transforms the value in the Just constructor and does nothing in the case of Nothing. Be aware that we cannot replace the last line with a simpler case of fmap  f  y  =  y because y is of the Maybe  a type, whereas the result should be of the Maybe  b type.

Type constructors of the *  ->  *  ->  * kind, such as (,), Either, and Map, also have a Functor instance, albeit only in their second parameter. Here's an example:

```
Prelude
instance Functor ((,) a) where
  fmap f (a,b) = (a, f b)
```

Here, the functorial map only transforms the second component of the tuple:

```
*Main> fmap show (1,2)
(1,"2")
```

While not part of the standard library, several library packages provide a notion of a bifunctor for `*`
`-> * -> *` that supports the transformation of both parameters.

The `IO :: * -> *` type constructor has a `Functor` instance too:

```
Prelude
instance Functor IO where
  fmap f p = p >>= \x-> return (f x)
```

This extends the computation, `p`, with a transformation of its result that uses the pure function, `f`.

Observe that the `IO` type constructor represents a computation with side effects. It is not appropriate
to think of it as a collection; we certainly cannot extract any elements from it. However, that is also
not required by the `Functor` type class. All that is required is that a lawful `fmap` function can be
defined of the appropriate type. That makes `Functor` more abstract than the somewhat informal
notion of a collection.

If you are curious, the one key element that makes a type constructor not a functor is if its parameter
appears to the left of a function arrow. For example, recall the type of endofunctions from the
previous chapter:

```
Data.Semigroup
newtype Endo r = Endo { appEndo :: r -> r}
```

Here, `r` appears to the left of the function arrow. The problem with writing `fmap` is that, given a
function, `f :: r -> s`, we cannot change `e :: r -> r` into `s -> s`. Yes, we can change `r`
on the right into `s` via function composition, `f . e :: r -> s`. However, there is no way we
can get rid of the remaining `r` with `f`. What we need is the opposite – a function, `f' :: s -> r`,
but that is the opposite of what `fmap` supplies.

Finally, like `Foldable`, we can automatically derive `Functor` by enabling the corresponding
language extension. Namely, if we write the `{-# LANGUAGE DeriveFunctor -#}` pragma at
the top of the file, we don't have to write the instance manually anymore:

```
data Pair a = MkPair a a
  deriving (Functor, Show)
```

As there is essentially no room for variation when writing the `Functor` instance, automatically
deriving the instance always gives the right behavior.

# Applicative functors

Just like the notion of `Functor` can be understood as a generalization of the map function for lists to other type constructors, the notion of `Applicative` functors is a generalization of the `zip`/`zipWith` functions for lists. However, for the sake of generality, it requires a variant of the `zip` and `zipWith` functions that we are already familiar with. Hence, we will explain that setup first before we dive into the general notion of `Applicative` functors.

## A family of zip functions

The standard library provides several `zip`-like functions to merge lists. The basic one is defined as follows:

```
Prelude
zip :: [a] -> [b] -> [(a,b)]
zip []     ys     = []
zip xs     []     = []
zip (x:xs) (y:ys) = (x,y) : zip xs ys
```

This merges the two given lists into a new list by combining the elements at the corresponding positions into a tuple. The new list comes to an end when one of the two lists runs out of elements:

```
*Main> zip [1..10] ["annie","bob","charlie"]
[(1,"annie"),(2,"bob"),(3,"charlie")]
```

What if you want to combine three, four, five, or more lists? The standard library provides similar functions for those occasions:

```
Prelude
zip3 :: [a] -> [b] -> [c] -> [(a, b, c)]
Data.List
zip4 :: [a] -> [b] -> [c] -> [d] -> [(a, b, c, d)]
zip5 :: [a] -> [b] -> [c] -> [d] -> [e] -> [(a, b, c, d, e)]
...
```

This only goes up to seven, so tough luck if you want to combine eight lists.

What if you are not interested in a tuple, but a different function of the corresponding elements? Then `zipWith` does the job:

```
Prelude
zipWith :: (a -> b -> c) -> [a] -> [b] -> [c]
zipWith f []     ys     = []
zipWith f xs     []     = []
zipWith f (x:xs) (y:ys) = f x y : zipWith f xs ys
```

This takes a function parameter that explains how the elements should be combined:

```
*Main> zipWith replicate [1..10] "abcd"
["a","bb","ccc","dddd"]
```

Again, there are variations for combining three to seven lists – that is, zipWith3, ..., zipWith7.

Do we need so many different functions? Can we provide a slimmer interface?

### *zip versus zipWith*

We don't need both the zip and zipWith variants as they can be interdefined. Firstly, zip is zipWith, where the function that's used is the tuple data constructor:

```
Prelude
zip :: [a] -> [b] -> [(a,b)]
zip = zipWith (,)
```

Conversely, zipWith can also be defined in terms of zip and map:

```
Prelude
zipWith :: (a -> b -> c) -> [a] -> [b] -> [c]
zipWith f xs ys = fmap (\(x,y) -> f x y) (zip xs ys)
```

This is maybe a little bit less interesting than the other way around because it creates an intermediate list of tuples that is immediately discarded again.

### *zipWith3, zipWith4, zipWith5, ...*

It is impossible to write a variant of zipWith for every number of lists. Fortunately, we can work around that with a special case of zipWith. This special case is as follows:

```
zipApply :: [b -> c] -> [b] -> [c]
zipApply []        xs      = []
zipApply fs        []      = []
zipApply (f:fs) (x:xs) = f x : zipApply fs xs
```

This takes a list of functions and a list of values and applies the corresponding function to the corresponding value. It can be defined as zipWith ($), where the ($) operator is the function application. More importantly, this function can be used to define zipWith itself:

```
Prelude
zipWith :: (a -> b -> c) -> [a] -> [b] -> [c]
zipWith f xs ys = zipApply (map f xs) ys
```

With `map f xs` , we combine the function and the first list into a list of functions of the `[b -> c]` type. Then, `zipApply` can produce the final result, similar to how we can define `zipWith3`:

```
Prelude
zipWith3 :: (a -> b -> c -> d) -> [a] -> [b] -> [c] -> [d]
zipWith3 f xs ys zs = zipApply (zipApply (map f xs) ys) zs
```

Now, `map f xs` combines the function and the first list into a list of functions of the `[b -> c -> d]` type. Next, `zipApply` combines that with `ys` into a list of functions, `[c -> d]`. The final `zipApply` incorporates the last list and yields the final result.

This approach works more generally. If we want to zip together n lists, we need 1 call to `map` and n-1 calls to `zipApply`. We can see `map` as `zipWith1`. Finally, there is also `zipWith0 :: a -> [a]`, which, given a function with zero inputs and zero lists, produces a list. It is called `repeat` and generates an infinite list. Together, these three functions form a minimal interface:

```
repeat   :: a -> [a]
map      :: (a -> b) -> [a] -> [b]
zipApply :: [a -> b] -> [a] -> [b]
```

The `Functor` type class already generalizes `map`. We will now do the same with `repeat` and `zipApply`.

## The Applicative type class

The `Applicative` type class provides an abstraction for type constructors that support a `zipApply`-like function:

```
Prelude
class Functor f => Applicative f where

    pure :: a -> f a

    (<*>) :: f (a -> b) -> f a -> f b
```

This type class has the `pure` and `(<*>)` methods, which generalize `repeat` and `zipApply`. Moreover, it is a subclass of `Functor`. This way, it also comes with the `fmap` generalization of `map`.

The standard instance of this type class is the one for lists that we started with. However, because the type class allows for some leeway, there is a second instance for lists. To distinguish them, the one we are interested in has a newtype `wrapper` called `ZipList`:

```
Control.Applicative
newtype ZipList a = ZipList { getZipList :: [a] }
    deriving Functor
```

This has the `zip`-based instance:

```
Control.Applicative
instance Applicative ZipList where
  pure x = ZipList (repeat x)
  ZipList fs <*> ZipList xs = ZipList (zipApply fs xs)
```

Before we see a range of (more) interesting instances, let's briefly review the laws that they need to satisfy.

## The applicative law

The `Applicative` type class comes with four laws. These laws capture the analogy with ordinary function application, written with whitespace or the (`$`) operator, between a function of the `a -> b` type and a parameter of the `a` type. The applicative counterpart is the (`<*>`) operator for application and the `f (a -> b)` function and the `f a` parameter live inside the type constructor, `f`. The name *applicative functor* comes precisely from this analogy.

### The identity law

The identity law lifts the definition of the identity function, (`id x = x`), to a law at the level of applicative functors. It states that `pure id` is the left identity of the (`<*>`) operator:

```
pure id <*> v = v
```

This explains the choice of `repeat` for `pure` in the case of `ZipList`: when zipping an infinite list with another list, the infinite list always has enough elements to line up with the other list and hence the result has the same shape as the other list.

### The composition law

Recall that function composition is defined as (`.`) `f g x = f (g x)`. The composition law lifts this to the applicative functor level:

```
pure (.) <*> u <*> v <*> w = u <*> (v <*> w)
```

### The homomorphism law

The third law says that `pure` relates ordinary function application and the `Applicative` operator, (`<*>`):

```
pure f <*> pure x = pure (f x)
```

We can either perform a pure function application and then wrap the result in an applicative functor, or we can wrap the function and its input first and then apply (`<*>`) to them.

### The interchange law

The last law states that we can swap the position of `pure` in a `(<*>)` composition:

```
u <*> pure y = pure ($ y) <*> u
```

It generalizes a similar property of pure functions: `f y = ($ y) f`. Here, `($ y)` is the right operator section of the `($)` operator.

One more relevant property concerns the relationship between `fmap` and `pure`:

```
pure f <*> u = fmap f u
```

Recall that `<$>` is the operator synonym of `fmap`, which somewhat resembles `(<*>)`. It is often used to write the following:

```
pure f <*> u = f <$> u
```

While these laws characterize the function application-like nature of applicative functors, they do not give us much of a sense of their practical use. We will explore this next while we review a range of different instances.

## Applicative functors and effects

While we have used `ZipList` and the family of `zip` functions as our initial intuition for the notion of applicative functors, there is a different notion that is helpful to understand most `Applicative` instances: *(computational) effects*. The idea is that, whereas A denotes a readily available value, F A denotes a computation that yields a value of A. Depending on the type of computation, F, other relevant effects may happen during the computation. For example, the computation may fail for some reason, and thus not produce a value at all. We will explore this and several other possible effects through different `Applicative` instances.

### Failing computations with Maybe

Failing computations may or may not yield a result. We have already modeled these using the `Maybe` type constructor, where `Just x` denotes a successful outcome with a result, x, and `Nothing` denotes failure to produce a result.

This type of constructor has the following `instance`:

```
Prelude
instance Applicative Maybe where
  pure x = Just x
  Nothing <*> _ = Nothing
  _ <*> Nothing = Nothing
  Just f <*> Just x = Just (f x)
```

With `pure`, we lift a readily available value, x, into a possibly failing computation. The application operator, (`<*>`), fails if either the function or its parameter fails, and only succeeds when both function and parameter can be produced.

For example, suppose we have a list of functions and a list of parameters, both associated with their names:

```
funs :: [(String, Float -> Float)]
funs = [("sine",sin),("cosine",cos),("increment",(+1))]

params :: [(String,Float)]
params = [("pi",pi),("zero",0),("x",5)]
```

Now, we can use the applicative interface to apply a named function to a named parameter, using `lookup :: Eq a => a -> [(a, b)] -> Maybe b` to fetch them by name:

```
fun :: String -> Maybe (Float -> Float)
fun f = lookup f funs

param :: String  -> Maybe Float
param p = lookup p params
```

```
*Main> fun "increment" <*> param "zero"
Just 1.0
```

If either the function name or the parameter name is not defined, the computation fails:

```
*Main> fun "decrement" <*> param "zero"
Nothing
*Main> fun "increment" <*> param "y"
Nothing
```

## Erroneous computations with Either

In the previous failure example, the result of `Nothing` does not tell us what went wrong: is the function missing or is the parameter missing? Errors are one level up from failure; they convey why the failure happened. We model such erroneous computations with the `Either :: * -> * -> *` type constructor. Here, `Right x :: Either e a` denotes a successful result, x, of the a type (like `Just x :: Maybe a` does). In case of failure, we get `Left r :: Either e a`, where `r :: e` is some error value that explains what went wrong.

The instance for `Either e` adapts that of `Maybe`:

```
Prelude
instance Applicative (Either e) where
  pure x = Right x
  Left r <*> _ = Left r
  _ <*> Left r = Left r
  Right f <*> Right x = Right (f x)
```

For our example, we can write a custom error with two data constructors for the two error cases:

```
data ApplicationError = MissingFunction String
                      | MissingParameter String
                      deriving Show
```

Let's write a little bit more infrastructure around the `lookup` calls:

```
fun :: String -> Either ApplicationError (Float -> Float)
fun f = maybe (Left (MissingFunction f)) Right (lookup f funs)


param :: String  -> Either ApplicationError Float
param p = maybe (Left (MissingParameter p)) Right
               (lookup p params)
```

This gives us more information when an error occurs:

```
*Main> fun "increment" <*> param "zero"
Right 1.0
*Main> fun "decrement" <*> param "zero"
Left (MissingFunction "decrement")
*Main> fun "increment" <*> param "y"
Left (MissingParameter "y")
```

## Implicitly parameterized computations with functions

Our previous two examples both depended on the globally defined lists of functions and parameters. A different approach is one where we can supply different values for the function and the parameter on different runs of the program. Let's define an environment that holds the two:

```
data ApplicationEnv = Env { fun :: Float -> Float
                          , param :: Float }
```

This gives us two (projection) functions that select the function and the parameter from the environment:

```
fun   :: ApplicationEnv -> (Float -> Float)
param :: ApplicationEnv -> Float
```

We can see both as computations that rely on an environment to produce a result. These form an `Applicative` instance for any type of environment:

```
Prelude
instance Applicative ((->) env) where
  pure x    = \ env -> x
  pf <*> px = \ env -> (pf env) (px env)
```

This allows us to write the following:

```
prog :: ApplicationEnv -> Float
prog = fun <*> param
```

On different runs, we can then supply different values to vary the behavior:

```
*Main> prog (Env { fun = (+1), param = 0 })
1.0
*Main> prog (Env { fun = (*2), param = 3 })
6.0
```

## Analyzing computations with the Const functor

We can analyze a computation *without actually executing it*, and just calculate some metrics about it. This involves using the Const functor:

```
Data.Functor.Const
newtype Const m a = Const { getConst :: m }
```

The Const functor is an edge case of a functor: Const m a does not actually contain or otherwise involve any value of the a type. We can see this in the following Functor instance:

```
Data.Functor.Const
instance Functor (Const m) where
  fmap f (Const m) = Const m
```

Here, the mapped function, f, goes unused because there is nothing to apply it to. The purpose of this constant functor is the actual payload of the m type. In the Applicative instance, we expect this type, m, to be a monoid:

```
Data.Functor.Const
instance Monoid m => Applicative (Const m) where
  pure x = Const mempty
  Const m1 <*> Const m2 = Const (m1 <> m2)
```

Because Const m a does not contain any a, pure x does not store x. Likewise, (<*>) does not apply any function to any value, because neither is available. Instead, pure allocates the mempty value and (<*>) aggregates those values.

As a small application, consider the well-known Fibonacci function:

```
fib :: Integer -> Integer
fib n
  | n < 2     = 1
  | otherwise = fib (n - 1) + fib (n - 2)
```

Suppose we wish to analyze how many recursive calls happen without actually computing the result. We can count with the `(Sum Integer)` monoid; the `Const (Sum Integer)` applicative functor only takes care of tracking that count and not computing the Fibonacci numbers. Using that, we can introduce a primitive operation tick that records a single call:

```
tick :: Const (Sum Integer) ()
tick = Const (Sum 1)
```

As the result value is irrelevant here, we use `()`. The actual purpose of `tick` is its side effect, counting `1`.

We introduce this `tick` in the definition of `fib`:

```
fib :: Integer -> Const (Sum Integer) Integer
fib n
  | n < 2     =  tick *> pure 1
  | otherwise =  tick *> (pure (+) <*> fib (n - 1) <*> fib (n -2))
```

We use the `tick *> p` combination because we only want the side effect of `tick` and then leave it up to p to produce a result. Here, `(*>)` is a predefined operator derived from `(<*>)` that discards the result of its left operand:

```
Prelude
(*>) :: Applicative f => f a -> f b -> f b
px *> py = pure (\x y -> y) <*> px <*> py
```

The operator has an obvious dual, `(<*)`, that discards the result of its second operand.

Let's see `fib` in action:

```
*Main> fib 5
Const {getConst = Sum {getSum = 15}}
```

This tells us that computing the 5th Fibonacci number takes 15 calls to `fib`.

## Logging computations with tuples

If we want to produce a metric, or a *log* of some sort, alongside the actual computation, we can use a variant on the `Const` functor, namely tuples:

```
Prelude
instance Monoid m => Applicative ((,) m) where
  pure x  = (mempty, x)
  (m1,f) <*> (m2,x) = (m1 <> m2, f x)
```

Here, a computation consists of a tuple where the first component is the log, which is a value of some monoid, and the second component is the result of the computation. The first component of the tuple behaves like the constant functor and the second component behaves like a pure computation.

In the case of the `String` monoid (that is, the list monoid), the log is conventional and accumulates text messages. In the case of the `Sum Integer` monoid, as we saw previously, we are counting. This requires a slightly modified definition of the `tick` operation:

```
tick :: (Sum Integer, ())
tick = (Sum 1, ())
```

It now produces a `()` value alongside the count.

The only thing we need to change in our applicative definition of `fib` is its type:

```
fib :: Integer -> (Sum Integer, Integer)
fib n
  | n < 2     = tick *> pure 1
  | otherwise = tick *> (pure (+) <*> fib (n - 1) <*> fib (n -2))
```

The modified type conveys that the result is computed alongside the count:

```
*Main> fib 5
(Sum {getSum = 15},8)
```

Now, we can see that the 5th Fibonacci number is 8 and, as before, that it took 15 calls for `fib` to compute this.

With a custom monoid, we can get more detailed statistics. This custom monoid is based on the `Map` data structure:

```
newtype MonoidMap k v = MM { runMM :: Map k v }
  deriving Show
```

We define the combination of two maps as their union:

```
instance (Ord k, Semigroup v) => Semigroup (MonoidMap k v) where
  MM m1 <> MM m2 = MM (unionWith (<>) m1 m2)
```

We require that the values in the map are elements of a semigroup. This way, when the two maps have a common key, the two values for that common key can be combined:

Moreover, the empty map is the neutral element of the union:

```
instance (Ord k, Semigroup v) => Monoid (MonoidMap k v) where
  mempty = MM empty
```

We can modify the definition of `tick` to record with which parameter, n, `fib` is called with this:

```
tick :: Integer -> (MonoidMap Integer (Sum Integer), ())
tick n = (MM (singleton n (Sum 1)),())
```

Now, `fib` can declare that its parameter is n with `tick n`:

```
fib :: Integer -> (MonoidMap Integer (Sum Integer), Integer)
fib n
  | n < 2     = tick n *> pure 1
  | otherwise =
      tick n *> (pure (+) <*> fib (n - 1) <*> fib (n -2))
```

This way, we can see how often `fib` is called recursively for different parameter values:

```
*Main> fib 5
(MM {runMM = fromList [(0,Sum {getSum = 3}),(1,Sum {getSum =
5}),(2,Sum {getSum = 3}),(3,Sum {getSum = 2}),(4,Sum {getSum =
1}),(5,Sum {getSum = 1})]},8)
```

As we can see, there are a lot of repeated calls.

## Stateful computations with State

We can avoid repeated calls by using a technique known as **memoization** or **tabulation**. This involves storing the intermediate results in a table and reusing them rather than recomputing them whenever possible. This requires stateful computation: the computation passes around a state that can be consulted and updated.

Let's model a stateful computation with the `State` type:

```
Control.Monad.State
newtype State s a = State { runState :: s -> (a,s) }
  deriving Functor
```

This is a `newtype` wrapper around the function type, `s -> (a,s)`. These functions take a state of the s type as input and use it to produce a result of the a type and an updated state.

The `Applicative` instance of `State s` threads the state through a computation:

```
Control.Monad.State
instance Applicative (State s) where
  pure x = State (\s -> (x,s))
  State pf <*> State px = State (\s0 -> let (f,s1) = pf s0
                                            (x,s2) = px s1
                                        in  (f x, s2))
```

In the `pure` definition, the input state is not used and is simply returned as-is. In the `(<*>)` definition, the input state, s0, is passed into the first computation, pf, which yields an intermediate state, s1, that is passed to the second computation, px, and results in the final state, s2.

For our running example, we use a state of the `Map Integer Integer` type to store the already computed results. We split the `fib` function into two mutually recursive parts. The first part checks whether the state already contains a result and uses that if possible. Otherwise, it calls the worker function to compute the state and stores it afterward:

```
fib :: Integer -> State (Map Integer Integer) Integer
fib n = State (\ s ->
  case Map.lookup n s of
    Just f  -> (f, s)
    Nothing -> let (f, s') = runState (fib' n) s
               in  (f, insert n f s'))


  where
    fib' n
      | n < 2      = pure 1
      | otherwise = (+) <$> fib (n-1) <*> fib (n-2)
```

This approach avoids repeated recomputation of the same Fibonacci number and is known as **memoization**.

## Nondeterministic computations with lists

The standard `Applicative` instance for lists is not that of `ZipList`, but one that uses lists to module *nondeterministic* computations. A nondeterministic computation does not have a single uniquely determined result. For several reasons, it may not be able to commit to a single result and simply offers several results. One reason can be that multiple results are valid, and it is left to the downstream consumers of the result to choose which one they want to use. Another reason can be that the precise value is not known, only that it is among those provided.

The `Applicative` instance treats such nondeterministic computations in a combinatorial fashion:

```
Prelude
instance Applicative [] where
  pure x = [x]
  pf <*> px = [f x | f <- pf, x <- px]
```

A `pure` computation is one with a single result, while the nondeterministic function application considers all possible combinations of the nondeterministic function and its nondeterministic parameter.

For example, when budgeting the renovation of a house, you don't know whether a cheap fix (1,000 euros) will do the trick or a more expensive solution (3,500 euros) is required. Also, you are uncertain whether you'll have to pay the standard 21% VAT or whether the house is older than 10 years and amenable to the reduced VAT of 6%.

We can model this as follows:

```
basePrice :: [Float]
basePrice = [1000,3500]

vat :: [Float]
vat = [0.06,0.21]
```

From this, we can see the total amount you have to pay will be as follows:

```
*Main> (\b v -> b * (1 + v)) <$> basePrice <*> vat
[1060.0,1210.0,3710.0,4235.0]
```

This result reflects the combination of each base price with each VAT amount. In contrast, ziplists would only pair the corresponding values: the base price of 1,000 euros with the 6% VAT and the base price of 3,500 euros with the 21% VAT.

## No effect

In addition to all the earlier examples, which all model different kinds of side effects, there is one applicative functor that models pure computations, which feature no effects. This is the `Identity` applicative functor, which is a trivial `newtype` wrapper around pure values:

```
Data.Functor.Identity
newtype Identity a = Identity { runIdentity :: a }
  deriving Functor
```

All its `Applicative` instance does is unwrap and wrap pure values; no actual side effects can happen:

```
Data.Functor.Identity
instance Applicative Identity where
  pure x = Identity x
  Identity f <*> Identity x = Identity (f x)
```

It is used in cases where an applicative functor must be provided, but no effect is required.

## Compositions

Now that we have seen an assortment of different types of effectful computation,

We will turn to the natural question, *"What if I want to use multiple effects in the same program?"*

This is possible by coming up with a custom representation and writing a new `Applicative` instance from scratch. However, much more conveniently, we can combine existing instances using either a *product* or a *composition*.

## The product of applicative functors

The product of two applicative functors, f and g, runs two computations, using f and g in parallel:

```
Data.Functor.Product
data Product f g a = Pair (f a) (g a)
```

This product of two computations is a functor when its two first parameters are functors:

```
Data.Functor.Product
instance (Functor f, Functor g) => Functor (Product f g) where
  fmap f (Pair x y) = Pair (fmap f x) (fmap f y)
```

In the same way, the `Applicative` instance defines its methods component-wise:

```
Data.Functor.Product
instance (Applicative f, Applicative g)
  => Applicative (Product f g) where
  pure x = Pair (pure x) (pure x)
  Pair pf qf <*> Pair px qx = Pair (pf <*> px) (qf <*> qx)
```

The definition of `(<*>)` shows that the two parallel computations happen in lockstep. However, data isn't exchanged between them; they are independent and each produces its own result.

We have already seen an example of this product construction, namely the `(m, )` tuple applicative functor. It is essentially a specialized definition of `Product (Const m) Identity`. While such a specialized definition does not reuse the existing instance code, it avoids the nested constructors. This makes it a bit more convenient to use and slightly more efficient.

## The composition of applicative functors

While a bit harder to wrap your head around, the composition of two applicative functors is often more useful than their product. It allows effects to interact and contribute toward a common result.

By looking at the composition of two functors, we can understand their nesting:

```
Data.Functor.Compose
newtype Compose f g a = Compose { getCompose :: f (g a) }
```

Its `Functor` instance maps through the two layers:

```
Data.Functor.Compose
instance (Functor f, Functor g) => Functor (Compose f g) where
  fmap f (Compose t) = Compose (fmap (fmap f) t)
```

The `Applicative` instance handles the two layers similarly:

```
Data.Functor.Compose
instance (Applicative f, Applicative g)
  => Applicative (Compose f g) where
  pure x = Compose (pure (pure x))
  Compose pqf <*> Compose pqx  =
    Compose ((\qf qx -> qf <*> qx) <$> pqf <*> pqx)
```

The `pure` method stacks two layers of pure computation, and the `(<*>)` operator uses a `zipWith` strategy on the outer layers that zips the corresponding inner layers.

Using this composition, we can define a variant of the Fibonacci function that involves both memoization and logging:

```
type Memoization = State (Map Integer Integer)
type Logging     = (,) (MonoidMap Integer (Sum Integer))
type Effect      = Compose Memoization Logging
```

The new definition that features the two effects is now essentially a merge of the two earlier definitions with their single effect:

```
fib :: Integer -> Effect Integer
fib n =
  Compose (State (\ s ->
    case Map.lookup n s of
      Just f  -> (pure f, s)
      Nothing -> let ((m,f), s') =
                        runState (getCompose (fib' n)) s
                 in ((m,f), insert n f s')))
  where
    fib' n
      | n < 2     = lift (tick n) *> pure 1
      | otherwise =
          lift (tick n) *> ((+) <$> fib (n-1) <*> fib (n-2))

    lift q = Compose (pure q)
```

The main addition to the earlier code is that we have to acknowledge the presence of the other code. This means applying the `lift` function to `tick`, to wrap it in the composition. Similarly, the memoization logic now acknowledges the presence of the log m.

Let's run this new Fibonacci function with a memoization table that is initially empty:

```
*Main> runState (getCompose (fib 10)) empty
((MM {ruMM = fromList [(0,Sum {getSum = 1}),(1,Sum {getSum =
1}),(2,Sum {getSum = 1}),(3,Sum {getSum = 1}),(4,Sum {getSum =
1}),(5,Sum {getSum = 1}),(6,Sum {getSum = 1}),(7,Sum {getSum =
1}),(8,Sum {getSum = 1}),(9,Sum {getSum = 1}),(10,Sum {getSum =
1})]},89),fromList [(0,1),(1,1),(2,2),(3,3),(4,5),(5,8),(6,13),(7,21),
(8,34),(9,55),(10,89)])
```

The result is a nested tuple of the form ((callstats, result), memotable):

- The call statistics are a table that associates a call count of 1 with each number in the range of 0 to 10

- The result is 89

- The memoization table associates each Fibonacci number with each number in the range of 0 to 10

Hence, we can confirm that memoization does its job and computes each Fibonacci number only once.

## Traversables

Recall that the functorial map (fmap) lifts pure functions of the a -> b type to functions on collections of the t a -> t b type. The Traversable type class generalizes this to effectful functions, a -> f b, with f as an applicative functor.

First, let's compare the two for lists (viewed as a collection, not as an effect):

```
fmap :: (a -> b) -> ([a] -> [b])
fmap f []     = []
fmap f (x:xs) = f x : fmap f xs


traverse :: Applicative f => (a -> f b) -> ([a] -> f [b])
traverse f []     = pure []
traverse f (x:xs) = pure (:) <*> f x <*> traverse f xs
```

As we can see, the structure is quite similar. The main difference is that traverse uses the application, (<*>), of applicative functors, and lifts the list constructors with pure.

## The Traversable class

The type class declaration looks as follows:

```
Prelude
class (Functor t, Foldable t) => Traversable t where
  traverse  :: Applicative f => (a -> f b) -> t a -> f (t b)
  sequenceA :: Applicative f => t (f a) -> f (t a)
  mapM      :: Monad m => (a -> m b) -> t a -> m (t b)
  sequence  :: Monad m => t (m a) -> m (t a)
```

The second method, `sequenceA`, is a special case of `traverse` where the elements are already computations. The two methods traverse and `sequenceA` can be inter-defined:

```
sequenceA = traverse id

traverse f = sequenceA . fmap f
```

A minimal complete definition comprises either of the two.

The other two methods, `mapM` and `sequence`, are special cases of the first two for the monad concept that we'll introduce in the next chapter. We won't discuss them any further here.

## Instances

The `Traversable` instances of other data types follow the same structure as those for lists. They follow that of their `Functor` instance, but wrap the constructor in the applicative functor with `pure`, and replace the ordinary function application with (`<*>`).

As a second example of this approach, let's look at the instance for `Maybe`:

```
Prelude
instance Traversable Maybe where
  traverse f Nothing = pure Nothing
  traverse f (Just x) = pure Just <*> f x
```

Because of the formulaic nature of these instances, they can be easily automated. We can enable automatic derivation with the {-# DeriveTraversable #-} pragma.

Then, we can just write a deriving clause when defining a new data type:

```
data Tree a = Leaf a | Fork (Tree a) (Tree a)
  deriving Traversable
```

This automatically generates the obvious instance for us:

```
instance Traversable Tree where
  traverse f (Leaf x)   = pure Leaf <*> f x
  traverse f (Fork l r) =
    pure Fork <*> traverse f l <*> traverse f r
```

The laws of `Traversable`, which we'll discuss next, do not leave us much leeway. There is rarely a reason to deviate from the automatically derived instance.

## The traversable laws

The `Data.Traversable` library lists three laws.

### Naturality

The **naturality** property allows us to incorporate a transformation, `t`, of the effect into the traversal:

```
t . traverse f = traverse (t . f)
```

Here, f is of the `A -> F B` type for some applicative functor, F, and types A and B. The t function is meant to be an *applicative transformation* from F to some other applicative functor, G. Such an applicative transformation is a polymorphic function of the `F a -> G a` type that satisfies two properties:

```
t (pure x) = pure x
t (u <*> v) = t u <*> t v
```

In other words, t maps the applicative functor methods, `pure` and `(<*>)`, of F to those of G.

An example of an applicative transformation from `Either ApplicationError` to `Maybe` forgets the errors:

```
eraseError :: Either ApplicationError a -> Maybe a
eraseError (Left r)  = Nothing
eraseError (Right x) = Just x
```

The naturality law allows us to perform this conversion either after the traversal or for every element.

### Identity

This law states that the identity traversal preserves the data structure; it adapts the identity law of functors (`fmap id = id`):

```
traverse Identity = Identity
```

This is expressed in terms of the `Identity` applicative functor that we saw earlier. To summarize, that law expresses that, if we don't change the elements and produce no side effects, we don't change the data structure.

## Composition

The composition law is an adaptation of the fusion law for functors (`fmap (g . f) = fmap g . fmap f`):

```
traverse (Compose . fmap g . f)
=
Compose . fmap (traverse g) . traverse f
```

Instead of two successive traversals with different effects, we can perform a single traversable with the composition of the two effects. The latter prevents the creation of an intermediate data structure.

# Case study – word count

As a small case study, we will write a program that collects several statistics of a piece of text. As an example text, we'll use Hokusai's haiku, *A Poppy Blooms*:

```
haiku :: String
haiku = unlines ["I write, erase, rewrite"
                ,"Erase again, and then"
                ,"A poppy blooms."]
```

## Character count

One of the simplest statistics is to count the number of characters in the text. For that, we can use the `Const (Sum Integer)` applicative functor:

```
type Count = Const (Sum Integer)
```

We count 1 for every character:

```
count :: Integer -> a -> Count b
count n _ = Const (Sum n)
```

With `traverse`, we can apply this to a whole string and the applicative functor will aggregate the counts:

```
charCount :: String -> Integer
charCount = getCount . traverse (count 1)
```

Here, getCount is a handy function to extract the integer value:

```
getCount :: Count a -> Integer
getCount = getSum . getConst
```

Here's an example:

```
*Main> charCount haiku
62
```

## Line count

Similar to the character count, we can count the number of lines in terms of the number of newline characters. For that, we can use the test function, which only counts those characters that satisfy a given predicate:

```
test :: (Char -> Bool) -> Char -> Count b
test p c = if p c then count 1 () else count 0 ()
```

With that in place, we can count the lines in a string as follows:

```
lineCount :: String -> Integer
lineCount = getCount . traverse (test (== '\n'))
```

Here's an example:

```
*Main> lineCount haiku
3
```

## Word count

Counting the number of words is the most tricky of the three statistics we collect. To know when to count a new word, we need to keep track of whether we are currently in a word or not. For that we use, in addition to Count, we must also use the state effect:

```
type WordCount = Compose (State Bool) Count
```

(Observe that constructing the composition the other way around, with Compose Count (State Bool), is not useful because the constant functor in Count would simply not keep track of the state.)

To get to the integer in this applicative functor, we need to unwrap quite a few more layers:

```
getWordCount :: WordCount a -> Integer
getWordCount p = getCount (fst (runState (getCompose p) False))
```

As you can see, `getWordCount` supplies the initial state, `False`, to indicate that we start out being not in a word. This way, the first non-space character we see gives rise to counting the first word:

```
newWord :: Char -> WordCount b
newWord c = let s' = not (isSpace c)
            in Compose (state (\s -> (test (not s && s'), s')))
```

The `newWord` function processes one character. Based on this character, it determines the new state, `s'`, and whether this character is part of a word. We define being part of a word as not being a space. Given the old state, `s`, and the new state, `s'`, we can determine whether we are starting a new word with the (`not s && s'`) condition, based on which we increase the word count.

It receives the previous state, `s`, which indicates whether we were in a word before.

By traversing with `newCount`, the `wordCount` function counts the number of words in a string:

```
wordCount :: String -> Integer
wordCount = getWordCount . traverse newWord
```

Here's an example:

```
*Main> wordCount haiku
11
```

## Everything all at once

Finally, we can combine the computation of all three statistics with a nested product of the three effects:

```
stats :: String -> (Integer, Integer, Integer)
stats = unpack . traverse f where

  f :: Char -> Product Count (Product Count WordCount) ()
  f c = Pair (count 1 ()) (Pair (test (c == '\n')) (newWord c))

  unpack :: Product Count (Product Count WordCount) a
            -> (Integer, Integer, Integer)
  unpack (Pair cc (Pair lc wc)) =
    (getCount cc, getCount lc, getWordCount wc)
```

Here's an example:

```
*Main> stats haiku
(62,3,11)
```

# Summary

In this chapter, we expanded our repertoire of type constructor classes. We studied a generalization of the list map function to another type of constructor, which is known as a functor. Next, we introduced a generalization of zipping, which is particularly useful for modeling a large range of different kinds of computational effects: applicative functors. Finally, we covered a generalization of mapping with pure functions to mapping with effectful functions, which is supported by the so-called traversable functors.

*Chapter 11, Monads*, continues with modeling effectful computations using type constructor classes. It introduces perhaps the main concept that Haskell is famous for: monads. These monads characterize a particular subset of applicative functors that are particularly flexible and general for effectful computations.

# Questions

Here are some questions and their answers so that you can test your knowledge of this chapter:

1.  What is a functor?
2.  What is an applicative functor?
3.  What effects can I model with applicative functors?
4.  What is a traversable functor?

# Further reading

To learn more about the topics that were covered in this chapter, take a look at the following resources:

- *The Control.Applicative library documentation*:

  ```
  https://hackage.haskell.org/package/base-4.18.1.0/docs/Control-
  Applicative.html
  ```

- *The Data.Traversable library documentation*:

  ```
  https://hackage.haskell.org/package/base-4.18.1.0/docs/Data-
  Traversable.html
  ```

## Answers

1.  A functor is a type constructor, f, with an instance of the Functor type class:

    ```
    class Functor f where
      fmap :: (a -> b) -> (f a -> f b)
      (<$) :: b -> (f a -> f b)
      x <$ t = fmap (\_ -> x) t
    ```

    This is subject to the identity and fusion laws:

    ```
    fmap id = id
    fmap f . fmap g = fmap (f . g)
    ```

2.  An applicative functor, f, is a functor with an instance of the Applicative type class:

    ```
    class Functor f => Applicative f where

      pure :: a -> f a

      (<*>) :: f (a -> b) -> f a -> f b
      fs <*> xs = liftA2 ($) fs xs

      liftA2 :: (a -> b -> c) -> f a -> f b -> f c
      liftA2 f xs ys = fmap f xs <*> ys

      (*>) :: f a -> f b -> f b
      xs *> ys = liftA2 (\_ y -> y) xs ys

      (<*) :: f a -> f b -> f a
      xs <* ys = liftA2 (\x _ -> x) xs ys
    ```

    This is subject to four laws:

    ```
    pure id <*> v = v
    pure (.) <*> u <*> v <*> w = u <*> (v <*> w)
    pure f <*> pure x = pure (f x)
    u <*> pure y = pure ($ y) <*> u
    ```

3.  The following table provides an overview of different effects and the applicative functors that model them:

| Effect | Applicative Functor |
|--------|---------------------|
| None (pure computation) | `Identity` |
| Failure | `Maybe` |
| Errors | `Either err` |
| Analysis | `Monoid m => Const m` |
| Logging | `Monoid m => (,) m` |
| Immutable environment | `(->) env` |
| Mutable state | `State s` |
| Nondeterminism | `[]` |
| Two effects in parallel | `(Applicative f, Applicative g) => Product f g` |
| Two effects composed | `(Applicative f, Applicative g) => Compose f g` |

4. A traversable functor, f, is a functor with an instance of the `Traversable` type class:

```
class (Functor t, Foldable t) => Traversable t where

    traverse  :: Applicative f => (a -> f b) -> t a -> f (t b)
    traverse f = sequenceA . fmap f

    sequenceA :: Applicative f => t (f a) -> f (t a)
    sequenceA = traverse id

    mapM      :: Monad m => (a -> m b) -> t a -> m (t b)
    mapM = traverse

    sequence  :: Monad m => t (m a) -> m (t a)
    sequence = sequenceA
```

This is subject to three laws:

```
t . traverse f = traverse (t . f)


traverse Identity = Identity
traverse (Compose . fmap g . f)
=
Compose . fmap (traverse g) . traverse f
```

Here, t is any applicative transformation that satisfies the following:

```
t (pure x) = pure x
t (u <*> v) = t u <*> t v
```

# 11
# Monads

This chapter introduces the king of the type constructor hierarchy: the monad. I see two main reasons for the prominent position and importance of monads:

- The first reason is an objective and pragmatic one—we can write more expressive effectful programs with monads than we can with applicative functors. In particular, the control flow of applicative functor programs is fixed upfront before it is run. Each step in an applicative program produces a result, and these results are combined to form the final result. In contrast, the control flow of monadic programs is more flexible. The result of a monadic step can determine what the next steps to take are. In essence, we have the same flexibility in monadic programs as we do in pure programs.

  This flexibility makes monads the first abstraction that Haskell programmers reach when writing effectful programs. Even when the same code can be written using either the monad or the applicative function abstraction, monad abstraction is often used. This way, it takes less time to refactor the code later when it turns out the extra flexibility of monads is needed after all. Even so, there is a trade-off to be made, as there are fewer monads than there are applicative functors.

- The second reason is that monads simply have a much longer history than applicative functors. They were the first purely functional model for effects that was explored and incorporated in Haskell at the end of the 1980s and the beginning of the 1990s. They were adopted as the unique approach to IO, which we saw in *Chapter 8, Input/Output*. In contrast, applicative functors were introduced much later, in 2008. By that time, monads were already firmly established, and applicative functors have never been as widely embraced and recognized, especially not to the extent that they have become well-known outside of the Haskell community.

If you have been going through the chapters of this book, monads will likely be less of a revelation for you. While we did not use the word, the IO type in *Chapter 8, Input/Output* was our first example of a monad. Moreover, in this chapter, we will see how monads are a step up from applicative functors, first by looking at two examples (Maybe and State) and then by discussing in their generality. Finally, we will review several more commonly used monads in the standard library.

In short, this chapter covers the following main topics:

- How do we model failing computations when the next step depends on the result of the previous step?

- How do we model stateful computations with a similar dependency between steps?

- What is the general concept of a monad and how does it differ from applicative functors?

- What are several important monads in the standard library and how do you use them?

## Failing with Maybe

In the previous chapter, we used the `Maybe` type constructor to model computations that can fail. We have illustrated this on two little *databases*, one of functions and another of parameters for those functions:

```
funs :: [(String, Float -> Float)]
funs = [("sine",sin),("cosine",cos),("increment",(+1))]

params :: [(String,Float)]
params = [("pi",pi),("zero",0),("x",5)]
```

With `lookup :: Eq a => a -> [(a, b)] -> Maybe b`, we would fetch these by name:

```
fun :: String -> Maybe (Float -> Float)
fun f = lookup f funs

param :: String  -> Maybe Float
param p = lookup p params
```

Using the applicative operator (`<*>`), we can perform the two lookups side-by-side and, if both are successful, perform the function application:

```
prog :: Maybe Float
prog = fun "increment" <*> param "zero"
```

The side-by-side aspect of (`<*>`) is not always appropriate. Sometimes there is a sequential dependency between two computations. For example, suppose we want to use Dutch names for the functions. To do that, we introduce a little database that maps Dutch names to English names:

```
dictionary :: [(String,String)]
dictionary = [("sinus","sine")
             ,("cosinus","cosine")
             ,("verhoog","increment")
             ,("verlaag","decrement")]
```

Finding the corresponding function by its Dutch name is now a two-step process, whereby we first translate the name from Dutch to English and then use the English name to find the function. Both steps may fail:

- The first-step fails when we look up a Dutch word that is not in the dictionary.
- The second step fails when there is no function for the given English name.

Moreover, if the first step fails, we simply cannot initiate the second step; we don't have an English function name to start from. This is where the second step depends on the first step and (<*>) cannot be used. Instead, we need a different combinator that captures this sequential structure:

```
andThen :: Maybe a -> (a -> Maybe b) -> Maybe b
andThen Nothing  f = Nothing
andThen (Just x) f = f x
```

Now we can express the two-step process as follows:

```
dutchFun :: String -> Maybe (Float -> Float)
dutchFun dutchName =
  lookup dutchName dictionary `andThen` \englishName ->
  lookup englishName funs
```

The same andThen combinator can be used for three-step processes, or for any number of steps. Say we want to translate the German name, via Dutch, to English and then find the corresponding function:

```
germanFun :: String -> Maybe (Float -> Float)
germanFun germanName =
  lookup germanName germanDutchDictionary `andThen` \dutchName ->
  lookup dutchName dictionary `andThen` \englishName ->
  lookup englishName funs
```

The combinator is powerful enough to replace the applicative operator (<*>):

```
(<*>) :: Maybe (a -> b) -> Maybe a -> Maybe b
pf <*> px = pf `andThen` \f ->
            px `andThen` \x ->
            pure (f x)
```

The same pattern of sequential dependency arises for other effects too. The next section explores this for the State effect.

# State-passing

In the previous chapter, we discussed the type `State s a` for computations that pass a state of type s and return a result of type a:

```
Control.Monad.State
newtype State s a = State { runState :: s -> (a,s) }
```

We have used this type to add memoization to the Fibonacci function:

```
fib :: Integer -> State (Map Integer Integer) Integer
fib n = State (\ s ->
  case Map.lookup n s of
    Just f  -> (f, s)
    Nothing -> let (f, s') = runState (fib' n) s
                  in  (f, insert n f s'))
  where
    fib' n
      | n < 2     = pure 1
      | otherwise = (+) <$> fib (n-1) <*> fib (n-2)
```

A benefit of using the `State s a` newtype is that it abstracts the actual representation, a function that passes a state, from the type signature. This same abstraction of the representation is upheld by the `<$>` and `<*>` operators; they allow the state-passing to be implicit.

Only the conditional logic that chooses between reusing an earlier result and calculating a new result breaks the encapsulation. It is defined directly in terms of the underlying function representation.

With three well-chosen *primitives*, we can provide an alternative definition. This arguably clear definition will preserve the encapsulation of `State s a` and bring the conditional logic above board.

The first two primitives we need to accomplish this are two functions, `get` and `put`, that respectively expose and overwrite the implicit state:

```
Control.Monad.State
get :: State s s
get = State (\s -> (s,s))

put :: s -> State s ()
put s = State (\_ -> ((),s))
```

These two primitives are the bridge between the explicit world (the encapsulated state) and the implicit world (the explicit parameters and the result).

The third primitive is a combinator that allows the result of a computation to determine what comes next.

```
andNext :: State s a -> (a -> State s b) -> State s b
andNext p k = State (\s0 -> let (x,s1) = runState p s0
                            in runState (k x) s1)
```

Compare this to the definition of the `(<*>)` operator where only the outgoing state `s1` of the earlier computation influences the next computation. Here, the result `x` of the earlier computation also influences the next.

Here is a useful derived function that combines the three primitives:

```
Control.Monad.State
modify :: (s -> s) -> State s ()
modify f = get `andNext` \s -> put (f s)
```

It modifies the implicit state using the given function `f` by getting the old state `s` and overwriting it with the transformed value.

Using this functionality, we can define the memorized Fibonacci function as follows:

```
fib :: Integer -> State (Map Integer Integer) Integer
fib n =
  get `andNext` \ s ->
    case Map.lookup n s of
      Just f  -> pure f
      Nothing -> fib' n                 `andNext` \f ->
                 modify (insert n f) `andNext` \_ ->
                 pure f
  where
    fib' n
      | n < 2     = pure 1
      | otherwise = (+) <$> fib (n-1) <*> fib (n-2)
```

This definition avoids acting on the actual representation. Thanks to `andNext`, we keep the control flow logic above board: the result of a step determines what comes next. We can of course still ignore the result. For example, the step after the call to `modify` does not depend on its trivial unit result.

## The monad type class

We now have seen not two, but *three* examples of the same pattern. The obvious two are the failure effect and the state effect. However, much earlier, in *Chapter 8, Input/Output* we saw the first example: `IO`. Clearly, there is another abstraction behind this that generalizes the three examples and extends to other effects.

This abstraction is known as *monad* and is captured in the Monad constructor type class:

```
Prelude
class Applicative m => Monad m where

  (>>=) :: m a -> (a -> m b) -> m b

  return :: a -> m a
  return = pure

  (>>) :: m a -> m b -> m b
  p >> q = p *> q
```

For legacy reasons, the Monad type class is equipped with a copy of the pure method called return. The concept of the applicative functor was conceived much later than that of the monad, and thus originally, Functor was the direct superclass of Monad. In the future, the return method might be dropped, although, given that it is still widely used, this may not be likely.

Similarly, the (>>) operator is an alias for the applicative functor operator (*>). It can also be defined in terms of (>>=), as suggested by the related operator names.

```
p >> q = p >>= \_ -> q
```

The lambda abstraction that ignores its input expresses that the second step does not depend on the result of the first.

## Monads vs applicative functors

The Monad type class is a subclass of Applicative because all monads are applicative functors. Indeed, as we have already illustrated for Maybe, we can define (<*>) in terms of (>>=) and pure:

```
pf <*> px = pf >>= \f -> px >>= \x -> pure (f x)
```

The opposite is not true; there are applicative functors that are not monads. We will see some examples later on.

There is an alternative way to characterize monads in terms of a *minimal* increment over applicative functors:

```
Prelude
join :: m (m a) -> m a
```

This function joins or collapses a composition of m with itself. The textbook example of this behavior is the standard library function concat for lists:

```
Prelude
concat :: [[a]] -> [a]
concat []       = []
concat (xs:xss) = xs ++ concat xss
```

This `join` function is a minimal increment in the sense that it cannot be used to define (`<*>`). Hence, it better captures the difference in expressive power between monads and applicative functors. Moreover, we can define (`>>=`) in terms of `join` and `fmap`:

```
p >>= f = join (fmap f p)
```

Conversely, and the way it is actually done in the standard library, we can define join in terms of (`>>=`):

```
join :: Monad m => m (m a) -> m a
join p = p >>= \q -> q
```

This runs computation p, which produces a follow-up computation q that is run subsequently.

Because of the additional expressive power of monads, most Haskell developers use monads by default and only turn to applicative functors when their use case demands it. However, for many purposes, the full power of monads is not needed, and may unnecessarily limit options. This was realized in the Haskell standard library, which contains some monad-specific functionalities that precede the introduction of applicative and traversable functors, namely:

```
mapM      :: Monad m => (a -> m b) -> [a] -> m [b]
sequence :: Monad m => [m a] -> m [a]
```

For example, we can read three integers this way:

```
*Main> sequence (replicate 3 (readLn :: IO Integer))
5
2
5
[5,2,5]
```

However, since then, we have realized that the monad constraint can be relaxed to an applicative functor constraint and that the list structure can be generalized to any traversable functor. Hence, we now prefer to use `traverse` and `sequenceA` to mapM and `sequence`. The latter two have only been kept around as derived methods in the `Traversable` type class for legacy reasons:

```
Data.Traversable
class (Functor t, Foldable t) => Traversable t where

    traverse   :: Applicative f => (a -> f b) -> t a -> f (t b)
    sequenceA :: Applicative f => t (f a) -> f (t a)

    mapM       :: Monad m => (a -> m b) -> t a -> m (t b)
    mapM = traverse

    sequence   :: Monad m => t (m a) -> m (t a)
    sequence = sequenceA
```

Nevertheless, you will still encounter programmers who use these legacy functions out of habit or because they are highly focused on monads.

## The monad laws

While we won't explore this any further, monads are, in a sense, a variant of monoids. That explains the name *monad*, but also the fact that monads have to satisfy three laws that resemble the three laws of monoids.

### Left and right identity

Firstly, the `return`/`pure` method is the identity of the monadic composition:

```
pure x >>= f = f x
p >>= \x -> pure x = p
```

### Associativity

When sequencing three steps, it does not matter which way we associate them.

```
(p >>= q) >>= r = p >>= \x -> (q x >>= r)
```

There is an operator that can be derived from `>>=` known as *Kleisli composition*, which is named after the Swiss mathematician Heinrich Kleisli, who studied monads:

```
(<=<) :: Monad m => (b -> m c) -> (a -> m b) -> (a -> m c)
f <=< g = \x -> f x >>= g
```

The operator is also called the *Kleisli fish* because of its shape. It is similar to the function composition operator (`.`) but acts on monadic rather than pure functions. It is used occasionally to write point-free monadic programs. For example, in the point-free style, the monad laws resemble even more closely those of monoids:

```
f <=< pure = f
pure <=< f = f
f <=< (g <=< h) = (f <=< g) <=< h
```

The operator also has a dual, which has its two parameters flipped:

```
(>=>) :: Monad m => (a -> m b) -> (b -> m c) -> (a -> m c)
f >=> g = \x -> f x >>= g
```

This *forward* composition is often more natural.

## Law-breakers

The laws can be used to show that some applicative functors do not form a monad. Take for example the constant functor. We could write this type-correct yet law-breaking monad instance for it:

```
-- invalid
instance Monoid m => Monad (Const m) where
  Const n >>= f = Const n
```

Because `Const m a` does not actually contain a value of type a, its definition for (`>>=`) does not have a value to invoke the function `f`. Nevertheless, we can produce a value of type `Const m b` by simply rewrapping the monoid value n at that type. Alas, this violates the left identity law. The left-hand side of that law simplifies as follows:

```
    pure x >>= f
 =
  Const mempty >>= f
 =
  Const mempty
```

This result is independent of `f`. In contrast, the right-hand side `f x` is entirely determined by `f`. For example, if we take `f = \_ -> Const (Sum 42)`, we get a value that is clearly different from the left-hand side of the law.

# The do notation

We saw the `do` notation earlier in *Chapter 8, Input/Output* where it made writing `IO` computations more convenient. The same `do` notation works for any monad. For example, here is the `germanFun` program, which uses the `Maybe` monad again now using the `do` notation:

```
germanFun :: String -> Maybe (Float -> Float)
germanFun germanName =
  do dutchName   <- lookup germanName germanDutchDictionary
     englishName <- lookup dutchName dictionary
     lookup englishName funs
```

The first two lines bind their results, which can be used in the following lines, and the last line provides the result for the whole computation.

Likewise, we can rewrite the `fib` program that uses the `State` monad:

```
fib :: Integer -> State (Map Integer Integer) Integer
fib n =
  do s <- get
     case Map.lookup n s of
```

```
        Just f  -> pure f
        Nothing -> do f <- fib' n
                      modify (insert n f)
                      pure f
   where
     fib' n
       | n < 2     = pure 1
       | otherwise = (+) <$> fib (n-1) <*> fib (n-2)
```

This definition features two do blocks. The first at the top-level of the function fetches the state and then decides how to proceed with a case analysis. The first branch consists of a single (pure) action and thus requires no do block. The second branch features three steps and does need a do block. As the result of modify is of no interest (only its side effect is), it is not bound to a variable.

## More monads

Besides Maybe and State, a number of other applicative functor examples we saw in the previous chapter also have a monad structure. We revisit them here.

### The Identity monad

Our first example is the Identity functor, which models pure computations. Its monad instance provides a sequential notation for function application:

```
Control.Monad.Identity
instance Monad Identity where
  Identity x >>= f = f x
```

When emphasizing the monad structure, this type is usually called the Identity monad rather than the Identity functor.

Instead of writing a nested function application h (g (f x)), we can write this in successive steps as Identity (f x) >>= (Identity . g) >>= (Identity . h). This isn't particularly convenient, but it looks a bit more familiar to imperative programmers when we use the do notation (and ignore the Identity wrappers):

```
do y <- Identity (f x)
   z <- Identity (g y)
   Identity (h z)
```

Be aware that the sequential notation does not fundamentally change the order in which this expression is executed. Lazy evaluation is still used, and if h ignores its input, then f x and g y are never computed.

As we don't need monads to perform pure computations in Haskell, the Identity monad does not see much use in practice. Its main use case is when we are given an interface that asks us to pick a monad and we don't actually need to perform any side effects.

## The Error (aka Exception) monad

The Either e a type models computations that can raise an error (or exception) of type e. Its monad structure is defined as follows:

```
Data.Either
instance Monad (Either e) where
  Left e  >>= f = Left e
  Right x >>= f = f x
```

When a value is available (Right x), we can pass it to the function f. However, when an error happens (Left e), we don't have a value to pass to the function and the error is propagated instead.

In the monadic setting, Either e is also called the *error monad* or the *exception monad*. In order to preserve the encapsulation of its representation, we often work with two primitive operations:

```
Control.Monad.Except
throwError :: e -> Either e a
throwError e = Left e

catchError :: Either e a -> (e -> Either e a) -> Either e a
catchError (Left e) h = h e
catchError (Right x) h = Right x
```

The throwError function throws or raises the given error of type e. Its type suggests it may deliver a result of any type a, but of course, it never does. The catchError function works like the try/catch blocks in imperative programming languages. If p executes normally, then catchError p h behaves like p. However, when p throws an error, the handler function h takes over and attempts to produce a result some other way.

Consider, for example, the following function, which computes the percentage of values that satisfy the given values in the given list:

```
data EmptyList = EmptyList

percentage :: (a -> Bool) -> [a] -> Either EmptyList Float
percentage p l
  | null l    = throwError EmptyList
  | otherwise = pure ( fromIntegral (length (filter p l))
                     / fromIntegral (length l))
```

If we are using this in an application where we are trying to guess the odds of throwing heads with a coin based on prior tosses, we can do the following:

```
data Toss = Heads | Tails deriving Eq


guessHeads :: [Toss] -> Either EmptyList Float
guessHeads tosses = catchError (percentage (== Heads) tosses)
                               (\EmptyList -> pure 0.5)
```

Here, we rely on percentage to compute the odds of heads, but if it throws an error because the list is empty, we recover by guessing the odds are 50/50.

The result of guessHeads is still Either EmptyList Float, which suggests that it could throw the EmptyList error. If we don't want that and want to basically exit the either monad, we have to resort to pattern matching or using the either :: (e -> b) -> (a -> b) -> Either e a -> b function from Data.Either:

```
guessHeads' :: [Toss] -> Float
guessHeads' tosses = either (\EmptyList -> 0.5) id
                           (percentage (== Heads) tosses)
```

The either function requires us to specify what to return in case of an error or a result. In the former case, we return 0.5. Because we don't use pure, this result will just be a plain Float. In the latter case, we just return the Float value we get using the identity function.

## The Reader (aka environment) monad

When using the monad structure of the partially applied function type (->) r, it is usually called the *Reader monad* or the *Environment monad*, and it is wrapped in a newtype:

```
Control.Monad.Reader
newtype Reader r a = Reader { runReader :: r -> a }
   deriving (Functor, Applicative)
```

The Reader newtype can derive the Functor and Applicative instances from the (->) r type if we provide the pragma {- LANGUAGE GeneralizedNewtypeDeriving -}.

However, the Monad instance is new:

```
Control.Monad.Reader
instance Monad (Reader r) where
  p >>= f = Reader (\r -> let x = runReader p r
                          in runReader (f x) r)
```

The monadic composition returns a function that takes the environment value r and passes it both into p and f.

## Asking nicely

The `Reader` monad is usually presented with two primitive operations. The first and foremost accesses the implicit environment:

```
Control.Monad.Reader
ask :: Reader r r
ask = Reader (\r -> r)
```

It is quite similar to the `get` operation for the `State` monad. For example, the following program computes the price of a purchase given the quantity of items, where each item costs `57.0` euro. It also takes `vat` as an implicit parameter:

```
price :: Int -> Reader Float Float
price qty =
   do vat <- ask
      pure (57.0 * (fromIntegral qty) * (1 + vat))
```

In a B2B transaction, no VAT has to be paid. We can model this as follows:

```
*Main> runReader (price 10) 0
570.0
```

However, the same transaction in a B2C context is subject to 21% VAT.

```
*Main> runReader (price 10) 0.21
689.7
```

The `Reader` monad is often used to implicitly pass around the configuration data (e.g., command-line flags) of an application. Such a configuration is often a composite data structure:

```
data AppConfiguration =
   MkAppConfiguration {
      verbosityLevel :: Int,
      userName :: String
   }
```

In most parts of the program, we only want to consult one component of the whole configuration structure. In those cases, the derived operation `asks` comes in handy:

```
Control.Monad.Reader
asks :: (r -> a) -> Reader r a
asks f = do r <- ask ; pure (f r)
```

Instead of returning the environment, `asks f` gives a derived value obtained by applying the function f to the environment. Often, this function f is a selector function. Here's an example:

```
warn :: String -> Reader AppConfiguration String
warn msg = do vl <- asks verbosityLevel
              if vl > 2 then pure (map toUpper msg)
                        else pure msg
```

Here, we select the verbosity level of the configuration structure and, if the value is greater than 2, we emphasize a message by turning it to uppercase.

## Local updates

The `Reader` monad differs from the `State` monad in that it is not possible for it to modify the environment; there is no counterpart to `put`. However, it does support a limited form of *local* modification:

```
Control.Monad.Reader
local :: (r -> r) -> Reader r a -> Reader r a
local f p = Reader (\r -> runReader p (f r))
```

The idea is that `local f p` modifies the environment given the using function f, but only for the computation p. When p finishes, the environment goes back to what it was before.

Here is a little example program to illustrate this:

```
localExample :: Reader Int (Int,Int,Int)
localExample = do x <- ask
                  y <- local (*2) ask
                  z <- ask
                  pure (x,y,z)
```

This program contains three `ask` calls, the second of which sees the locally modified environment:

```
*Main> runReader localExample 1
(1,2,1)
*Main> runReader localExample 5
(5,10,5)
```

## Example

We now show off what we can do with `ask` and `local` in a small pretty-printing example. Recall the rose trees that we discussed in *Chapter 9, Monoids and Foldables*

```
data Rose a = RNode a [Rose a]
```

Our objective is to take an example rose tree like this one:

```
example = RNode 1 [RNode 2
                    [RNode 4
                      [RNode 7 []
                      ,RNode 8 []
                      ,RNode 9 []]
                    ,RNode 5 []]
                  ,RNode 3
                    [RNode 6 []]]
```

Then, we have it pretty-printed as follows:

```
*Main>  example
- 1
  - 2
    - 4
      - 7
      - 8
      - 9
    - 5
  - 3
    - 6
```

The indentation level of each line should be proportional to the depth in the tree. To keep track of this indentation level, we use an implicit environment of type Int. The indent function consults this environment to prefix a string with the appropriate number of spaces:

```
indent :: String -> Reader Int String
indent s = do n <- ask
              pure (replicate n ' ' ++ s)
```

When processing a node, we indent its value and recursively process its subtrees. Those subtrees see a locally modified indentation level. The modification is only local because the siblings of the node should see the original indentation level:

```
goN :: Show a => Rose a -> Reader Int [String]
goN (RNode x xs) = do y  <- indent ("- " ++ show x)
                      ys <- local (+2) (goL xs)
                      pure (y:ys)
```

Processing the list of subtrees is a straightforward effectful traversal. This is followed by the concatenation of the resulting list of lists:

```
goL :: Show a => [Rose a] -> Reader Int [String]
goL l = concat <$> traverse goN l
```

Finally, the Show instance kicks off the computation in the reader monad with an initial indentation level of 0.

```
instance Show a => Show (Rose a) where
  show n = unlines $ runReader (goN n) 0
```

Here, the unlines :: [String] -> String function concatenates all the lines and puts newline characters between them.

## The Writer monad

Like in the case of the reader monad, the Writer monad is usually presented as a newtype wrapper:

```
Control.Monad.Writer
newtype Writer w a = Writer { runWriter :: (a, w) }
```

Observe that the two components of the tuple are swapped compared to the Applicative structure we saw in the previous chapter. I am not aware of any good reason for this difference.

Just like the Applicative structure, the Monad structure requires the parameter w to be a monoid:

```
Control.Monad.Writer
instance Monoid w => Monad (Writer w) where
  p >>= f = Writer (let (x, w1) = runWriter p
                        (y, w2) = runWriter (f x)
                    in (y, w1 <> w2))
```

The bind operator concatenates the monoid values of the two subcomputations p and f.

The main primitive operation that is used with the writer monad is called tell:

```
Control.Monad.Writer
tell :: Monoid w => w -> Writer w ()
tell w = Writer ((),w)
```

As a small application, let us add logging to the factorial function. We use a list of strings to represent the log and add a message to this log as follows:

```
log :: String -> Writer [String] ()
log msg = tell [msg]
```

To avoid our function clashing with the logarithm function from the `Prelude` library, which is also called `log`, we can explicitly hide the one from the `Prelude` with the following `import` declaration:

```
import Prelude hiding (log)
```

Now we can call our own `log` function from the factorial function without a hitch:

```
fac :: Integer -> Writer [String] Integer
fac n =
  do log ("Calling: fac " ++ show n)
     r <- go n
     log ("Returning: fac " ++ show n ++ " = " ++ show r)
     pure r
  where
    go n
      | n <= 0    = pure 1
      | otherwise = do r <- fac (n-1)
                       pure (n * r)
```

Here, we have moved the logic of the factorial function into a local function called `go` and wrapped the logging calls around it.

The `displayLog` function extracts the log and shows it:

```
displayLog :: Writer [String] a -> IO ()
displayLog p = let (_, l) = runWriter p
               in mapM_ putStrLn l
```

Here, `mapM_ :: (Foldable t, Monad m) => (a -> m b) -> t a -> m ()` is a variant of `mapM` and `traverse` that applies an effectful function (here, `putStrLn`) to the elements of a data structure. It only cares about the side effect of the function and discards its results:

```
*Main> displayLog (fac 3)
Calling: fac 3
Calling: fac 2
Calling: fac 1
Calling: fac 0
Returning: fac 0 = 1
Returning: fac 1 = 1
Returning: fac 2 = 2
Returning: fac 3 = 6
```

## The list (aka nondeterminism) monad

Finally, the list monad, or nondeterminism monad, is an extension of the applicative functor structure of lists that models nondeterminism. It is not based on the ziplist structure:

```
Prelude
instance Monad [] where
  p >>= f = concatMap f p
```

Here, `concatMap` is defined as the composition of `concat` and `map`:

```
Prelude
concatMap :: (a -> [b]) -> [a] -> [b]
concatMap f = concat . map f
```

The idea is that `p >>= f` models a nondeterministic computation where each of the results x of p leads to many results f x. For example, suppose we want to buy two storage boxes where one is smaller than (and thus can be stored inside) the other. There are five box sizes. We can model the possibilities as follows:

```
boxes :: [(Int,Int)]
boxes = do large <- [1..5]
           small <- [1..(large-1)]
           pure (large,small)
```

Observe that this do notation is very similar to the list comprehension notation:

```
boxes' :: [(Int,Int)]
boxes' = [ (large, small)
         | large <- [1..5]
         , small <- [1..(large-1)]
         ]
```

We can write this list comprehension in a different style by using a guard:

```
boxes' :: [(Int,Int)]
boxes' = [ (large, small)
         | large <- [1..5]
         , small <- [1..5]
         , small < large
         ]
```

Guards are also supported in the monadic style—use the `guard` primitive:

```
Control.Monad
guard :: Bool -> [()]
guard False = []
guard True = [()]
```

Depending on the Boolean value, this function returns no result or one trivial unit result. In a larger program, this actually discards or preserves the results computed by the context in which it is used. We can use it as follows:

```
boxes :: [(Int,Int)]
boxes = do large <- [1..5]
           small <- [1..5]
           guard (small < large)
           pure (large,small)
```

Whether you use the list comprehension notation or the do notation for the list monad is a matter of choice. In fact, GHC has a language extension, called `MonadComprehension`, which extends the comprehension notation to other monads.

## Summary

In this chapter, we have taken a further step in the functor–applicative hierarchy with monads. Monads model effects where the next step in a computation can depend on the previous step. This makes them very expressive for modeling effects, and they are often the go-to effect model for Haskell programmers. Besides the `IO` monad, which we have already studied in a chapter of its own, we have reviewed several monads provided by the standard library here.

*Chapter 12, Monad Transformers* considers how we can combine multiple effects in the same monad. In the previous chapter, we saw two ways of combining applicative functors, namely products and compositions. Neither of these approaches is effective for monads. Instead, we require a new approach, called *monad transformers*, around which a framework has been created.

## Questions

1. What is a monad?
2. What are important monads in the standard library and their primitive operations?

# Answers

1.  A monad is a type constructor m with an instance of the Monad type class:

```
class Applicative m => Monad m where
  (>>=) :: m a -> (a -> m b) -> m b
  return :: a -> m a
  return = pure
  (>>) :: m a -> m b -> m b
  p >> q = p *> q
```

It is subject to three laws:

```
return x >>= f = f x
p >>= return = p
(p >>= q) >>= r = p >>= (\x -> q x >>= r)
```

2.

| Effect | Monad | Primitive Operations |
|---|---|---|
| No effect, pure | `Identity` | - |
| Failure | `Maybe` | - |
| Exceptions, errors | `Either e` | `throwError, catchError` |
| State | `State s` | `get, put, modify` |
| Environment | `Reader r` | `ask, asks, local` |
| Logging | `Writer w` | `tell` |
| Nondeterminism | `[]` | `guard` |

# 12
# Monad Transformers

This chapter shows how the functionality of different monads can be combined into a single monad. Creating such combinations is relatively straightforward for applicative functors. We have seen that two different constructions can be used for this purpose – products and compositions. Unfortunately, neither works for monads. The product of two monads is not a monad and the composition of two monads is not a monad.

For the first few years of Haskell's existence, there was no other way to create custom monads with combined effects than to write them from scratch. This involved a lot of boilerplate and required substantial expertise. Hence, researchers have long sought a way to make it possible to combine existing monads. This would avoid the boilerplate and make custom monads more widely accessible.

Eventually, an out-of-the-box solution was found: *monad transformers*. The idea is no longer to combine monads but rather to transform an existing monad into a new one. The purpose of this transformation is to augment the existing monad with additional functionality. As a consequence, the units of functionality are no longer monads but monad transformers.

In this chapter, we will learn how this monad transformer mechanism works and review the transformer counterparts for the monads we covered in the previous chapter. On top of that, we will see how our application code can abstract over the specific monads and the monad transformers it uses using monad subclasses. This will allow us to reuse the code in more contexts and evolve it more easily. Finally, we will point out two important gotchas when combining multiple monad transformers.

In short, this chapter covers the following main topics:

- Writing custom monads that combine the functionality of different basic monads

- Using monad transformers as a reusable mechanism to define custom monads

- Using common off-the-shelf monad transformers

- Abstracting concrete monads with monad subclasses and instantiating them in different ways to achieve different behavior

- Being aware of and exploiting the ability to compose monad transformers in different ways to obtain different interactions

# Combining monadic effects

Before we solve the problem of combining different monadic effects in the standard Haskell way, let's illustrate the problem on a small example application. We'll also discuss the solution of writing a custom monad, which seems the most obvious but is not a best practice.

## Logging revisited

Let's make the logging functionality from the previous chapter a bit more sophisticated by adding several requirements. Recall that previously, we used the `Writer [String]` monad for logging. To accommodate the new requirements, we will have to come up with a custom monad, which we'll call App.

These are the requirements:

1. We want to distinguish different levels of importance for the logged messages:

   ```
   data LogLevel = Mundane | Important | Critical
     deriving (Eq, Ord, Show)
   ```

2. When we record a message in the log, we have to supply the logging level:

   ```
   log :: LogLevel -> String -> App ()
   ```

   It is convenient to set up a few derived functions that partially apply `log` to different logging levels:

   ```
   mundane, important, critical :: String -> App ()
   mundane   = log Mundane
   important = log Important
   critical  = log Critical
   ```

3. We want to be able to configure what messages should be logged, depending on their level. For this purpose, we will use a configuration data type:

   ```
   data Config = MkConfig { shouldLog :: LogLevel -> Bool }
   ```

   For example, the following configurations log all messages, no messages, and only the critical messages, respectively:

   ```
   cfgAll, cfgNone, cfgCritical :: Config
   cfgAll      = MkConfig (\_ -> True)
   cfgNone     = MkConfig (\_ -> False)
   cfgCritical = MkConfig (== Critical)
   ```

4. When we run an application, we supply the configuration and get back both the application's result and its log:

   ```
   runApp :: Config -> App a -> (a, Log)
   ```

The log is a list of messages and their logging level:

```
type Log = [(LogLevel, String)]
```

Given an implementation for these requirements, we can write a new version of the logged factorial function from the previous chapter:

```
fac :: Integer -> App Integer
fac n =
  do mundane ("Calling: fac " ++ show n)
     r <- go n
     important ("Returning: fac " ++ show n ++ " = " ++ show r)
     pure r
  where
    go n
      | n < 0     = do critical ("Negative input: " ++ show n)
                       pure 1
      | n == 0    = pure 1
      | otherwise = do r <- fac (n-1)
                       pure (n * r)
```

Here, we classify the different log entries at different levels:

- The entry for calling the function is *mundane*

- The entry with the function result is *important*

- The entry with the negative input is *critical*, as this should not happen

Now, we can run the application with different configurations:

```
*Main> runApp cfgNone (fac 3)
(6, [])
*Main> runApp cfgCritical (fac 3)
(6, [])
*Main> runApp cfgCritical (fac (-1))
(1, [(Critical, "Negative input: -1")])
```

The key question that remains is how we define the App monad in a way that satisfies our requirements.

## A custom monad

There is an *obvious* approach: simply define a new monad from scratch that models the desired combination of effects. While this is a viable approach in principle, it is usually not so obvious what the custom monad should look like in practice. Nevertheless, it is a good staging point toward a more modular approach and, incidentally, a way to avoid the boilerplate that comes with modularity.

Here is a custom definition of the App monad that satisfies our requirements:

```
newtype App a = MkApp { unApp :: Config -> (a, Log) }
  deriving Functor
```

We represent this monad with a function that takes the configuration and returns a tuple of the result and the log. This way, it combines elements of both Reader Config and Writer Log.

With this representation, we can define the log function as follows:

```
log :: LogLevel -> String -> App ()
log lvl msg = MkApp (\cfg ->
  if shouldLog cfg lvl
    then ((), [(lvl,msg)])
    else ((), []))
```

The configuration value and the log level specify whether the message is put in the log or not.

The runApp function is just a flipped version of unApp:

```
runApp :: Config -> App a -> (a, Log)
runApp cfg app = unApp app cfg
```

The trickiest part of the whole definition is writing the definition of (>>=):

```
instance Monad App where
  p >>= f = MkApp (\cfg ->
    let (x, log1) = runApp cfg p
        (y, log2) = runApp cfg (f x)
    in (y, log1 ++ log2))
```

Again, this definition combines elements from Reader and Writer. The configuration is passed to both steps, and the logs of both steps are concatenated.

Finally, we are missing an Applicative instance:

```
instance Applicative App where
  pure x = MkApp (\cfg -> (x, []))
  (<*>) = ap
```

Our definition of pure returns the result, x, without consulting the configuration and with an empty log. As we saw in the previous chapter, the (<*>) operator can be defined in terms of (>>=).

The ap function from the `Control.Monad` library provides this definition in a reusable form:

```
Control.Monad
ap :: Monad m  => m (a -> b) -> m a -> m b
ap mf mx = do f <- mf
              x <- mx
              pure (f x)
```

Coming up with these definitions requires (substantial) experience with the definitions of existing monads.

## Changed requirements

We can make the problem more challenging by evolving our requirements. The change we want is to write the log directly to standard output or a file, rather than to collect all the messages in a list. This way, we can observe the messages as they arrive, and still see them even if the application crashes. Concretely, this involves two changes:

- The configuration gets a second field, namely a function that explains how to emit the messages:

```
data Config =
        MkConfig { shouldLog :: LogLevel -> Bool
                 , output :: (LogLevel, String) -> IO ()}
```

  The default configuration could output all levels and print them on standard output:

```
defaultCfg :: Config
defaultCfg = MkConfig { shouldLog = \lvl -> True
                      , output    = print }
```

- The function to run the application now evaluates to the IO monad:

```
runApp :: Config -> App a -> IO a
```

We are not only interested in how to change our representation to reflect these new requirements but also in how to do this with minimal upheaval to the existing definitions.

## Changes to the custom monad

To support the new requirements with our custom monad, we must change its representation so that it makes use of IO for reporting the log:

```
newtype App a = MkApp { unApp :: Config -> IO a }
  deriving Functor
```

With this representation, we can define the `log` function as follows:

```
log :: LogLevel -> String -> App ()
log lvl msg = MkApp (\cfg ->
  do when (shouldLog cfg lvl)
       (output cfg (lvl,msg)))
```

Now, we can use the `output` function from the configuration to emit the message. This makes use of the when function from `Control.Monad` to perform an action conditionally:

```
Control.Monad
when :: Applicative f => Bool -> f () -> f ()
when True  act = act
when False act = pure ()
```

The `runApp` function remains a flipped version of unApp, now with a different result type:

```
runApp :: Config -> App a -> IO a
runApp cfg app = unApp app cfg
```

The definition of (`>>=`) is affected more substantially:

```
instance Monad App where
  p >>= f = MkApp (\cfg ->
    do x <- runApp cfg p
       runApp cfg (f x))
```

We no longer have to work with explicit logs here, but we do have to switch from pure function calls to using the `do` notation for the `IO` monad. Finally, the definition of `pure` in the `Applicative` instance undergoes a similar change:

```
instance Applicative App where
  pure x = MkApp (\cfg -> pure x)
  (<*>) = ap
```

While these changes may not seem so bad, there is a more convenient approach.

# Monad transformers

While two monads cannot be combined easily to form a third monad, there is a different mechanism, called *monad transformers*, that allows us to augment an existing monad with additional functionality.

# The Reader transformer

As a first example of a (monad) transformer, we will visit the monad transformer, which adds the reading effect to an existing monad. This transformer is represented as follows:

```
Control.Monad.Trans.Reader
newtype ReaderT r m a = ReaderT { runReaderT :: r -> m a }
  deriving Functor
```

As we can see, this looks a lot like the definition of `Reader r a` from the previous chapter. The main difference is that it takes an additional type parameter, m, for the monad that is being augmented. For example, we would use this as `ReaderT Config (Writer Log)` to augment the `Writer Log` monad with an implicit environment. That would give us our first App representation. Similarly, we get the second App representation by transforming `IO` into `ReaderT Config IO`.

The key point of the monad transformer is that the transformed monad is, again, a monad:

```
Control.Monad.Trans.Reader
instance Monad m => Monad (ReaderT r m) where
  p >>= f = ReaderT (\env ->
    do x <- runReaderT p env
       runReaderT (f x) env )
```

This looks a lot like the monad instance for our second App representation, but now for a more general type.

Of course, a monad has to be an applicative functor too:

```
Control.Monad.Trans.Reader
instance Monad m => Applicative (ReaderT r m) where
  pure x = ReaderT (\env -> pure x)
  (<*>) = ap
```

Because we are defining `(<*>)` here with `ap`, we require m to be a monad. It is possible to give a direct definition that only requires m to be an applicative functor.

## *The writer-based application*

Now, let's reimplement our first challenge. As we have already said, the definition of App is as follows:

```
type App = ReaderT Config (Writer Log)
```

To define `log`, we can use `ask`, or rather the derived `asks`, operation of `ReaderT` to inspect the configuration:

```
Control.Monad.Trans.Reader
ask :: Monad m => ReaderT r m r
```

```
ask = ReaderT (\env -> pure env)

asks :: Monad m => (r -> a) -> ReaderT r m a
asks f = do r <- ask
            pure (f r)
```

Now, we can write the following:

```
log :: LogLevel -> String -> App ()
log lvl msg =
  do p <- asks shouldLog
     when (p lvl)
       (lift (tell [(lvl,msg)]))
```

This definition makes use of the `lift` function, which transforms a computation in the underlying monad (here, `tell [(lvl,msg)] :: Writer log ()`) into a computation in the transformed monad:

```
Control.Monad.Trans.Reader
lift :: Monad m => m a -> ReaderT r m a
lift act = ReaderT (\env -> act)
```

To define `runApp`, we need to peel away the newtype constructors of both `ReaderT` and `Writer`:

```
runApp :: Config -> App a -> (a, Log)
runApp cfg app = runWriter (runReaderT app cfg)
```

### The IO-based application

We will reconfigure our transformed monad to use `IO` as the basis:

```
type App = ReaderT Config IO
```

We must also adapt the definition of log:

```
log :: LogLevel -> String -> App ()
log lvl msg =
  do p <- asks shouldLog
     when (p lvl)
       (do out <- asks output
           lift (out (lvl, msg)))
```

Finally, `runApp` becomes a little simpler because we do not have to unwrap `IO`:

```
runApp :: Config -> App a -> IO a
runApp cfg app = runReaderT app cfg
```

As we can see, the `ReaderT` definition and its type class instances are much more reusable than when we write a custom monad.

## The MonadTrans type class

The `MonadTrans` type class generalizes from the preceding `ReaderT` example:

```
Control.Monad.Trans
class MonadTrans t where
  lift :: Monad m => m a -> t m a
```

It requires that any monad transformer, `t`, has a `lift` function like the one we saw for `ReaderT`. Moreover, it comes with the implicit requirement that `t m` is a monad when `m` is.

Hence, previously, we should have written the following:

```
Control.Monad.Trans.Reader
instance MonadTrans (ReaderT r) where
  lift act = ReaderT (\env -> act)
```

The class comes with two laws. The first law expresses that `lift` should map `pure` of the underlying monad to `pure` of the transformed monad:

```
lift (pure x) = pure x
```

Here, the left-hand `pure x` is a computation in the underlying monad, `m`, while the right-hand `pure x` is a computation in the transformed monad, `t m`.

Similarly, the second law expresses that `lift` should map the `(>>=)` operator of the underlying monad to the `(>>=)` operator of the transformed monad:

```
lift (p >>= f) = lift p >>= (lift . f)
```

## The Reader monad revisited

The standard definition of the `Reader` monad isn't the one we saw in the previous chapter. In reality, its definition is based on `ReaderT`:

```
Control.Monad.Trans.Reader
type Reader r a = ReaderT r Identity a
```

Here, the identity monad, which contributes no effects, serves as the basis. Hence, there is no Reader constructor. Instead, there is a constructor function:

```
Control.Monad.Trans.Reader
reader :: (r -> a) -> Reader r a
reader f = ReaderT (\r -> Identity (f r))
```

Similarly, the field projection function, `runReader`, is the composition of two projections:

```
Control.Monad.Trans.Reader
runReader :: Reader r a -> r -> a
runReader p r = runIdentity (runReaderT p r)
```

The same approach is followed for most other monads we saw in the previous section; they are defined in terms of their monad transformer and the identity monad. We'll review these transformers next.

# Other monad transformers

With the notable exception of the `IO` monad, which is a special case because it is built into the language, most other monads have a corresponding monad transformer. As they mostly follow the same approach as `ReaderT`, we'll only review them briefly.

## The StateT and WriterT transformers

The transformers for the state and writer effects have the closest resemblance to `ReaderT`:

```
Control.Monad.Trans.State
newtype StateT s m a = StateT { runStateT :: s -> m (a, s) }
Control.Monad.Trans.Writer
newtype WriterT w m a = WriterT { runWriterT :: m (a, w) }
```

As monad transformers, they have appropriate `Monad` instances:

```
Control.Monad.Trans.State
instance Monad m => Monad (StateT s m)
Control.Monad.Trans.Writer
instance (Monad m, Monoid w) => Monad (WriterT w m)
```

We haven't shown the implementation because it is very similar to the ones for `State s` and `Writer w` from the previous chapter. Instead, we will show the full `MonadTrans` instances:

```
Control.Monad.Trans.State
instance MonadTrans (StateT s) where
  lift act = StateT (\s -> act >>= \x -> pure (x, s))
Control.Monad.Trans.Writer
instance Monoid w => MonadTrans (WriterT w) where
  lift act = WriterT (act >>= \x -> pure (x, mempty))
```

Both of these instances wrap the `act` computation in the appropriate structure of the additional monad transformer.

# The MaybeT and ExceptT transformers

Two monad transformers allow us to abort computations – the first without and the second with an exception value to explain the cause of the abortion:

```
Control.Monad.Trans.Maybe
newtype MaybeT m a = MaybeT { runMaybeT :: m (Maybe a) }
Control.Monad.Trans.Except
newtype ExceptT e m a = ExceptT { runExceptT :: m (Either e a) }
```

We won't show the monad instances as they are similar to the ones we saw previously, but we will show the `MonadTrans` instances:

```
Control.Monad.Trans.Maybe
instance MonadTrans MaybeT where
  lift act = MaybeT (act >>= \x -> pure (Just x))
Control.Monad.Trans.Except
instance MonadTrans (ExceptT e) where
  lift act = ExceptT (act >>= \x -> pure (Right x))
```

Again, these instances wrap the `act` computation in the appropriate additional structure.

# The ListT transformer

The monad transformer version for the list monad requires a special warning. Several libraries contain a definition that should be avoided:

```
-- do not use
newtype ListT m a = ListT { runListT :: m [a] }
```

This representation follows the example of `MaybeT` and `EitherT e`. Unfortunately, it does not yield a proper monad for most choices of m. Unless m is a *commutative* monad (which I won't go into here), the `(>>=)` operator of `ListT m` violates the associativity law.

Instead, there is a more involved representation, sometimes referred to as *ListT done right*, that does yield a proper monad for every choice of m:

```
ListT
newtype ListT m a = ListT (m (Maybe (a, ListT m a)))
```

I won't show the type class instances as they are beyond the scope of this book. If you are interested, you can study the implementation of the `list-t` package. Otherwise, you can restrict yourself to simply using the API provided by that library.

We now have a good idea of monad transformers. Next, we will see that it is a good idea not to write programs that directly rely on them. Instead, we will introduce an abstraction layer, based on type classes, that allows us to easily replace and evolve the monad stack.

# Monad subclasses

The six monad transformers, together with an appropriate base monad such as `Identity` or `IO`, allow us to put together a large number of different monads. Given the many choices for the monad that's used by an application, we often do not want to fix the monad up front:

- We may not have a full overview of the effects that are required by the application before we start writing parts of it

- We may want to reuse different programs or parts of programs with different monads

- We may want to quickly adapt an existing program to additional requirements, which may entail incorporating additional effects

To support these and similar scenarios, Haskell programmers can make use of type classes to abstract over the particular monad being used while still imposing requirements on it. These type classes are known as `Monad` subclasses, and there is one for each effect.

## The MonadReader type class

Our first `Monad` subclass is for the reader effect:

```
Control.Monad.Reader.Class
 class Monad m => MonadReader r m | m -> r where
   ask   :: m r
   local :: (r -> r) -> m a -> m a
```

The `MonadReader r m` class expresses that m is a monad that supports the reader effect, with an implicit environment of the r type. Supporting the reader effect means providing the two primitive reader operations, `ask` and `local`.

The special notation "`| m -> r`" is known as a *functional dependency*. It expresses the requirement that r should be uniquely determined by m. In other words, if the compiler knows what m is concretely, then it should be able to tell what r is concretely.

### MonadReader instances

The obvious instance for this is the following for `ReaderT`:

```
Control.Monad.Reader.Class
 instance Monad m => MonadReader r (ReaderT r m) where
   ask = ReaderT (\r -> pure r)
   local f p = ReaderT (\r -> runReaderT p (f r))
```

However, there is also an instance for `WriterT`:

```
Control.Monad.Reader.Class
instance (Monoid w, MonadReader r m)
 => MonadReader r (WriterT w m) where
  ask = lift ask
  local f p = WriterT (local f (runWriterT p))
```

The idea is that (`WriterT w m`) can support the reader effect if the underlying monad, m, does. The primitive reader operations are then all delegated to m and appropriately adapted (often using `lift`) in the transformed monad.

There are similar `MonadReader` instances for the other monad transformers.

### MonadReader use

The `MonadReader` class encourages us to write programs like the following:

```
type VAT = Float

priceWithVAT :: MonadReader VAT m => Float -> m Float
priceWithVAT p = do vat <- ask
                    pure (p * (1 + vat))
```

Here, we have not fixed the type of the monad; it is a type parameter, m. However, we require it to be a monad (because we use the do notation) and support the reader effect (because we use `ask` to fetch VAT). Hence, m is constrained by `MonadReader VAT m`.

Now, we can choose to instantiate m with `Reader VAT` (which is `ReaderT VAT Identity`):

```
*Main> runReader (priceWithVAT 5.2) 0.21
6.292
```

The instantiation of m happens implicitly. The type of `runReader` forces it to be `Reader r` for some r, and the functional dependency of the `MonadReader VAT m` constraint forces r to be VAT.

However, we can also include the program in a larger application that includes logging:

```
orderWidgets
   :: (MonadReader VAT m, MonadWriter [String] m)
   => Int -> m Float
orderWidgets n = do tell ["Order of " ++ show n ++ " widgets"]
                    p <- priceWithVAT 5.2
                    tell ["  at unit price " ++ show p]
                    pure (fromIntegral n * p)
```

This program can be run as follows:

```
*Main> runWriter (runReaderT (orderWidgets 10) 0.21)
(62.92, ["Order of 10 widgets", "  at unit price 6.292"])
```

This instantiates the monad to `ReaderT VAT (Writer [String])`.

## More Monad subclasses

The other monadic effects we have reviewed have similar `Monad` subclasses and instances.

### MonadState and MonadWriter

The type classes for the state and writer effects are quite straightforward variations of `MonadReader`:

```
Control.Monad.State.Class
class Monad m => MonadState s m | m -> s where
  get :: m s
  put :: s -> m ()
Control.Monad.Writer.Class
class (Monoid w, Monad m) => MonadWriter w m | m -> w where
  tell :: w -> m (    )
```

Hence, the primitive operations, `get`, `put`, and `tell`, which we discussed in the previous chapter are overloaded type class methods.

### MonadError

The naming scheme for errors or exceptions isn't entirely consistent. It can't make up its mind between the words *error* and *exception*. While the monad transformer uses the latter, the type class and its methods are named after the former. The reason for this is a now deprecated library called `Control.Monad.Error` that is superseded by `Control.Monad.Except`:

```
Control.Monad.Error.Class
class Monad m => MonadError e m | m -> e where
  throwError :: e -> m a
  catchError :: m a -> (e -> m a) -> m a
```

We have the following instance for the `ExceptT` monad transformer of the form:

```
Control.Monad.Error.Class
instance Monad m => MonadError e (ExceptT e m)
```

However, we also have a special instance for the `Maybe` monad:

```
Control.Monad.Error.Class
instance MonadError () Maybe where
```

```
throwError () = Nothing
catchError (Just x) h = Just x
catchError Nothing  h = h ()
```

As the `Nothing` value does not hold any information regarding the error, this instance states that the errors are of the `()` type.

### Alternative and MonadPlus

For nondeterminism, there are two relevant type classes. Historically, the `Monad` subclass, `MonadPlus`, came first. Later, when `Applicative` was introduced, it got an analogous subclass called `Alternative`. Today, the latter is preferred because it is more general – it applies both to applicative functors that are monads and to those that are not monads:

```
Control.Applicative
class Applicative f => Alternative f where
  empty :: f a
  (<|>) :: f a -> f a -> f a
```

The type class features two primitive methods: `empty` denotes that there is no alternative (that is, failure or a dead-end) and the `(<|>)` operator chooses between two alternative courses of action.

The list functor, which collects all alternative results, has the following instance:

```
Control.Applicative
instance Alternative [] where
  empty = []
  (<|>) = (++)
```

However, there is also an instance for `Maybe`, which expresses a left-biased choice:

```
Control.Applicative
instance Alternative Maybe where
  empty = Nothing
  Just x   <|> other  = Just x
  Nothing <|> other  = other
```

This instance is in line with the exception semantics of `Maybe`: the left alternative is the default one; only when it fails do we resort to the right alternative.

The `guard` function we saw in the previous chapter for encoding list comprehensions works for any `Alternative` instance:

```
Control.Monad
guard :: Alternative f => Bool -> f ()
guard False = empty
guard True  = pure ()
```

You may encounter uses of `MonadPlus` in the wild. This type class is a restriction of `Alternative` to monads, with clones of the two operations:

```
Control.Monad
class (Alternative m, Monad m) => MonadPlus m where
  mzero :: m a
  mzero = empty
  mplus :: m a -> m a -> m a
  mplus = (<|>)
```

I don't recommend using it anymore.

# Monad transformer gotchas

There are two aspects of monad transformers that you will run into sooner or later. I will share them here so that you'll be prepared.

## Effect interaction

When stacking two different monad transformers, `T1` and `T2`, to combine two effects, you have a choice. Do you use `T1 (T2 Identity)` or `T2 (T1 Identity)`? Does it matter which one you choose?

In some cases, it doesn't matter. For instance, in our earlier example of logging with levels, we combined the reader and writer effects, like so:

```
type App = ReaderT Config (Writer Log)
```

Recall that, because `Writer w` is defined as `WriterT w Identity`, this comes down to the following:

```
type App = ReaderT Config (WriterT Log Identity)
```

However, we could also have written the following:

```
type App = WriterT Log (ReaderT Config Identity)
```

As we have only interacted with this monad through the overloaded `ask` and `tell` operations, the only thing we need to change is the implementation of `runApp`:

```
runApp :: Config -> App a -> (a, Log)
runApp cfg app = runReader (runWriterT app) cfg
```

With these definitions, the behavior of the program will be indistinguishable from the original version.

However, we have to carefully choose the order when failure, exceptions, or nondeterminism are paired with either the state or the writer effect. Consider, for example, these two alternative monad stacks:

```
type M1 = StateT Int (MaybeT Identity)
type M2 = MaybeT (StateT Int Identity)
```

If we write functions to run computations in these two monads, we already get an inkling of their difference:

```
runM1 :: M1 a -> Int -> Maybe (a, Int)
runM1 p s = runIdentity (runMaybeT (runStateT p s))


runM2 :: M2 a -> Int -> (Maybe a, Int)
runM2 p s = runIdentity (runStateT (runMaybeT p) s)
```

The type signatures tell us that when failure (`Nothing`) happens, M1 does not give us a final state, but M2 does. Let's write a small program to experiment with this:

```
p :: (MonadState Int m) => m ()
p = do s <- get
       put (s + 1)
```

When the computation succeeds, we get the same information, just structured slightly differently:

```
*Main> runM1 p 0
Just ((),1)
*Main> runM2 p 0
(Just (),1)
```

However, when it fails, M1 does not show us the last value of the state anymore while M2 does:

```
*Main> runM1 (p >> empty) 0
Nothing
*Main> runM2 (p >> empty) 0
(Nothing,1)
```

When we provide an alternative to recover from the failure, we will see that M1 has rolled back the state to its initial value:

```
*Main> runM1 ((p >> empty) <|> get) 0
Just (0,0)
*Main> runM2 ((p >> empty) <|> get) 0
(Just 1,1)
```

In contrast, with M2, `get` always sees the effect of all the preceding `put` operations.

The behavior of M1 is called *backtracking* or *rollback*. It is useful when we want the alternative branches in the computation to have state values that are independent of each other. In contrast, M2 is useful when we want to share information across branches.

## Multiple copies

When combining two copies of the same monad transformer in a monad stack, things get a little tricky. Suppose we have to keep track of both a federal tax (10%) and a city tax (5%) on property, and we use one reader effect for each:

```
type FederalTax = Float
type CityTax = Float


type M = ReaderT FederalTax (ReaderT CityTax Identity)
runM :: M a -> a
runM p = runIdentity (runReaderT (runReaderT p 0.10) 0.05)
```

We may try to compute the overall tax as follows:

```
propertyTax :: Float -> M Float
propertyTax value = do fTax <- ask
                       cTax <- ask
                       pure (value * (fTax + cTax))
```

Unfortunately, this does not do what we want:

```
*Main> runM (propertyTax 100000.0)
20000.0
```

This result is wrong; it should be 15000.0. What goes wrong is that both calls to ask retrieve the federal tax because it is stored in the outermost ReaderT transformer. Recall that ask is an overloaded operation whose behavior is determined by the available MonadReader type class instances. There is only one such instance for ReaderT:

```
instance Monad m => MonadReader r (ReaderT r m)
```

Hence, for the monad, M, the ask operation retrieves the federal tax.

How do we make the program behave correctly? I have two relatively modest workarounds. The first approach is to merge the two copies of the reader effect into a single one, with a combined environment value:

```
data Taxes = MkTaxes { federalTax :: Float
                     , cityTax    :: Float }

type M = ReaderT Taxes Identity
```

```
runM :: M a -> a
runM p = runIdentity (runReaderT p (MkTaxes 0.10 0.05))
```

This requires making a small adjustment to the program – that is, switching from `ask` to `asks`:

```
propertyTax :: Float -> M Float
propertyTax value = do fTax <- asks federalTax
                       cTax <- asks cityTax
                       pure (value * (fTax + cTax))
```

This way, we get the desired behavior:

```
*Main> runM (propertyTax 100000.0)
15000.001
```

Alternatively, we keep the monad stack, M, as-is with two copies of `ReaderT`, but we have the program explicitly acknowledge their relative positions in the stack:

```
propertyTax :: Float -> M Float
propertyTax value = do fTax <- ask
                       cTax <- lift ask
                       pure (value * (fTax + cTax))
```

The difference is that we now retrieve the city tax with `lift ask`. With this, we are saying that `ask` should not be performed concerning M, but concerning the `ReaderT CityTax Identity` monad under the surface. This way, it correctly retrieves the city tax:

```
*Main> runM (propertyTax 100000.0)
15000.001
```

These two are not the two only workarounds. There are other, more onerous approaches, such as setting up a custom monad transformer, but those require a bit more experience to carry out.

## Summary

In this chapter, we studied how custom monads, which combine several effects, can be assembled using monad transformers. These transformers augment a monad with the specified functionality, typically of an additional effect.

*Chapter 13, Domain-Specific Languages*, starts the final part of this book. We will move on from studying Haskell's hierarchy of type constructor classes and focus our attention on application-oriented aspects. The first topic, which we studied in this chapter, is a language-oriented approach to problem-solving. By creating a new language tailored to a particular problem domain, we can more easily solve problems in that domain.

## Questions

Answer the following questions to test your knowledge of this chapter:

1. What is a monad transformer?
2. What are the important monad transformers?
3. What is a monad subclass?
4. What are the important monad subclasses?

## Further reading

To learn more about the topics that were covered in this chapter, take a look at the following resources:

- The monad transformer library documentation: `https://hackage.haskell.org/package/mtl-2.3.1`

- The `list-t` library documentation: `https://hackage.haskell.org/package/list-t`

## Answers

Here are the answers to this chapter's questions:

1. A monad transformer is a type constructor, T, that transforms any monad, M, into a new monad, T M. Moreover, T must be an instance of the MonadTrans type class:

```
class MonadTrans t where
      lift :: Monad m => m a -> t m a
```

   Monad transformers are typically used to augment existing monad with the functionality of an additional effect.

2. The important monad transformers are:

| Effect | Monad Transformer | Key Operations |
|---|---|---|
| Reader/environment | `ReaderT r` | `ask, local` |
| Writer | `Monoid w =>` `WriterT w` | `tell` |
| State | `StateT s` | `put, get` |
| Failure | `MaybeT` | `empty, (<\|>)` `throwError, catchError` |

| Effect | Monad Transformer | Key Operations |
|---|---|---|
| Errors/exceptions | `ExceptT e` | `throwError, catchError` |
| Nondeterminism/failure | `ListT (done right)` | `empty, (<\|>)` |

3. A monad subclass is a type constructor class that subclasses the Monad type class. They require that a monad provides some additional operations. The purpose of monad subclasses is to write monadic code that is polymorphic in the particular choice of monad, but still uses particular operations. Constraint polymorphism allows the monad to be instantiated in different ways, in particular by stacking monad transformers in different ways or by including additional monad transformers.

4. The important monad subclasses are:

| Effect | Monad Subclass | Key Operations |
|---|---|---|
| Reader/environment | `MonadReader r m` | `ask, local` |
| Writer | `Monoid w => MonadWriter w m` | `tell` |
| State | `MonadState s m` | `put, get` |
| Errors/exceptions | `MonadError e m` | `throwError, catchError` |
| Nondeterminism/failure | `Alternative` | `empty, (<\|>)` |

# Part 4:
# Practical Programming

In this part, you explore four practical programming techniques, with a distinct functional programming flavor. First, you will develop **domain-specific languages** (**DSLs**) by leveraging lightweight programming language implementation techniques and increase programmer productivity. Then, you will turn textual input into structured data by means of parser combinators. Next, you will reach deep into data structures by means of lenses, a powerful data accessor mechanism. Finally, you will not write tests but generate them with property-based testing.

This part has the following chapters:

- *Chapter 13, Domain-Specific Languages*

- *Chapter 14, Parser Combinators*

- *Chapter 15, Lenses*

- *Chapter 16, Property-Based Testing*

# 13
# Domain-Specific Languages

As software developers, languages are one of the most fundamental and powerful tools at our disposal. When we say *languages*, we likely think of **general-purpose programming languages (GPLs)** such as Haskell, Python, and Java. While these GPLs differ in many ways, they have all been designed to tackle a wide range of tasks well, but not to excel at any one particular task. In other words, they are jacks of all trades, but masters of none. This is useful when we don't know in advance what tasks we will face or when we are facing a wide range of different tasks. However, when the tasks we are facing are highly similar and drawn from the same problem domain, GPLs are not optimal. Indeed, we may end up repeating a lot of scaffolding code across tasks and be unnecessarily distracted from the task at hand.

This is where **domain-specific languages (DSLs)** come in. A DSL is a language that has been designed to excel at a particular kind of task, or a range of tasks, within a particular domain (but is likely useless outside of its scope). Often, this means that the DSL is a rather minimal language, stripped of the wide range of common general-purpose features of GPLs. Instead, the DSL provides primitive language features that correspond directly to the key concepts in the problem domain. This way, the programmer can directly start working, without having to work out a translation from domain concepts to GPL language features. This means that programmers become more efficient when they use a DSL.

Developing a language requires a substantial investment in terms of development time. Think of writing parsers, compilers or transpilers, documentation, IDE integration, and other tooling. In the case of DSLs, such an investment often does not make business sense. After all, compared to GPLs, DSLs for small niches will have many orders of magnitude fewer users and fewer programs written in them. Only in the case of a large user population, big organizations, and/or a large expected return is such an investment worthwhile. A few examples of these are HTML, CSS, and SQL.

Fortunately, there is a less costly approach for developing DSLs, known as *embedded DSLs*. An embedded DSL piggybacks on an existing GPL, known as the *host language*, and reuses its existing tooling and language features (data types, abstraction mechanism, and so on). The downside is that the designer of an embedded DSL does not have complete liberty and must abide by the rules of the host language in terms of the type system, syntax, error messages, and so on.

Embedded DSLs are where Haskell comes in. Many of the language features we have studied so far in this book are very useful for designing and implementing a DSL. Since the 1990s, Haskell has been a testbed and trailblazer for embedded DSL development. Several early embedded Haskell DSLs have been widely copied to other host languages.

In this chapter, we will look at several examples of DSLs that are tailored to different problem areas, both programming-oriented and otherwise. Then, we'll focus on implementation techniques for DSLs. The most general and flexible approach is deep embedding. It contrasts with shallow embedding, which is a more lightweight and efficient technique.

In short, this chapter covers the following main topics:

- What do DSLs embedded in Haskell look like?

- What are several interesting embedded DSLs?

- How does the general-purpose deep embedding implementation of DSLs work?

- How does shallow embedding work?

# A DSL for formatting

We'll start with a relatively simple programmer-oriented DSL, one for pretty-printing source code. Pretty-printing means generating a textual layout that is nicely formatted.

## Overview

The Haskell DSL we'll study is available in the `Text.PrettyPrint` module in the `pretty` package. It combines three elements that distinguish this module from arbitrary other libraries and characterizes it as an embedded DSL:

- The DSL revolves around an **abstract data type** (or multiple ones). An abstract data type is a data type whose representation is hidden from the user. The only way it can be manipulated is through the API of the library. The user can't perform any pattern matching on it or invoke constructors directly.

- In our DSL, the abstract data type is `Doc`; this is the type of the (formatted) document. Such a document combines textual content with layout directives.

- To create values of the abstract data type, the DSL provides several **constructor functions**. These values can be created either directly or from one or more existing values of the abstract data type. The constructor functions are also called **combinators.**

Let's look at two examples of combinators for documents:

- First, we have `text :: String -> Doc`, which creates a basic document from a given string. Then, we have `sep :: [Doc] -> Doc`, which, if there is enough room, puts the given documents side by side, separated by whitespace. Otherwise, if there is not enough room, it puts the documents below each other.

- We can now write a small example document:

```
hw :: Doc
hw = sep [text "hello", text "world"]
```

- Lastly, the DSL provides one or more **interpretation functions** that turn values of the abstract data type into something concrete. For example, the following function computes the actual layout of a document:

```
renderStyle :: Style -> Doc -> String
```

Here, the `Style` type conveys some configuration information. A default `style` is also provided:

```
*Main> renderStyle style hw
"hello world"
```

The default style allows lines that are up to 100 characters, and at most two-thirds of a line can be content and the rest whitespace. If we reduce the line length to 14, this horizontal layout will no longer fit:

```
*Main> renderStyle style {lineLength = 14} hw
"hello\nworld"
```

The 10 characters of content take up more than two-thirds of 14 characters. This violates the whitespace requirement. For that reason, the function generates a different, vertical layout that puts the two words on separate lines. (In fact, because of floating-point imprecision, the switch already happens at a line length of 15 characters.)

Working with an embedded DSL typically has two phases. First, we build up a structure (of the abstract data type), after which we interpret it. Different DSLs for the same domain can distinguish themselves in two ways according to two phases: the range of combinators they provide and the range of different interpretations they support.

## Data format example

The expressiveness of the pretty printing library mainly stems from its range of available combinators. Let's explore this a bit further using a small example.

Suppose we have the following JSON-like data type of values:

```
data Value = Primitive String | Record [(String, Value)]
```

A primitive value is a string, and a recursive value is a record of key-value pairs. Here's an example:

```
card :: Value
card = Record [("name",
                Record [("first", Primitive "Tom")
                       ,("last", Primitive "Schrijvers")])
              ,("role", Primitive "author")
              ]
```

We would like to format these values in a JSON-like fashion. For this purpose, we'll write a formatting function that turns a value into a document:

```
format :: Value -> Doc
format (Primitive s) =
  doubleQuotes (text s)
format (Record l)    =
  sep [lbrace, (nest 2 (sep [entry e | e <- l])), rbrace]
    where
      entry :: (String, Value) -> Doc
      entry (k, v) =
        doubleQuotes (text k) <+> colon <+> format v <> comma
```

The first case turns a primitive value into a text document surrounded by double quotes. The second case turns a record into a left brace, followed by the entries and a right brace. These three elements are laid out horizontally or vertically. The entries are nested with two spaces of indentation and separated horizontally or vertically. Each entry consists of a double-quoted key followed by a colon, the value, and a comma.

This makes use of the following combinators, in order of appearance:

- Surround the document with double quotes

  ```
  doubleQuotes :: Doc -> Doc
  ```

- Turn the string into a document

  ```
  text :: String -> Doc
  ```

- Layout documents horizontally (separated by a space) or vertically

  ```
  sep :: [Doc] -> Doc
  ```

- A left brace character '{'

  ```
  lbrace :: Doc
  ```

- Left margin of nested document is indented given number of spaces

  ```
  nest :: Int -> Doc -> Doc
  ```

- A right brace character '}'

  ```
  rbrace :: Doc
  ```

- The two documents are put side by side, separated with a space

```
(<+>) :: Doc -> Doc -> Doc
```

- A colon character ':'

```
colon :: Doc
```

- The two documents are put side by side, without separator

```
(<>) :: Doc -> Doc -> Doc
```

- A comma character ','

```
comma :: Doc
```

We can observe different layouts if we set the line length at different values:

```
putStrLn $ renderStyle style {lineLength = 50 } $ format v
{ "name" : { "first" : "Tom",
             "last" : "Schrijvers",
           },
  "role" : "author",
}
*Main> putStrLn $ renderStyle style {lineLength = 90 } $ format v
{ "name" : { "first" : "Tom", "last" : "Schrijvers", },
  "role" : "author",
}
*Main> putStrLn $ renderStyle style {lineLength = 100 } $ format v
{ "name" : { "first" : "Tom", "last" : "Schrijvers", },
  "role" : "author",
}
```

As we can see, the format we have put together can flexibly adapt itself to the given line length.

In the next section, we'll study a rather different DSL that is targeted at investment banking.

# A DSL for financial contracts

The domain-specific nature of the language means that programs can be more easily understood, and often also written or modified, by domain experts who do not have a background in programming. In this section, we'll discuss such a DSL – one for financial contracts.

The idea for this DSL was first presented in 2000 in the paper *Composing Contracts* and has since been highly influential. Many (investment) banks have adopted this approach and set up in-house variants of the DSL (in a much more sophisticated form than what we'll see here). It has carved out an important job market for functional programmers in the financial sector.

## Compositional contracts

A contract is an agreement between two parties: the *holder* and the other party. (It can be generalized to more than two parties, but we won't go that far in this book.) A contract is always formulated from the point of view of the holder. Here is an example contract that, while simplified, is representative of contracts that commonly occur in the finance industry:

```
C: the right to choose on 30 June 2024 between:
C1: Both of:
            C11: Receive €100 on 29 Jan 2025.
            C12: Pay €105 on 1 Feb 2026.
    C2: An option exercisable on 15 Dec 2024 to choose one of:
        C21: Both of:
                C211: Receive €100 on 29 Jan 2025.
                C212: Pay €107 on 1 Jun 2026.
        C22: Both of:
                C221: Receive €100 on 29 Jan 2025.
                C222: Pay €112 on 1 Feb 2027.
```

A key observation we can make is that larger contracts, such as C, are created by composing smaller contracts, such as C1 and C2. These are, in turn, created by combining elementary contracts, such as C11 and C12.

The finance industry employs an extensive vocabulary for describing various specific forms of financial contracts (swaps, futures, caps, floors, American options, and European options, to list but a few). The benefit of exploiting the compositional nature of contracts is that we can describe and reason about all these (and more) with only a small set of primitive combinators.

The original presentation consisted of only 10 combinators. These not only allow us to express the commonly used types of contracts but also provide the flexibility of expressing new ones.

## Zero-coupon bonds

As a basic example of a compositional contract, we'll consider the so-called **zero-coupon bond**. A zero-coupon bond states that the holder receives a particular amount of money in a particular currency on a particular date. Examples of these are C11, C211, and C221 in the preceding code. For example, we can define C11 as follows:

```
c11 :: Contract
c11 = zcb (date "29 Jan 2025") 100 EUR
```

Here, the zcb function creates a zero-coupon bond from a date, an amount, and a currency:

```
zcb :: Date -> Double -> Currency -> Contract
```

Here, `Contract` is the abstract data type around which the DSL revolves. The `Date` type of dates is an auxiliary predefined type. Values of this type can be obtained through the `date :: String -> Date` function, which parses a string representation of the date. It also assumes a `Currency` type, which is defined as an enumeration of the different currencies of interest:

```
data Currency = EUR | GBP | JPY | USD | …
```

Even though it is fairly basic, the zero-coupon bond is not a primitive contract. It is defined in terms of several primitive combinators that can also be used to define other contracts:

```
zcb :: Date -> Double -> Currency -> Contract
zcb day amount currency =
  scale amount (get (truncate day (one currency)))
```

The `scale`, `get`, `truncate` and `one` combinators are four of the nine primitive building blocks that our contract DSL provides. We'll explain all nine next, starting with these four.

## Contract combinators

Here, we'll provide an overview of the nine contract combinators, but first, we need to explain two important dates related to contracts:

- **Acquisition date**: The acquisition date is the date at which the holder of the contract enters the contract with the other party. It is the date when the contract becomes active. Many consequences of the contract depend on this acquisition date because any stipulations in the contract regarding earlier dates will have no effect. For example, if `C1` is acquired on January 30, 2025, the holder no longer receives €100.

- **Expiry date**: The expiry date is the earliest point in time at which a contract can no longer be acquired. Each combinator will indicate how it affects the expiry date. Be aware that the expiry date is not quite the same as the end of the contract; a contract may still have consequences after its expiry date. An example is a contract known as an option, such as "*the right to decide on December 26, 2024, whether or not to acquire contract C.*" This contract must be acquired before December 26, 2020 – its expiry date – but the underlying contract, `C`, may have consequences much later than December 26, 2024.

All contracts have an acquisition date and an expiry date, and some combinators explicitly interact with these dates.

### *one*

The `one` primitive pays out one unit of the given currency immediately, at the time of acquisition:

```
one :: Currency -> Contract
```

This contract never expires.

## truncate

The truncate combinator affects the expiry date of the given contract. The expiry date of truncate d c is the soonest of d and the original expiry date of c:

```
truncate :: Date -> Contract -> Contract
```

For example, in the truncate date (one currency) combination, the expiry date becomes the given date because one itself never expires.

## get

The get combinator forces the holder to acquire the given contract, c, on its expiry date, right before c expires. Importantly, it cannot be acquired any earlier:

```
get :: Contract -> Contract
```

The expiration date of get c is the same as that of c.

For example, while truncate date (one currency) can be acquired any time before or on date, get (truncate date (one currency)) can only be acquired on date.

## scale

The scale combinator multiplies all the amounts in the given contract by the given factor:

```
scale :: Double -> Contract -> Contract
```

The expiry date of scale f c is the same as that of c.

For example, scale 100 (one EUR) gives the holder €100 at the time of acquisition, rather than just €1.

We have now covered the four combinators needed for the zero-coupon bond:

```
zcb day amount currency =
  scale amount (get (truncate day (one currency)))
```

From right to left, we read: *We get one unit of the given currency (one), cannot acquire it any later than day (truncate), and not earlier (get), and multiply by amount (scale).*

Another basic contract we can create with scale is the zero contract:

```
zero :: Contract
zero = scale 0 (one EUR)
```

This contract bestows neither rights nor obligations. On its own, it is pointless, but as we'll see shortly (when we show the European option), it is a useful building block for larger contracts.

To express other interesting contracts, we'll cover the other contract combinators, several of which are needed to construct our initial example contract.

### give

This combinator swaps the roles of the two parties in the given contract. The expiry date remains the same:

```
give :: Contract -> Contract
```

For example, while one  EUR means that the holder receives €1 from the other party, give  (one EUR) means that the holder has to pay €1 to the other party. This way, we can express C12 from the initial example:

```
c12 :: Contract
c12 = give (zcb (date "1 Feb 2026") 105 EUR)
```

Contracts without give are too good to be true. Why would the other party enter the contract if it would not get anything in return?

### both

This combinator combines two contracts in a way that the holder is forced to acquire both or neither. They can't have one without the other. The acquisition of the two contracts is immediate upon the acquisition of their combination:

```
both :: Contract -> Contract -> Contract
```

The expiry date of both c and c' is the earliest expiry date of c and c'.

For example, both (one EUR) and (give (scale 2 (one EUR))) means that the holder receives €1 and has to pay (back) €2. Similarly, we can set up the example contract, C1, as follows:

```
c1 :: Contract
c1 = both c11 c12
```

### or

This combinator is the dual of both. When acquiring or  c  c', the holder must immediately acquire c or c', but not both. This forces a choice; unless c or c' has already expired, then only the other can be acquired:

```
or :: Contract -> Contract -> Contract
```

The expiry date of or c c' is the latest expiry date of c and c'.

A European option makes use of this combinator:

```
european :: Date -> Contract -> Contract
european d c = get (truncate d (c `or` zero))
```

This gives the holder the choice of date, d, to either acquire the underlying contract, c, or not. Not acquiring c is captured in the zero contract we defined earlier, which bestows no rights or obligations.

It is also worth pointing out that the give operator we saw earlier affects the or combinator. Namely, because give swaps the roles of the two parties, it also affects who gets to make the choice. For example, in the contract, or c11 c12, the holder chooses whether they get money (c1) or pay money (c12). In the contract, give (or c11 c12), the roles are fully reversed: it is the other party that chooses whether they get or pay money.

### thereafter

This combinator provides a kind of sequential composition of contracts. When you acquire c `thereafter` c', you acquire c if it has not expired yet. If c has already expired, then you acquire c' instead:

```
thereafter :: Contract -> Contract -> Contract
```

The whole is expired when both underlying contracts have expired.

Here's an example:

```
truncate (date "1 Jan 2024") (scale 2 (one EUR)) `thereafter` one EUR
```

If you acquire this contract before January 1, 2024, you get €2. If you acquire it later, you only get €1.

### anytime

This combinator forces the underlying contract to be acquired but allows the holder to choose when it is acquired. Of course, the acquisition has to happen before the underlying contact expires:

```
anytime :: Contract -> Contract
```

The expiry date of anytime c is the expiry date of c.

With this combinator, we can express the *American option*. Like the European option, the American option allows the holder to decide whether they acquire an underlying contract or not. On top of that, it also allows the holder to choose when to acquire within a given time interval. In other words, american d1 d2 c means the holder can choose between d1 and d2 whether they want to acquire c or not:

```
american :: Date -> Date -> Contract -> Contract
american d1 d2 c = before `thereafter` after where
```

```
before = get (truncate d1 after)
after  = anytime (truncate d2 (c `or` zero))
```

There are two parts to this contract. The second part, `after`, allows you to choose whether to acquire `c` or not, any time before `d2`. The first part, `before`, requires you to make that choice on `d1`. The two parts are combined thereafter, meaning that the first part applies until `d1` and the second part applies after `d1` (and until `d2`).

## Interpreting contracts

The advantage of having contracts in a machine-readable form is that they can be automatically processed to extract all kinds of information. Let's consider two.

### ExpiryDate

As we have seen, every contract has an associated expiry date. With this function, we can extract that information from a given contract:

```
expiry :: Contract -> ExpiryDate
```

Here, `ExpiryDate` is either a concrete date or indicates that the contract never expires:

```
data ExpiryDate = ExpiresOn Date | ExpiresNever
  deriving Show
```

Here's an example:

```
*Main> expiry (one EUR)
ExpiresNever
*Main> expiry (truncate (date "1 Jan 2025") (one EUR))
ExpiresOn 1 Jan 2025
```

This way, we know which contracts we urgently have to acquire (if at all), and which we should throw away because they have already expired.

### Valuation

The key interpretation of financial contracts is their valuation: how much money does the primary party (typically, the investment bank) stand to make or lose when it engages in the contract? Doing this accurately is impossible as it requires knowledge of the future. In practice, educated guesses have to be made based on extrapolations of the past and models of how the market evolves. Unfortunately, we do not have access to the actual valuation functions that are used in practice; these are the carefully guarded trade secrets of the banks that develop them.

A simplified model would calculate the value of a contract on a given date in a given reference currency:

```
value :: Contract -> Currency -> Date -> Double
```

For example, given our example contract, c, we could compute its value in Japanese yen on May 5, 2024, with `value c JPY (date "5 May 2024")`. This would be a prediction involving future exchange rates between the euro and the yen, and future inflation, which makes €1 tomorrow worth less than €1 today.

More elaborate models could explore multiple scenarios about future evolutions together with their likelihood and yield a probability distribution of a contract's worth.

Now that we have studied two more advanced DSLs from the perspective of a DSL user, we will turn our attention to developing DSLs ourselves.

## Implementing DSLs

There are two main techniques for implementing an embedded DSL in Haskell: **deep embedding** and **shallow embedding**. Each has its advantages and disadvantages, and we will study both.

### Running example

To illustrate the deep embedding technique, and later the shallow embedding, we will use a small DSL for describing geometric regions. This DSL was originally developed for a prototype system in a US Navy study. The prototype had to keep track of where different entities (ships, planes, and so on) were concerning each other. Different regions (also called zones) have different significance: coming too close to friendly units is interpreted as hostile intent, certain corridors are reserved for airline routes, and so on.

The core abstract data type in this DSL is `Region`. There are several combinators for constructing such regions. For the sake of minimality, we'll only consider three here:

- A primitive region is a circular shape around the origin, with a given radius:

  ```
  type Radius = Double

  circle :: Radius -> Region
  ```

- We can *dualize* a given region, covering every point that is outside of the given region:

  ```
  outside :: Region -> Region
  ```

- Finally, we can take the intersection of two given regions. This covers every point that's present in both regions:

  ```
  (/\) :: Region -> Region -> Region
  ```

In practice, there will be more primitives, but these three will do to serve our point. Moreover, they can already be used to derive other relevant regions, such as `annulus`:

```
annulus :: Radius -> Radius -> Region
annulus r1 r2 = outside (circle r1) /\ circle r2
```

An annulus is a band-shaped region; it is the circular part between the smaller radius, `r1`, and the larger radius, `r2`.

The key interpretation function for regions is `inRegion :: Point -> Region -> Bool`, which checks whether a given point lies in the region. This way, we can check, for example, whether a hostile entity is in a region that it should not be. A point is defined here simply as a tuple of its coordinates:

```
type Point = (Double, Double)
```

Now, let's consider how we can implement this small DSL with one abstract data type, three combinators, and one interpretation function.

## Deep embedding

The straightforward idea of deep embedding is to represent the abstract data type with an algebraic data type. Then, we can include each primitive combinator as a constructor of that data type. If we apply this approach to our running example, we get the following:

```
data Region
  = Circle Radius
  | Outside Region
  | Region :/\ Region
```

This data type represents the (abstract) syntax of our region language; any value of the `Region` type that we construct will be an abstract syntax tree.

Hence, we can define the combinator functions by applying the corresponding constructor:

```
circle  = Circle
outside = Outside
(/\)    = (:/\)
```

This is pretty straightforward. The only part that requires some effort is defining the interpretation function, `inRegion`. This function is defined as an interpreter that gives meaning to the abstract syntax:

```
inRegion :: Point -> Region -> Bool
(x,y) `inRegion` Circle r    = sqrt (x**2 + y ** 2) <= r
p     `inRegion` Outside r   = not (p `inRegion` r)
p     `inRegion` (r1 :/\ r2) = p `inRegion` r1 && p `inRegion` r2
```

All the business logic of the DSL is essentially captured in this interpreter function.

Besides the relative ease of the deep embedding approach, it also has the advantage that we can easily write other functions that process regions using pattern matching. For example, we could write a function that generates a graphical representation of the region, or one that computes a region's area. Hence, adding additional interpretation functions is easy: it does not require us to modify any of the existing code.

A disadvantage that the deep embedding approach shares with all uses of algebraic data types is that adding more primitives is less convenient. When we add another primitive as a constructor, we need to update all the functions that perform pattern matching.

## Shallow embedding

The shallow embedding approach trades off several advantages and disadvantages with deep embedding. Its definition is less straightforward but more efficient. Moreover, it becomes easy to add more primitives, but at the same time only supports one interpretation function.

The core idea of shallow embedding is that we use the interpretation function as a representation for the abstract data type. In our running example, the interpretation is to check whether given points occur in the region. Hence, the representation we use is as follows:

```
type Region = Point -> Bool
```

Now, the formal interpretation function has no work:

```
p `inRegion` r = r p
```

As the region is its own interpretation, we can just apply it as a function.

A consequence of this representation choice is that every combinator creates an interpretation function:

```
circle r  = \(x,y) -> sqrt (x**2 + y ** 2) <= r

outside r = \p -> not (r p)

r1 /\ r2  = \p -> r1 p && r2 p
```

As we can see, the business logic is now distributed among these combinators. This choice of representation comes with a performance benefit: it delivers the interpretation directly without performing a pattern match on an abstract syntax tree. It also becomes easy to add additional primitives. For example, we can define a combinator that sets up a square region around the origin:

```
type Side = Double

square :: Side -> Region
square s = \(x,y) -> abs x <= s/2 && abs y <= s/2
```

However, because the choice of interpretation function is baked into the representation, it is impossible to provide additional ones.

## The best of both worlds

With the help of type class overloading, we can combine the best of both worlds (except for the conceptual simplicity) into a single approach, which is sometimes called the *finally tagless* approach. It is based on shallow embedding but uses type classes to overload the interpretation.

Instead of using a concrete representation, we can use a type parameter, r, that is constrained by a type class. The type class, which we now call Region, has the combinators as its methods:

```
class Region r where
    circle  :: Radius -> r
    outside :: r -> r
    (/\)    :: r -> r -> r
```

Derived combinators, such as annulus, get similarly overloaded types:

```
annulus :: Region r => Radius -> Radius -> r
annulus r1 r2 = outside (circle r1) /\ circle r2
```

We can support an interpretation by instantiating the Region type class:

```
instance Region (Point -> Bool) where
    circle r  = \(x,y) -> sqrt (x**2 + y ** 2) <= r
    outside r = \p -> not (r p)
    r1 /\ r2  = \p -> r1 p && r2 p
```

As before, the interpretation function, inRegion, applies the region as a function:

```
inRegion :: Point -> (Point -> Bool) -> Bool
inRegion p r = r p
```

To support additional interpretations, we must provide additional instances of the type class. For instance, if we have an image representation, we could write an instance that generates it:

```
instance Region Image where
    ...
```

Moreover, we can support additional combinators by introducing additional type classes. For example, to add the square primitive, we can create a Square type class:

```
class Square r where
    square :: Side -> r
```

Code that combines primitives from multiple type classes gets multiple constraints on the representation:

```
someRegion :: (Region r, Square r) => Radius -> Side -> r
someRegion r s = circle r /\ outside (square s)
```

A representation just supports the additional primitives through an instance of the new type class:

```
instance Square (Point -> Bool) where
   square s = \(x,y) -> abs x <= s/2 && abs y <= s/2
```

This way, it is relatively easy to support additional primitives and additional interpretations to the DSL.

## Summary

In this chapter, we studied DSLs embedded as libraries in Haskell. We saw two examples of such embedded DSLs – one for pretty-printing source code and one for financial contracts. Both revolve around an abstract data type, several combinators to construct values of that abstract data type, and one or more interpretation functions. We also studied two implementation techniques, deep and shallow embedding, as well as a refinement of the latter ("finally tagless") for additional flexibility.

*Chapter 14, Parser Combinators*, complements this chapter. It introduces another example of a DSL for parsing that has been copied from Haskell to other programming languages. Moreover, this DSL is quite useful for processing standalone DSLs with a custom syntax.

## Questions

Answer the following questions to test your knowledge of this chapter:

1.  What is a DSL?
2.  What is an embedded DSL?
3.  What is deep embedding?
4.  What is shallow embedding?

## Further reading

To learn more about the topics that were covered in this chapter, take a look at the following resources:

*   The pretty-printing library documentation
*   `https://hackage.haskell.org/package/pretty-1.1.3.6/docs/Text-PrettyPrint.html`
*   The original paper on the contracts DSL
*   *Simon L. Peyton Jones, Jean-Marc Eber, Julian Seward: Composing contracts: an adventure in financial engineering, functional pearl. ICFP 2000: 280-292*

# Answers

Here are the answers to this chapter's questions:

1.  As opposed to a GPL, a DSL is a language tailored toward a particular problem domain. It features concepts of that problem domain as primitives and aims to be more effective than a GPL for problem-solving within that domain.

2.  Embedding is a lightweight implementation technique for DSLs that makes use of the facilities of a general-purpose programming language, called the host language.

    Typically, an embedded DSL is set up as a library of the host language. This way, it has to abide by the syntax, type system, and abstraction mechanisms of the host language. In exchange, the development effort is very low as no custom facilities for parsing syntax, type-checking programs, and low-level code generation have to be created; the host language takes care of this.

    Typically, an embedded DSL revolves around one or more abstract data types. It provides a range of combinators for creating values of this abstract data type and one or more interpretation functions.

3.  Deep embedding is an implementation technique for embedded DSLs. The idea is that the DSL's abstract data types are represented by concrete algebraic datatypes that model their abstract syntax. That is to say, each combinator is realized as a data constructor, and interpretation functions pattern match on those constructors to interpret them.

4.  Shallow embedding is an alternative implementation technique for embedded DSLs. The idea is to bake a fixed interpretation into the definition of the DSL. The abstract data types are represented directly by their interpretation. This means that the combinators build interpretation functions.

# 14
# Parser Combinators

Parsing is the act of turning a usually human-readable structured text into a data structure that can be easily processed in software. The best-known application of parsers is in compilers. A compiler frontend takes the text written by programmers, the source code, and turns it into an abstract syntax tree, which is a more convenient data structure to work with in the next stages of the compiler. Besides parsing source code, many other structured text formats are parsed, such as JSON, YAML, and XML, which are used for all kinds of data entry, data exchange, and configuration.

To make parsing possible, the text cannot take on an arbitrary form. It needs to be structured in a particular way, and follow certain rules. Formally, the expected text structure is sometimes codified in a grammar, which serves as a non-executable specification for the parser. This formal background, together with the development of many sophisticated and intricate parsing approaches for compiler development, has cast somewhat of a stigma on parsing as an arcane task that is best left to experts, and out of reach of most programmers. Instead, they stick to existing text-based formats, such as JSON, and their readily available parsers. While this is often convenient for the programmer, it is not always an ideal choice for those who have to write structured text. This is especially true for domain-specific languages, where, for example, there's a YAML-based encoding of a function call such as the following:

```
- type: method_call
  receiver: obj
  method: foo
  arguments:
    - tuple:
      - 1
      - true
```

This is rather clunky compared to the more conventional option:

```
obj.foo((1,true))
```

Fortunately, a much more lightweight and accessible approach to parsing was invented in the 1990s in the context of Haskell: *parser combinators*. A parser combinator is an embedded DSL for writing parsers that leverages several abstractions we have covered in earlier chapters, such as monads and applicative functors. The approach has been immensely popular and copied to many other programming languages.

We'll become familiar with parser combinators in this chapter. Based on an example, we will see what the main job of a parser is, how such a parser can be written in Haskell, and what happens under the hood. We'll start with a small hand-rolled parser combinator implementation to master the basics, and then move on to one of the most robust and widely used libraries, Parsec. We will have a look at Parsec's more advanced and convenient features, and consider some parsing challenges and gotchas.

In short, this chapter covers the following main topics:

- What is parsing and what is it used for?
- How can we define and use a basic definition of parser combinators?
- How can we use the full-fledged Parsec library of parser combinators?
- How can we solve common parsing challenges?

# Parsing

Before we dive into parser combinators, let's briefly review what parsing is, and consider some alternative options for obtaining Haskell parsers.

## What is parsing?

The basic idea of parsing is to take a string representation of some data and turn it into the corresponding value of a structured data type. For example, consider the `"1 + 2"` string. With a parser, we could turn this into a value, `Plus (Lit 1) (Lit 2)`, of the `Expr` algebraic data type:

```
data Expr = Lit Int | Plus Expr Expr
```

Typically, the textual value is convenient for humans, but further programmatic processing is much easier on the structured value. For example, it is much easier to write an evaluation function that takes `Expr` than a string.

Because the string can easily be ill-formed – for example, `"1 +"` or `"1 ++ 2"` – parsing is an operation that may fail. We model this in Haskell with the result type, `Maybe Expr`. Thus, the basic parsing interface would look like this:

```
parseExpr :: String -> Maybe Expr
```

A more informative interface would return `Either ParseError Expr`, where the `ParseError` type explains the cause of the failure. Sometimes, depending on how the parser is set up, it may also produce multiple results. For example, if we don't take association into account, then the `"1 + 2 + 3"` string could be parsed to both `Plus (Lit 1) (Plus (Lit 2) (Lit 3))` and `Plus (Plus (Lit 1) (Lit 2)) (Lit 3)`. There's ambiguity here, and we can model it with `[Expr]` to return all possible results. However, ambiguity is usually undesirable and indicates a flaw in either the language that needs to be parsed or in the implementation of the parser.

Typically, there is no one-to-one mapping between a string representation and a structured representation of the same value. For instance, in our expression example, the amount of white space should play no role. `"1+2"`, `"1 + 2"` and `"1    +\n2"` should parse to the same expression. Besides whitespace, parentheses are other common characters that are not explicitly represented in the structured value but may influence which structured value is produced. For example, the parentheses in `"(1 + 2) + 3"` and `"1 + (2 + 3)"` disambiguate between the two expression trees.

## How to get a parser

There are three main ways to create a parser in Haskell.

### Hand-write a parser

The first approach, which I discourage, is to write the parser function by hand. While this is sometimes done for applications that are used on a large scale, it is a high-effort, error-prone undertaking that is not easy to evolve.

### Generate a parser

The second approach is to use a parser generator, such as Happy for Haskell. Parser generators follow a two-phase approach. In the first phase, the generator takes a specification for the parser, written in a standalone DSL, and generates source code for the parser function. In the second phase, this source is compiled and linked against the user code, which can now use the parser function.

This parser-generator approach has several important advantages:

- It generally produces highly efficient code with predictable performance characteristics by leveraging complicated parsing algorithms
- Writing similar code by hand is not practical
- Before code generation, the parser generation can analyze the specification and report issues, such as ambiguity

### Use parser combinators

Given the many advantages of parser generators, why do we need anything else, such as parser combinators? This question becomes even more pressing when we realize that parser combinators lack many of the advantages of parser generators.

Indeed, parser combinators are often less efficient, sometimes pathologically so, because they use simpler algorithms. Moreover, they typically do not and cannot analyze the parser up front; they have to discover problems when they arise at runtime. Finally, they also have some pitfalls, such as left recursion, that are annoying and need to be worked around all the time.

The main thing parser combinators have going for themselves is that their barrier to entry is much lower. They can be used directly, without learning the syntax of a standalone DSL; it is just an embedded DSL packaged as a library. This approach does not require the two-stage compilation whenever the parser is modified, which facilitates exploration. Moreover, because simpler algorithms are used, it is easier for the programmer to understand what is going on in the parser. Finally, in some instances, parser combinators can be a bit more powerful and flexible because they allow the parser to be created or adapted dynamically (for example, based on what it has read so far).

Because of this low barrier to entry, and because it presents another compelling example of an embedded DSL, we'll study parser combinators in the remainder of this chapter.

# Parser combinators

Parser combinators are a compositional approach for defining parsers in the style of the embedded DSLs, which we covered in the previous chapter. In this section, we will cover basic combinators and the essence of their implementation.

## A parser for sums

A **parser** is a kind of data structure that is assembled from combinators. The (abstract) type of the parser is `Parser a`; this type denotes a parser that processes a string and produces a result of the a type. For example, to parse sum expressions, we want a parser, `exprP`, of the `Parser Expr` type.

Once we have a parser, we can apply it to an input string using the following interpretation function:

```
parse :: Parser a -> String -> Maybe a
```

Because the input string may not be in the expected format, the parser can fail; this is modeled with the `Maybe a` result type.

We expect the following behavior:

```
*Main> parse exprP "1+2"
Just (Plus (Lit 1) (Lit 2))
*Main> parse exprP "1++2"
Nothing
```

The first primitive parser combinator we will use to define `exprP` is as follows:

```
satisfy :: (Char -> Bool) -> Parser Char
```

This combinator checks whether the next character in the input satisfies the given predicate. If it does, that character is returned. If it does not, the parser fails. For example, with the `isDigit` predicate from `Data.Char`, we can check whether the input is a single digit:

```
digit :: Parser Char
digit = satisfy isDigit
```

This works as expected:

```
*Main> parse digit "1"
Just '1'
*Main> parse digit "a"
Nothing
```

When parsing a digit, it is often useful to get back its numeric value rather than its character representation. Because Parser has a functor instance, we can transform the parse result with fmap:

```
digitValue :: Parser Int
digitValue = fmap digitToInt digit where
  digitToInt c = ord c - ord '0'
```

Our conversion makes use of the fact that digits have consecutive character codes, given by ord, starting at '0'. Now, we get integers when parsing digits:

```
*Main> parse digitValue "1"
Just 1
```

We can further specialize satisfy to check for a specific character:

```
char :: Char -> Parser Char
char c = satisfy (== c)
```

For example, we can check for a plus operator:

```
plus :: Parser Char
plus = char '+'
```

This works as follows:

```
*Main> parse plus "1"
Nothing
*Main> parse plus "+"
Just '+'
```

Now we have the two main ingredients for parsing sums: digits and plus signs. How do we combine them into one parser? Well, Parser forms a monad, where ( >>= ) is the composition operator that performs two parsing steps in sequence. Hence, we can write a simple sum parser as follows, using do notation instead of ( >>= ) for convenience:

```
simpleSumP :: Parser Expr
simpleSumP =
  do x <- digitValue
     plus
     y <- digitValue
     pure (Plus (Lit x) (Lit y))
```

Observe that we are not interested in the result of the `plus` parser because we already know what it is. Also, the `pure` parser simply returns a result without consuming any input.

The parser now yields the desired result:

```
*Main> parse simpleSumP "1+2"
Just (Plus (Lit 1) (Lit 2))
```

However, it still has several limitations:

- The numbers are only one digit long
- The sum has to contain exactly two terms
- Whitespace around the numbers and operators is not allowed

Let's start with the last issue. To support white space, we can add a parser for a whitespace character:

```
space :: Parser Char
space = satisfy isSpace
```

We can add this to our simple sum parser:

```
simpleSumP :: Parser Expr
simpleSumP  =
  do x <- digitValue
     space
     plus
     space
     y <- digitValue
     pure (Plus (Lit x) (Lit y))
```

Now, it admits spaces around the operator:

```
*Main> parse simpleSumP "1 + 2"
Just (Plus (Lit 1) (Lit 2))
```

However, the spaces are compulsory. We can't omit them:

```
*Main> parse simpleSumP "1 + 2"
Nothing
```

This is not what we want. We want the spaces to be `optional`. We can make this possible by using Parser's `Alternative` instance. It provides a choice operator:

```
(<|>) :: Parser a -> Parser a -> Parser a
```

This way we can provide two alternative parsers. If the first one fails, we fall back on the second one. This is used in the generic optional combinator:

```
optional :: Alternative f => f a -> f (Maybe a)
optional p = fmap Just p <|> pure Nothing
```

With this combinator, we can request optional spaces around the operator:

```
simpleSumP :: Parser Expr
simpleSumP  =
  do x <- digitValue
     optional space
     plus
     optional space
     y <- digitValue
     pure (Plus (Lit x) (Lit y))
```

This way, both forms of input work:

```
*Main> parse simpleSumP "1 + 2"
Just (Plus (Lit 1) (Lit 2))
*Main> parse simpleSumP "1+2"
Just (Plus (Lit 1) (Lit 2))
```

While we can have zero or one space on either side of the operator, we can't have many:

```
*Main> parse simpleSumP "1  +  2"
Nothing
```

To support many spaces, we must add recursion to the mix:

```
spaces :: Parser ()
spaces = (space >> spaces) <|> pure ()
```

This definition defines `spaces` as being either one `space` followed by more `spaces` or nothing (`pure`). As spaces do not contain relevant information, we simply return `unit` here.

Generally, there are two useful repetition patterns for parsers: zero-or-more and one-or-more. These are captured in the `many` and `many1` combinators, respectively:

```
many, many1 :: Parser a -> Parser [a]
many  p = many1 p <|> pure []
many1 p = do x <- p
             xs <- many p
             pure (x:xs)
```

For example, we can define `number` as being one or more digits:

```
number :: Parser Int
number = fmap digitsToNumber (many1 digitValue) where
  digitsToNumber :: [Int] -> Int
  digitsToNumber = foldl (\x y -> 10 * x + y ) 0
```

We use `many1` here because we want at least one digit in a number. Finally, we can write the version of the parser that incorporates all these improvements, as well as allowing zero or more additions:

```
exprP :: Parser Expr
exprP = do spaces
           x <- literalP
           spaces
           more x <|> pure x
  where
        literalP :: Parser Expr
        literalP = fmap Lit number

        more :: Expr -> Parser Expr
        more x = do plus
                    y <- exprP
                    pure (Plus x y)
```

The expression can start with several spaces followed by a literal and some more spaces. Then, we can either have a `plus` operator and another expression, or we are done.

Now, we can parse arbitrarily long sums of multidigit numbers with any amount of whitespace:

```
*Main> parse exprP " 1  + 23 +456 "
Just (Plus (Lit 1) (Plus (Lit 23) (Lit 456)))
```

Now that we have an idea of what basic parser combinators are available and how they are combined into larger parsers, let's take a look under the hood and see how parser combinators work.

## Parsers under the hood

A basic representation for compositional parsers combines elements of the state monad and the maybe monad:

```
newtype Parser a = P { runP :: String -> Maybe (a, String) }
```

This representation takes an input string and maybe produces a result. Because we want to sequentially compose parsers, a parser does not necessarily consume the whole input string. It may leave a remainder of the input string for the next parser. This remainder is captured by the string result.

How the composition works is best seen in the Monad instance:

```
instance Monad Parser where
  p >>= f = P (\s -> case runP p s of
                       Nothing -> Nothing
                       Just (x, s') -> runP (f x) s')
```

If the first parser, p, fails, the composition fails. If the first parser succeeds, its result, x, as well as the remainder of the input, s', is passed to the second parser, f.

The Alternative instance shows how choice works:

```
instance Alternative Parser where
  empty = P (\s -> Nothing)
  p <|> q = P (\s -> case runP p s of
                       Nothing -> runP q s
                       r        -> r)
```

When the first parser succeeds, the alternative composition commits to its result. When it fails, the second parser is used instead.

The satisfy primitive is the only one that looks at the input:

```
satisfy :: (Char -> Bool) -> Parser Char
satisfy p =
  P (\s -> case s of
             (c:s') -> if p c then Just (c,s')
                              else Nothing
             []     -> Nothing)
```

If the input is empty or the first character does not satisfy the predicate, nothing is returned. Otherwise, both the first character and the remainder are.

Finally, running the parser just discards the remaining string:

```
parse :: Parser a -> String -> Maybe a
parse p s = fmap fst (runP p s)
```

This means that the parser may not consume the whole input as we might expect. The following example illustrates this unintuitive behavior:

```
*Main> parse exprP "1-2"
Just (Lit 1)
```

Here, the parse does not recognize the `'-'` character. However, because `"1"` is a valid parse, the parser still succeeds and discards the remainder `"-2"`. If we don't want this, we have to use a special primitive:

```
eof :: Parser ()
eof = P (\s -> if null s then Just ((),"") else Nothing)
```

This primitive only succeeds when the end of the input (end of file) is reached. We use it as follows to fail when the input is not fully consumed:

```
*Main> parse (exprP <* eof) "1-2"
Nothing
```

Recall that `(<*)` sequentially composes two computations and returns the result of the first:

```
*Main> parse (exprP <* eof) "1+2"
Just (Plus (Lit 1) (Lit 2))
```

Thanks to the basic hand-rolled parser definition, we now have a good idea of how parsing works. In the next section, we'll move on to a much more sophisticated *industrial-strength* parser combinator library.

# The Parsec library

In practice, you will want to use an off-the-shelf parser combinator library. In this chapter, we'll study Parsec, which is one of the older and more established libraries. On Hackage, you can find various new libraries with more bells and whistles, but Parsec will do nicely as a starting point.

## Different types of parsers

To provide additional flexibility and expressive power, Parsec's parser type features three additional type parameters beyond the a parameter for the result type:

```
ParsecT s u m a
```

Let's discuss the three additional parameters from right to left:

- The monad parameter, m, signals that `ParsecT s u` is a monad transformer; it can be layered on top of a monad, m. For basic uses, we don't need any underlying monad and can default to using the trivial `Identity` monad. For that, Parsec provides a type synonym:

  ```
  type Parsec s u = ParsecT s u Identity
  ```

- The u parameter is for a user-defined state. Indeed, some parsers may wish to modify their behavior based on information they keep track of. For that reason, the parser representation has a state monad transformer built-in, which can be accessed with the `getState` and `putState` functions. However, often, this functionality is not needed. In those cases, we can default the u parameter to the unit type `()`.

- The s parameter generalizes from String to other sources of characters. This generalization is captured in the Stream type class:

```
class Monad m => Stream s m t | s -> t where
    uncons :: s -> m (Maybe (t, s))
```

The idea is that the stream of type s contains elements, called tokens, of type t, and accessing these tokens may require a particular monad, m. In the case of String, we have the following instance:

```
instance Monad m => Stream String m Char
```

Here, the tokens are of the Char type, and no particular monad is required; any monad will do. Despite the generalization of the token type here, all combinators that involve the token type, such as satisfy, actually assume that the token type is Char:

```
satisfy :: Stream s m Char
        => (Char -> Bool) -> ParsecT s u m Char
```

In summary, for many basic use cases, the following type will do:

```
type Parser = Parsec String ()
```

There are three functions for running the parsers, from more general to less general:

1. The most general function is as follows:

```
runParserT :: Stream s m t
           => ParsecT s u m a -> u -> SourceName -> s
           -> m (Either ParseError a)
```

This takes a parser, the initial user-defined state, the source name, and the stream as inputs. It produces either an error or a result in the stream's monad, m. The source name is some descriptor of the source of the data, such as the name of the file, which can be used in error messages; the SourceName type is just a synonym for String.

2. The next function specializes runParserT for the Identity monad:

```
runParser :: Stream s Identity t
          => Parsec s u a -> u -> SourceName -> s
          -> Either ParseError a
```

3. Finally, the most specific form further specializes runParser to the point where the user-defined state is not relevant and defaults to unit:

```
parse :: Stream s Identity t
      => Parsec s () a -> SourceName -> s
      -> Either ParseError a
```

This is the function you will want to use most often.

## Parsec particulars

Parsec provides the same type class instances (`Functor`, `Applicative`, `Alternative`, and `Monad`), as well as all the additional combinators (`satisfy`, `char`, `space`, `spaces`, `many`, `many1`, and `eof`) that we saw in the previous section. However, because the underlying representation is more sophisticated, the implementations are different. Yet the behavior is by and large the same, apart from two major aspects – the notion of character consumption and the mechanism for error messages. We'll explain these two here.

### To consume or not to consume, that is the question

One of the problems with parsers is that alternative branches revisit large parts of the input repeatedly. For example, suppose we have the `p = p1 <|> p2` parser, where we have the following:

```
p1 = many (char 'a') *> char 'b'
p2 = many (char 'a') *> char 'c'
```

If we have a very long string of `'a'` characters followed by `'c'`, then the `p1` branch of `p` will run down the whole string and fail when it sees `'c'` at the end. Then, `p2` will start over, run down the whole string again, and finally accept it. For more complex parsers, repeatedly revisiting parts of the string easily becomes pathological to the extent that the parser is simply unusable.

To avoid this pitfall and to enforce better practice, Parsec disables the possibility of revisiting parts of the input string by default. This is where the notion of *consumption* comes in. Once a part of the input has been consumed, it cannot be revisited. This matters for alternatives such as `p1 <|> p2`: if `p1` has already consumed part of the input before it fails, then `p2` is not tried as an alternative because it is not allowed to revisit that already consumed input.

The `satisfy` combinator is a main primitive that consumes a character. When the character satisfies the predicate, it is consumed. When it does not, it isn't. This means that the following parser is pointless:

```
abac = ab <|> ac where
  ab = char 'a' *> char 'b'
  ac = char 'a' *> char 'c'
```

It aims to parse both the `"ab"` and `"ac"` strings. When encountering `"ac"`, `char 'a'` (which is defined as `satisfy (=='a')`) in the first branch will consume the first `'a'`. The subsequent `char 'b'` fails when seeing `'c'`. Yet, the second branch won't be tried because the first branch has consumed a character. This way, the parser can never accept the `"ac"` string.

A way around this problem is to factor out the common prefix, `char 'a'`, of the two alternatives:

```
abac = char 'a' *> (char 'b' <|> char 'c')
```

When encountering "ac", char 'a' consumes 'a'. Then, the parser tries char 'b' on 'c', which fails. Nothing is consumed in that first alternative, so the second alternative, char 'c', is applied and succeeds. This way, "ac" is accepted.

Factoring out common prefixes is often not very convenient. It breaks abstractions and prevents reuse. For this reason, Parsec provides a primitive combinator that temporarily disables consumption:

```
try :: ParsecT s u m a -> ParsecT s u m a
```

The idea is that try p executes p but defers its consumption until the end. If p fails midway through, then try p does not consume anything. If p succeeds, then try p consumes everything that p does. This way, we can make the example work as follows:

```
abac = try ab <|> ac where
  ab = char 'a' *> char 'b'
  ac = char 'a' *> char 'c'
```

Thanks to try, the ab parser does not consume anything when seeing "ac". It simply fails, and the ac alternative can successfully accept the input.

### Error messages

One of the useful features of Parsec is that it issues error messages when a parse fails. For example, let's say that we want to check for a digit:

```
*Main> parse (satisfy isDigit) "" "a"
Left (line 1, column 1):
unexpected "a"
```

The error message informs of the position where the unexpected character is encountered. Compare this to Parsec's predefined digit parser, whose error message is more informative than this. It not only tells us what is not expected but also what is expected instead:

```
*Main> parse digit "" "a"
Left "file" (line 1, column 1):
unexpected "a"
expecting digit
```

Parsec provides a combinator to annotate our parsers with a description of what they expect:

```
(<?>) :: ParsecT s u m a -> String -> ParsecT s u m a
```

We can use it as follows:

```
*Main> parse (satisfy isDigit <?> "digit") "" "a"
Left "file" (line 1, column 1):
unexpected "a"
expecting digit
```

This functionality is already built into Parsec's predefined parsers for various character classes: `space`, `tab`, `newline`, `upper`, `lower`, `hexDigit`, `alphaNum`, and so on. Yet even if the expected character class is already given, we can still provide better descriptions for composite parsers. For example, compare the following two:

```
*Main> parse (traverse char "hello") "" "world"
Left (line 1, column 1):
unexpected "w"
expecting "h"
*Main> parse (string "hello") "" "world"
Left (line 1, column 1):
unexpected "w"
expecting "hello"
```

The second parser, which is predefined, is essentially defined as follows:

```
string s = traverse (\c -> char c <?> s) s
```

It helpfully reports the whole string it expects rather than any of its characters. This works because the outer use of `(<?>)` overrides the one inside `char`.

Moreover, the `(<|>)` combinator helpfully combines the descriptions of its alternatives:

```
*Main> parse (string "hello" <|> string "world") "" "sun"
Left (line 1, column 1):
unexpected "s"
expecting "hello" or "world"
```

Hence, with a little effort, we can make the Parsec error messages a lot more helpful.

With the particulars of Parsec down, let's revisit the problem of parsing arithmetic expressions and face several challenges in the process.

# Parsing challenges – expressions revisited

In this section, we'll revisit the parser for simple arithmetic expressions, now using Parsec. We explore several variations and extensions, consolidate earlier lessons, and handle new challenges.

As our starting point, consider again the simple type for arithmetic expressions:

```
data Expr = Lit Int | Plus Expr Expr
```

We could write a very naive parser for it that follows the structure of the data type definition:

```
exprP = literalP <|> sumP
literalP = Lit <$> number
sumP = do x <- exprP
          plus
```

```
            y <- exprP
            pure (Plus x y)
```

When used naively, the parser does not consume all the input:

```
*Main> parse exprP "1+2"
Right (Lit 1)
```

To amend this, we have to check for the end of the file:

```
*Main> parse (exprP <* eof) "" "1+2"
Left (line 1, column 2):
unexpected '+'
expecting digit or end of input
```

The problem is that `literalP` has accepted `"1"`, but the subsequent `eof` does not accept `"+"`. Yet, the `sumP` alternative is not explored because `literalP` has consumed a character. Wrapping `literalP` in `try` does not change anything because it succeeds; it's `eof` that fails.

An idea could be to try `sumP` first, by swapping the two alternatives. We'll even wrap `sumP` in `try`. This way, we can fall back to a plain literal when there is no `'+'` operator:

```
exprP = try sumP <|> literalP
```

Now, parsing goes into an infinite loop:

```
*Main> parse (exprP <* eof) "" "1+2"
```

This problem is known as *left recursion*. The first thing `exprP` does is call `sumP`, which, in turn, first calls `exprP`. In other words, we get a loop that does not make any progress.

The solution is to factor out the common prefix of `sumP` and `literalP`, which is `literalP`. This eliminates the left recursion:

```
exprP =
  do x <- literalP
     f <- rest
     pure (f x) where
  rest = (do plus
             y <- exprP
             pure (`Plus` y)
         ) <|> (pure id)
```

Now, parsing a sum just works:

```
*Main> parse (exprP <* eof) "" "1+2"
Right (Plus (Lit 1) (Lit 2))
```

Well, it right-associates addition:

```
*Main> parse (exprP <* eof) "" "1+2+3"
Right (Plus (Lit 1) (Plus (Lit 2) (Lit 3)))
```

In contrast, Haskell left-associates it. If we want to replicate that behavior, we have to refactor the parser a little so that it uses an accumulator:

```
exprP = exprP' id where
  exprP' f  =
    do x <- literalP
       rest (f x)
  rest x = (do plus
               exprP' (Plus x)
            ) <|> (pure x)
```

Now, we get a left-associated expression tree:

```
*Main> parse (exprP <* eof) "" "1+2+3"
Right (Plus (Plus (Lit 1) (Lit 2)) (Lit 3))
```

Parsec offers a convenient combinator that captures this pattern:

```
chainl1
  :: Stream s m t
  => ParsecT s u m a -> ParsecT s u m (a -> a -> a)
-> ParsecT s u m a
```

It parses a sequence of elements separated by operators in a left-associative fashion. (For right-association, you can use chainr1.) It can be used as follows in our running example to yield a very concise definition:

```
exprP = literalP `chainl1` plusP
plusP = pure Plus <* plus
```

Let's go a step further and add multiplication to our expression data type:

```
data Expr = Lit Int | Plus Expr Expr | Times Expr Expr
```

A naive adjustment to the parser would allow either operator in the chain:

```
exprP = literalP `chainl1` opP
opP = plusP <|> timesP
timesP = pure Times <* char '*'
```

This does not take the precedence of times over `plus` into account:

```
*Main> parse (exprP <* eof) "file" "1+2*3"
Right (Times (Plus (Lit 1) (Lit 2)) (Lit 3))
```

To achieve proper precedence, we can view an expression as a sum chain where the elements (terms) are multiplication chains:

```
exprP = termP `chainl1` plusP
termP = literalP `chainl1` timesP
```

This stratification does the right thing:

```
*Main> parse (exprP <* eof) "file" "1+2*3"
Right (Plus (Lit 1) (Times (Lit 2) (Lit 3)))
```

We'll stop here, but this needn't be your final version. You can grow this parser further with additional operators, parentheses, and additional expression forms, as well as more helpful error messages.

## Summary

In this chapter, we learned how parser combinators make it easy to turn strings into structured data. We covered how to write parsers and also looked under the hood of a minimal parser combinator implementation to get a basic understanding of how the approach works. Then, we moved on to the industrial-strength Parsec library for parser combinators. We studied its character consumption behavior and its support for error messages. Finally, we explored how to satisfy several requirements and avoid common pitfalls when writing parsers.

*Chapter 15, Lenses*, presents an elegant, purely functional approach to a mundane but ubiquitous programming task: data access in nested data types. First, we'll identify the disadvantages of Haskell's built-in support for record access and then present the concept of lenses as a much more convenient alternative for both reading and updating fields. We'll not only show that lenses compose trivially to reach deep into data structures but that they can also be used to seamlessly define virtual fields. Finally, we'll cover the main lens combinators provided by the well-known `lens` library.

## Questions

Answer the following questions to test your knowledge of this chapter:

1. What is parsing?
2. What are parser combinators?
3. What are the advantages and disadvantages of parser combinators?
4. What are the particular features of Parsec?

# Further reading

To learn more about the topics that were covered in this chapter, take a look at the following resource:

- The Parsec library documentation: `https://hackage.haskell.org/package/parsec`

# Answers

Here are the answers to this chapter's questions:

1. Parsing is the act of turning a, usually human-readable, structured text into a data structure that can be easily processed in software.

2. Parser combinators are an embedded DSL for parsing. They define parsers in a compositional way, assembling primitive parsers into larger ones.

3. Parser combinators have several advantages:

   - They are more convenient to write than hand-rolling your own parser

   - As an embedded DSL, they are easily integrated into a code base and do not hamper the development process

   - They do not require learning a new language and have a low threshold for entry

   - Monad parsers are very flexible and expressive; the parsing behavior can be determined dynamically

4. Parser combinators also have several disadvantages compared to parser generators:

   - Their performance is usually not as good as that of parser generators and can be pathologically bad if we aren't careful (for example, in the case of left recursion)

   - Due to their flexibility, monadic parser combinators can provide few static guarantees about their well-behavedness, such as the absence of ambiguity

   We focused on two particular features of Parsec:

   - To prevent pathological behavior, parsers consume their input, which prevents the input from being revisited by alternative parsers. This behavior can be overridden by the `try` combinator.

   - Using the `(<?>)` combinator, parsers can be annotated with a description of what they are parsing. This is used to improve the error message when the parse fails.

# 15
# Lenses

Data access in nested data types is one of the most common and mundane activities in real-world programs. In imperative and object-oriented programming languages, reaching deep inside nested objects or records is relatively frictionless. This is not the case in Haskell. Because data structures are immutable, updating a field means rebuilding the data structure around the new value for that field. This is especially painful when the field appears deeply nested inside the structure.

The concept of **lenses** was developed to remedy this problem. In its basic form, a lens is a data accessor that can be used to both inspect and modify the value of a field in a data structure. Unlike the typical data accessors built into programming languages, lenses are first-class: they can be composed, passed around, and used on different instances of the same data structure. Of course, this wouldn't be Haskell if we didn't take the idea to the next level. Indeed, lenses can perform all kinds of computations, point at fields that are not there (virtual fields), or point at many fields at once. These advanced forms of lenses, also collectively called **optics**, make it worth using the approach in languages that already have reasonable support for data accessors. For example, lenses are used in Java to convert old data formats of Minecraft maps into the current format.

This chapter reviews the basic approach for records that is built into Haskell and identifies its disadvantages. Next, we'll cover the concept of lenses as a much more convenient alternative for both reading and updating fields. We'll show that lenses not only compose trivially to reach deep into data structures but that they can also be used to seamlessly define virtual fields and perform side effects. Finally, we'll cover advanced forms of lenses and their combinators.

In short, this chapter covers the following main topics:

- Using records and their field accessors and updates, and being aware of their limitations
- Using and composing lenses for field access and updates
- Using lenses for virtual fields and performing side effects
- Using advanced forms of lenses and their combinators

## Technical requirements

Support for lenses is not part of the Haskell standard library but needs to be installed as a separate package. Hackage features many lens packages. The most widely used and most feature-rich package is simply called `lens`. Its enormous size and dependency on many other packages is sometimes a reason not to use it. For that reason, and to keep things accessible, I recommend starting with a smaller package that only provides the essential functionality of the `lens` package: `microlens`. This is the package we will be using in this chapter.

## Records and deep access

Before we dive into lenses, let's review Haskell's built-in support for data access and its shortcomings.

Haskell's built-in support for data access is the named fields of record types that we first saw in *Chapter 2, Algebraic Data Types*. Here is a small example of this:

```
data Employee = MkEmployee { firstName :: String
                           , lastName  :: String
                           , salary    :: Int
                           }
```

This `Employee` type has one data constructor, `MkEmployee`, with three fields. Each field has been given a name, which can be used to access that field. Suppose we have a particular employee:

```
director = MkEmployee "Parker" "Jones" 3500
```

We can use a field name as a (projection) function to extract the field's value:

```
*Main> firstName director
"Parker"
*Main> salary director
3500
```

With the record update notation, we can also modify one or more fields:

```
*Main> director {salary = 4000}
MkEmployee {firstName = "Parker", lastName = "Jones", salary = 4000}
*Main> director {firstName = "Patty", lastName = "Smith"}
MkEmployee {firstName = "Patty", lastName = "Smith", salary = 3500}
```

Things get a bit more involved when we need to reach deeper into a data structure. Suppose we have a data type for companies that contains a distinguished employee, namely the CEO:

```
data Company = MkCompany { name  :: String
                         , ceo   :: Employee
                         , motto :: String
                         }
```

Now, we get a nested structure, like so:

```
fiberCo =
  MkCompany
    { name = "FiberCo"
    , ceo = MkEmployee { firstName = "Lux"
                       , lastName = "Cable"
                       , salary = 3000 }
    , motto = "We are the light at the end of your cable." }
```

To query the salary of the CEO, we can compose the projection functions:

```
*Main> salary (ceo fiberCo)
3000
```

This is not too bad, but updating the salary is much more awkward:

```
*Main> fiberCo { ceo = (ceo fiberCo) { salary = 3500} }
MkCompany {name = "FiberCo", ceo = MkEmployee {firstName = "Lux",
lastName = "Cable", salary = 3500}, motto = "We are the light at the
end of your cable."}
```

What is quite verbose is that we have to refer to the CEO of the company twice:

- To extract the old `Employee` value from the company so that we can update it
- To write the updated `Employee` value into the `ceo` field of the company

This only gets worse as we have to reach deeper into a data structure. In the next section, we'll show that lenses provide a cleaner and more convenient approach to this problem.

# Lenses and their composition

Lenses are convenient abstractions for data access that are composed nicely. This way, they facilitate deep data access.

## Basic lenses

In essence, we can think of a lens as a pair of two functions – one for retrieving a component of a larger data type and another for replacing that component with a new value:

```
data Lens' s v = MkLens' { view :: s -> v
                         , set  :: v -> s -> s }
```

The larger data type is sometimes called `source`. Here, this is indicated with the s type variable. The component that the lens focuses on is then called `view`, which is indicated by the v type variable here.

When using lenses, the convention is to prefix the regular field names with an underscore, and to the regular names themselves for the lenses. For example, instead of the previous definition of Employee, we could write the following:

```
data Employee = MkEmployee { _firstName :: String
                           , _lastName  :: String
                           , _salary    :: Int
                           }
```

Additionally, we can write lenses for the three fields:

```
salary :: Lens' Employee Int
salary = MkLens' { view = _salary
                 , set = \s e -> e { _salary = s } }
```

We can use this code as follows for querying and updating the salary:

```
*Main> view salary director
3500
*Main> set salary 4000 director
MkEmployee {_firstName = "Parker", _lastName = "Jones", _salary =
4000}
```

With the combination of view and set, we can define the derived operator, over:

```
over :: Lens' s v -> (v -> v) -> (s -> s)
over l f s = set l s (f (view l s))
```

This modifies the field with the given function. For example, to double the director's salary, we can write the following:

```
*Main> over salary (*2) director
MkEmployee {_firstName = "Parker", _lastName = "Jones", _salary =
7000}
```

## Lens composition

The key feature of lenses is that they compose nicely, which allows us to reach deeper into data structures.

The composition operator encapsulates the awkward definition of the composite set operation:

```
composeLens :: Lens' s m -> Lens' m v -> Lens' s v
composeLens l1 l2 =
  MkLens' { view = view l2 . view l1
          , set = \s v -> set l1 s (set l2 (view l1 s) v)
          }
```

If we had a second lens, ceo :: Lens' Company Employee, for the CEO of a company, we could modify the CEO's salary as follows:

```
*Main> set (composeLens ceo salary) fiberCo 3500
MkCompany {_name = "FiberCo", _ceo = MkEmployee {_firstName = "Lux",
_lastName = "Cable", _salary = 3500}, _motto = "We are the light at
the end of your cable."}
```

This code is much cleaner than that using the record update notation.

## Change of representation

What's still a bit awkward and verbose is the name composeLens. This is one of the reasons why existing lens packages, such as lens and microlens, use a different representation for lenses. In the rest of this chapter, we'll use microlens and its representation:

```
type Lens' s v =
    forall f. Functor f => (v -> f v) -> (s -> f s)
```

This is an oddly abstract representation. How does this relate to the representation we saw earlier? Well, we can recover both view and set by making appropriate choices for the functor, f.

over is the easiest to recover – just plug in the Identity functor:

```
over :: Lens' s v -> (v -> v) -> (s -> s)
over l f s = runIdentity (l (Identity . f) s)
```

Then, set is just a special case that ignores the old view value:

```
set :: Lens' s v -> v -> (s -> s)
set l v s = over l (\_ -> v) s
```

The view function is recovered using the constant functor:

```
view :: Lens' s v -> s -> v
view l s = getConst (l Const s)
```

Writing the lens definition for a field such as salary is not that much harder:

```
salary :: Lens' Employee Int
salary t (MkEmployee f l s) =
    fmap (\s' -> MkEmployee f l s') (t s)
```

Yet, a key point of this change of representation is that lenses are just functions and as a consequence, we can compose two lenses using the function composition operator, ( . ):

```
*Main> set (ceo . salary) 3500 fiberCo
MkCompany {_name = "FiberCo", _ceo = MkEmployee {_firstName = "Lux",
_lastName = "Cable", _salary = 3500}, _motto = "We are the light at
the end of your cable."}
```

The composition of lenses now looks quite easy on the eyes. However, that's not the only advantage of the new representation. Another is that it naturally lends itself to further generalization. We will explore the possibilities of this generalization shortly.

## Lens operators

While we have used ordinary function names such as view and set for our lenses, lenses are often used with operators – lots of operators. Here, we'll review the main ones.

The first operator we'll consider is a synonym of view, with its parameters flipped:

```
(^.) :: s -> Lens' s v -> v
s ^. l = view l s
```

This way, we can write the following:

```
*Main> director ^. salary
3500
```

This notation is meant to resemble the director.salary notation that's used by many object-oriented languages.

Because set takes three parameters and an operator can take only two parameters, we have to use two operators to replace set. The first operator takes care of the first two parameters and returns a partially applied set function that still expects the third parameter. The operator notation is meant to resemble an assignment operator:

```
(.~) :: Lens' s v -> v -> (s -> s)
l .~ v = set l v
```

The second operator is a reverse function application, which is used for the third parameter:

```
(&) :: a -> (a -> b) -> b
x & f = f x
```

Together, they allow us to write a field, as follows:

```
*Main> director & salary .~ 4000
MkEmployee {_firstName = "Parker", _lastName = "Jones", _salary =
4000}
```

For `over`, we use `(&)` together with the following:

```
(%~) :: Lens' s v -> (v -> v) -> (s -> s)
l %~ f = over l f
```

This leads to the following code for doubling the director's salary:

```
*Main> director & salary %~ (*2)
MkEmployee {_firstName = "Parker", _lastName = "Jones", _salary =
7000}
```

There are a few specialized versions of `(%~)` for particular kinds of updates:

- The first operator mimics the imperative `+=` assignment operator. It adds a given value to the field:

  ```
  (+~) :: Num v => Lens' s v -> v -> (s -> s)
  l +~ x = l %~ (+x)
  ```

- In the same vein, the second operator mimics the `-=` operator, which subtracts a value from the field:

  ```
  (-~) :: Num v => Lens' s v -> v -> (s -> s)
  l -~ x = l %~ (subtract x)
  ```

- Finally, we have a more generic variant that uses the semigroup operator, `(<>)`, to update the field with a given value:

  ```
  (<>~) :: Semigroup v => Lens' s v -> v -> (s -> s)
  l <>~ x = l %~ (<> x)
  ```

While these can be very convenient, the many different operators can quickly become overwhelming.

## Generating boilerplate

The definitions of the lenses for data type fields are quite mechanical. For example, the lenses for the other two fields of `Employee` look as follows:

```
firstName :: Lens' Employee String
firstName t (MkEmployee f l s) =
  fmap (\f' -> MkEmployee f' l s) (t f)

lastName :: Lens' Employee String
lastName t (MkEmployee f l s) =
  fmap (\l' -> MkEmployee f l' s) (t l)
```

The microlens add-on package, microlens-th, has automated this boilerplate for us. Instead of writing the three lenses for Employee, you can simply write the following:

```
makeLenses ''Employee
```

Here, makeLenses is a TemplateHaskell function that generates the lens definitions. TemplateHaskell is a Haskell language extension that's enabled with the following pragma:

```
{-# LANGUAGE TemplateHaskell #-}
```

TemplateHaskell code is executed at compile time. It generates Haskell source code that is included in the module where it appears and has access to the code that appears earlier in the file. We pass makeLenses the name of the data type for which it should generate lenses. Using this name, it looks up the definition of the data type, figures out what field names start with an underscore (for example, _salary), and then generates lens definitions for these fields using the same name without the underscore (for example, salary). For this to work, the makeLenses call has to appear after the definition of the data type.

## Polymorphic lenses

The lenses we have been using so far are limiting what we can do with polymorphic data types. Take, for example, tuples of the (a,b) type, for which we can define two lenses – one for each of its components:

```
_1 :: Lens' (a,b) a
_2 :: Lens' (a,b) b
```

We can update a component as follows:

```
*Main> (3,True) & _1 %~ (+1)
(4,True)
```

However, what we cannot do is transform a component into another type:

```
*Main> (3,True) & _1 %~ show
```

This would change the type of the view from Int to String, and at the same time, it would change the type of the source from (Int,Bool) to (String,Bool). The Lens' type allows neither. However, the more general type of polymorphic lenses does allow this:

```
type Lens s t v w =
    forall f. Functor f => (v -> f w) -> (s -> f t)
```

The additional generality comes at the cost of a more complicated type. While Lens' has only two type parameters, Lens has four. Here, v is the type of the view before transformation, and w is the type after. Similarly, s is the type of the source before transformation and t after.

In lens libraries, this more general type of lens is used wherever possible. For example, for tuples, we have the following:

```
_1 :: Lens (a,b) (a',b) a a'
_2 :: Lens (a,b) (a,b') b b'
```

This allows type to change:

```
*Main> (3,True) & _1 %~ show
("3",True)
```

The _1 lens is overloaded to work not only for 2-tuples but also for 3-tuples, 4-tuples, and 5-tuples. This is achieved with a type class. Similar lenses (_2 to _5) exist that focus on other components of tuples.

So far, we have looked at basic lenses that behave essentially like built-in data accessors. In the next section, we'll explore what additional behavior can be packed into lenses so that we can go beyond conventional field access.

# Programmatic data access

Unlike the built-in field access functionality in programming languages, lenses are defined entirely programmatically. In the previous section, we used them rather rigidly to access actual fields of data types. Nothing forces those fields to be present, and we can deviate from them if we want.

## Virtual fields

Consider the following data type for claiming car trip expenses:

```
data Trip = MkTrip { _origin      :: String
                   , _destination :: String
                   , _distanceInKm :: Float }
```

The distance is stored in kilometers and comes with an appropriate lens:

```
distanceInKm :: Lens' Trip Float
distanceInKm t (MkTrip o d km) =
  fmap (\km' -> MkTrip o d km') (t km)
```

However, to accommodate the users of imperial miles, we can supply an alternative lens that pretends the field is stored in miles:

```
distanceInMi :: Lens' Trip Float
distanceInMi t (MkTrip o d km) =
  fmap (\mi' -> MkTrip o d (mi' * kmmi)) (t (km / kmmi))
    where kmmi = 1.60934
```

Internally, the lens transforms the stored kilometers to miles before exposing them, and, vice versa, converts miles back to kilometers before storing them.

Likewise, a lens can split information from one into multiple virtual fields. For example, suppose we store the time of day as the number of seconds since midnight:

```
data Time = MkTime { _daySeconds :: Int }
```

With lenses, we can pretend that the time is stored as a classic 24-hour clock and provide lenses for hours, minutes, and seconds. For example, that for hours would be implemented as follows:

```
hours :: Lens' Time Int
hours t (MkTime ds) =
  fmap update (t (div ds 3600)) where
    update h' = MkTime (mod ds 3600 + 3600 * (mod h' 24))
```

This lens extracts the hours out of the second-based representation before presenting them, and, vice versa, for storing them. In the latter case, it also maintains the invariant of the 24-hour clock that hours only ranges from 0 to 23.

Another interesting lens is the one for the Map data structure, which associates keys and values:

```
at :: k -> Lens' (Map k v) (Maybe v)
```

With at k, we focus on the value that is associated with the key, k. Because the key may not be present in the map, the view type is Maybe v.

For example, we can look up the value associated with a key as follows (this example requires installing the microlens-ghc extension package):

```
*Main> let m = fromList [("tom",5),("kevin",7)]
*Main> m ^. at "tom"
Just 5
*Main> m ^. at "patrick"
Nothing
```

The lens also allows us to insert or delete a value:

```
*Main> m & at "tom" .~ Nothing
fromList [("kevin",7)]
*Main> m & at "patrick" .~ Just 9
fromList [("kevin",7),("patrick",9),("tom",5)]
```

This is not the behavior you'd expect from a conventional data accessor.

## Side effects

The generality of the lens type also allows side effects during field access. This is facilitated by the `traverseOf` combinator. The following example illustrates its use, where we modify the director's salary by reading a new value from the standard input:

```
*Main> director & traverseOf salary (\s -> readLn)
4010
MkEmployee {_firstName = "Parker", _lastName = "Jones", _salary =
4010}
```

If we are not interested in producing a new value, we can use `traverseOf_`. The following code prints the old value:

```
*Main> director & traverseOf_ salary print
3500
```

The `lens-action` package even introduces a more general form of lens where accessing the data involves a side effect. Think of a lens that focuses on the content of a file, which would involve `IO` for reading and writing.

In the next section, we'll explore advanced forms of purely functional lenses that deviate from the `Lens` definition, as well as their combinators.

## Advanced lenses

One of the interesting insights of the function-based lens representation is that we can both generalize and specialize in various ways. These variations are often still compatible: they can be composed. We have already seen one example of this:

```
type Lens' s v
  = forall f. Functor f => (v -> f v) -> (s -> f s)
type Lens s t v w
  = forall f. Functor f => (v -> f w) -> (s -> f t)
```

The polymorphic lens is a generalization of the monomorphic one. When we have a monomorphic and a polymorphic lens of compatible types, they can be combined to yield a new monomorphic lens. For example, if we combine the `_1` lens with the `salary` lens, we get a new lens that focuses on the salary of the employee in the first component of a tuple:

```
_1 . salary :: Lens' (Employee, b) Int
```

Another way in which specialization is possible is through the functor type parameter, `f`, in the lens definition.

## Getters and setters

Earlier, we saw that we can recover the `view` and `set` functions from the `Lens'` and `Lens` representations by instantiating the functor parameter, `f`. In some cases, we can or want to provide only read-only or write-only access. We can use those types in their instantiated form.

For example, a simpler read-only lens has the following `type`:

```
type SimpleGetter s v =
    forall r. (v -> Const r v) -> (s -> Const r s)
```

Such a read-only lens makes sense when particular information can be easily extracted from a data structure, but not obviously modified. For example, we can easily compute the length of a list, but there is no usually clear-cut way in which we can modify a list so that it has a given length:

```
_length :: SimpleGetter [a] Int
_length t l = Const (getConst (t (length l)))
```

This way, we can use `_length` with the `view` function or its operator alias:

```
*Main> [2..6] ^. _length
5
```

On its own, it is perhaps silly to write this instead of `length [2..6]`. Yet, it is practical and consistent when computing the length of a list that appears inside a larger data structure.

Generalizing from the `length`/`_length` example, any `s -> v` function can be used to construct a getter:

```
to :: (s -> v) -> SimpleGetter s v
to f t s = Const (getConst (t (f s)))
```

Hence, we could have just written the following:

```
_length :: SimpleGetter [a] Int
_length = to length
```

A similar approach exists for write-only lenses, known as setters, though it has fewer use cases.

## Traversals

We can also partly specialize the functor, `f`, by requiring it to be an applicative functor:

```
type Traversal s t v w =
    forall f. Applicative f => (v -> f w) -> (s -> f t)
```

Unlike a regular lens, a traversal can point at multiple values inside a data structure. Indeed, traversals generalize the type signature of `traverse`, which visits all elements in a data structure:

```
traverse :: Applicative f => (v -> f  w) -> (k v -> f (k w))
```

Hence, we can readily construct traversals for all traversable functors:

```
traversed :: Traversable k => Traversal (k v) (k w) v w
traversed = traverse
```

For example, we can use this to update the elements of a list:

```
*Main> [1,2,3] & traversed .~ 0
[0,0,0]
*Main> [1,2,3] & traversed %~ (*2)
[2,4,6]
```

But traversals are more general than this. They can be used with any data structure, not just traversable functors. For example, we can create a traversal for the two parts of an employee's name:

```
names :: Traversal Employee Employee String String
names t (MkEmployee f l s) =
  (\f' l' -> MkEmployee f' l' s) <$> t f <*> t l
```

This definition transforms the first name and last name of an employee. Because `Employee` is not a type constructor, we can't change the type of the two name fields. They have to remain strings. In a case like this, where the types of both the source and the view remain the same, we can use the `Traversal'` type synonym to avoid repetition:

```
type Traversal' s v = Traversal s s v v
```

With this name traversal we can, for example, modify both names at the same time:

```
*Main> director & names %~ map toUpper
MkEmployee {_firstName = "PARKER", _lastName = "JONES", _salary =
7000}
```

We can also extract the names, as follows:

```
*Main> director ^. names
"ParkerJones"
```

The reason the strings are concatenated is that (`^.`) uses the `Const String` functor, whose `Applicative` instance uses the monoidal structure to combine the values. If the element type does not have a **Monoid** instance, this operator won't work.

Instead, we can use the `(^..)` operator, which extracts a list of elements:

```
*Main> director ^.. traversed
["Parker","Jones"]
```

To print the names, we can use `traverseOf_`, like before, but now on multiple elements:

```
*Main> director & traverseOf_ names putStrLn
Parker
Jones
```

Finally, as a slightly larger example, suppose we have departments:

```
data Department = MkDepartment { _deptName  :: String
                               , _deptStaff :: [Employee] }
```

We equip this type with a lens for a department's staff:

```
staff :: Lens' Department [Employee]
```

Now, we can give all the staff members in the `sales` department a €100 raise, as follows:

```
*Main> sales & staff . traversed . salary %~ (+100)
```

The key here is the composite lens, where we have the following:

- `staff` focuses on the staff list of the department
- `traversed` focuses on *each* employee in that list
- `salary` focuses on the salary of that employee

A small but more readable variation uses the `each` lens instead of `traversed`:

```
*Main> sales & staff . each . salary %~ (+100)
```

Here, `each` is a type class member:

```
class Each s t a b | s -> a, t -> b, s b -> t, t a -> s where
  each :: Traversal s t a b
```

It not only has an instance for lists but also for homogenous tuples:

```
instance Each (a,a) (b,b) a b
```

# Prisms

Prisms are lenses for data types such as `Maybe a` that have multiple constructors (`Just` and `Nothing`) where only one of the constructors contains the relevant data. The `microlens` package models these prisms as traversals that contain zero or one element. For example, for `Maybe`, there are two traversals for the two constructors:

```
_Just :: Traversal (Maybe a) (Maybe b) a b
_Nothing :: Traversal' (Maybe a) ()
```

Going through the `_Just` lens only affects the value if it was created with the `Just` constructor:

```
*Main> Just 1 & _Just %~ (+1)
Just 2
*Main> Nothing & _Just %~ (+1)
Nothing
```

We can write similar lenses for our algebraic data types. For example, recall our data type of shapes from *Chapter 2, Algebraic Data Types*:

```
data Shape = Circle Double
           | Rectangle Double Double
```

We can have a `radius` lens for the field of the `Circle` constructor:

```
radius :: Traversal' Shape Double
radius t (Circle r) = Circle <$> t r
radius t s          = pure s
```

To retrieve the radius, neither the `(^.)` nor `(^..)` operator is very practical:

```
*Main> Circle 2.0 ^. radius

<interactive>:3:15: error:
    • No instance for (Monoid Double) arising from a use of 'radius'
    • In the second argument of '(^.)', namely 'radius'
      In the expression: Circle 2.0 ^. radius
      In an equation for 'it': it = Circle 2.0 ^. radius
*Main> Circle 2.0 ^.. radius
[2.0]
```

The first approach does not work because `Double` does not have an instance of `Monoid`. Recall from *Chapter 9, Monoids and Foldables*, that only newtype-wrapped types such as `Sum Double` and `Product Double` have such an instance.

The second approach gives us a singleton list, which isn't very convenient. After all, we are only expecting zero or one radius value. The list type forces us to consider the possibility of more than one radius being returned.

For prisms, the (^?) operator is a better choice:

```
*Main> Circle 2.0 ^? radius
Just 2.0
*Main> Rectangle 1.0 3.0 ^? radius
Nothing
```

This operator returns the value wrapped in Maybe to account for its possible absence. For arbitrary traversals, with more than one value, it only returns the first:

```
*Main> [1,2,3,4] ^? each
Just 1
```

When we are sure the value has a radius, we can use the unsafe (^?!) operator:

```
*Main> Circle 2.0 ^?! radius
2.0
```

However, this crashes on rectangles.

Something else that's useful is the has operation, which checks whether there is a value:

```
*Main> Circle 2.0 `has` radius
True
*Main> Rectangle 1.0 3.0 `has` radius
False
*Main> [1,2,3] `has` each
True
*Main> [] `has` each
False
```

This concludes our review of more advanced lens forms.

# Summary

In this chapter, we looked at data access in deeply nested data structures. We saw how updating fields with the built-in `record` field functionality is awkward. As an alternative, we introduced lenses as first-class, easily composable data accessors. We saw that they not only allow purely functional updates of record fields but also support virtual fields and side effects. Moreover, besides focusing on one field, they can also focus on multiple fields or values at once.

*Chapter 16, Property-Based Testing*, concludes this book with another viral idea that was developed in the context of Haskell: property-based testing. It is a powerful alternative to ordinary unit testing. The idea is to not write unit tests manually but generate them automatically from a more high-level description – a property. From most properties, an unbounded number of unit tests can be automatically generated, either randomly or more systematically. This makes testing more thorough and fun.

# Questions

Answer the following questions to test your knowledge of this chapter:

1. What is a lens?
2. What is a polymorphic lens?
3. What is a traversal?

# Further reading

To learn more about the topics that were covered in this chapter, take a look at the following resources:

- The `microlens` package documentation:

  `https://hackage.haskell.org/package/microlens`

- The `lens` package documentation:

  `https://hackage.haskell.org/package/lens`

## Answers

Here are the answers to this chapter's questions:

1.  A lens is a first-class data accessor. In its standard form, it focuses on a particular field in a data structure and allows you to both retrieve and modify the value of that field.

    Packages such as `lens` and `microlens` use the following function-based representation for (monomorphic) lenses:

    ```
    type Lens' s v =
       forall f. Functor f => (v -> f v) -> (s -> f s)
    ```

    Here, the `s` type parameter denotes the source type (the data structure) and the `v` parameter denotes the view type (the field).

    A key property that makes working with lenses convenient is that they compose. The preceding function-based representation lens composition is simply function composition, `(.)`.

2.  A polymorphic lens is a lens that allows you to modify the value of a view in a way that changes its type, from `v` to `w`. As a consequence, the type of the source changes as well, from `s` to `t`.

    Packages such as `lens` and `microlens` use the following function-based representation for polymorphic lenses, which generalizes that of monomorphic lenses:

    ```
    type Lens s t v w =
       forall f. Functor f => (v -> f w) -> (s -> f t)
    ```

3.  A traversal is a lens that can focus on zero or more values, rather than on a single value.

    Packages such as `lens` and `microlens` use the following function-based representation for polymorphic lenses, which generalizes that of ordinary lenses:

    ```
    type Traversal s t v w =
       forall f. Applicative f => (v -> f w) -> (s -> f t)
    ```

# 16
# Property-Based Testing

Testing is an important aspect of software quality assurance. It exercises the software to expose bugs, ideally early on in the development process where they can be mitigated relatively cheaply. Unfortunately, there are several negative stereotypes associated with testing: it is seen as tedious, time-consuming, and costly. For these reasons, testing is often looked down upon and neglected.

This negative perception is likely due to a particular testing approach: unit testing. Unit testing is rather labor intensive as individual test inputs and expected outputs have to be devised one by one. Typically, a large suite of such unit tests is needed to test the software thoroughly. Some cleverness can go into choosing appropriate inputs, but on the whole, the challenges are limited and the work rather repetitive.

As Haskell programs can also contain bugs, software testing is recommended. However, instead of resorting to unit testing, we have a much more fun and productive testing approach at our disposal: property-based testing. The original property-based testing approach, in the form of the QuickCheck library, was devised in 2000 by Koen Claessen and John Hughes. Since then, the idea has spread far outside Haskell and libraries are available for many other, functional and non-functional, programming languages.

The essence of the approach is summarized by John Hughes' slogan "Don't write tests! Generate them." Indeed, the tester no longer has to come up with the test inputs for individual unit tests. The framework takes care of this automatically and does in seconds what takes a human hours. Instead of working out the expected outputs for corresponding inputs, the tester has to think of more general properties of their code. This is more fun and more useful than writing unit tests manually. Indeed, the properties document the code to some extent: they can capture both the requirements of the code and our understanding of how it works. The fact that this challenges us a bit more to think about what we are doing is also not a bad thing.

This chapter reviews unit testing in Haskell, identifies its shortcomings, and presents property-based testing as a better alternative. We'll learn how to configure property-based testing for our applications by creating generators and a shrinking approach for our data types. Finally, we'll explore how to formulate properties to uncover bugs in a system under test.

In short, this chapter covers the following main topics:

- Knowing what the advantages of property-based testing are over unit testing
- Setting up generators to automatically generate random test inputs for properties
- Automatically shrinking counterexamples of properties down to their essence
- Formulating properties to effectively test your code

# Unit testing versus property-based testing

In this section, we'll review unit testing, probably the most common and well-known form of software testing, and identify several important shortcomings. Then, we'll introduce property-based testing and explain how it improves upon those shortcomings.

## Unit testing

Unit testing is perhaps the most familiar and most obvious way of testing code, especially in the setting of functional programming.

In Haskell, the smallest meaningful unit of code that can be tested is a function. The way to test a function is to supply it with an input and see whether it produces the corresponding expected output. If not, there is either something wrong with the function's implementation or with our understanding of how it should behave. Either way, we have identified a problem that needs to be investigated further.

### Manual testing

With the GHCi interactive shell, such unit testing often happens naturally. When we have written a function, we can immediately play around with it in GHCi, as we have already illustrated many times in this book.

For example, suppose we represent a polynomial, $c_0 + c_1x + c_2x^2 + \ldots + c_nx^n$ as its list of coefficients, $[c_0,c_1,c_2,\ldots,c_n]$. For example, we represent the polynomial $1 + 3x^2$ as a list, $[1,0,3]$. The following function aims to evaluate such a polynomial for a given value of x:

```
horner :: [Int] -> Int -> Int
horner coeffs x = foldl (\r c -> c + x * r) 0 coeffs
```

This makes use of a clever technique, Horner's rule, to evaluate the polynomial without using exponentiation. The correctness of the implementation of this technique, in particular using the higher-order foldl function, is not at all obvious.

We can manually check whether it works correctly on the polynomial $1 + 3x^2$ when x = 1:

```
*Main> horner [1,0,3] 1
4
```

This is the correct answer because $1 + 3 \times 1^2 = 4$. However, the implementation is wrong. We can discover this when we have the discipline to try another situation:

```
*Main> horner [1,0,3] 0
3
```

This is wrong because $1 + 3 \times 0^2 = 1$. Hence, something is wrong in our implementation that we need to investigate further.

While these manual experiments are a worthwhile exploratory activity, they lack many qualities we expect from rigorous testing:

- Because GHCi sessions are not stored, they don't keep track of the tests we have formulated. This is a problem because we often want to repeatedly test the same code – for example, every time it is modified.

- For instance, in our running example, we may diagnose that we should have used `foldr` instead of `foldl` as the coefficients appear to be used in the wrong order. We might change the code as follows:

```
horner :: [Int] -> Int -> Int
horner coeffs x = foldr (\r c -> c + x * r) 0 coeffs
```

Now, we want to rerun the earlier tests to see whether the change fixes the observed problem and does not cause any new problems:

```
*Main> horner [1,0,3] 1
4
*Main> horner [1,0,3] 0
0
```

As we can see from rerunning the checks, the problem has not been fixed. After some thought, we observed that when switching from `foldl` to `foldr`, we should also have switched the order of the parameters in the anonymous function:

```
horner :: [Int] -> Int -> Int
horner coeffs x = foldr (\c r -> c + x * r) 0 coeffs
```

Now, we want to run the checks again:

```
*Main> horner [1,0,3] 1
4
*Main> horner [1,0,3] 0
1
```

Finally, both results are as expected. Is the code correct? We can't be sure with testing alone, and two tests are probably not enough. Yet, we can check with some more inputs to increase our confidence.

- It is not natural to perform many unit tests at once, such as for a whole module of functions, if we have to formulate individual tests each time. We can also easily miss out on performing tests for some functions within a module.

- We don't get a report of the tests we have performed that we can consult to identify issues in the code and check whether we have forgotten to test anything.

For that reason, we typically use a framework for unit testing. This provides a systematic way of writing tests and repeatedly invoking these tests. Moreover, tests can be grouped and performed together, yielding convenient reports.

### The HUnit framework

In Haskell, there are several unit testing frameworks. We shall use the basic `HUnit` package here to explain the general approach.

This is what a test looks like in `HUnit`:

```
test1 :: Test
test1 = TestCase (assertEqual "for horner [1,0,3] 1"
                  4
                  (horner [1,0,3] 1))
```

Here, `TestCase :: Assertion -> Test` is a constructor that creates a test out of a single test case. We use `assertEqual :: (Eq a, Show a) => String -> a -> a -> Assertion` to create an assertion out of a string label, an expected value, and the value under test. The value under test (as well as the expected value) can be an expression such as `horner [1,0,3] 1`. Thanks to lazy evaluation, it won't be evaluated until the test is run.

The idea of this test is to check whether `horner [1,0,3] 1` yields 4. The label is printed as part of the report to indicate which test is being performed. It is common practice to include the expression being tested in the label.

We can run the test as follows:

```
*Main> runTestTT test1
Cases: 1  Tried: 1  Errors: 0  Failures: 0
Counts {cases = 1, tried = 1, errors = 0, failures = 0}
```

The `runTestTT :: Test -> IO Count` function prints a test report and returns a value of the `Count` type with a summary. Because the test succeeds, the report and the summary value are essentially the same: one test case was tried, and no errors or failures occurred.

Let's write our second test case as well:

```
test2 :: Test
test2 = TestCase (assertEqual "for horner [1,0,3] 0"
```

```
                    1
             (horner [1,0,3] 0))
```

Because this test fails for the buggy definition of `horner`, it generates a more extensive report:

```
*Main> runTestTT test2
### Failure:
Main.hs:10
for horner [1,0,3] 0
expected: 1
 but got: 3
Cases: 1  Tried: 1  Errors: 0  Failures: 1
Counts {cases = 1, tried = 1, errors = 0, failures = 1}
```

This prints which test failed by referring to line 10 in the `Main.hs` source file where it is defined. It also prints the label, the expected value, 1, and the value that was actually obtained – that is, 3. In the summary, we can see that one failure occurred.

Because it's tedious to run the individual tests separately, we can group them into lists of tests with the `TestList :: [Test] -> Test` constructor:

```
hornerTests :: Test
hornerTests = TestList [test1,test2]
```

Running the list of tests works the same way as running the individual tests:

```
*Main> runTestTT hornerTests
### Failure in: 1
Main.hs:10
for horner [1,0,3] 0
expected: 1
 but got: 3
Cases: 2  Tried: 2  Errors: 0  Failures: 1
Counts {cases = 2, tried = 2, errors = 0, failures = 1}
```

We can now see that two test cases were tried, of which one failed. The failure is reported as occurring in 1, which is the second element in the list.

Finally, we can also label our tests with the `TestLabel :: String -> Test -> Test` constructor:

```
hornerTests :: Test
hornerTests =
  TestLabel "horner"
    (TestList [ TestLabel "x=1" test1
              , TestLabel "x=0" test2])
```

These labels are printed to explain where a failure happened:

```
*Main> runTestTT hornerTests
### Failure in: horner:1:x=0
Main.hs:10
for horner [1,0,3] 0
expected: 1
 but got: 3
Cases: 2  Tried: 2  Errors: 0  Failures: 1
Counts {cases = 2, tried = 2, errors = 0, failures = 1}
```

Here, the failure happened in the horner:1:x=0 case.

While it's easy to get the hang of unit testing, the approach has several important downsides:

- Unit testing is rather labor-intensive. To rigorously test a function, we have to write a lot of individual test cases for it.

- Unit tests are a rather low-level way of describing what a unit of code should do. Each test case only covers one input/output pair. From seeing such expected input/output pairs, it is hard to glean what the purpose of the function is. In other words, documenting our code requires a double effort. For programmers, we have to write a specification, and for the test framework, we have to write test cases.

- The test writer determines what cases are tested, based on their anticipation of where bugs might be. This human bias may overlook bugs where they are not expected.

To address these three shortcomings, a new approach was introduced: property-based testing.

## Property-based testing

Property-based testing was introduced in Haskell in 2000 through the Quickcheck library by John Hughes and Koen Claessen. The idea is to formulate a test at a more abstract level than a unit test, in the form of a so-called property. From this property, the framework automatically generates many unit tests. This generation happens on the fly when executing the tests. Moreover, by using randomness to generate the unit tests, the programmer's unconscious bias is avoided.

One way to abstract our earlier test1 into a property is by doing the following:

```
prop_sum_at_one :: [Int] -> Bool
prop_sum_at_one cs = horner cs 1 == sum cs
```

In its simple form, a property is a function whose name starts with the prop_ prefix by convention. It should take several parameters and return a Boolean. The expectation is that, provided the code under test is correct, the property should return True for every possible choice of parameters.

Here, we have expressed that when evaluating a polynomial at x = 1, the result should be the sum of its coefficients. We can mimic `test1` by providing the specific polynomial, [1,0,3]:

```
*Main> prop_sum_at_one [1,0,3]
True
```

Because the property is parameterized in the polynomial, we can easily use it with other polynomials. Yet, the whole point is that *we* don't. Instead, we have the framework pick the polynomials:

```
*Main> quickCheck prop_sum_at_one
+++ OK, passed 100 tests.
```

Here, we have asked `QuickCheck` to exercise our property. In the blink of an eye, it reports back to us that it has tested the property with 100 randomly picked polynomials, and that the test passes in all cases.

Similarly, we can abstract `test2` into a property:

```
prop_at_zero :: Int -> [Int] -> Bool
prop_at_zero c cs = horner (c:cs) 0 == c
```

Here, we express that, when we evaluate a polynomial at x = 0, we should get back the value of the first coefficient.

This property is violated by our implementation:

```
*Main> quickCheck prop_at_zero
*** Failed! Falsified (after 3 tests and 2 shrinks):
0
[1]
```

Here, `QuickCheck` reports that, with its third test attempt, it has found inputs for which the property does not hold. Subsequently, it has been able to perform two shrinking steps to this counterexample, before presenting it to us. The point of shrinking is to make the counterexample smaller and thus easier to understand, making diagnosing the problem easier. The final counterexample consists of the 0 and [1] parameters. In other words, `prop_at_zero 0 [1]` fails. After some consideration, we can see that it fails because `horner [0,1]` should yield 0, but it yields 1.

The random tests mean that `QuickCheck` does not always find the same counterexample. For example, we may find a different one for the second property:

```
*Main> quickCheck prop_at_zero
*** Failed! Falsified (after 3 tests and 2 shrinks):
1
[0]
```

In general, when there is a counterexample, there is no guarantee that QuickCheck will find it. Yet, with the same programmer effort, QuickCheck is usually much more thorough in its testing than unit testing would be. By default, it makes 100 test attempts for a property, with only a little bit more programming effort than a single unit test.

# Generators

In this section, we'll teach QuickCheck to generate test inputs for new data types.

## Arbitrary

Out of the box, QuickCheck does not support properties of all types. It only supports the common data types in the standard library. Suppose we define a custom data type, say for the two states of a button:

```
data Button = On | Off deriving (Eq, Show)
```

We have written a simple function to toggle a button:

```
toggle :: Button -> Button
toggle On  = Off
toggle Off = On
```

We want to test this function using the following property:

```
prop_toggle b = toggle (toggle b) == b
```

This expresses that toggling the button twice brings it back to its original state. Unfortunately, QuickCheck cannot work with this property:

```
*Main> quickCheck prop_toggle

<interactive>:3:1: error:
    • No instance for (Arbitrary Button)
        arising from a use of 'quickCheck'
    • In the expression: quickCheck prop_toggle
      In an equation for 'it': it = quickCheck prop_toggle
```

The problem is that QuickCheck does not know how to randomly generate values of the Button type as test input for the property. It is taught how to do so through the Arbitrary type class. Hence, the type error raised here complains that Button does not have an Arbitrary instance.

# Generators

The Arbitrary type class has a method called arbitrary that explains how to generate random values of the type:

```
class Arbitrary a where
  arbitrary :: Gen a
```

The type of the arbitrary method is Gen a, a generator for values of the a type.

## A simple generator

Because our Button type only has two values, we can define the generator using the predefined elements :: [a] -> Gen a combinator:

```
instance Arbitrary Button where
  arbitrary = elements [On,Off]
```

Each time the elements combinator has to generate a value, it randomly selects an element from the given list. We can observe this behavior with the sample :: Show a => Gen a -> IO () function, which generates and prints 11 values:

```
*Main> sample (elements [On,Off])
Off
On
Off
On
On
Off
Off
On
Off
Off
Off
```

Thanks to the Arbitrary instance, we can now run our test:

```
*Main> quickCheck prop_toggle
+++ OK, passed 100 tests.
```

## Generators for composite types

Let's move on from an enumerate type to a composite type:

```
data Point = MkPoint Int Int deriving (Show, Eq)
```

Every point has two coordinates of the Int type. As Int already has an Arbitrary instance, we can rely on its generator when defining one for Point. We can combine the generators for the two coordinates into one for a point by exploiting the fact that Gen is a monad:

```
instance Arbitrary Point where
  arbitrary = do x <- arbitrary
                 y <- arbitrary
                 pure (MkPoint x y)
```

Because Gen is a monad, it is also an applicative functor, and we can write the preceding code a bit more succinctly:

```
    arbitrary = MkPoint <$> arbitrary <*> arbitrary
```

A slightly more involved composite data type is that of shapes, which we looked at in *Chapter 2, Algebraic Data Types*:

```
data Shape
  = Circle Double
  | Rectangle Double Double
  deriving (Show, Eq)
```

It has two constructors to choose from. Here, we can use the oneof :: [Gen a] -> Gen a combinator:

```
instance Arbitrary Shape where
  arbitrary = oneof [circle, rectangle]
    where circle    = Circle    <$> arbitrary
          rectangle = Rectangle <$> arbitrary <*> arbitrary
```

Here, the oneof combinator chooses to generate either a circle or a rectangle, with equal probability.

### Generators for recursive types

Generators for recursive types are harder to set up. For instance, consider this basic type of binary tree:

```
data Tree = Leaf Int | Fork Tree Tree deriving (Show, Eq)
```

Let's also write two functions over trees that we can test:

```
toList :: Tree -> [Int]
toList (Leaf x) = [x]
toList (Fork l r) = toList l ++ toList r

mirror :: Tree -> Tree
mirror (Leaf x) = Leaf x
mirror (Fork l r) = Fork (mirror r) (mirror l)
```

The first function collects the elements of a tree in a list, while the second function mirrors a tree by recursively swapping the left and right branches of forks.

We expect that these functions are related as follows:

```
prop_mirror_toList :: Tree -> Bool
prop_mirror_toList t = toList (mirror t) == reverse (toList t)
```

In other words, the elements of the mirrored tree should be in the reverse order of the elements of the original tree.

To test this property, we have to write an `Arbitrary` instance. For that, we could follow the same strategy as for `Shape`:

```
instance Arbitrary Tree where
   arbitrary = oneof [leaf, fork]
     where leaf = Leaf <$> arbitrary
           fork = Fork <$> arbitrary <*> arbitrary
```

Before testing the property with this instance, we must modify it a little bit to observe what is going on:

```
prop_mirror_toList :: Tree -> Property
prop_mirror_toList t =
   label ("tree height is " ++ show (height t))
     (toList (mirror t) == reverse (toList t))

height :: Tree -> Int
height (Leaf x)   = 0
height (Fork l r) = 1 + max (height l) (height r)
```

We use the `label` combinator to attach a text label to each test instance. `QuickCheck` uses these labels to produce a more informative report:

```
*Main> quickCheck prop_mirror_toList
+++ OK, passed 100 tests:
47% tree height is 0
11% tree height is 2
 9% tree height is 1
 5% tree height is 3
 5% tree height is 5
 4% tree height is 4
 2% tree height is 12
 2% tree height is 6
 2% tree height is 8
 1% tree height is 10
 1% tree height is 103
```

```
1% tree height is 133
1% tree height is 14
1% tree height is 150
1% tree height is 17
1% tree height is 29
1% tree height is 344
1% tree height is 38
1% tree height is 63
1% tree height is 7
1% tree height is 9
1% tree height is 98
```

As we can see, the generator generates leaves about half of the time and very shallow trees most of the time. Only a few larger, even huge, trees are generated as well. Overall, we don't get a very good distribution of trees. After all, errors are often not found in leaves or shallow trees as they are easier to foresee by programmers and easier to discover during manual experimentation.

We can tweak the distribution by replacing the `oneof :: [Gen a] -> Gen a` combinator with the `frequency :: [(Int, Gen a)] -> Gen a` combinator. The latter also chooses from a list of given generators, but it respects the given relative likelihood rather than assigning equal likelihood to each. For example, we could say the following:

```
arbitrary = frequency [(1,leaf), (2,fork)]
  where leaf = Leaf <$> arbitrary
        fork = Fork <$> arbitrary <*> arbitrary
```

Now, forks are generated twice as often as leaves. This is not a good choice of relative frequency because it generates huge trees, which may take forever. We can try to adjust the relative frequency until we are happy, but there is a better way.

The Gen monad provides access to an implicit size parameter. We can use this size to influence what we generate. Here is one possible approach:

```
arbitrary =
  sized (\s ->
    if s > 0 then resize (s-1) (
                   frequency [(1,leaf),(9,fork)]
                 )
             else leaf
  )
```

Here, we use `sized :: (Int -> Gen a) -> Gen a` to access the current size. If it is non-zero, we are nine times as likely to generate a fork than a leaf. If the current size is zero, we always generate a leaf. With `resize :: Int -> Gen a -> Gen a`, we decrement the size for the recursive calls. This approach only generates trees whose height is equal to or less than the initial size, with the former more likely than the latter.

We can control the maximal size that QuickCheck uses if we use the quickCheckWith function. This takes an additional first parameter of the Args record type, which contains all the configuration data that can be supplied. The standard value of Args that the plain quickCheck function uses is stdArgs. The field in this type that controls the size is maxSize (default: 100). When running successive tests, QuickCheck will go through different sizes up to this maximum value.

The standard value of 100 is still problematic as a full binary tree of height 100 contains $2^{100}-1$ nodes (more than $10^{30}$). So, it helps to bring the maximum size down considerably:

```
*Main> quickCheckWith (stdArgs {maxSize = 10}) prop_mirror_toList
+++ OK, passed 100 tests:
20% tree height is 0
10% tree height is 4
10% tree height is 5
10% tree height is 6
10% tree height is 7
 9% tree height is 2
 8% tree height is 1
 8% tree height is 8
 8% tree height is 9
 7% tree height is 3
```

As we can see, our last approach gives a good distribution of tree sizes.

To work with the standard maximum size of 100, an alternative size-based strategy is helpful:

```
arbitrary =
  sized (\s ->
    if s > 0
      then
        resize (s `div` 2) (
          frequency [(1,leaf),(9,fork)]
        )
      else
        leaf
  )
  where leaf = Leaf <$> arbitrary
        fork = Fork <$> arbitrary <*> arbitrary
```

This halves the size for every recursive step. Starting from an initial size of 100, we reach 0 in the 8th level of recursion. Hence, we get trees with, at most, $2^8-1 = 255$ nodes:

```
*Main> quickCheck prop_mirror_toList
+++ OK, passed 100 tests:
31% tree height is 7
28% tree height is 6
15% tree height is 5
14% tree height is 0
 5% tree height is 3
 5% tree height is 4
 2% tree height is 2
```

As we can see, some thought has to go into designing generators for recursive types to avoid excessive generation times.

## Custom generators

While convenient, the disadvantage of using a type class to obtain a generator for a type is that the same generator is used for all properties. This may not always be appropriate. Sometimes, we want to use a different generator because it is more relevant to test particular values.

For example, suppose a property should only hold for positive integers. Say we have written a more efficient version of the Fibonacci function that we want to compare to the more naive version:

```
fibSlow :: Integer -> Integer
fibSlow 0 = 1
fibSlow 1 = 1
fibSlow n = fibSlow (n-1) + fibSlow (n-2)


fibFast :: Integer -> Integer
fibFast n = go n 0 1 where
  go 0 _ r = r
  go n a b = go (n-1) b (a+b)
```

These two functions only make sense for positive inputs. We can codify this requirement in the property itself with a conditional expression:

```
prop_fib :: Integer -> Bool
prop_fib n = if n >= 0 then fibFast n == fibSlow n else True
```

This property always succeeds trivially when the number is negative. The actual test is only performed when the number is positive. QuickCheck provides the (==>) operator to express such conditional properties more succinctly:

```
prop_fib :: Integer -> Property
prop_fib n = n >= 0 ==> fibFast n == fibSlow n
```

The conditional operator also has an impact on QuickCheck's approach and test report (we have limited the maximum size because fibSlow is slow for larger values):

```
*Main> quickCheckWith (stdArgs {maxSize = 20}) prop_fib
+++ OK, passed 100 tests; 54 discarded.
```

The test is performed 100 times on positive inputs and passes each time. However, in the process of generating 100 positive inputs, it also generates 54 negative inputs, which it discards because they do not satisfy the condition.

In this case, the condition is rather easy to satisfy. The generator for the Integer produces positive numbers about twice as often as negative numbers. However, in the case of more tricky conditions, it can be hard to find 100 satisfying inputs.

Instead of the conditional approach, we can write a custom generator that always yields a valid test case:

```
positive :: Gen Integer
positive = fmap abs arbitrary
```

Here, we generate an integer with arbitrary and then use abs to make it positive. Of course, we cannot write a new Arbitrary instance for Integer that uses this generator as there already is one. However, we can supply the custom generator explicitly when testing the property using the forAll combinator:

```
*Main> quickCheckWith (stdArgs {maxSize = 20})
                      (forAll positive prop_fib)
+++ OK, passed 100 tests.
```

Now, all test inputs satisfy the condition; none are discarded.

## Shrinking

Once QuickCheck has found a counterexample, it's the tester's or programmer's job to figure out why the test fails. The purpose of shrinking is to reduce the size of a counterexample as much as possible to make this more manageable.

## Shrinking in action

To see what shrinking does, let's return to the failing `prop_at_zero` property. We'll contrast the same test run. When executed with `quickCheck` and with `verboseCheck`, the verbose version of `quickCheck` gives us a blow-by-blow account of the test run. The first gives a short report:

```
*Main> quickCheck prop_at_zero
*** Failed! Falsified (after 3 tests and 3 shrinks):
1
[0]
```

The second also shows the steps that precede the generation of that report:

```
*Main> verboseCheck prop_at_zero
Failed:
-2
[2,0]

Failed:
2
[2,0]

Passed:
0
[2,0]

Failed:
1
[2,0]

Passed:
0
[2,0]

Passed:
1
[]

Failed:
1
[0]

Passed:
0
[0]
```

```
Passed:
1
[]


*** Failed! Falsified (after 3 tests and 3 shrinks):
1
[0]
```

As we can see, `QuickCheck` does not immediately find the counterexample of 1 and `[0]`. First, it finds the counterexample of -2 and `[2,0]`. However, before reporting that counterexample, it (successfully) attempts to shrink it. Shrinking is a trial and error process, where various *smaller* versions of the test inputs are tried out. If such a smaller version passes the tests, it is a dead end for shrinking and discarded. If it fails the test, `QuickCheck` tries to shrink it even further. At a certain point, either no smaller variant fails anymore, `QuickCheck` has run out of ways to shrink the counter example (it is already deemed minimal), or `QuickCheck` has exceeded the maximum number of shrinks configured in `Args`. In the preceding example, shrinking ends because of the first scenario: all smaller variants pass the test and the one found is truly minimal.

## User-defined shrinking

The way to shrink a data type has to be specified in the `Arbitrary` type class's `shrink :: a -> [a]` method. Given a value, it should produce a list of smaller values. The default implementation returns an empty list; no shrinking happens.

Most predefined types in the standard library do have a non-trivial definition. For example, for `Int`, the `shrink` function produces several smaller values:

```
*Main> shrink 100
[0,50,75,88,94,97,99]
```

For our user-defined algebraic data types, we have to come up with a shrinking strategy ourselves. For example, we can do the following for the binary tree type:

```
instance Arbitrary Tree where
  arbitrary = … -- as before
  shrink (Leaf x)   = [Leaf y | y <- shrink x]
  shrink (Fork l r) = l : r : [Fork l' r | l' <- shrink l]
                           ++ [Fork l r' | r' <- shrink r]
```

The only way we can make a leaf any smaller is by shrinking the value contained in the leaf. In contrast, we offer four different ways to shrink a fork:

- Replace it with the left branch
- Replace it with the right branch

- Keep the right branch and shrink the left branch

- Keep the left branch and shrink the right branch

We can see this shrinking in action if we break the definition of `mirror`, as follows:

```
mirror :: Tree -> Tree
mirror (Leaf x) = Leaf x
mirror (Fork l r) = Fork (mirror l) (mirror l)
```

Absent-mindedly, we forgot to swap the two branches in the recursive calls. This function simply returns the tree as-is.

`QuickCheck` manages to find this bug fairly quickly:

```
*Main> quickCheck prop_mirror_toList
*** Failed! Falsified (after 7 tests and 4 shrinks):
Fork (Leaf 1) (Leaf 0)
```

The counterexample it finds after 7 tests is a tree of height 6 with 65 constructors. After shrinking, `QuickCheck` brings it down the presented tree of height 1 with 3 constructors. This is much less overwhelming and allows us to easily identify the mistakes we've made in `mirror`.

## Test properties – a case study

In this section, we'll explore writing different test properties by employing a small case study.

### System under test

Our system under test is a compiler from a small expression language to a corresponding stack language.

We can use the following type of expression:

```
data Expr
  = Lit Int
  | Add Expr Expr
  | Sub Expr Expr
  | Mul Expr Expr
  deriving Show
```

It features literals, addition, subtraction, and multiplication.

The stack language features similar functionality, but the parameters of the binary operators are not explicitly given. Instead, they are taken from a stack:

```
data Instr = Push Int | Plus | Minus | Times
type Prog  = [Instr]
type Stack = [Int]
```

A program in the stack language is a sequence of instructions that are executed consecutively:

```
exec :: Prog -> Stack -> Maybe Stack
exec []      s = Just s
exec (i:is) s = instr i s >>= exec is
```

Each instruction transforms the stack by taking whatever operands it needs from the top of the stack and pushing its result back on the stack:

```
instr :: Instr -> Stack -> Maybe Stack
instr (Push n) stack          = Just (n : stack)
instr Plus     (x : y : stack) = Just (x + y : stack)
instr Minus    (x : y : stack) = Just (x - y : stack)
instr Times    (x : y : stack) = Just (x * y : stack)
instr _        _              = Nothing
```

We use the `Maybe` monad to model the fact that execution may crash when there are not enough operands available on the stack.

The compiler between the two languages is defined as follows:

```
compile :: Expr -> Prog
compile (Lit n)     = [Push n]
compile (Add e1 e2) = compile e1 ++ compile e2 ++ [Plus]
compile (Sub e1 e2) = compile e1 ++ compile e2 ++ [Minus]
compile (Mul e1 e2) = compile e1 ++ compile e2 ++ [Times]
```

It maps a literal to a program that pushes the literal's value on the stack. For the binary operators, the corresponding stack program first sets up the two operands on the stack and then performs the operation that fetches them from the stack.

## Properties

There is a subtle bug hidden in the preceding code. Our mission now is to uncover it by exploring various properties.

### Same size

The first property we propose is based on the observation that the stack program must perform the same number of operations as the original expression. The former can be obtained as the program's `length`. For the latter, we must define a new function:

```
exprSize :: Expr -> Int
exprSize (Lit _) = 1
exprSize (Add e1 e2) = 1 + exprSize e1 + exprSize e2
```

```
exprSize (Sub e1 e2) = 1 + exprSize e1 + exprSize e2
exprSize (Mul e1 e2) = 1 + exprSize e1 + exprSize e2
```

Now, the property can be expressed as follows:

```
prop_same_size :: Expr -> Bool
prop_same_size e =
  exprSize e == length (compile e)
```

Before we can test this property, we have to provide a generator for expressions:

```
instance Arbitrary Expr where
  arbitrary = sized go where
    go :: Int -> Gen Expr
    go 0 = Lit <$> arbitrary
    go n = oneof
      [ Lit <$> arbitrary
      , Add <$> go (n `div` 2) <*> go (n `div` 2)
      , Sub <$> go (n `div` 2) <*> go (n `div` 2)
      , Mul <$> go (n `div` 2) <*> go (n `div` 2) ]
```

This generator follows a similar strategy as that for binary trees. We use the `size` parameter to restrict the size of the expression rather than the height, as we did for the trees. When the size is zero, we only generate a literal. When the size is non-zero, we generate each constructor with the same likelihood. In the case of the binary operators, we halve the size for each parameter.

With this generator in place, we can see that the size property succeeds on 100 tests:

```
*Main> quickCheck prop_same_size
+++ OK, passed 100 tests.
```

We have to look further.

### Successful execution

While a stack program may fail because the stack does not contain enough values, this should never be the case for compiled expressions. Indeed, compiled expressions should be self-contained and put all the values they need on the stack and in time for when they are needed. We can express this with the following property:

```
prop_exec_compile_succeeds :: Expr -> Bool
prop_exec_compile_succeeds e =
  isJust (exec (compile e) [])
```

Here, we use the `isJust :: Maybe a -> Bool` function from the `Data.Maybe` library to check for success.

As it turns out, `QuickCheck` confirms that this property is satisfied on 100 test inputs:

```
*Main> quickCheck prop_exec_compile_succeeds
+++ OK, passed 100 tests.
```

But we can be more precise about the stack discipline of compiled expressions than this.

### Stack discipline

Not only does a compiled expression push all the data it needs on the stack, but it does not push any more than it needs. At the end, we get back the original stack, with one additional value top, namely the result of the expression:

```
prop_stack_discipline :: Expr -> Stack -> Bool
prop_stack_discipline e s =
   fmap tail (exec (compile e) s) == Just s
```

Here, we executed the compiled expression with an arbitrary initial stack. At the end, we check that the tail of the final stack is the same as the initial stack.

This property holds too:

```
*Main> quickCheck prop_stack_discipline
+++ OK, passed 100 tests.
```

Yet, we have not said anything about the element at the top of the final stack.

### Same result

Of course, we expect that the stack program yields the same result as the original expression. Hence, we can compare against the basic evaluation function for expressions:

```
eval :: Expr -> Int
eval (Lit n)     = n
eval (Add e1 e2) = eval e1 + eval e2
eval (Sub e1 e2) = eval e1 - eval e2
eval (Mul e1 e2) = eval e1 * eval e2
```

We state that the result should be the same with the following property:

```
prop_same_result :: Expr -> Bool
prop_same_result e =
   exec (compile e) [] == Just [eval e]
```

Now, we are getting somewhere:

```
*Main> quickCheck prop_same_result
*** Failed! Falsified (after 6 tests):
```

```
Add (Sub (Lit 3) (Sub (Lit 5) (Lit (-2)))) (Add (Add (Lit (-2)) (Lit
(-4))) (Add (Lit 3) (Lit 3)))
```

We have found a counterexample! Unfortunately, it is rather large.

## Shrinking

Let's simplify the counterexample by implementing a shrinking approach:

```
shrink (Lit n)       = [Lit n' | n' <- shrink n]
shrink (Add e1 e2) =
  [e1, e2] ++ [Add e1' e2' | (e1', e2') <- shrink (e1, e2)]
shrink (Sub e1 e2) =
  [e1, e2] ++ [Sub e1' e2' | (e1', e2') <- shrink (e1, e2)]
shrink (Mul e1 e2) =
  [e1, e2] ++ [Mul e1' e2' | (e1', e2') <- shrink (e1, e2)]
```

This is essentially the same shrinking approach we used for binary trees. This formulation is a little bit more compact as it uses the shrinking strategy for tuples to combine the two alternatives of shrinking either the left or the right subexpression.

This shrinking pays off as we get a much smaller counterexample:

```
*Main> quickCheck prop_same_result
*** Failed! Falsified (after 4 tests and 5 shrinks):
Sub (Lit 0) (Lit 1)
```

The test case says that 0 - 1 goes wrong. We can confirm this ourselves:

```
*Main> eval (Sub (Lit 0) (Lit 1))
-1
*Main> exec (compile (Sub (Lit 0) (Lit 1))) []
Just [1]
```

We can see that the evaluator behaves correctly, but the compiler performs the subtraction the wrong way around. The problem is in this line of code:

```
compile (Sub e1 e2) = compile e1 ++ compile e2 ++ [Minus]
```

The two subexpressions should appear in the opposite order:

```
compile (Sub e1 e2) = compile e2 ++ compile e1 ++ [Minus]
```

Indeed, by coming second, the value for e1 will appear on top of that for e2. This is consistent with the corresponding instr case:

```
instr Minus (x : y : stack) = Just (x - y : stack)
```

The order does not matter for addition and multiplication, but morally, we should alter their `compile` cases as well.

Either way, with the problem fixed, our property now succeeds:

```
*Main> quickCheck prop_same_result
+++ OK, passed 100 tests.
```

In fact, for good measure, we should rerun all properties. This is facilitated by adding the following two lines at the end of the program:

```
return []
runTests = $quickCheckAll
```

Here, `quickCheckAll` is a `TemplateHaskell` macro that gathers all the properties in the module, provided their names start with `prop_`. To enable `TemplateHaskell`, you also need to include the following pragma at the beginning of the file:

```
{-# LANGUAGE TemplateHaskell #-}
```

The line with `return []` is a `TemplateHaskell` peculiarity that ensures the subsequent line can see all the prior definitions.

With `runTests` in place, we can run all tests in one go:

```
*Main> runTests
=== prop_same_size from Compiler.hs:44 ===
+++ OK, passed 100 tests.

=== prop_exec_compile_succeeds from Compiler.hs:48 ===
+++ OK, passed 100 tests.

=== prop_stack_discipline from Compiler.hs:52 ===
+++ OK, passed 100 tests.

=== prop_same_result from Compiler.hs:56 ===
+++ OK, passed 100 tests.

True
```

Isn't this satisfactory?

# Summary

In this chapter, we explored testing in Haskell. In particular, we contrasted unit testing with property-based testing in `QuickCheck`. The latter allows more thorough testing with less effort, but writing test properties requires a bit more abstraction. We have seen that, to support properties of user-defined types, we should instantiate the `Arbitrary` type class to supply a generator for test inputs. Ideally, we also supply a shrinking strategy, which `QuickCheck` uses to derive smaller, more manageable counterexamples.

Although still relatively little known outside of the Haskell community, there are clones of the `QuickCheck` library available for many other programming languages. Also, for Haskell, several variants exist, such as `SmallCheck`, which replaces random generation with systematic enumeration of small values. Moreover, modern testing frameworks such as `hspec` combine property-based and unit testing under the same roof.

# Questions

Answer the following questions to test your knowledge of this chapter:

1.  What are the advantages and disadvantages of property-based testing over unit testing?
2.  How does `QuickCheck` generate test inputs?
3.  What is shrinking?

# Further reading

To learn more about the topics that were covered in this chapter, take a look at the following resources:

- *The HUnit package documentation*:

    `https://hackage.haskell.org/package/HUnit`

- *The QuickCheck package documentation*:

    `https://hackage.haskell.org/package/QuickCheck`

- *The hspec package documentation*:

    `https://hackage.haskell.org/package/hspec`

# Answers

Here are the answers to this chapter's questions:

1. Property-based testing has several key advantages over unit testing:

   - Writing a single property requires a little bit more thought than writing a single unit test, but from it, QuickCheck can generate an arbitrary number of unit tests. Hence, property-based testing is more productive.

   - Properties are often a form of documentation of the code under test. Their parametric nature means that they convey insight into many situations, whereas a unit test covers a single situation and thus offers little insight.

   - The random generation of test inputs reveals problems in unexpected corners where human testers would not have looked.

   There are also some disadvantages or costs associated with property-based testing:

   - Writing properties requires thinking at a more abstract level and having more insight into the code. It is debatable whether this is an advantage.

   - There is a setup cost when defining the QuickCheck framework with new data types. We have to define a generator and, ideally, a shrinking strategy.

   - By default, random testing is not repeatable. Different test inputs are generated on each run. This can be mitigated by manually initializing the random number generator.

2. QuickCheck generates test inputs of a given type, A, using generators of the Gen A type. Types can be equipped with a standard generator through the `arbitrary :: Gen a` method in the Arbitrary type class.

   The QuickCheck library provides various combinators for defining such a generator, most of which are based on some random choice among alternatives. Notably, to contain their size when generating values of recursive data types, the Gen monad provides a `size` parameter.

3. Once QuickCheck has found a counterexample for a property, it does not outright present it to the user. Instead, it first attempts to find a smaller counterexample by using repeated shrinking. Shrinking derives smaller test inputs from the given failing test input. Its behavior is defined through the `shrink :: a -> [a]` type class method in the Arbitrary type class and defined separately for each type. The default behavior is that no shrinking happens.

   The underlying idea of shrinking is that smaller counterexamples are easier to understand and simplify the subsequent debugging process.

# Index

# J

**Java Virtual Machine (JVM) 10**
**juxtaposition 12**

# K

**kinds 208**

# L

**lambda abstractions 102**
**lambda calculus 7**
**lambda functions 102**
**lawful instances 131**
  extensionality 132
  negation 132
  reflexivity 132
  symmetry 132
  transitivity 132
**laws 132**
**lazy evaluation 158**
  programming with 164
  versus input/output (I/O) 177
**lazy memory leaks 168**
  increased laziness 171, 172
  leaking accumulator 168
  strictness annotation 169
**left recursion 333**
**lenses 337, 339**
  advanced lenses 347
  basic lenses 339-341
  boilerplate, generating 343, 344
  change of representation 341
  composition 339
  lens operators 342, 343
  polymorphic lenses 344, 345

**library functions**
  by example 188
  guessing game 192, 193
  list membership functions 142, 143
  Map library 144, 145
  numbers, summing 188
**Lisp 8**
**listable collections 213**
  instances based on foldr 213-215
  minimum complete definition,
    with foldr 213
**list (aka nondeterminism) monad 274, 275**
**list comprehensions 54**
  generators 54, 55
  guards 55
  guard scheduling 56
  interdependent generators 56
  symmetry breaking 56
**lists 51**
  predefined functions 52-54
  strings-as-lists approach 57
  structural recursion 61, 62
  syntax 51
  syntax desugared 51, 52
**ListT transformer 287**

# M

**Maybe datatype 44, 45**
**MaybeT transformer 287**
**Maybe type constructor**
  failing with 258, 259
**memoization 158, 242, 243**
**memory leak 168**
**Meta Language (ML) 8**
**monadic effects**
  changed requirements 281
  combining 278

www.packtpub.com

Subscribe to our online digital library for full access to over 7,000 books and videos, as well as industry leading tools to help you plan your personal development and advance your career. For more information, please visit our website.

## Why subscribe?

- Spend less time learning and more time coding with practical eBooks and Videos from over 4,000 industry professionals

- Improve your learning with Skill Plans built especially for you

- Get a free eBook or video every month

- Fully searchable for easy access to vital information

- Copy and paste, print, and bookmark content

Did you know that Packt offers eBook versions of every book published, with PDF and ePub files available? You can upgrade to the eBook version at packtpub.com and as a print book customer, you are entitled to a discount on the eBook copy. Get in touch with us at customercare@packtpub.com for more details.

At www.packtpub.com, you can also read a collection of free technical articles, sign up for a range of free newsletters, and receive exclusive discounts and offers on Packt books and eBooks.

# Other Books You May Enjoy

If you enjoyed this book, you may be interested in these other books by Packt:

**C++20 STL Cookbook**

Bill Weinman

ISBN: 978-1-80324-871-4

- Understand the new language features and the problems they can solve
- Implement generic features of the STL with practical examples
- Understand standard support classes for concurrency and synchronization
- Perform efficient memory management using the STL
- Implement seamless formatting using std::format
- Work with strings the STL way instead of handcrafting C-style code

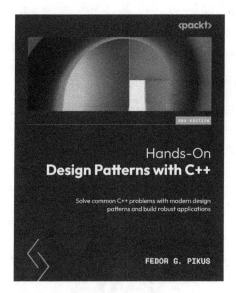

**Hands-On Design Patterns with C++ - Second Edition**

Fedor G. Pikus

ISBN: 978-1-80461-155-5

- Recognize the most common design patterns used in C++
- Understand how to use C++ generic programming to solve common design problems
- Explore the most powerful C++ idioms, their strengths, and their drawbacks
- Rediscover how to use popular C++ idioms with generic programming
- Discover new patterns and idioms made possible by language features of C++17 and C++20
- Understand the impact of design patterns on the program's performance

## Packt is searching for authors like you

If you're interested in becoming an author for Packt, please visit `authors.packtpub.com` and apply today. We have worked with thousands of developers and tech professionals, just like you, to help them share their insight with the global tech community. You can make a general application, apply for a specific hot topic that we are recruiting an author for, or submit your own idea.

## Share Your Thoughts

Now you've finished *Soar with Haskell*, we'd love to hear your thoughts! Scan the QR code below to go straight to the Amazon review page for this book and share your feedback or leave a review on the site that you purchased it from.

`https://packt.link/r/1805128450`

Your review is important to us and the tech community and will help us make sure we're delivering excellent quality content.

# Download a free PDF copy of this book

Thanks for purchasing this book!

Do you like to read on the go but are unable to carry your print books everywhere? Is your eBook purchase not compatible with the device of your choice?

Don't worry, now with every Packt book you get a DRM-free PDF version of that book at no cost.

Read anywhere, any place, on any device. Search, copy, and paste code from your favorite technical books directly into your application.

The perks don't stop there, you can get exclusive access to discounts, newsletters, and great free content in your inbox daily

Follow these simple steps to get the benefits:

1. Scan the QR code or visit the link below

https://packt.link/free-ebook/9781805128458

2. Submit your proof of purchase

3. That's it! We'll send your free PDF and other benefits to your email directly

www.ingramcontent.com/pod-product-compliance
Lightning Source LLC
LaVergne TN
LVHW081511050326
832903LV00025B/1449

*9781805128458*